Kansas

A Land of Contrasts

Kansas

A Land of Contrasts

Fourth Edition

Robert W. Richmond

Harlan Davidson, Inc.
Wheeling, Illinois 60090-6000

Copyright © 1974, 1980, 1989
Forum Press, Inc.
Copyright © 1999
Harlan Davidson, Inc.

Library of Congress Cataloging-in-Publication Data
Richmond, Robert W.
    Kansas, a land of contrasts / Robert W. Richmond. — 4th ed.
      p.   cm.
    Includes bibliographical references and index.
    ISBN 0-88295-949-2
    1. Kansas—History.   I. Title
F681.R52   1999
978.1—dc21   98-49693
                                                          CIP

All illustrations are courtesy of the Kansas State Historical Society,
Topeka, unless otherwise noted.
Cover photo: Butterfly milkweed and primrose in the Flint Hills tallgrass
prairie (Butler County), by Steve Mulligan.
Cover design: De Pinto Graphic Design

Manufactured in the United States of America
00 99 1 2 3 VP

For Peter and Douglas
readers and critics
who put up with a writing father . . .
all those years ago

Contents

Preface

Kansas, A Land of Contrasts appears here in its fourth edition. The state has seen innumerable changes since the book's initial publication in 1974 and I have tried to record those changes. Many Kansas citizens have come to prominence in recent years and I have attempted to recognize them, whether their contributions have been in politics or in the arts. Although the basic facts of the state's early history remain the same, new research has revealed some things about our more distant past that are worthy of inclusion here. Much of that recent research and writing is identified in the suggested readings at the end of each chapter. Also, I committed some sins of omission in the earlier editions. I hope that those have been corrected and that this edition provides new perspectives for the reader of Kansas history.

This book remains a personal kind of history because after more than forty-five years of writing, teaching, and working intimately with the history of one's native state it is difficult not to view it personally. *Kansas, A Land of Contrasts* owes much to the substantial work of others, but I have attempted to shed additional light on certain aspects of Kansas history, particularly those events of the twentieth century. While it is not possible to present all the details on a number of subjects in a survey such as this, the major issues and themes are covered with emphasis upon people and personalities. For more specific information and complete analysis of particular developments, the reader should refer to the suggestions at the end of each chapter.

In several cases the readings apply to more than one chapter of this book. That is especially true of biographies of people whose careers spanned several decades, such as Alf Landon, Arthur Capper, Clifford Hope, and William Allen White. Some of the articles cover a broader time frame also. While I have repeated some entries, I have tried to list the readings with the eras to which they seem most closely tied, leaving it to the reader to absorb whatever additional information applies to the wider scope of Kansas history.

Certain topics have received detailed attention—prohibition, for example, because it was a burning issue in Kansas for so long. William Allen White is quoted frequently because no other Kansas commentator had so much to say about what went on for a half century nor did anyone say it quite as well. I have tried to present Kansas history in its proper chronology but some subjects were better presented in a topical way. My choice of the title stems from years of noting that Kansas has often embodied contrast—conservative on one hand but in the front ranks of change on the other; a desert to Zebulon Pike but Eden to many settlers.

This book would not have been possible without the collections of the Kansas State Historical Society, the assistance of its staff, and its various publications. The Society's periodical of many years, *The Kansas Historical Quarterly*, ended in 1977, and it has been replaced by *Kansas History: A Journal of the Central Plains*. Although its format has changed, the contents continue to provide the same kind of valuable data carried in years past. In addition, *Kansas: The First Century*, edited by John D. Bright, contains comprehensive studies on several facets of state history, and the work of James Drury, Marvin Harder, and Carolyn Rampey provides detailed examinations into the workings of state government. James C. Malin's studies of the territorial period and Great Plains development are valuable, while *Kansas Folklore* by Samuel Sackett and William Koch and Koch's more recent *Folklore From Kansas* deal with an often overlooked aspect of the state's story.

Louise Barry's *The Beginning of the West* chronicles much of what went on prior to 1854 in what is now Kansas, and two general works have appeared since the first edition of this book, both of which are good. These are The *34th Star*, edited by Nyle H. Miller, and Kenneth S. Davis, *Kansas: A Bicentennial History*. Three valuable compilations have been published in the 1990s: Homer E. Socolofsky and Virgil W. Dean, *Kansas History, An Annotated Bibliography*; Homer E. Socolofsky, *Kansas Governors*; and Dave Webb, *399 Kansas Characters*. Also, *Kansas First Families at Home*, edited by Nel Lindner Richmond, provides information on the state's first ladies and the executive residences.

I wish to thank the scholars of Kansas and western American history, past and present, who have made my writing easier and most of them are listed in the readings following each chapter.

I owe particular thanks to Joseph W. Snell, James L. Forsythe, Donald R. McCoy, Richard D. Pankratz, and William Unrau, all of whom read portions of the original manuscript and offered valuable suggestions. Randall Thies provided revised information on Kansas archeology for this edition. Thomas Fox Averill once more was helpful in identifying current Kansas authors of note. My wife, Nel, again offered both criticism and encouragement. Unless otherwise credited, all illustrations are from the State Historical Society's files.

My feelings about the history of Kansas have not changed since 1974 so this edition reflects the same viewpoints of the first publication. I still hope that it gives a clearer picture of Kansas for those who wish to know more about the state and that it eliminates some misconceptions. I also hope that it continues to make the study and teaching of Kansas history easier for those who believe that state and local history play important roles in the understanding of our national story.

Robert W. Richmond
Topeka, Kansas

The Land and Its Native People

Although history is the study of human actions, one cannot consider that story without first considering the land in which it has taken place. Kansas must be viewed as something more than the familiar 200 by 400 mile rectangle outlined on a map. Climate and geography have affected all who have inhabited what is now Kansas. There is beauty and variety whether one considers the shifting sands in areas south of the Arkansas River or the red hills of the gypsum country west of present Medicine Lodge. All of it has helped make people what they were, what they are, and what they may become.

THE LAND

The casual traveler sees Kansas as a kind of tabletop—flat and monotonous with few differences in its surface features and soil. This is not a true picture of the state. It rises from under 700 feet above sea level in its southeastern corner to more than 4,100 feet at its western border, and it contains a wide variety of terrain.

Kansas has no mountains, not much natural surface water, and a comparatively small amount of native timber, but it holds some of the most beautiful scenery in the United States if one takes time to look at it. Because of its distance from east to west, it has a great diversity of terrain, climate, soil, native plants, and animals, although most of it lies within that region generally referred to as the Great Plains.

1

The extreme southeastern part of Kansas is on the fringe of what the geologist refers to as the Ozark Plateau, an area resembling the rugged country of southern Missouri and northern Arkansas. The northeastern portion of the state with its rolling hills assumed its present appearance as a result of glacial activity hundreds of thousands of years ago. The Kansan glacier, the second one to enter the area during the Ice Age, moved south to the Kansas River and west to the Blue. It wore away some rock formations and carried others along with it. From that action came the hills and bluffs that mark the country along the rivers of northeastern Kansas.

Whatever a scientist may choose to call the rest of the state's geological areas—central lowlands, Flint Hills, Blue Hills, or Arkansas River lowlands, among others—it is easy to remember this simple fact. The eastern and central areas of hills and native long grasses, like the Bluestem, give way to the flatter, short grass (Buffalo and Grama) country west of the 100th meridian, known as the High Plains. In each part of Kansas one can observe different types of grass, trees, and rock.

The state is drained by two major river basins, the Kansas (a part of the larger Missouri River system) and the Arkansas (part of the Arkansas-Red-White system). The Kansas, or Kaw, River does not really come into existence until the Republican and Smoky Hill rivers, both of which begin in Colorado, come together in the Junction City vicinity. Downstream from there the major tributaries are the Blue, Delaware, and Wakarusa, but many other streams empty into the Kaw between Manhattan and Kansas City. All the tributaries of the Republican, Smoky Hill, Saline, and Solomon rivers in northern and western Kansas are a part of the Kansas River system.

The Blue flows through a deep, narrow valley as does the Delaware. The lower Republican, Solomon, Saline, and Smoky Hill rivers all have valleys two or three miles wide, lined by bluffs. Some of the streams in north-central Kansas flow at times through regions containing salt springs and marshes that give the water a brackish quality. The Saline River is one of the saltiest streams in the United States.

The Arkansas has its beginning high in the Rocky Mountains, but it is fed by a number of streams as it makes its way across southwestern and south-central Kansas. The Pawnee, Ninnescah, Walnut, Cimarron, Cottonwood, Neosho, and Verdigris all contribute to the flow of the Arkansas although some of the tributaries do not join it until after it has gone beyond the southern border of the state.

The tributaries of the Arkansas in western and south-central Kansas have firm, low banks and their valleys are generally wide and flat, bordered by bluffs. When they cut through rocky country their channels are deeper and narrower, with rocky ledges and cliffs along them. It is sandy along the south side of the Arkansas from the Colorado line to the area east of Dodge City. Sand dunes reappear around Hutchinson.

During long, dry periods many of these streams do not really look like rivers, but at times—in 1844, 1903, and 1951, for example—they have produced monstrous floods. Regardless of their levels, they have meant life to a variety of creatures throughout the history of the area. Although many of the Kansas rivers flow through areas in western Kansas that are not well-suited to farming, the major streams generally have valleys that are agriculturally productive.

Along the banks of eastern Kansas streams grow a variety of trees. Cottonwood, willow, elm, green ash, box elder, hackberry, walnut, burr oak, and red cedar were here before the white man came. Rainfall was great enough that this timber could also flourish in the uplands away from the water courses. It was of tremendous value to the first settlers, just as it had been to the earlier native people. In the west there were fewer trees, and along some of the streams that moved through sandy, less fertile soil only the cottonwood and willow were found. The Indians, and later the settlers, were pleased to find wild plum, papaw, elderberry, chokecherry, Indian turnip, plantain, several other plants, and a variety of nuts, all of which provided food. Some of these, at times, served as a basis for medicine. Poison ivy was also present, but it has never brought happiness to Kansas residents, ancient or modern.

There were grouse, prairie chicken, wild turkey, bald eagle, crow, and a number of hawks, owls, ducks, and geese, as well as many smaller birds. It is interesting to note that although some of these creatures, in their natural habitat, are gone forever from this part of the Plains, others have come back or have been reintroduced in recent years. Once again, deer, beaver, wildcat, turkey, and antelope are a part of the Kansas scene.

Kansas had a large animal population. At one time the antelope, elk, white-tailed and mule deer, black bear, prairie wolf, cougar, wildcat, beaver, otter, and badger could all be found, along with smaller animals such as rabbits, squirrels, prairie dogs, and coyotes. Also, Kansas was in the center of the great bison (or buffalo) herd range until humans and machines triumphed over that beast in the 1870s.

Kansas geography and climate affected life in the past, and still do. The drought-resistant grasses of the High Plains have encouraged utilization of the area for grazing animals, and only when farmers used irrigation for crops have they really prospered consistently with grain farming in western Kansas.

The trees of eastern Kansas, the Bluestem grass of the Flint Hills (described as belly deep to a horse as late as the 1850s and 1860s), the

Paleontologist George Sternberg (right) of Hays at work in the field. Sternberg died in 1969.

Dakota sandstone of west central Kansas, the chalk bluff area in extreme western Kansas, and the mineral contents of the geological depths that underlie the surface of what was once all part of a great prehistoric sea have all played some part in the development of the region.

The chalk bluffs of Logan and Gove counties contained rich deposits of fossils which provided material for study and exhibition beginning in the nineteenth century. Much of the early work was done by the Kansas paleontologists Charles and George Sternberg, and dramatic discoveries resulting from their efforts are preserved in the Sternberg Museum at Fort Hays State University.

Walnut timber provided the army, missionaries, and the first white settlers in eastern Kansas with logs for building and later supplied manufacturers the raw material for furniture. Limestone and sandstone have been quarried extensively for a century, and certain clays have provided the material for brickmaking in the days before Kansas Territory was created. All of these products have gone into the construction of homes, businesses, and government buildings.

Kansas limestone has also provided the basis for a large cement manufacturing industry. Sand makes glass manufacture possible, native phosphates have produced commercial fertilizers, gypsum led to wallboard manufacture, and lead, zinc, coal, volcanic ash, helium, salt, and oil have created great numbers of finished products vital to American industry and life.

THE PEOPLE

There were many different cultures which occupied the land that is presently Kansas before the first permanent settlers came in the nineteenth century. Much of what is known today about these people has come through archeological work, a great deal of it done in recent years. Since the 1950s, the construction of large reservoirs in the state and ambitious programs of highway construction made it important to do archeological salvage work before these projects covered the land with water or asphalt. Consequently, vast amounts of information about early people have been recovered by archeologists working ahead of construction. Cooperative efforts between professional and amateur archeologists have allowed additional sites to be excavated. These kinds of efforts continue to contribute to an expanding understanding of the state's prehistoric and early historic past. The first Kansans have been called by archeologists the Paleo-Indians. They entered the central Plains about 11,000 years ago and occupied the area until approximately 7000 B.C. The earliest of these groups were hunters who pursued big game like the mammoth or ancient forms of the bison. Although evidence of these people is scarce in Kansas, numerous finds of their distinctive spear points show that they once lived in all parts of the state.

The Archaic period followed, lasting until about 1 A.D. The people of this period, too, were hunters, but they pursued more modern animals. They were also gatherers—using berries, fruit, roots, and seeds to supplement their diets. Abundant evidence of Archaic peoples has been found in Kansas in the form of campsites where they once lived and occasional burial sites. Well-preserved remains of Archaic campsites have been discovered throughout east-central Kansas and less frequently elsewhere in the state. Excavation of these sites has provided much new information on how these people lived. Fired-clay figurines found in an Archaic campsite in Council Grove reservoir predate the production of pottery vessels and are among the first fired-clay objects known in North America. Archaic period burials provide evidence for the social and religious sophistication of these people.

The next general period of Indian history is defined as the Woodland, so called because of influences from the woodlands of eastern America. Cultural changes that came from the East during this period included the introduction of the bow and arrow, pottery making, and

Little White Bear, Kansa Chief

Top: Earth lodges, typical of Pawnee Indian dwellings in what is now northern Kansas.
Courtesy of the Bureau of American Ethnology, Smithsonian Institution.
Bottom: Dwellings similar to this were used by the Quiviran (Wichita) Indians.

possibly domestication of plants in a primitive form of agriculture. Social innovations also occurred, such as the beginnings of community living and the construction of burial mounds. Dwelling sites from this period have been found frequently across Kansas, and archeologists have provided a detailed view of how these people lived in the eastern part of the state. In northeastern Kansas, for example, these people were living in well-built, oval houses with a pole framework that was probably covered with a grass thatching plastered in places with mud.

With the increased use of domesticated plants the Indians became, at least in part, food producers instead of food gatherers, making possible a more settled existence, larger populations, and permanent houses. This cultural stage is identified by archeologists as that of the Village Farmers. These people lived in Kansas from approximately A.D. 1000 until 1500. As their life became more sophisticated, so did their utensils and tools. They occupied earth lodges in northern Kansas and dwellings built of poles and grass, plastered with clay, in southern Kansas.

Finally came the Protohistoric Indians, who lasted only about a hundred years. These peoples were the forerunners of the tribal groups that one hears and reads about today: the Great Bend (the Wichita), the Oneota (the Kansa, or Kaw, and the Osage), the Lower Loup (the Pawnee, also known as Harahey), and the Dismal River (the Plains Apache). The grass lodge, the earth lodge, and the tipi were all built by these various groups who hunted the buffalo, and grew some varieties of corn and vegetables, but also lived off the land as had the earlier "gatherers."

Some of the most extensive archeological work in Kansas has involved the Protohistoric Wichita. These digs have confirmed the existence of these people throughout south-central Kansas. At some sites evidence of early contact with the earliest Spanish explorers, possibly Coronado, has been found. These sites have also yielded information on the grass-covered lodges and pit houses in which these people lived. Their agricultural acumen was shown by the numerous underground storage pits. Here they stocked surplus food for later use. Pottery, turquoise, and obsidian from the Southwest, as well as copper from the Great Lakes region, show the involvement that these early Kansans had with other people and places.

As European and American explorers entered the Plains the historic period (that time from which written accounts have been preserved) began. The beginning of the historic period varied from 1541 in central Kansas to 1700 on the eastern border. Among the tribes present were the Wichita, Kansa, Osage, Republican Pawnee (so called because the Republican River valley was their homeland), and the Cuartelejo Apache. Some years later came the Comanche, the Kiowa, and the Kiowa Apache, who pushed the Wichita into Texas and the Cuartelejo Apache into eastern New Mexico. By the 1820s groups such as the Southern Cheyenne and the Arapaho began to appear on the central Plains. These familiar tribes, portrayed in conflict with whites so many times on motion picture and television screens, were in the setting where the confrontations would begin.

These people, who were purely nomadic and who depended mainly on the buffalo as well as deer and antelope, were set apart from the earlier Indians because they had horses. This mobility gave them a superior ability to hunt and wage war. In the summer they were on the move, following the buffalo herds, visiting with their friends, and warring with their enemies, but in the winter they often established semipermanent, seasonal camps. In the winter, however, feed for their horses posed a problem. Their use of cottonwood bark and other woody vegetation as fodder is thought to have denuded the Plains, creating or significantly accenting the treeless landscape that greeted the early settlers.

It is difficult to say exactly when Indians acquired horses, but by 1719 the Pawnee had about three hundred horses, some marked with Spanish brands. The first horses owned by the Plains tribes came from the vicinity of Santa Fe, New Mexico, where the Spanish had built up herds descended from the animals they brought with them from Europe in the sixteenth century. Some horses were probably taken north by Pueblos escaping from Spanish rule while others were undoubtedly stolen by raiders in both the Southwest and the southern Great Plains.

While it is not possible to make general statements about Native Americans that will apply to all tribes or cultures, it is useful to note that

Indian Nations of Kansas, 1500–1850
Locations of the Indian tribes native to present Kansas (in larger capital letters) and "emigrant" Indians who came to the area after 1830 (smaller letters).

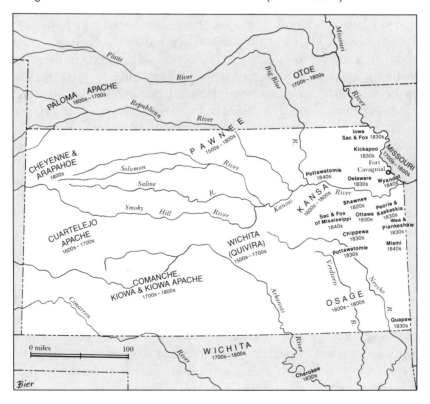

Hide paintings chronicled important events in tribal history. This one depicts a raid by the Kansas on a Pawnee village to get horses. The raiders were killed by the mounted Pawnee defenders.

they used similar weapons for both hunting and war in the period before the acquisition of firearms. They had spears, arrows, axes, and clubs, all with stone heads or points at first and later metal ones after contact with whites.

The furs and the skins of animals they hunted provided clothing, which was supplemented with blankets and other forms of cloth after trading began with whites. Skins also were used for covering tepees, as furnishings for the interiors of the different kinds of dwellings, for bedding, and for containers of various kinds. Beginning perhaps in the Woodland period, smoking became common among the tribes. Pipes were the smoking instruments of the Plains and were used socially and in rituals, particularly during religious ceremonies and when supernatural aid or enlightenment was sought.

Although religious customs varied among the Indians, all of them believed in a Great Spirit of some sort that represented the power of nature and, at times, the Creator. This mystical figure was called Wakanda, Waconda, or Wakan, depending on the people or the interpretation. There was also a belief that everything in nature had life—rocks, trees, and hills—and that the various gods were sometimes represented in animals. In addition to the serious Indian beliefs there was also a tradition of folklore that was often humorous. Humankind's foolish qualities were often illustrated by animal stories that were similar to Aesop's fables.

Indians differed from each other in many ways. They wore varying hairstyles and different kinds of clothing, ate different foods, and created different forms of art. These differences depended on their interests, the time in which they lived, and where they lived. Like other cultures, they were shaped by their respective times and environments.

There is one unique chapter in the Indian history of Kansas. In the state park north of Scott City on Ladder (or Beaver) Creek are the remains of a stone and adobe pueblo. This pueblo, a seven-room structure, has been known to archeologists since 1898. Nearby are traces of shallow ditches extending from some of the many springs that line the valley, presumably once used to irrigate crops in nearby flatlands. The first archeologists to study the pueblo concluded that it had been built and occupied by

Nomadic Plains Indians with lodges (tipis) made of animal hides. Courtesy of the National Archives.

Pueblan Indians from the Rio Grande valley in the late seventeenth or early eighteenth century, who escaped Spanish oppression to find a temporary home with the Plains Apaches. The settlement was referred to by the Spanish as El Cuartelejo. These Pueblo Indians undoubtedly came from the Taos and Picuris pueblos in what is now New Mexico. A group of Indians is known to have left the Southwest about 1664 and later were taken back to their homeland by Spanish soldiers, but the path of their journey cannot be established definitely. In 1696 a group from Picuris evaded the Spanish and spent about ten years among the Plains Apaches. When they were gathered up again by the Spanish in 1706, the Spanish commander wrote that they were dwelling in housing of a permanent type. Archeologists currently believe the Scott County pueblo to be that structure.

The stage is set. Kansas is the stage, and its landscape provides the scenery and the props. The first actors in the play named History have been described and it is time to introduce a new set of characters, all of whom made contact with some members of the first cast during different acts in this drama.

Suggestions for Reading

Robert Baughman, *Kansas in Maps* (1961); Rex Buchanan, ed., *Kansas Geology* (1984); R. Douglas Hurt, *Indian Agriculture in America: Prehistory to Present* (1987); Kelly Kindscher has written two volumes on the flora of the region: *Edible Wild Plants of the Prairie* (1997) and *Medicinal Wild Plants of the Prairie* (1992); Grace Muilenburg, *The Kansas Scene* (1953); O. J. Reichman, *Konza Prairie: A Tallgrass Natural History* (1987); Katherine Rogers, *The Sternberg Fossil Hunters: A Dinosaur Dynasty* (1991); Waldo R. Wedel, *An Introduction to Kansas Archeology* (1959); Waldo R. Wedel, *Prehistoric Man on the Great Plains* (1961); Waldo R. Wedel, *Central Plains Prehistory* (1986); and Frank W. Wilson, *Kansas Landscapes: A Geologic Diary* (1978).

A brief article by Randall M. Thies, "Earth, Wind, and Fire: Kansas Archeology," appeared in *Kansas Heritage* (Spring, 1997).

2

Exploration of the Great Plains

Between 1541 and 1830 a number of explorers—Spanish, French, and American—visited, examined, and recorded information about the land that is now Kansas. They were in search of gold, trade with the Indians, and knowledge. They recorded much of what they saw and, in the case of the Americans, brought to their fellow citizens the first information on such things as the prairie dog and the sunflower.

THE SPANISH EXPLORERS

In the early spring of 1540 a large Spanish expedition set out from northwestern Mexico, under the command of a *conquistador* named Francisco Vasquez de Coronado, to search for the fabulously wealthy Seven Cities of Cibola. The Spanish in North America were interested in acquiring wealth and an empire for their King, and they had been told stories of cities with streets paved with gold.

In July, Coronado reached the first city, which turned out to be a poor Zuñi Indian village in what is now western New Mexico. Disappointed, though not discouraged, Coronado stayed with the Zuñi and sent out parties to see if other cities might exist. They discovered the Grand Canyon and more Indian pueblos, but found that the legendary Cibola was just that—a legend. Coronado spent the winter of 1540–1541 in the Rio Grande valley and made plans for a second exploration to the kingdom of Quivira. An Indian slave called "the Turk," because, according to one Spaniard, "he looked like one," reported that this also was a land of riches.

In April 1541 Coronado set out for the north. Much of the country through which he marched was so barren and food supplies became so short that the commander was forced to send part of his men back to Mexico. He continued with a selected group of thirty, all of whom hoped to find Quivira. With this small force of soldiers and a Franciscan priest, Coronado moved into the High Plains country.

According to the most reliable authorities, Coronado went through what is now west Texas and the Oklahoma panhandle beyond the 100th meridian, entering Kansas in the vicinity of Liberal. He passed near the modern towns of Plains, Meade, Fowler, and Minneola and crossed the Arkansas River near present Dodge City on June 29, 1541. From the river the expedition swung to the northeast, and on July 2, encountered some Quiviran Indians (the Wichitas) between present Kinsley and Larned. The natives were at first frightened by the Spaniards for they had not seen horses before and believed that these strange new creatures were a combination of man and beast.

After his meeting with these people, Coronado journeyed past Pawnee Rock and the great bend of the Arkansas River and followed its course until he reached other villages, presumably near Lyons. He found practically naked Indians living in grass lodges. The people were without gold or silver. By that time it was apparent to the Spaniards that the stories told by the Turk were false, and he was killed.

However, Coronado marched for another twenty-five leagues (a league is slightly more than two-and-a-half miles) and crossed the Smoky Hill River. He found more villages, but they were like the ones he had already seen, without wealth. Coronado did not go farther than the site of Lindsborg, although some writers have believed that he did. He was tired and his men were discouraged. After about thirty days in Quivira he prepared to return to the Southwest—his quest for gold and silver had been in vain.

Despite the shortage of the kind of riches the Spaniards longed for, they were impressed with the land in central Kansas. They saw thousands of buffalo and recognized their value. They also noted the fertility of the soil and the native plants. Pedro de Casteñeda, one of Coronado's soldiers, commented on the land:

> . . . Judging from what was seen on the borders of it, this country is
> very similar to that of Spain in the varieties of vegetation and fruits.
> There are plums like those of Castile, grapes, nuts, mulberries, oats,
> pennyroyal, wild marjoram, and large quantities of flax, but this
> does not do them [the Indians] any good, because they do not know
> how to use it. The people . . . have villages like those in New Spain.
> The houses are round, without a wall, and they have one story like a

Coronado's march into present Kansas, painted by Albert T. Reid, a noted Kansas artist.

loft, under one roof, where they sleep and keep their belongings. The roofs are of straw. . . .

In August 1541, Coronado left Kansas and made his way back to the Rio Grande valley where he rejoined his original force. During the summer of 1542, suffering from injuries received in a fall from his horse, Coronado made his final report to his superiors. He brought no wealth but his expedition served to increase interest in the country he had seen, and in later years his exploration gave Spain a claim to the Plains country.

Father Juan Padilla, the priest who accompanied Coronado, returned to Quivira in the spring of 1542, hoping to bring Christianity to the Indians. He had with him a few assistants and servants as well as a half-dozen Indians who had served Coronado as guides on his return march. He spent some time among the friendly Quivirans and then decided to move farther east in an effort to expand his missionary efforts. Unfortunately, he met some hostile natives who killed him. The time and place of his death are unknown, but memorials to this first Christian martyr on Kansas soil have been erected at Council Grove and Lyons.

In 1593 or 1594, an unauthorized and ill-fated Spanish expedition, led by two men (Leyva and Humaña), went from New Mexico to Kansas in search of gold. Little is known about the group except that all but one of them were killed.

In June 1601, Juan de Oñate, governor of New Mexico, with more than seventy men and a number of wagons, marched in a northeasterly direction guided by the lone survivor of the Leyva-Humaña expedition. One group of Indians, whom they called Escanjaques, accompanied them farther into present Kansas where they fought with another tribe (probably the Wichitas). Oñate turned back to New Mexico, presumably from the area between what is now Wichita and Kingman. Oñate's expedition accomplished nothing more than the earlier Spanish ones, but he, like Coronado, was favorably impressed with the agricultural possibilities of central Kansas:

> The cornstalks were as tall as those of New Spain and in some
> places even taller. The land was so fertile that even though the corn
> had just been harvested, there was a second crop about six inches
> high, without other cultivation or preparation of the soil than
> pulling up the grass and making some holes in which the corn was
> planted. There were many beans and some calabashes [gourds], and
> plum trees between the planted fields. . . .

The Spanish influence was little felt on the Great Plains. The Indians were not as easily conquered as those in the Southwest, and the resources were not the kind that could be exploited—soil, grass, and buffalo were not like gold, silver, and copper and could not fill the treasure chests of Spanish rulers. Spain could claim the area but could not impose its will upon the land.

THE FRENCH EXPLORERS

In June 1673, Louis Jolliet and Jacques Marquette, with five other Frenchmen from Canada, were traveling by canoe down the Mississippi. Suddenly they reached the mouth of a great river pouring its muddy waters into the "Father of Waters" and became the first whites to see the Missouri. About a year later Jolliet drew a map, and the names Kansas and Missouri made their first appearance in recorded history. Although these French explorers did not personally examine present Kansas, they gathered information that would be of value to later travelers in the West.

The French were interested in expanding their fur trade with the Indians through the Missouri valley. From their posts in the Illinois country they attempted to penetrate the land beyond the Missouri River. In 1719, Charles Claude du Tisné went up the Missouri and contacted Indians in western Missouri and in Kansas. His expedition was filled with difficulties, caused mostly by the fact that the tribes he met—Osages and Pawnees—did not like each other and that affected their dealings with the French. He planted a French flag, probably in southeastern Kansas, and thus established a contact which the French hoped would lead to future Indian friendships and a profitable trade.

In that same year war broke out between France and Spain, and the Spanish were worried about the possible increase of French influence with the Plains tribes. Pedro de Villasur was sent with a small force in 1720 to try to discover what the French were doing. Villasur marched all the way to the Platte River, in what is now Nebraska, where he was defeated in battle by the Pawnees. Although the defeat took place in Nebraska it affected Kansas history because it seriously damaged Spanish military influence in this area.

The French were now in a position to strengthen their contacts and trade with the western Indians. They sent Étienne Veniard de Bourgmont up the Missouri in 1723 to establish Fort Orleans on the river in what is now Carroll County, Missouri. The next year Bourgmont led an expedition as far west as Saline and Ellsworth counties and there, in October, he met with the Padouca, the name then given by the French to the Plains Apaches. The Indians promised their friendship; Bourgmont felt that he had effectively blocked Spanish influence and opened the way for the French to trade with the southwestern settlements.

For fifteen years the French maintained their trade west of the Missouri River, in the vast area they called Louisiana. Then, in 1739, a party of French traders led by Paul and Pierre Mallet, traveled all the way from the Platte River to Santa Fe, crossing Kansas in a southwesterly direction, partly along the route later followed by the Sante Fe Trail.

In 1744 the French built Fort Cavagnial, a combined military and trading post at the Kansas village near where Fort Leavenworth is now. Details are not complete on the fort, but it had five log buildings, surrounded by a log stockade, in which the soldiers and traders lived. Fort Cavagnial, named for the governor of New France, was established to control the fur trade and to make trading contact with the Spaniards.

The fort became the commercial and military center of the area, which now includes most of Kansas, Missouri, and Nebraska. It was served by several military commanders, who ordinarily had only about ten soldiers, and its traders dealt with several tribes of Indians. The French trapped very little themselves but they distributed great quantities of trade goods to Indians who brought their furs to the fort. The post's residents led an isolated life in the winter, but during the summer there were Indians coming and going and French-Canadian traders up and down the Missouri River.

Fort Cavagnial remained important to the French in North America until the end of the French and Indian War in 1763. Then France gave up Canada to the English and the Louisiana country (which included the Mississippi and Missouri valleys from the Gulf of Mexico to Canada) to the Spanish. The fort was small but it was the first white outpost of any permanency in what is now Kansas. It also was extremely important to the fur trading industry of Louis XV's American empire.

Spain once again governed the Plains, but the trading contacts with the Indians continued to be French, who operated out of their little settlement in St. Louis. Auguste and Pierre Chouteau traded with the Kansas after 1790, and other Frenchmen dealt with the Osages and the Otoes. In 1792, Pierre Vial, a Frenchman employed by Spain, went from Santa Fe to St. Louis. The next year he traveled from the Pawnee country in Nebraska, through Kansas, to Santa Fe. Like the earlier Mallets he helped lay out a part of the later Santa Fe Trail.

As the eighteenth century drew to a close, there were Englishmen in Canada casting envious eyes south to the central Plains and Americans who were looking beyond the Mississippi and Missouri rivers. Spain's power in international politics was declining, which meant that Spain would have difficulty in exerting control in North America. Also Spain believed that the wilderness of Louisiana was a drain on the treasury, so Spanish diplomats did not object to selling the area if a reasonable price could be agreed upon. In 1800 Spain and France signed the Treaty of San Ildefonso, and France got Louisiana. However, no public announcement of the sale was made because both countries thought it better to keep the news from both England and the United States.

Napoleon had plans for a new colonial empire, and after he made peace with England in 1802 he was ready to make a move in North America. He first sent troops to Santo Domingo, and rumors of the transfer of Louisiana from Spain flew like wildfire in the American West. Some westerners talked about going to war to control Louisiana and to protect American interests on the Mississippi, but President Jefferson, at the same time, was trying to keep peace and also buy Louisiana. When Napoleon's army had trouble with rebels and disease in Santo Domingo, and, when he found that he might again be at war with England, the United States was able to purchase Louisiana.

AMERICAN EXPLORERS APPEAR— THE LEWIS AND CLARK EXPEDITION

Early in 1803, President Thomas Jefferson asked Congress for funds to send an exploring expedition from the Missouri River to the Pacific Northwest. When Congress approved, the president chose Meriwether Lewis and William Clark to lead the party. Four months later, on April 30, representatives of the United States and France completed arrangements for the sale of Louisiana to the United States, but the American flag was not raised officially over New Orleans until December 20. Included in Jefferson's great real estate bargain was most of Kansas, leaving only that portion south of the Arkansas River and west of the 100th meridian in Spanish hands.

The Louisiana Territory was mostly unknown to the U.S. government at the time of the purchase. The headwaters of the Mississippi had not been thoroughly explored, and most of the Far West was a mystery. Fur traders had traveled up the Missouri into present North Dakota, but most Americans were ignorant of what they had found. The fact that the United States had doubled its size for approximately fifteen million dollars did not impress some people. One Boston newspaper said that the territory was "a great waste, a wilderness unpeopled with any beings except wolves and wandering Indians."

Lewis and Clark, with forty-three men, left their camp near St. Louis on May 14, 1804, and on June 26 reached the junction of the Kansas and Missouri rivers. There they stayed for three days while they gathered information on the area, including facts about the Kansas Indians. They camped on the north bank of the Missouri on June 29 and the next night stopped on the Kansas side. By July 1 they were opposite the site of Leavenworth, and on July 3 they stayed in present Atchison County.

To greet the Fourth of July the explorers fired a shot from the "swivel gun" (a small cannon) on their keelboat. During the day they named two creeks—Fourth of July and Independence—and had one member of the party bitten by a snake. Their camp that night was on the Missouri bank, opposite Doniphan, and they closed the day with another cannon shot

Zebulon Pike and his men in council with the Pawnee Indians, 1806.

and "an extra Gill [measure] of whiskey." On July 5, 7, and 9, their camps were on the Kansas side, but shortly after that they moved beyond the borders of the state. Although the Kansas portion of the famous journey was brief, Lewis and Clark did gather considerable information about eastern Kansas and its inhabitants. They also provided a map that, despite its inaccuracies, gave the federal government more data than it previously had.

THE PIKE EXPEDITION

The United States government decided also to explore the southern portion of the Louisiana Purchase. Consequently, General James Wilkinson, then governor of Louisiana Territory, issued orders to Lieutenant Zebulon M. Pike on June 24, 1806, sending him to the Plains. Wilkinson told Pike to return some Osage Indians, who had been prisoners, to their home in western Missouri and to meet with chiefs of both the Osages and Kansas for the purpose of making peace between them. Pike also was to establish friendly relations with the Comanches, and for that purpose he was to visit the Pawnees from whom he might get interpreters and information on how best to deal with the Comanches. Wilkinson's orders to Pike also said:

> In the course of your tour, you are to remark particularly upon the geographical structure, the natural history, and population of the country through which you may pass, taking particular care to collect and preserve specimens of everything curious in the mineral or botanical worlds, which can be preserved and are portable. . . .
>
> It is an object of much interest with the executive to ascertain the direction, extent, and navigation of the Arkansaw and Red rivers; as far, therefore, as may be compatible with these instructions and practicable to the means you may command, I wish you to carry your views to those subjects; and should circumstances conspire to favor the enterprise, that you may detach a party with a few Osage to descend the Arkansaw under the orders of Lieutenant [James B.] Wilkinson [son of the general], or Sergeant Ballinger, properly instructed and equipped to take the courses and distances, to remark on the soil, timber, etc. and to note the tributary streams. . . .

In September 1806, while Lewis and Clark were still on their way home, the Pike expedition entered Kansas in the southeastern part of the state, near present Fort Scott, and marched to the northwest. Pike crossed the Neosho and Verdigris rivers and camped on the Cottonwood in what is now Chase County. He then moved on to the Smoky Hill, Saline, and

Solomon rivers. He and his men recorded information on the geography of the Flint Hills and noted a large number of animals. Pike was of the opinion that eastern Kansas would be good grazing land.

While on the march Pike learned from a Pawnee hunter that a large body of Spanish soldiers had been in the vicinity recently. But the Americans did not make contact with the Spaniards, who had also gone north to hold a council with the Pawnees. On September 23, Pike was in the area west of present Glasco, and the next day he was met by a party of Pawnees. Six days later, on the Republican River, Pike sat at a grand council with the Pawnees and persuaded them to fly an American flag instead of a Spanish one. For several days Pike stayed among the Pawnees, working for peace among the Indians, gathering additional information, and making preparations to set out for the Arkansas River.

For many years a controversy existed concerning the location of the Pawnee village where Pike held his meeting. On the Republican River in Republic County, near the towns of Belleville and Republic, is the site of a Pawnee village of the early 1800s. In the 1890s many Kansans decided that this was the place where Pike had convinced the Pawnees to fly the American flag, and in 1901 a monument was dedicated to the event.

Thirty-five miles away, in Webster County, Nebraska, near Red Cloud, is another Pawnee village site. Here, Nebraskans claimed, was where Pike had been. In 1936, Waldo R. Wedel, a native Kansan and one of the nation's leading archaeologists, stated that the Nebraska site probably had the best claim to where Pike stopped. More recent scholarship, which has dealt in great detail with Pike's march, supports that idea.

As far as Kansas is concerned there is no great value in claiming that Pike stopped south of the present Nebraska border. Most important is that the Pawnee village in Republic County is one of the notable archeological sites in the United States. It contained between thirty and forty earth lodges and probably had a thousand residents. One of those lodges, with displays that interpret Pawnee life, is now a part of a unique museum devoted to the historical and archeological picture of the Indians that Zebulon Pike met, and it represents their style of living as he would have found it in 1806.

On October 15, Pike and two men were separated from the rest of the expedition but they were reunited on the great bend of the Arkansas, where they stayed for another ten days. On October 28, Lieutenant Wilkinson, five soldiers, and two Indians left the camp and started downstream in canoes. Shallow water, cold weather, and a combination of bad luck made their journey difficult, but they did see the valleys of the Arkansas and the Ninnescahs before moving into Oklahoma and Arkansas.

Pike and the rest of his men went west, up the Arkansas and by mid-November were beyond the Kansas border. They sighted but did not climb the Rocky Mountain peak that bears Pike's name. They suffered with the mountain winter, and they were captured by Spanish authorities who held them in Santa Fé and later in northern Mexico. The Spanish took away Pike's papers except for a few letters and his journal, which he managed to hide. But he was able to remember much of the information the expedition had accumulated. Finally, in July 1807, the Americans were released.

Zebulon Pike was not a trained explorer and he made a great many mistakes on the expedition but he did gather and eventually publish valuable scientific facts that were previously unknown to the United States government. He also indicated that there were great possibilities for trade with the Spanish Southwest, and he increased interest in the future development of that trade.

Pike was not impressed with much of the land through which he marched, particularly the western part of Kansas. He wrote:

> . . . On the rivers Kanses, La Platte, Arkansaw, and their various branches, it appears to me to be only possible to introduce a limited population on their banks. The inhabitants would find it most to their advantage to pay attention to the multiplication of cattle, horses, sheep, and goats, all of which they can raise in abundance, the earth producing spontaneously sufficient for their support . . . but the wood now in the country would not be sufficient for a moderate share of population more than 15 years, and it would be out of the question to think of using any of it in manufacture. . . .
>
> In that vast country of which I speak, we find the soil generally dry and sandy, with gravel, and discover that the moment we approach a stream the land becomes more humid, with small timber. I therefore conclude that this country never was timbered. . . . These vast plains of the western hemisphere may become in time as celebrated as the sandy deserts of Africa; for I saw in my route, in various places, tracts of many leagues where the wind had thrown up the sand in all the fanciful form of the ocean's rolling wave, and on which not a speck of vegetable matter existed.
>
> But from these immense prairies may arise one great advantage to the United States, viz: The restriction of our population to some certain limits, and thereby a continuation of the Union. Our citizens being so prone to rambling and extending themselves on the frontiers will, through necessity, be constrained to limit their extent on the west to the borders of the Missouri and Mississippi, while they leave the prairies incapable of cultivation to the wandering and uncivilized aborigines of the country.

With these comments, Pike began the discussions—and the arguments—about the "Great American Desert." These discussions would go on for decades and would influence the thinking of many Americans. The explorer who reinforced Pike's opinions was Major Stephen H. Long, who was in the West in 1819 and 1820 under orders from John C. Calhoun, secretary of war. Long was an experienced army engineer who had earlier examined rivers in the upper Mississippi valley.

THE LONG EXPEDITION

The war department planned to establish a fort on the upper Missouri (in present Montana) to help police Indians and keep out British fur traders. A part of the army's plan was to conduct additional scientific studies west of the Missouri. Long's orders read:

> The object of the expedition is to acquire as thorough and accurate knowledge as may be practicable of a portion of the country which is daily becoming more interesting but which is as yet imperfectly known. . . . You will enter in your journal everything interesting in relation to soil, face of the country, water courses and productions, whether animal, vegetable, or mineral.

Long's first responsibility was to ascend the Missouri River to its junction with the Yellowstone but on August 6, 1819, a company of thirteen men was detached from the main group at Fort Osage (east of Independence, Missouri) and directed overland into Kansas "to extend our examination between Fort Osage and the Konza River, also between that river and the Platte." The commander of the party was Thomas Say, a zoologist. Others in the group were a geologist, a naturalist, an artist, and assorted interpreters, guides, and soldiers. Say and his group crossed Johnson, Douglas, and Shawnee counties and probably camped near Lecompton on the Kansas River on August 13. They became familiar with the Kansas summer heat and some of the prairie creatures—including flies and rattlesnakes. On August 19, they reached the Vermillion (in Pottawatomie County) and were forced to make a meal "of a black wolf." The following day they came to a large village of Kansas just east of Manhattan where they participated in a pipe-smoking ceremony, a conference, and a meal of buffalo and corn. Say was in the village four days and during that time collected valuable information about the Kansas and their way of living.

Say's group proceeded up the Blue River and were met by a large band of hostile Pawnees who stole their baggage and food and scattered their pack horses, but left them unharmed. They went back to the Kansas' village where they again enjoyed the tribe's hospitality. Say decided to abandon the march to the Platte and on August 26 set out for the Missouri where they caught up with the expedition's steamboat, the *Western Engineer,* in present Doniphan County. Major Long, aboard the steamboat, had made several stops along the way and had held a council with Kansas at Cow Island near present Atchison.

The entire party proceeded to Council Bluffs, where they spent the winter. In the spring they traveled up the Platte and South Platte to the Rocky Mountains. Long discovered the peak that is named for him, and some of his men climbed Pike's Peak for the first time. Long divided his party and sent one group down the Arkansas River while he took another south of present Kansas, down the Canadian River, which he thought was the Red. Both parties met at Fort Smith in Arkansas and went from there to the Mississippi where they disbanded.

Long's trained scientists recorded large amounts of technical data, which added to the general knowledge of all phases of the territory that he covered. But his agreement with Pike on the barrenness of part of the country was emphasized by this statement concerning the country between the Missouri and the Red:

> In regard to this extensive section of country, I do not hesitate in giving the opinion, that it is almost wholly unfit for cultivation, and of course uninhabitable by a people depending on agriculture for their subsistence. Although tracts of fertile land considerably extensive are occasionally to be met with, yet the scarcity of wood and water, almost uniformly prevalent, will prove an insuperable obstacle in the way of settling the country. . . . This region, however, . . . may prove of infinite importance to the United States, inasmuch as it is calculated to serve as a barrier to prevent too great an extension of our population westward, and secure against the machinations or incursions of an enemy. . . .

When Long published a map of the area he had explored he put the name "Great American Desert" on it, and there it would remain in atlases and school geographies until after the Civil War.

Just as Long finished his explorations another expedition set out from Fort Smith under the command of Jacob Fowler. He marched up the Arkansas River to south-central Colorado and observed some regions missed by the earlier travelers. On his return he hit the headwaters of the Whitewater and Verdigris rivers, crossed the Neosho and struck out for the Missouri near present Kansas City. But his reports were no more favorable than Pike's and Long's. He said the country was lacking in vegetation and the hills were mostly "hard black soil with some progecting rocks and covered with vigetation mostly a short grass something like blew grass."

A member of the Stephen Long expedition made this drawing of a Kansa dance near present Manhattan in 1819. It is believed to be the first picture ever printed depicting a scene in present Kansas.

All of the negative comments made by government explorers concerning the lack of agricultural prospects for the western portion of Kansas (and other areas of the Great Plains) lent strength to two major theories, both of which were tied up with national politics. There were many Americans who believed that the expansion of the United States should stop at the Missouri River, just as Pike and Long had suggested, and if the land were uninhabitable for white settlers then there was no reason to worry about occupying the land.

There were others who thought that the Indians could easily be removed to this region where they would not bother white Americans nor would white Americans bother them. As it turned out both theories were unrealistic but, for a time, they affected the thinking of a number of people who controlled the political power of the nation, and they led to the experiment of Indian relocation.

Suggestions for Reading

There is a tremendous amount of published material dealing with explorations on the Great Plains, but the following references will give the interested reader representative information on the various people and conditions discussed in this chapter. Stephen Ambrose, *Undaunted Courage: Meriwether Lewis, Thomas Jefferson, and the Opening of the American West* (1997); John E. Bakeless, *Lewis and Clark, Partners in Discovery* (1947); Maxine Benson, ed., *From Pittsburgh to the Rocky Mountains: Major Stephen Long's Expedition, 1819–1820* (1988); Donald J. Blakeslee, *Along Ancient Trails: The Mallet Expedition of 1739* (1995); Herbert E. Bolton, *Coronado on the Turquoise Trail* (1949); Elliott Coues, *History of the Expedition under the Command of Lewis and Clark* (1893); Leroy R. Hafen and Carl C. Rister, *Western America* (1941); George P. Hammond and Agapito Rey, *Narratives of the Coronado Expedition* (1940); W. Eugene Hollon, *The Lost Pathfinder: Zebulon Montgomery Pike* (1949); Donald Jackson, *The Journals of Zebulon Montgomery Pike* (1966); A. P. Nasatir, *Before Lewis and Clark* (1952); Walter P. Webb, *The Great Plains* (1931); and Waldo R. Wedel, *An Introduction to Kansas Archeology* (1959). Charles E. Hoffhaus, "Fort de Cavagnial: Imperial France in Kansas, 1744–1764," *Kansas Historical Quarterly* (Winter, 1964), summarizes a little-known aspect of French efforts on the Plains. Milton Reichart, "Bourgmont's Route to Central Kansas: A Reexamination" *Kansas History* (Summer, 1979) deals with French exploration. The story of the first permanent U.S. military post in Kansas is told in Arthur J. Stanley, Jr., "Fort Leavenworth: Dowager Queen of Frontier Posts" *Kansas Historical Quarterly* (Spring, 1976).

3

Indian Removal and Christian Missionary Efforts

By 1814 there was peace (at least temporarily) between Indians and whites east of the Mississippi River, and so settlement increased in the areas bordering the river. Consequently, the federal government's Indian policy had to be revised. In theory, the government treated the tribes as though they were nations, which meant that the United States Senate ratified treaties just as they did with foreign powers. But advancing settlement generally meant that there would be additional conflict, and treaties were often used by the government as ways for removing tribes from their homelands.

As early as 1803, President Thomas Jefferson proposed a plan that would offer the eastern Indians lands west of the Mississippi in exchange for those on which they were living. This was tried on a voluntary basis after 1815, but without success. The actual relocation of the tribes began after Congress passed an act in 1825 that was supplemented by the Removal Act of 1830. Removal did not take place without great difficulty. Several of the eastern tribes had reached a high level of political organization and, in some cases, dealt with both social and governmental problems on a basis superior to their white neighbors'. President Andrew Jackson expressed the opinion of most westerners when he said that the treaty lands had been reserved only as Indian hunting grounds. When the game was gone then the Indians should also go so that settlement could take place. In addition, he said the plan was a humane one because it would remove the Indians from the influences of immoral whites and save them from destruction.

INDIAN REMOVAL TO KANSAS

The story of Indian removal and the establishment of missions to transplanted eastern tribes cannot be considered without giving attention to a Baptist preacher and teacher named Isaac McCoy. McCoy, who by 1818 was working among the Miami Indians in Indiana, believed that the influence of white men upon red would bring about the disintegration of the tribes, and that they would face both cultural and moral poverty. He thought that the only solution was the establishment of an Indian state beyond the Mississippi where the tribes could become Christian farmers.

After he left the Miami mission, McCoy worked among the Weas, the Delawares, and the Potawatomis. In 1822 he went to the Carey Mission for the Potawatomis in Michigan Territory, where he came in contact with three men who would also be important in the Kansas Baptist missions at a later date—Robert Simerwell, Jotham Meeker, and Johnston Lykins. McCoy decided to take his ideas to Washington after he had discussed them with the Baptist Mission Board. He presented his conclusions to John C. Calhoun, secretary of war, who passed them on to President James Monroe. Both men thought that McCoy's ideas were good, and the federal government moved ahead with plans for Indian removal.

In June 1825, William Clark, of Lewis and Clark expedition fame, arranged a treaty with the Kansas and Osages that resulted in their giving up large areas of land in what is now Kansas. Clark was at that time Superintendent of Indian Affairs in St. Louis and responsible for all Indian relations beyond the Mississippi River. This treaty opened the way for a wholesale moving of eastern Indians to the West.

In 1828, Isaac McCoy was appointed one of the commissioners for the government to assist certain tribes to examine the western country and to select locations for their new homes. Two tours were made, and delegations of Potawatomis, Ottawas, Creeks, Chickasaws, and Choctaws were taken into the West. In 1830 McCoy was appointed surveyor and agent to assist in the migration. He was to devote more than ten years to the work. During that period he selected and surveyed locations for various tribes and established missions and schools. He traveled through the valleys of the Kansas, Smoky Hill, and Solomon rivers. He also made maps and recorded information about those regions.

In the light of what is known about race relations and its problems today, McCoy's ideas about a separate land for Indians were unrealistic, but he cannot be severely criticized for what he tried to do. He earnestly wanted to do something good for the Indians, and he did not try to make money for himself. He did not wish to remove the Indians just to make more land available for advancing white settlers, and he fought for Indian welfare. The plan did not work out as McCoy had hoped. There were too many tribes, too little land, and too much white contact too soon.

McCoy's concern about the Indians, and his reaction to some of the whites hired by the government to help him, are expressed in this paragraph written during his 1828 survey in Kansas:

> I have for myself, a lonesome time. No one is with me who feels interested in the enterprise beyond his own immediate comfort, or with whom I can indulge as an associate. The Indians are exceedingly careless and improvident. Willing to do anything I tell them, but will not put themselves to the trouble of thinking. Like children, some of them think the distance great and appear to be somewhat homesick. I almost daily show them on the map where we are, and whither we are going. Were it not for this, some would be ready to fancy themselves near the edge of the world. Upon the whole, however, they are generally cheerful. The two white men hired as packmen are poor sticks and give me trouble. Scarce a day passes that I have not to reprove one of them and sometimes threaten to discharge them there in the wilderness. . . .

Great numbers of Indians were not moved from the East until after 1830, but the Delawares signed a treaty in 1829 that gave them land in present Kansas. From then until almost time for the opening of Kansas Territory (1854), the area and Indian removal were closely tied together. Nearly thirty tribes were assigned reservations in eastern Kansas although, in some cases, very few of their members occupied the land. The Cherokees acquired 800,000 acres in southeastern Kansas, but they never lived there. Known as the "Cherokee Neutral Tract," that land was later involved in a great controversy as settlers and railroad promoters struggled to get it by any means possible.

From the Great Lakes region and the Ohio valley came the once-powerful Shawnees, Delawares, Wyandots, Ottawas, and Potawatomis, along with the Kickapoos, Chippewas, Peorias, Kaskaskias, Weas, Piankashaws, Quapaws, Iowas, Sacs and Foxes, and the "New York Indians." Some of these tribes had already experienced one move. Included in the New York group were remnants of the Iroquois nations and the Munsees and Stockbridges, from New York and New England. They were all assured by the federal government that they would not be moved again and could live in peace indefinitely, west of the Missouri. All those promises would disappear during the next thirty years.

Many of the Indians made the trip to their new homes without too much physical difficulty though it was hard for them to leave areas where

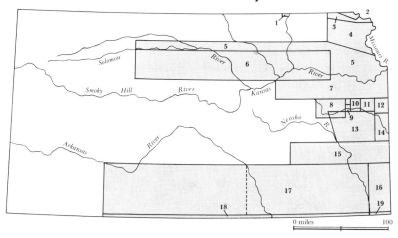

Indian Reservations in Kansas, 1846

1. Otoes and Missourias. 2. Iowas, 1837. 3. Sacs and Foxes of Missouri, 1837. 4. Kick-apoo Reserve, established under treaty of 1833. 5. Delaware Reserve and Outlet, established under treaty of 1831. 6. Kansa Reserve, established under treaty of 1825. 7. Shawnee Reserve, established by treaty of 1825. 8. Sacs and Foxes of Mississippi. 9. Chippewa Reserve, 1830. 10. Ottawa Reserve, 1832. 11. Peorias and Kaskaskias, 1833. 12. Weas and Piankeshaws, 1833. 13. Potawatomi Reserve, established under treaty of 1837. 14. Miami Reserve, 1839 and 1841. 15. New York Indian Lands, con-veyed under treaty of 1838. 16. Cherokee Neutral Lands, conveyed under treaty of 1838. 17. Osage Reserve established by treaty of 1825. (The western boundary, originally the dotted line, was arbitrarily extended by the surveyors to the old Mexican line.) 18. Cherokee Strip, conveyed under treaty of 1835. 19. Quapaw Strip, 1834.

they had lived so long. Some who had no trouble on the journey suffered after reaching Kansas. For example, the Ottawas found the change in cli-mate and in living conditions disastrous. The agent who conducted them reported that "out of about 600 emigrants, more than 300 died within the first two years, because of exposure, lack of proper food, and the great dif-ference between the cool, damp woods of Ohio and the dry, hot plains of Kansas." Ottawa births could not keep pace with deaths and so their num-bers decreased. They also suffered loss of life and property in the Marais des Cygnes River flood of 1844.

There were unscrupulous whites involved in removal who managed to make money for themselves while Indians did not receive the supplies and medical care they were promised. There were also sympathetic whites who understood the Indians' sadness, who were genuinely concerned about their welfare, and who looked unfavorably on dishonest dealing and wor-ried about the government's seeming lack of humanity. James B. Gardiner, superintendent of Indians being moved from Ohio (Shawnees and Otta-was), was one of the concerned whites. He wrote in October 1832:

. . . With very few exceptions, the Indians are on horseback, and in *their own* wagons and carriages. We have seventy-five public horses and ten public wagons, to assist in the transportation of the baggage, and the conveyance of the aged, sick, and decrepit.

The Indians are generally healthy, and, so far, are contented and pleased with the prospect of reaching their new homes, before the severity of winter. . . .

We have, as yet, received but ten thousand dollars, which sum, according to the report of the disbursing agent, was nearly exhausted in the preparatory measures. . . . This gentleman left us at Indianapolis for Cincinnati, for the avowed purpose of procuring funds, and has not been heard of since.

From the time of leaving Indianapolis up to the present period, we have subsisted ourselves, the Indians, and about six hundred horses, principally on funds *borrowed from the Indians themselves!* Still, we have managed so as to prevent any real want, or any delay in our operations.

A great proportion of the emigrants . . . consists of women and children. Several of the former are very aged and infirm, and many of the latter helpless infants. A few deaths . . . have occurred on the road. . . .

Deeply sensible of the responsibility which devolves upon me . . . I am extremely solicitous to exercise all possible prudence and caution, in preserving the lives and the health of the eight hundred defenceless human beings committed to my care. . . .

It would have been well if all the people responsible for removal procedures had been as concerned as Gardiner. Removal generally was difficult to manage, and many delays took place. Conflict, like the Black Hawk war in Illinois and the Second Seminole war in the southeastern United States, fought because the Sacs and Foxes and the Seminole tribes wished to retain their homelands, took more lives and increased bad feelings on both sides. The price of Indian removal was high, but by the 1840s nearly 100,000 Indians had been moved from the path of white settlement, and what the government chose to call a "permanent Indian frontier" had been established.

THE MISSIONARIES

Although most of the work of Christian missionaries in the Kansas area was closely tied to the post–1825 Indian removal policy, the first missionary station was established slightly earlier. In September 1824, a mission was started among the Osage Indians by the United Foreign Missionary Society, an organization supported by three Protestant groups, including the Presbyterians. This first effort was called Mission Neosho and was located in Neosho County, near where the town of Shaw now stands.

The people who came to build Mission Neosho had been working among the Osages in Missouri. The missionaries, Benton Pixley and his wife Lucia, came with their two small children and chose the location near the Neosho River. He began cutting timber for a log house where they would live, but they stayed in an abandoned trader's cabin through the first winter. In the spring of 1825 a group of fellow missionary workers came from Missouri and helped build large log buildings; one was used as a school room for Osage children and the other as a church for the adults.

The following year Daniel Bright arrived as an instructor in farming. Ground was broken and crops were planted and cultivated. The Indians helped with the farming and raised beans, watermelons, pumpkins, and corn. Another teacher, Cornelia Pelham, came that year and for the next several months Mission Neosho was a busy place. Indian children came daily for two months each year to go to school and the mission was responsible for feeding them. Some Osages came to beg (mostly women and little children), and others ignored the mission much of the time.

Pixley learned the Osage language and he made an honest effort to understand how the Indians thought and lived, which was something that not all missionaries bothered to do. He also taught and preached but the preaching was difficult because the Osages were not really interested in the white's God. Pixley wrote of the Indians' relation to Christianity:

> When I tell them I came to teach them the word of God, they
> sometimes sneeringly ask, "Where is God? Have you seen him?"—
> and then laugh that I should think of making them believe a thing
> so incredible, as a being who sees and takes knowledge of them,
> while they cannot see him. They indeed call the earth, the sun and
> moon, thunder and lightning, God; but their conceptions on this
> subject are altogether indefinite and confused. Some old men, who
> are more given to seriousness and reflection, frankly declare that
> they know nothing about God—what he is, or where he is, or what
> he would have them do. . . .
> Of a future state of rewards and punishments, they have no
> conception. Some, indeed, perhaps the generality of them, have
> some confused ideas of a future state of existence, and suppose if
> they are painted when they die according to the particular mark of
> their family, they shall be known, and join those of their relatives
> who have died and gone before them. But these ideas are only what

might be called the traditions and superstitions of the common people, and are regarded as foolishness by others. . . .

Besides the general lack of interest in Christianity on the part of the Osages, Pixley was caught in a situation between two rival chiefs. A young chief, Clermont, was unfriendly to the missionaries and encouraged his men to annoy them. White Hair, an older chief, was friendly to Pixley and encouraged him in his work. Religious services were often disturbed and broken up by young Indian men. On one occasion a group of them stopped a meeting and destroyed the log seats in the church room. Complaints were filed with the Indian agent who did nothing because he had no sympathy for Pixley's work. Finally, Pixley closed Mission Neosho in 1828, hoping that he could reopen it, but it was completely abandoned in 1829.

Mission Neosho, as a religious institution, was a failure. It did not convert many Osages to Christianity nor did it revolutionize their living habits. The mission's importance lay in the fact that it was the first one and that it opened the way for the establishment of similar institutions at a later time. It was also important because Benton Pixley left written comments that tell a great deal about Indian life and customs. In addition to his observations on religious attitudes he wrote:

> You ask how this people live. If by living he meant place, manners, and accommodations—in the summer it is on the prairies, in the winter in the village huts; three months perhaps in these huts, and betwixt two or three months on the prairie; the rest of the time they are scattered here and there, a few families together, hunting, moving every day or two, and lodging where night overtakes them. Their accommodations are few and simple. A few wooden dishes, two or three horn-spoons, a knife, and a kettle or two, make up the amount of their household furniture. Their houses and manner of building them is equally crude. They set two rows of the little poles in the ground, of sufficient width for their accommodation, and bring them together in a curve at the top. These they cover with flags or buffalo hides, and when in their towns have mats laid upon the ground to recline and sleep upon. Their food, while in the town, is principally jerked meat, boiled corn, dried pumpkins, and beans. Wild fruits, acorns, and other nuts, in the season of them, make up what is lacking, and when their provisions are exhausted they move off on their hunts. If they kill nothing the second or even the third day, they are not alarmed. . . . The fear of starving is the last thing that would be likely to enter an Osage mind.
>
> The women plant the corn, fetch the wood, cook the food, dress the deerskins, dry their meat, make their moccasins, do all the

business of moving, pack and unpack their horses, and even saddle and unsaddle the beasts on which their husbands and other male kindred ride; while the men only hunt and war, and, when in their towns, go from lodge to lodge to eat, and drink, and smoke, and talk, and play at cards, and sleep; for with them it is no mark of ill manners to doze away some hours of the day in their neighbor's lodge. And were you here now, just to go through their towns on a tour of observation, you would probably find more than four-fifths of the men employed in gaming, and scarcely one engaged to any useful purpose.

The record of the establishment of Baptist missions in Kansas begins directly with Isaac McCoy. In August 1830 he was greatly encouraged while talking to a group of Shawnees about plans for a mission, and later that same year he gained additional support from them. On July 7, 1831, the mission to the Shawnees was opened by Johnston Lykins in present Johnson County, and it became the central point for additional Baptist missionary activity.

In the autumn of 1833, Jotham Meeker arrived in Kansas, bringing with him the first printing press to be used west of the Missouri. The press was operated first at the Shawnee mission, and, when Meeker moved on to a mission among the Ottawas four years later, he took it with him. It was used to print hymnals, the scriptures, and a newspaper in the Shawnee language.

McCoy did not believe that his church moved rapidly enough in expanding its missionary efforts —a common complaint among most Protestant missionaries in the West. Money was slow in coming, and McCoy felt that the kind of encouragement he needed did not come at all. Consequently, he led a movement to establish a new Baptist missionary organization. When the Baptists split over the

The Shawnee Sun, first printed in 1835 by Jotham Meeker at the Shawnee Baptist Mission.

slavery question in 1845, the new southern church offered its help to McCoy's organization, but he decided to operate independently. Work began among the Weas and Potawatomis, and a mission for the latter was built in 1848 on the Kansas River just west of present Topeka. Unfortunately for both Indians and whites, McCoy died in 1846, at the age of sixty-two, but it can be said that he did all that was within his power to make the unhappy story of Indian removal as painless as possible.

At the same time that McCoy and the Baptists were establishing missions in Kansas other denominations were engaged in the same kind of work. One of the most important missions was the Methodist one to the Shawnees, supervised by the Reverend Thomas Johnson. First built in 1830 in present Wyandotte County, it was moved to the Shawnee lands in Johnson County where building began in 1839. Children of many tribes came to learn English and vocational skills—agriculture and what today would be called industrial arts and home economics. At its peak the mission had sixteen buildings, took in two thousand acres, and served an enrollment of about two hundred Indian boys and girls.

For many years the Shawnee Methodist Mission was an outpost of civilization on the western frontier. Branches of the Santa Fe and Oregon trails passed by its doors, and many of the important figures in western history were guests there. School began in October 1839, and, generally speaking, the school days followed a pattern of six hours of instruction, Monday through Friday. On Saturdays there was teaching for three hours. The boys worked in the shops or on the farm and the girls helped with the domestic chores. The day began at 4 A.M. and ended at 8 P.M.

A young woman, who began teaching at the school in 1850, wrote to a friend shortly after her arrival:

I am much pleased with the school. The girls are perfectly quiet and easily managed. They were never known to sauce a teacher and are quite affectionate and kind, harmless and playful. The male school is taught by two young gentlemen, one a Methodist preacher.

I never had better accommodations. . . . I live in a stately brick house that has 13

Isaac McCoy, Baptist missionary.

One of the three remaining buildings at the Shawnee Methodist Mission in Johnson County, dating from the 1840s.

rooms. . . . I have a very neat room with window blinds and nicely carpeted floor and as nice a stand and as good a bed as I ever wish to have. . . .

Could you see the difference it makes in these children . . . to have the benefit of Christian education I think you would with me be ready to bless the first missionaries that erected the first rude hut . . . in these plains. . . .

Indian students were not much different from any others. The major barriers to their education were described as the "ignorance, prejudice, instability and apathy of their parents." It was difficult to keep the children in school for an extended length of time. The younger children learned English more rapidly than the older ones and they were more adaptable to what the missionaries believed was the "right way" to live.

In 1848 the mission school branched out and organized a "classical department," which resembled a modern high school. Known as Western Academy, the branch lasted three years and instead of Indians most of its students were young white men and women from nearby Missouri who wanted a formal education but could not afford to go to school in the East.

Shawnee Methodist Mission continued in operation until 1862, when it was closed at the request of the federal government. During most of its life the mission was under the leadership of Thomas Johnson, although several other Methodist missionaries played major roles in its development. It also served as a base of operation for additional Methodist efforts among other Indian tribes in Kansas.

The Shawnees were served by another major mission, one run by the Society of Friends (Quakers), also in Johnson County. It opened in 1837 and lasted until 1869, offering instruction similar to that given at the Shawnee Methodist Mission. Richard Mendenhall, one of the teachers at the Friends school, took a dim view of his Methodist neighbors because they tolerated slavery. On May 14, 1854, Mendenhall wrote a letter to the Washington, D.C. *National Era* which said in part:

> There is in this territory an extensive missionary establishment . . .
> under the Methodist Church South, at which slaves have long been
> kept to do the menial service of the mission. . . .
>
> It would seem, to a candid thinker, a difficult matter to conceive
> a grosser inconsistency than to go forth to preach Christianity to
> the heathen, and to carry slaves along to assist in the glorious work.
> Thus, while they would hold up the gospel . . . with one hand, with
> the other they bind fast the yoke of bondage on the neck of the
> poor slave. . . .
>
> This Christian missionary . . . would plant Slavery here; yes, had
> introduced it here, in violation of the laws of the land, and yet, we
> are to believe that he is a minister of the Gospel of Christ. . . .

Slavery did disappear at the Shawnee Methodist Mission, and by the time the Civil War began Thomas Johnson was against secession. Mendenhall's letter does point out that the favorable attitude of many southern churches toward slavery was in conflict with some denominations' ideas concerning the purposes of Christianity.

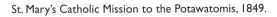

St. Mary's Catholic Mission to the Potawatomis, 1849.

Other Protestant missionary leadership was centered in Presbyterianism. In 1837, Samuel M. Irvin and his wife established a mission to the Iowa, Sac, and Fox Indians near what is now Highland in Doniphan County. The Iowa tribe, originally from north of the Great Lakes, had settled along the Missouri River in the nineteenth century and were neighbors of the Sacs and Foxes of the Missouri. A treaty of 1836 removed both groups from their lands in northwestern Missouri and sent them to a new reserve in northern Kansas and southern Nebraska.

Irvin's work was difficult and often discouraging. The Iowas were more interested in hunting than in education, and, along with the Sacs and Foxes, had been subjected to disease, bad whiskey, and dishonesty by previous contacts with whites. Although the brick building completed in 1846 could accommodate a hundred students there were seldom more than forty at the mission. Lessons were taught in both the Iowa and English languages and when the mission acquired a printing press in 1843, a hymnal and several grammar books were printed in Iowa. As at the other mission schools, the "three R's," agriculture, and religion were standard courses.

Eventually disease among the Indians, the additional reduction of Indian lands, and the further separation of Indians from the immediate vicinity of the mission led to its decline. It was operated for a time after 1860 as a home for Indian orphans but that was unsuccessful and by 1866 all operations ceased. Samuel Irvin diverted his interest to the ministry of the Presbyterian church in Highland and to the operation of the Highland Presbyterian Academy, later Highland University.

Representatives of the Roman Catholic church, which had a long history of missionary work throughout North America, began to serve among the Potawatomis in present eastern Kansas (Miami County) in 1838. A year later the site shifted to Linn County, and ten years later, when the tribe was moved to a new reserve farther west, the church moved with it and established a mission and school at St. Marys. Until 1871 it operated with some success and in the 1850s was described by a visitor:

> I had the pleasure of visiting the school . . . and was much pleased with the appearance of the pupils—they are all neatly and cleanly clad, and their appearance would be an honor to any community— but here on the frontier reflects greater credit upon the managers and assistants of this charitable institution. The pupils are taught the rudiments of a common English education, with the addition of farm work for the boys. . . .
>
> There is in the whole establishment fourteen buildings, including a very respectable church. The Mission field contains one hundred and seventy acres, of which one hundred and ten are under cultiva-

tion. . . . The Mission had about three hundred head of horned
cattle. . . .

The Indians about the Mission appear to partake of its influence
to a great extent—they have better fields, more stock, and appear to
be more industrious. So much for the model Indian Mission.

The Jesuit order, which operated St. Mary's, also founded a mission at present St. Paul in Neosho County among the Osages living
along the Neosho and Verdigris rivers. A separate girls' department
was established by the Sisters of Loretto, and the institution lasted
from 1847 until 1870, with its enrollment reaching nearly 240 at one
point. Under the direction of Mother Bridget Hayden and Father Paul
Ponziglione the school had greater success with the Osages than did
the teachers at Mission Neosho, primarily because the Indians had lived
for another twenty years in closer contact with whites. Catholic missionaries also worked among the Kickapoos and Miamis in Leavenworth
and Miami counties.

Other religious efforts included the Baptist missions to the
Stockbridges (Leavenworth County), to the Weas (Miami County), and
to the Delawares. The latter lasted from 1832 until 1867 and occupied two
different locations in Wyandotte County. It benefitted from the able direction of John G. Pratt who served as both missionary and Indian agent.
The Methodists worked among the Potawatomis along the Miami-Franklin
county line, the Kickapoos in Leavenworth County, the Delawares in
Wyandotte County, the Peorias in Franklin County, and the Kansas in
Morris County, with the mission school located at Council Grove. Although the school at Council Grove was in operation only from 1851 until 1854, the church had provided missionary contact with the Kansas several years previously. The Kansas were also served briefly by the Society of
Friends, and the Kickapoos received attention from the Presbyterians in
present Brown County in the 1850s and 1860s. A small group of Munsees
in Wyandotte County received aid and schooling from the Moravian
(United Brethren) church.

WHAT THE MISSIONS ACCOMPLISHED

Many of the missions had little lasting effect on the Indians with whom
they dealt but all of them served some purpose, even though they may not
have provided the religious and educational life for which their founders
had hoped. Most of the people who came to preach and teach stayed in
Kansas and several of them provided leadership during the territorial pe-

riod and the early years of statehood. Not all of them followed the teachings of Christianity as closely as one might wish in their dealings with their Indian charges. In fact, several of them were involved in land speculation that did no service to the Indians.

Not all that was done wrong by missionaries in the West can be blamed entirely on those individuals. The national denominations were often involved in competition for federal funds, which could be used to help support the mission stations and their employees. The churches were playing politics at times when they should have been more concerned with the welfare of the tribes. Often the Indians recognized those situations and also understood that the white's churches could not agree on either policy or theology. Consequently, Indians had difficulty understanding just why their lives would be better if they accepted the white's God. Too, the Indians had lived happily with their own religions for a long time and had spiritual values that did not seem to be inferior to Christianity. The Indians could communicate in their own languages, so English did not seem as important to them as it was to the missionaries, some of whom did not make a serious effort to understand the Indian tongues.

Some of the missions served as stopping places and offered assistance to travelers on the major western trails. They were outposts of civilization in a mostly unknown land. Three of them were to become institutions of higher learning—Highland University (now Community College), Ottawa University, and St. Mary's College, now closed, which served as both a liberal arts college and a Jesuit seminary.

Even with their numerous shortcomings, the missions eased some of the problems of the transplanted tribes and many missionaries tried to protect the Indians. The missions and the honest missionaries should be given credit for their contributions, most of which did not have to do with church membership.

INDIAN REMOVAL FROM KANSAS

Shortly before Kansas territory was opened for settlement and during the first two years of the territory's existence several treaties were drawn up between the federal government and tribes that further reduced the land held by Indians. The government did not wish to push the Indians out of Kansas at that time but it wanted to make more land available to settlers and hoped that the Indians would be satisfied with smaller reservations. The details of what was done and how it was arranged are very complex, and often confusing, but hundreds of thousands of acres were taken from the tribes.

In addition to the individual settlers who wanted to buy farmland, there were railroad and town promoters and other speculators who hoped to purchase large quantities of land and resell it at huge profits. In some cases land was not to be resold by the federal government until the Indians had a chance to receive permanent title to land of their own and had been properly paid for the land they were giving up. Other tribal land was to be held in trust by the government, and when it was sold the money was to go to the Indians. However, both settlement and speculation often were ahead of government planning, and when Indians and whites laid claim to the same property, the Indians usually lost.

The Delawares, Shawnees, Kickapoos, Miamis, and Wyandots were among the tribes who first signed treaties reducing their land holdings. Delaware, Potawatomi, Osage, and Cherokee land was particularly attractive to groups promoting railroads, and at times the government helped make the land available to them. In some cases the tribes simply sold their land to the promoters. Although railroads were not completely honest in their efforts to acquire Indian lands they would not have been able to get the land without the assistance of the federal government and politicians who granted favors to special economic interests.

After a treaty the federal government made arrangements for annuities—payments made over a period of years rather than a lump settlement in cash. Often the annuities were paid with cheap trade goods, substandard food, government credit, and very little actual money. This comment about annuity payments and illegal settlement on Indian land is from the Burlington *Kansas Patriot*, May 9, 1868:

> The semi-annual payment of annuities to the Sacs and Foxes took place at the agency, on Wednesday of last week. They received $20,000—or rather they were supposed to receive that amount. In point of fact, the trader received the money and carried it off in a carpet-bag. The Indians got their credit renewed. . . . A delegation of the tribe together with their agent, recently returned from Washington, where they negotiated a treaty, which if ratified, will open the entire reservation to settlement and pre-emption. Hundreds of whites are already upon the reservation and have taken claims. According to the provisions of the treaty, no settlement upon these lands can be legal, until one year after the ratification of the treaty.

The great numbers of settlers who moved west after the Civil War hurried the final removal of the Indians from Kansas. The following editorial, from the Emporia *News*, January 26, 1867, expresses the attitude of most white Kansans of the time toward the use of Indian lands:

Negotiations are now pending having in view the complete extinction of the Indian titles to lands in Kansas. We are glad to see this movement inaugurated. It must be confessed that the schemes of reservation and civilization have thus far proved to be sad and silly failures. It is well known that several years since, our government made very costly attempts to better the conditions of these tribes. Comfortable stone houses were built, sufficient in number and size to accommodate all; but in a few months the doors and partitions had been used up for fuel and the ponies were stabled in the houses, while their owners were lodging in tents outside. . . .

The earth belongs to the workers. These human weeds have no right to withhold from tillage and improvement the magnificent domain they now occupy. We are glad to chronicle their approaching removal. . . .

Their reservations, comprising millions of acres of the best land in the world, will be opened to settlement. We are especially interested in the Kaw Reserve, which extends northward from Americus, up the Neosho, including a vast area of valuable timbered land and prairie bottoms. . . . We want to see them fully occupied by bona fide settlers. . . .

One by one, the tribes left Kansas for new homes in the Indian Territory (Oklahoma) to the south. By the 1870s nearly all the Indians were gone from eastern Kansas. The tribes who had come from the East had been moved again and the natives—the Kansas and the Osages—joined them in the journey to a new home. They would all continue to meet the same kinds of problems that they had experienced in Kansas and they would be burdened with some new difficulties as they tried to conform to what the government said was the proper way of life.

A small number of Indians, divisions of larger tribal groups, remained in Kansas. Some Kickapoos, Sacs and Foxes of the Missouri, and members of the Prairie band of the Potawatomis stayed in Kansas and retained a small amount of their original reserves. In the twentieth century they have made additional changes in living, and they have sold more of their land. In recent years they have made an effort to revitalize and preserve their native culture.

The debates over Indian lands and its value have not ended. Cases have been in the courts of the United States since the 1870s, and tribes are still attempting to get payments that are more realistic than those of the nineteenth century. A Kansas editor of the late 1860s said that the Indians were "receding at the advance of civilization," but he might have added that such a recession needed to be treated with more honesty and humanity than was then being shown by state and federal governments.

Suggestions for Reading

A good detailed analysis of Indian land titles, treaties, and final removal is Anna H. Abel's "Indian Reservations in Kansas and the Extinguishment of Their Titles," *Kansas Historical Collections*, vol. 8, pp. 76–88, but these books cover the Indian situation very well: Martha B. Caldwell, *Annals of Shawnee Methodist Mission* (1939); Berlin B. Chapman, *The Otoes and Missourias* (1965); Russell D. Edmunds, *The Potawatomis, Keepers of the Fire* (1978); Grant Foreman, *The Last Trek of the Indians* (1946); Paul W. Gates, *Fifty Million Acres* (1954); A. M. Gibson, *The Kickapoos* (1963); Joseph B. Herring, *The Enduring Indians of Kansas: A Century and a Half of Acculturation* (1990); Ruth Landes, *The Prairie Potawatomi* (1970); John J. Mathews, *The Osages* (1961); H. Craig Miner and William E. Unrau, *The End of Indian Kansas* (1977); Leo Oliva, *Fort Scott on the Indian Frontier* (1984); George A. Schultz, *An Indian Canaan* (1972); William Unrau, *The Kansas Indians* (1971). Other articles pertaining to missionary efforts are scattered throughout the *Kansas Historical Collections*, and these articles in the *Kansas Historical Quarterly* are of particular interest: Lela Barnes, "Journal of Isaac McCoy for the Exploring Expedition of 1828" and "Journal of Isaac McCoy for the Exploring Expedition of 1830" (August and November, 1936); James M. Burke, S. J., "Early Years at St. Mary's Pottawatomie Mission" (August, 1953); T. F. Morrison, "Mission Neosho: The First Kansas Mission" (August, 1935); and M. Lilliana Owens, S. L., "The Early Work of the Lorettines in Southeastern Kansas" (August, 1947). These articles in *Kansas History* are also of interest: Kevin Abing, "A Holy Battleground: Methodist, Baptist, and Quaker Missionaries Among Shawnee Indians, 1830–1844" (Summer, 1998); Charles R. King, "Physician to Body and Soul: Jotham Meeker—Kansas Missionary" (Winter, 1994–1995); Joseph T. Manzo, "Emigrant Indian Objections to Kansas Residence" (Winter, 1981); George A. Schultz, "Kennekuk, the Kickapoo Prophet" (Spring, 1980); Sr. M. Evangeline Thomas, "The Role of Women Religious in Kansas History, 1841–1891" (Spring, 1981); and Stephen A. Warren, "The Baptists, the Methodists, and the Shawnees: Conflicting Cultures in Indian Territory, 1830–1834" (Autumn, 1994).

4

Trails and Early Transportation

For the first three-fourths of the nineteenth century, two great trails and their various branches carried thousands of Americans to the Far West. These roads, the Santa Fe and the Oregon-California, were of great importance in the history of the United States, and their story is closely tied to Kansas.

THE SANTA FE TRAIL

Trade with the Spanish Southwest attracted the interest of a number of people long before the 1820s, but the reports of later American explorers and the participation of Americans in the fur trade increased that interest. William Becknell, a Missouri trader, can be called the "father of the Santa Fe Trail," because he was the first to follow the general route and the first to use wagons instead of pack mules or horses to take trade goods over the trail. On September 1, 1821, Becknell and a handful of men left Franklin, Missouri, for Santa Fe. They reached the Arkansas River, in present Barton County, on September 24, and by mid-November they were in Santa Fe where they received a friendly reception.

Becknell was so encouraged by his first trip, using pack animals, that he made the journey again the next year using wagons. His second expedition was more difficult because he met unfriendly Osage Indians, and when the caravan attempted to take a shortcut across the dry plains between the Arkansas and the Cimarron rivers they ran out of water. Despite their hardships they reached Santa Fe and made satisfactory profits. Encouraged by Becknell's success, a group of trading partners ordered $30,000 worth of goods (mostly hardware and cotton cloth) and on May 16, 1824, started a wagon train for Santa Fe. These they traded for gold, silver, and furs and the trading partners made a 600 percent profit on their merchandise.

Becknell briefly described both his 1821 and 1822 trips for the Franklin, Missouri, *Intelligencer,* April 22, 1823, and he made these comments concerning the difficulties on the second expedition:

> No obstacle obstructed our progress until we arrived at the Arkansas, which river we crossed with some difficulty, and encamped on the south side. About midnight our horses were frightened by buffaloes, and all strayed. . . . Eight of us, after appointing a place of rendezvous, went in pursuit of them in different directions, and found eighteen. Two of this company discovered some Indians, and being suspicious of their intentions, thought to avoid them by returning to camp; but they were overtaken, stripped, barbarously whipped, and robbed of their horses, guns and clothes. They came in about midnight, and the circumstance occasioned considerable alarm. We had a strong desire to punish these rascally Osages, who commit outrages on those very citizens from whom they receive regular annuities. . . .
>
> After six days of incessant fatigue in endeavoring to recover all our horses, we once more left our camp, and after traveling eight days up the Arkansas, struck a south-west course for the Spanish country. . . .

Josiah Gregg, the first historian of the Santa Fe Trail, and author of *Commerce of the Prairies,* described Becknell's problems on the Cimarron desert:

> The adventurous band pursued their forward course without being able to procure any water, except from the scanty supply they carried in their canteens. As this source of relief was completely exhausted after two days' march, the sufferings of both men and beasts had driven them almost to distraction. The forlorn band were at last reduced to the cruel necessity of killing their dogs and cutting off the ears of their mules, in the vain hope of assuaging their burning thirst with the hot blood. This only served to irritate the parched palates, and madden the senses of the sufferers. . . .
>
> Frequently led astray by the deceptive glimmer of the mirage, or false ponds, as those treacherous oases of the desert are called, and not suspecting (as was really the case) that they had already arrived near the banks of the Cimarron, they resolved to retrace their steps

to the Arkansas. But they now were no longer equal to the task, and would undoubtedly have perished in those arid regions, had not a buffalo, fresh from the river's side, and with a stomach distended with water, been discovered by some of the party, just as the last rays of hope were receding from their vision. The hapless intruder was immediately dispatched, and an invigorating draught procured from its stomach. I have since heard one of the parties to that expedition declare, that nothing ever passed his lips which gave him such exquisite delight as his first draught of that filthy beverage. . . .

Becknell's success opened the way for more and more wagons on the Santa Fe Trail, and men named Chouteau, St. Vrain, Pratte, and Bent, all of whom gained fame in the fur trade, would use the trail to make more money. It also opened the way for added trade with the mountain men who came to the Southwest—people such as Jedediah Smith and Kit Carson.

A large trading party headed for Santa Fe in late 1822 and was caught in a blizzard on the Arkansas River near the site of Dodge City. They were forced to stay there for three months and when they were able to proceed they dug large holes where they stored the merchandise they had with them. These *caches* (a French word meaning concealed storage places) were emptied by the traders in the summer after they had obtained more pack animals, but the excavations remained visible for years and were a landmark on the trail.

"Arrival of the Caravan," from Josiah Gregg's *Commerce of the Prairies* (1844), shows a Santa Fe Trail wagon train at its destination.

So many people became involved in the Santa Fe trade that it was suggested the federal government survey the trail. On March 3, 1825, President James Monroe signed a bill authorizing a survey and a commission was appointed to take charge of the project. The commission set out from Fort Osage in western Missouri in July 1825. At Council Grove the Osages signed a treaty that permitted trail traffic to cross their lands, and on Dry Turkey Creek, in present McPherson County, a similar treaty was drawn up with the Kansas. The survey took two years and by the time it was finished traffic had increased even more.

The Santa Fe Trail, with two-thirds of its length in Kansas, had several beginnings in Missouri—Arrow Rock, Old Franklin (present Boonville), Fort Osage, Independence, and Westport Landing (present Kansas City). It went to what is now Gardner in Johnson County and on west through present Overbrook and Burlingame to Council Grove. From there it ran to the great bend of the Arkansas River and followed the river west. In the vicinity of present Ingalls, Cimarron, and Dodge City there were river crossings for the shortcuts to the Cimarron and another near Hartland for an alternate route that ran straight south to the Cimarron. The longer, and safer, route continued along the Arkansas to Bent's Fort near LaJunta, Colorado, and then headed south through Raton Pass to Santa Fe.

The trail had several natural landmarks and well-known stopping places in Kansas where good water was available. Council Grove, on the Neosho River, became the gathering place for wagon trains banding together for protection on the Plains and it also had the last good stand of timber from which wood for repairs was available. Josiah Gregg was at Council Grove in 1831 and wrote:

> Early on the 26th of May we reached the long looked-for rendezvous of Council Grove, where we joined the main body of the caravan. . . . On the day of our departure from Independence, we passed the last human abode upon our route; therefore, from the borders of Missouri to those of New Mexico not even an Indian settlement greeted our eyes. . . .
>
> During our delay at the Council Grove, the laborers were employed in procuring timber for axle-trees, and other wagon repairs, of which a supply is always laid in before leaving this region of substantial growths; for henceforward there is no wood on the route fit for these purposes. . . . The supply procured here is generally lashed under the wagons, in which way a log is not unfrequently carried to Santa Fe, and even sometimes back again. . . .

In what is now Barton County stood Pawnee Rock. As a lookout and ambush, where vast herds of buffalo provided easy hunting for Indians, the rock was one of the dangerous points on the trail. Most of the travelers on the route mentioned the rock in their diaries. As railroad builders and settlers arrived in the area the top of the rock was quarried away so that it is much smaller now than it was more than a century ago.

Between the towns of Lakin and Hartland there was once an island in the Arkansas River. In 1816 a fur trading party under the leadership of Auguste P. Chouteau was attacked by Pawnee Indians, and the trappers retreated to the island where they successfully defended themselves. When the government survey of the trail was made, Chouteau's Island was listed as a place to turn off for the Cimarron River. To the south on the Cimarron, in present Grant County, was Wagon Bed Springs, so named because at one time a wagon box was set in the springs as a tank. Jedediah Smith, the famous mountain man, was killed by Comanches near there in 1831.

The final landmark on the trail before it left Kansas was Point of Rocks, a high bluff rising above the bed of the Cimarron. It marked a campground that was used frequently because good water was always available there from the "middle spring" of the Cimarron. Point of Rocks marked the southern end of the trail's "dry route" or *La Jornada* across the Cimarron desert. Other landmarks and campgrounds included Elm Grove in Johnson County, Diamond Spring in Morris County, Lost Spring in Marion County, the crossings of Cow and Walnut creeks in Rice and Barton counties, and the junction of the Pawnee and Arkansas rivers in Pawnee County. Different travelers stopped at different places through the years, of course, but some places served caravans continuously through the trail's history.

Military protection for the Santa Fe Trail during its early years was limited. Several caravans suffered losses from attacks by Indians and at times there was trouble with Mexican outlaws on the southern portion of the road. In the spring of 1829, troops of the Sixth United States Infantry, under the command of Major Bennet Riley, marched ahead of a wagon train all the way to Chouteau's Island. There Riley camped because the country south of the river was Mexican territory. However, the wagon train was attacked by Indians south of the river the next day so Riley marched to the rescue and escorted the traders for several additional miles.

The army detachment stayed on the Arkansas until mid-October when it returned to Fort Leavenworth. Life on the trail was peaceful for the next three years, but in 1832 Indian attacks took place again and the government sent more troops to guard the Santa Fe trade. Circumstances were similar in 1834, but then nine years passed before the army was needed again. In the 1840s there was trouble with some Texans who raided both Mexican and American wagon trains, but the army effectively stopped that activity.

In 1847 civilians built Fort Mann, the first fort on the Kansas portion of the trail, just west of present Dodge City. It lasted only a year, but in that time it was under attack by Indians. On almost the same location the army built Fort Atkinson in 1850, and it was in existence until 1853, manned by regular troops. Although the two posts were short-lived they did give travelers a greater sense of security than they had had previously.

In 1859 a more permanent fort, Camp Alert, renamed Fort Larned, was built. It existed until 1878. It served as a major stopping point on the trail and was also important as a supply base for the army during the Civil War and the Plains Indian wars of the 1860s and 1870s. Several of the stone buildings still survive and are a part of the Fort Larned National Historic Site under the supervision of the National Park Service.

For five years, 1864–1869, Fort Zarah offered additional protection to the trail from its location near present Great Bend, and Fort Dodge, just east of Dodge City, was active from 1865 until 1882. Like Fort Larned these posts provided escorts for mail service and wagon trains. Except for two or three isolated trading posts, these forts were the only outposts west of Council Grove during the years when the trail traffic was at its heaviest.

The Mexican War (1846–1847) increased the use of the Santa Fe Trail because of the great volume of military supplies that were transported from the Missouri River towns to the Southwest. Troops under the command of Colonel Alexander Doniphan and Colonel Stephen Watts Kearny also used the trail on their way to help secure California for the United States. The Mormon Battalion, enlisted from westward emigrating members of the Church of Jesus Christ of Latter Day Saints, originally bound for the Great Salt Lake Basin in Utah, left their footprints on the trail as did innumerable other military units.

After the treaty of Guadelupe-Hidalgo was signed with Mexico in 1848 and Santa Fe became an American city, the traffic grew heavier. Following the discovery of gold in California in 1848 the trail was used by many Forty-Niners (so called because they went to the gold fields in 1849). Ten years later, people seeking their fortunes in the Colorado mining country traveled the road to Bent's Fort and from there went to the mountains. Some idea of the volume of traffic during the trail's later years can be gleaned from this report in the Cottonwood Falls *Kansas Press*, July 25, 1859:

> We are indebted to S. M. Hays & Co., of Council Grove, for a statement of the Santa Fe trade through Council Grove, from June 28th, 1859, to July 15th, 1859, a period of 17 days. There passed the Grove during this time 415 men, 289 wagons, 56 horses, 744 mules, 2,251 oxen and 23 carriages engaged in this trade, and they transported over the plains over 1,700 tons of freight.
>
> Add those previously reported, and there have passed the Grove this season, engaged in this trade, 1,970 men, 1,510 wagons, 361 horses, 3,707 mules, 14,515 oxen, 51 carriages and transported over

the plains 4,920 tons of freight or 9,840,000 pounds of freight. These amount to a total of $1,263,112. Then there is the wages of 1,970 men, incidental expenses, etc., which will swell the amount at least to $1,400,000, or enough to build 140 miles of railroad, at $10,000 per mile.

In the 1860s the trail was shortened at its eastern end. Other roads fed into it in eastern Kansas, and with the coming of the railroad it was no longer necessary to transport goods by wagon all the way from the Missouri River. The farther west the railroad went the more starting points for the trail came into existence. By 1870 many travelers were using branch roads from places such as Junction City, Ellsworth, Salina, and Hays, which joined the main Santa Fe Trail farther south. When the Santa Fe railroad was completed to the Colorado border in 1872 the Santa Fe Trail as a main thoroughfare was finished, but it continued in use between Kansas communities and in Colorado and New Mexico for several years after 1872.

THE OREGON-CALIFORNIA TRAIL

This road to the West was known by many names. It was called the Oregon Trail, the California Trail, the Platte Trail, and the Mormon Trail by people who traveled it. The Plains Indians had names for it also, including the "White-Topped Wagon Road." It was primarily a trail of emigrants but it, too, was used by the army and was followed, in part, by stagecoaches and the Pony Express. The valley of the Platte River, in present Nebraska and Wyoming, became a thoroughfare for thousands who sought California gold, Oregon land, or a Christian mission field in the Far West. Many of those people began their journeys by traveling through eastern Kansas.

What was to become the Oregon Trail was used by fur traders returning from the mouth of the Columbia River in 1813, but it was not until 1830 that William Sublette, a noted fur trader, took the first wagons along the route to the Rocky Mountains. By the middle of the 1840s, traffic on the trail was tremendous and the California gold rush increased its use even more in 1849 and 1850. The trail was a relatively easy one through present Kansas, although river crossings could sometimes be hazardous. Emigrants found little in the way of shelter or assistance, and at times they were forced to throw away valuable possessions that were too heavy for the long trip. Many of the travelers did not live to see the new land they had set out for, while others, after 1854, decided to go no farther than Kansas Territory and settled there.

The emigrants moved west from the Missouri River at several points but all the Kansas branches of the trail met near present Marysville at the Independence crossing of the Big Blue River. Many of the travelers who

The "wind wagon" was designed to sail over the Plains to the Pike's Peak gold fields in the late 1850s.

stayed south of the Kansas (or Kaw) River went past the sites of Lawrence and Tecumseh and crossed the river where Topeka now stands, using a ferry operated by a French-Indian family named Papin. Others went on west, past the Potawatomi Baptist mission, to the Uniontown crossing, near where Willard is today.

North of the Kansas River the trail passed present St. Marys, Westmoreland, and Blue Rapids before it reached Marysville. It crossed the Vermillion at a ford named for Louis Vieux, a Potawatomi, who later operated a toll bridge there. Near Westmoreland was a large campground served by the excellent springs in the area. To the northwest of Blue Rapids was Alcove Spring, named in 1846 by emigrants, one of whom described the spring as "a beautiful cascade of water." The area was well known to early traders and mountain men as well as to later travelers to the Far West. John C. Frémont and his 1842 exploring expedition camped at the spring, and the missionary Marcus Whitman, with a thousand emigrants to Oregon, stopped there in 1843. The ill-fated Donner party, most of whom later froze or starved in the Sierra Nevada mountains, buried one of its members, Sarah "Grandma" Keyes, near the spring in 1846.

Then came the crossing of the Blue River. Thousands of covered wagons with settlers and gold seekers bound for the Far West forded and ferried the river. In 1849 a ferry and trading post were established at the ford by Frank J. Marshall. Two years later the military road between Fort Leavenworth, and Fort Kearny (in Nebraska) crossed the river a mile farther west. Marshall, for whom Marshall County was named, built another ferry. From Independence Crossing the trail went on northwest past what is now Hanover and left Kansas south of where Fairbury, Nebraska, now stands.

Many wagon trains crossed the Missouri River at St. Joseph, Missouri, and headed for the Blue River along a branch of the trail that paralleled present U.S. Highway 36. They crossed Wolf Creek near the Presbyterian mission at Highland and the Nemaha River near the site of Seneca. Other emigrants joined the main trail from the vicinity of Atchison and Leavenworth. Most of the travelers used oxen to pull their wagons, although mules and horses were also employed. The ox-drawn wagons usually traveled about twelve miles a day but bad weather, sickness, or breakdowns often made for even slower travel.

Travel on the Oregon-California Trail is illustrated by the following quotations from a diary kept by a Forty-Niner:

> SUNDAY, May 6—Started at 5 a.m., and reached the Kansas river, at 4 p.m. This is a long, wide, muddy river, and very rapid. There is a ferry kept here by some Frenchmen [the Papins] who will reap a rich harvest this Spring at $1 per wagon, and 10 cents per head for cattle.
>
> We have been out twelve days, having accomplished one hundred miles. . . . The boys all like the trip well, and I am determined, if successful in California, to recross the plains. We are all sun-burnt . . . and upon our return I think it will be necessary to take along some acquaintances to identify us.
>
> MONDAY, 7—Occupied the larger part of the day in being ferried across the river. Encamped four miles from the Kansas, on Soldier's creek, in the country of the Potawatomies. . . .
>
> Today, we had the misfortune to break down our wagon, making it impossible to proceed farther; but, as good fortune would have it, we found a French settler, who, Yankee like, was ready for a trade. . . .
>
> TUESDAY, 8—Moved fifteen miles and encamped at Cross creek. Today, while the train was crossing a creek, I rode to the upper Kansas ferry, at a trading post, called by the traders Uniontown. It contains about thirty buildings, six of which are stores. . . .
>
> We are now getting along finely; have plenty of wood, water, and grass, and will soon be in the Pawnee country, the most dangerous

Indians we will have to encounter; but we apprehend no danger, as we have a well organized train of 25 wagons, and 105 men, all well armed. . . .

THURSDAY, 10—Refreshed our animals today. The Vermillion contains some fine large fish and many a large cat-fish filled our hungry maws, in order, as some said, "to save our bacon."

The camp today, presented such a spectacle as would have caused our mothers and sisters, could they have looked on, to laugh heartily. From wagon to wagon were stretched clotheslines, with sundry shirts and stockings thereon, while along the banks of the river might have been seen any quantity of the boys with sleeves rolled up, and making hickory shirts and rosin soap fly with great gusto.

FRIDAY, 11—Struck our tents at 3 o'clock a.m., halted at 10 a.m. to rest our teams, and repair a wagon in the train that had broken an axle. . . . During our forenoon's march we passed a newly-made grave, at the head of which was a rudely cut stone, bearing this inscription "To the memory of Henry Roushi, of Illinois, who departed this life, May 8th, 1849." He was wounded in the leg, a few days previously, by the accidental discharge of a pistol in the hands of an acquaintance. . . .

SUNDAY, 13—Traveled 18 miles today. . . . Encamped on the plain with no wood, bad water, and very good grass.

About three and a half miles from Independence [crossing] we struck the prairie, and our route ever since has been across a succession of prairies, occasionally fording some beautiful streams, skirted by a dense foliage, affording a relief to the eye, after gazing for days upon nothing but everlasting plains.

MONDAY, 14—Struck our tents at 6 a.m. and in a few minutes drive arrived at the junction of the St. Joseph and Independence roads. We are now carried along by a perfect tide of emigration and while I write there is some eight trains in sight, numbering from twenty to forty wagons each. There are about 600 wagons ahead of us, while between our rear and St. Joseph there is 850 more, and no one knows how many on the Independence road.

This afternoon we gave chase to some fine antelope, but did not succeed in shooting them. Traveled sixteen miles. . . .

Although the diary shows some aspects of trail travel it does not point out the tragedy that often came to the migrants. John H. Clark, who used the branch from St. Joseph in 1852, made these entries in his diary, which emphasize the sadder aspects of the journey:

Historic Roads and Trails

Republican R.

MORTON STANTON HAMILTON GREELEY WALLACE CHEYENNE SHERMAN RAWLINS

Fort Wallace

Arkansas River

Smoky Hill

STEVENS GRANT KEARNY WICHITA LOGAN THOMAS SHERIDAN DECATUR NORTON

Leavenworth & Pikes Peak

SEWARD HASKELL FINNEY SCOTT LANE GOVE GRAHAM ROOKS OSBORNE PHILLIPS SMITH

North Fork

Smoky Hill River

Fort Dodge

MEADE GRAY FORD HODGEMAN NESS TREGO ELLIS RUSSELL

Fort Hays

Trail

Parallel

Fort Larned

Santa Fe

CLARK KIOWA EDWARDS PAWNEE RUSH BARTON MITCHELL LINCOLN CLOUD JEWELL REPUBLIC

Fort Zarah

Express

Solomon River

COMANCHE BARBER PRATT STAFFORD RICE ELLSWORTH SALINE OTTAWA WASHINGTON

Fort Harker

Arkansas River

HARPER KINGMAN RENO McPHERSON DICKINSON CLAY

Republican R.

Ft. Riley

Trail

Ft. Kearny

Fort Riley

Big Blue R.

SEDGWICK HARVEY MARION MORRIS GEARY WABAUNSEE JACKSON POTTAWATOMIE MARSHALL

Oregon

Road

SUMNER BUTLER CHASE LYON

Kansas R.

California

Pony

River

COWLEY ELK GREENWOOD WOODSON COFFEY OSAGE SHAWNEE JEFFERSON ATCHISON DONIPHAN

Express

CHAUTAUQUA MONTGOMERY WILSON NEOSHO ALLEN ANDERSON FRANKLIN DOUGLAS JOHNSON WYANDOTTE LEAVENWORTH BROWN NEMAHA

Trail

Fort Leavenworth

Missouri River

CHEROKEE LABETTE CRAWFORD BOURBON LINN MIAMI

Fort Scott

Ft. Leavenworth— Ft. Gibson Road

0 miles   50   100

May 10—Saw the first dead ox on the road today, and passed two or
three graves, the occupants of which, it is said, died of small pox.
Met a young man with two small children returning to the states;
said he had buried his wife and one child just beyond. We felt for
the poor fellow as he every now and then turned his look toward the
wilderness where lay his beloved ones. . . .

May 11—Had some emigrant neighbors near us whom we
intended to visit but for the rain, which fell in torrents. . . .About
midnight our neighbor approached our campfire and told us that his
only child had just died and he had come to solicit aid to bury it. . . .
We had an empty cracker box which we made answer for a coffin,
dug a grave in the middle of the road and deposited the dead child
therein. The sun had just risen and was a spectator to that mother's
grief as she turned slowly but sadly away from that little grave to
pursue the long journey before her. . . .

May 14—Camped last night on the bank of the Nemaha river,
and this morning were called upon to bury a man who had died of
cholera during the night. There have been many cases of this
disease, or something very much like it; whatever it may be it has
killed many persons on this road already. . . .

The traveler crossed the Blue River at Marshall's ferry and made this
comment:

It was a tedious journey of six miles from camp to the Big Blue. Here
we set fire to a pile of driftwood, cooked our dinner and smoked our
pipes. On the east bank of this river is located a private post-office,
a dramshop [saloon], hotel and ferry, the business all under one roof.
If we mail a letter we pay $1; if we take a dram of good whiskey,
seventy-five cents; a square meal (?), $1.50; if it is a wagon we want
carried over the river, $4 and no grumbling. The proprietor is doing
a rushing business.

Death was frequent on the trail and, as the diarist mentioned, it came
from smallpox and cholera, along with other diseases such as diphtheria
and measles. What the emigrants called cholera was not always a virus
infection that reached epidemic proportions. Often it was severe dysentery or diarrhea brought on by impure water, bad food, or severe changes in
weather and temperature. Whatever the cause, "cholera" killed great numbers of Oregon- and California-bound travelers in Kansas, many of whom
died at the river crossings while they were in camp. Burial sites of some of
the victims may still be seen in the vicinity of the Louis Vieux crossing of

the Vermillion and near Westmoreland in Pottawatomie County, as well as near the Uniontown crossing of the river in Shawnee County.

The heavy use of the Oregon-California road led to additional efforts on the part of the federal government to learn more about the West while establishing military posts to protect overland traffic. In 1842 and 1843, John C. Frémont traveled thousands of miles between the Missouri River and the Pacific Coast. His expeditions were recorded in publications and on maps and gave the American public a much better idea of what the Plains and the Rockies were like. Frémont was not as critical of Kansas as Pike and Long had been, and he indicated that the region had great agricultural possibilities.

Through the Civil War the trail continued to be heavily traveled, but as the Union Pacific railroad built along the Platte through Nebraska in the late 1860s, and as rails began to appear in eastern Kansas, the use of the trail declined. By 1870 parts of it were still used locally, but it was no longer the great through highway it once had been.

RIVER TRAFFIC

The Missouri River was a natural highway from the Mississippi to the Great Plains and the northern Rocky Mountains. The first vessels on the Missouri and on other streams in present Kansas were Indian canoes and the pirogues (a kind of canoe) of the French fur traders. Even very shallow water did not handicap these forms of transportation.

Next came the keelboats, which were used by both explorers and fur traders. The cigar-shaped keelboats were anywhere from forty to seventy-five feet long and eight to eighteen feet wide, and they could carry up to forty or fifty tons of freight. They had sails but if the wind was not strong enough to move them they were hauled along upstream by crew members walking along the shore or they were pushed along by poles. They moved downstream with the current. Even though they were good sized they did not need much water and so could navigate shallow streams. Keelboats were used by Lewis and Clark on the Missouri and by the fur-trading Chouteau family to take goods up and down the Kansas River between their posts near present Bonner Springs and on Mission Creek (west of Topeka) and the Missouri River. The boats were also the means for transporting supplies in 1827 to Daniel Morgan Boone, son of Daniel Boone and a government farmer for the Kansa Indians, who lived in what is now Jefferson County.

Steamboats became important to western transportation after 1840, although a few frequented the Missouri before then. The construction of

Albert T. Reid's drawing of the steamboat *Lightfoot of Quindaro,* a vessel designed for use on the Kansas River.

Fort Riley in 1853 made people begin to think about the possibilities of steamboat travel from the Missouri up the Kansas River. In April 1854, a stern-wheeler, the *Excel,* carried more than a thousand barrels of flour to Fort Riley, and it made several more trips that year. At one time it even navigated the Smoky Hill River for a few miles.

By 1856 the traffic on the Missouri was described as "immense," with sixty boats running between St. Louis and the Kansas River towns "all filled with passengers and freight." However, the navigation of the Kaw was a different story, and, despite the high hopes of many Kansans, the river never became a major waterway. Between 1854 and 1866 thirty-four steamboats carried people and freight on the Kaw, but some of those boats made only one trip and some did not complete even one. Uncertain water depth and great numbers of sand bars proved to be overwhelming obstacles for the boats and their captains.

In 1855, the *Emma Harmon* took six days to steam from Lawrence to Topeka and on its return to Kansas City it ran aground. Another steamboat spent several days on a sand bar near Fort Riley. The *Lightfoot of Quindaro,* which was built specifically for use on the Kaw, had trouble, too, and took more than a month to make a round trip from Kansas City to Lawrence in 1857.

One of the steamboats for which Kansans predicted a bright future was the *Hartford,* which headed up the Kaw for Manhattan in May 1855. It got stuck on a sand bar a mile above the mouth of the Big Blue and there it stayed for a month waiting for the river to rise. When the *Hartford* could finally start back downstream its owners decided that they would give up on the Kaw. Opposite the Catholic mission at St. Mary's, it ran aground again, caught fire, and burned completely. A steamboat that was sent up the river to salvage the *Hartford* never made it past Lecompton. As one Lawrence editor put it, the Kansas River was a "hard road to travel."

A kind of water transportation that was important to Kansas was the ferry boat, which was in use on almost every stream of any consequence. Ferries varied in size and in their methods of propulsion. Some ran with ropes and pulleys, pulled by men or horses, and some were simply rowed or poled across. Steam ferries were used on the Missouri at the major towns like Atchison and Leavenworth. Bridges eventually replaced ferries but a few were still in use as late as the 1890s.

EARLY FREIGHTING AND STAGECOACHING

Overland freighting in Kansas and on the Great Plains began with the Santa Fe trade, as we have already seen, and after the Mexican War the freighters prospered.

Most noted among the freighting firms based in Kansas was Russell, Majors and Waddell. That company was at one time the largest in the West. It employed hundreds of men and owned thousands of oxen that pulled its wagons, and it transported millions of tons of goods, both civilian and military.

Leavenworth and Atchison in the late 1850s were great depots for freighters, and from there the heavily loaded wagons were trailed west over the Oregon and Santa Fe trails and the military roads that led to forts in Kansas and on to Nebraska, Colorado, Wyoming, and Utah. One resident of Atchison, writing shortly before the Civil War, said:

> No one could question the commercial importance of Atchison. . . .
> It was nothing unusual to see two or three steamboats lying at the
> levee discharging freight, and as many more on the river in sight,
> either above or below the city. . . . It was no uncommon thing . . . to
> see great quantities of freight, in the shape of thousands of wagons
> and ox-yokes, mining machinery, boilers, and other material, and
> the provisions necessary to supply the thousands of people then
> flocking to the Great West. Tons of stuff were piled on the levee
> and in the warehouses. It was common to see immense quantities of
> heavy freight stacked up for several blocks along the levee, and
> every warehouse was packed with groceries, provisions, clothing,
> boots and shoes, etc., awaiting transportation. . . .

The freighting business continued to boom through the Civil War and the late 1860s as more and more settlements were developed in the West and as the army continued to be involved in warfare with Indians. But with the coming of the railroads and the completion of transcontinental lines the wagons were no longer vital and so the freighters, who had moved west ahead of the railroads beginning in the early 1800s, disappeared.

Some of the people involved in freighting became interested in organizing stagecoach lines and the same towns along the eastern border of Kansas that were important in freighting maintained their importance with stagecoaching.

During the winter of 1858–1859, Russell, Majors and Waddell, in connection with John Jones of Leavenworth, founded the Leavenworth and Pike's Peak Express Company. The company bought enough mules and stages for service between the Missouri River and Denver. The route ran from Leavenworth to a station on Chapman Creek in Dickinson County and there northwest to a junction with the "Parallel Road," which went through the northern tier of counties into present Colorado. Said the Denver *Rocky Mountain News*, May 14, 1859:

> This is the beginning of the stupendous enterprise undertaken by the . . . Company—the making of a new road, over a comparatively unknown country, and immediately stocking it with a working force of men, animals and wagons, sufficient to forward with promptness and dispatch a daily mail and passenger coach from each end of the line. The coaches which we have seen are the very best of Concord coaches, finished in the best style, and perfectly new, having never turned a wheel until their departure from Leavenworth. . . .

Stages of the Reynolds line, which ran between Ashland and Dodge City in the 1880s.

> The whole length of the road is 687 miles . . . but it will probably be shortened 75 miles by cut-offs in various places. . . . The company have 52 coaches, one of which will leave each end of the route each day, except Sunday, at six A.M., and make the trip in ten to twelve days. . . .

The Leavenworth and Pikes Peak Express ran until February 1860, when its business was assumed by the Central Overland California & Pike's Peak Express Company. In 1862 another change took place when Ben Holladay, known as the "Stagecoach King," gained control of the company and renamed it the Overland Stage Line. On the Smoky Hill Trail, that followed approximately the route of the Union Pacific railroad and U.S. Highway 40 through Kansas, David Butterfield operated a stage line known as the Butterfield Overland Despatch. However, hostile Indians often caused trouble for the coaches on the Smoky Hill Trail and so the line was never very successful.

Holladay continued to be the leading stagecoach operator for several years and in 1866 bought out the almost bankrupt Butterfield line. However, Holladay could see that the railroads were sure to build in the near future and so he sold all his interests to Wells, Fargo and Company. Until after 1900, when the automobile replaced them, stagecoaches continued to provide transportation in parts of Kansas not served by railroads.

The stagecoach was never a comfortable way to travel. Although the drivers often were dashing figures, and coaches pulled with good mules or horses can still make an exciting movie or television scene, the passengers put up with a great deal of discomfort. The ride was generally either too hot or too cold, too wet or too dusty, and the coaches never rode with much smoothness or stability. The stopping places where meals, and sometimes overnight accommodations, were available generally left a good deal to be desired. Horace Greeley, the famed New York editor, made a stage trip through Kansas in 1859, and at one stop noted that he had a meal that was the worst he had ever eaten for a half-dollar. And another Kansas traveler commented that he had paid the same amount for a meal of corn bread and tough beef and had been waited on by "an innocent looking female about the size of a four year old elephant." He added: "I should think she was something over six feet in her stockings, and weighed at least two hundred and seventy-five pounds. Her whiskers are visible across a large room."

John J. Ingalls, who came to Kansas before the Civil War and later served the state as a United States senator, rode a stagecoach from Denver to Atchison in 1861 under conditions that were uncomfortable. He described his trip:

Nature had its way at last and discussion yielded to drowsiness and the vain pursuit of sleep. It is astonishing how rapidly the human animal degenerates into the hog under circumstances favorable to this retrograde development; what a totally disgusting disregard of others' rights, what brutal invasions of decency and propriety men can be guilty of when a selfish assertion of their own comfort is necessary to its own enforcement. Legs are well enough in their place, but thrust across one's private lap, they become impertinent and offensive. . . .

On Monday we breakfasted at sunrise and passed Rock Creek at noon, which put us at last in the hospitable boundaries of Kansas; after dinner we passed through Marysville . . . and took supper at Guittard's. The night was so magnificent that I couldn't resist the temptation to ride outside till after midnight, when I crawled into the front on the mail bags and covering with blankets enjoyed a very comfortable nap. I had just wakened on Tuesday morning and was considering the propriety of uncoiling when somebody inside fired a pistol from a window, the animals sprang, breaking the coupling-bars, turning sharply to the left and upsetting the coach. . . . I thought my back was broken . . . I was insensible for a few moments and have suffered extreme pain ever since, but the physicians assure me that I have sustained no serious injury.

It took Ingalls six days to make his trip from Denver to Atchison and he probably paid about $75 for his limited space on the stagecoach. He, too, complained about the meals he ate along the way and was unhappy that his only opportunity to clean up came from a bucket of cold water at the morning stops. A stagecoach ride could be exciting but it never qualified as first-class travel.

THE PONY EXPRESS

On January 30, 1860, the Leavenworth *Daily Times* carried a story headlined "Great Express Enterprise! From Leavenworth to Sacramento in Ten Days! Clear the Track and Let the Pony Come Through!" This was the public announcement for the short-lived but famous experiment in fast mail service that began operation on April 3, 1860.

The Pony Express was first created by William H. Russell, who involved his freight and staging partners, Alexander Majors and William Waddell. The service operated over a two-thousand-mile route connecting the eastern states at the Missouri River town of St. Joseph, with the

Telegraph line builders are saluted by a passing Pony Express rider.

state of California. Averaging less than ten days per run, traveling through the storms and heat of summer, and the snow and cold of winter, with Indians and other hazards thrown in, the Pony Express became one of the West's most colorful stories.

For nearly eighteen months the Express was in operation over a route that crossed northeastern Kansas on its way to a junction with the Platte valley trails. The departure of the first rider was a cause for celebration, even though his starting time was delayed because the train from the East was late. The first rider carried with him forty-nine letters, nine telegrams, and some newspapers. On April 16, the Leavenworth Times stated: "A marvel feat has been accomplished! The Pony Express has galloped across half the continent, and today the Pacific is in close neighborhood to the Atlantic. History will record this event as one of the gigantic private enterprises of our day."

Unfortunately, Russell, Majors and Waddell could not afford the experiment in fast mail service. It required approximately five hundred horses, nearly two hundred stations and a similar number of station employees, plus eighty riders. Even with charges of $5 for each letter carried the company made enough to cover only about one-tenth of its expenses. One of the purposes of the Pony Express was to publicize the route followed by the company's stagecoaches but as advertising it was far too expensive.

As the transcontinental telegraph line was built the route of the Pony Express grew shorter. By the fall of 1861 the wires stretched clear across the country. On November 21, 1861, the Atchison *Champion* said:

It was thought last year, and truly too, that the pony had accomplished wonders when he had given us a communication with the Pacific coast. . . . But now the Pony has become a thing of the past—his last race is run. Without sound of trumpets, celebrations, or other noisy demonstrations, the slender wire has been stretched from ocean to ocean. . . .

Kansas Territory had some telegraph service as early as 1859, but by 1861 the Kansas towns were in wire communication with all parts of the Union. The end of the Pony Express closed the final chapter in the history of Russell, Majors and Waddell. The losses sustained by the company in its operation of the mail service finished it and the once prosperous firm closed its business forever.

Suggestions for Reading

William Y. Chalfant, *Dangerous Passage: The Santa Fe Trail and the Mexican War* (1994); Arthur Chapman, *The Pony Express* (1932); William E. Connelley and Frank Root, *The Overland Stage to California* (1901); Seymour V. Connor and Jimmy M. Skaggs, *Broadcloth and Britches: The Santa Fe Trail* (1977); Everett N. Dick, *Vanguards of the Frontier* (1941); Robert L. Duffus, *The Santa Fe Trail* (1930); J. V. Frederick, *Ben Holladay: The Stagecoach King* (1940); William Ghent, *The Road to Oregon* (1929); Josiah Gregg, *Commerce of the Prairies*, ed. by Max Moorhead (1954); Kate L. Gregg, ed., *The Road to Sante Fe* (1952); David S. Lavender, *Bent's Fort* (1954); Wayne C. Lee and Howard C. Raynesford, *Trails of the Smoky Hill* (1980); Alexander Majors, *Seventy Years on the Frontier* (1893); Dale Morgan, *Jedediah Smith and the Opening of the West* (1953); Leo E. Oliva, *Fort Larned on the Santa Fe Trail* (1982); Leo Oliva, *Soldiers on the Santa Fe Trail* (1967); Francis Parkman, *The Oregon Trail* (1875); Raymond W. and Mary L. Settle, *Empire on Wheels* (1949); Marc Simmons, *On the Santa Fe Trail* (1986); George R. Stewart, *The California Trail* (1962); and John D. Unruh, Jr., *The Plains Across* (1979).

Innumerable diaries of overland travel have been published but one of the most complete is John Hawkins Clark, "Overland to the Gold Fields of California in 1852," ed. by Louise Barry, *Kansas Historical Quarterly* (August, 1942). *Kansas History* contains an article by David K. Clapsaddle, "The Wet and Dry Routes of the Santa Fe Trail (Summer, 1992) while most of the Winter, 1996–1997 issue of *Kansas History* is devoted to Santa Fe Trail History. In addition, the *Overland Journal*, the quarterly publication of the Oregon-California Trails Association, now in its fifteenth year, contains a wealth of information. River transport is covered in Phil E. Chappell, "A History of the Missouri River," and Albert R. Greene, "The Kansas River—Its Navigation," both in *Kansas Historical Collections*, vol. 9; in Edgar Langsdorf, "A Review of Early Navigation on the Kansas River" *Kansas Historical Quarterly* (May, 1950); and in James H. Thomas and Carl N. Tyson, "Navigation on the Arkansas River, 1719–1886" *Kansas History* (Summer, 1979).

5

"Bleeding Kansas"— The Territorial Period

The term "Bleeding Kansas" refers to a period in Kansas history that drew the attention of the entire nation. It is true that there was a certain amount of violence in Kansas Territory, but "Bleeding Kansas" came into use mostly because of newspaper editorials and politicians' speeches. How many deaths can be blamed on the controversies between supporters of the free-state or the proslavery causes is difficult to say, but, presumably, approximately fifty persons died violently during the territorial period. Considering that Kansas Territory was on the American frontier the number is not excessive when compared to similar areas.

Politics did play a part in unnecessary violence, but if certain very active newspapermen, both East and West, had not written such sensational stories the violent events that did occur might have been at least partially lost in other news of the 1850s. Although publicity about the bloodshed may have been overdone, there is no question about the violent expressions of opinion that were a part of the Kansas territorial story.

In December 1853, U.S. Senator A. C. Dodge of Iowa introduced a bill to organize the territory of Nebraska, of which present Kansas was to be a part. In January 1854, a revision of the bill came before the Senate. The new bill, introduced by Stephen A. Douglas of Illinois and supported by the administration of President Franklin Pierce, called for the creation of two territories to be called Kansas and Nebraska. The territories would be divided by the 40th parallel, the present northern boundary of Kansas.

The bill also specifically repealed the Missouri compromise of 1820, which had provided for the admission of Missouri as a slaveholding state, but prohibited slavery north of 36° 30´—the southern boundary of Missouri–in the rest of the Louisiana Purchase. Instead, the Kansas-Nebraska bill called for the use of "popular sovereignty"—the resident voters would decide for themselves whether or not slavery would be allowed in the territories.

The introduction of the popular sovereignty theory and the division of the area into two territories caused many people to assume, wrongly, that Senator Douglas intended Nebraska to be free while Kansas, Missouri's neighbor, would be controlled by the slaveholders. The lengthy debates in Congress that followed the introduction of the bill were bitter, and the fight was a sectional one, with political party membership forgotten in many cases. The free-soil newspapers of the North, led by such editors as William Lloyd Garrison in Boston and Horace Greeley in New York, violently attacked Douglas, the South, and the Pierce administration, while newspapers of the South and the Missouri border country replied with equally nasty comments.

The battle of words continued throughout the period of congressional discussion of the bill and during the months that followed, when people began to migrate to the new territories. The newspapers of 1854 were filled with exaggerated statements and opinions, which made for more sectional bad feeling. In the minds of some editors, ministers, and active abolitionists in the North, the passage of the Kansas-Nebraska bill was the worst thing that had happened to the nation in many years. During the congressional debates, meetings were held and resolutions were passed throughout the North in opposition to the bill. Stephen A. Douglas was compared both to Benedict Arnold and Judas Iscariot for his role in the political struggle. Typical of the resolutions that came out of the meetings was this one, the product of a Pittsburgh gathering:

> Resolved, that the disgrace clinging to the name of Benedict Arnold, will lose its pre-eminence in American history, and be measurably hid in the blacker and more hideous infamy that will forever stamp the characters of northern statesmen, who . . . sell themselves to pro-slavery fanaticism . . . and aim a fearful stab at the Union of the States, whose value the people of the North have ceased to consider greater than the value of human liberty and American honor.

May 26, 1854, was a dark day for those who opposed the bill, for that morning it passed Congress. While it did not actually become law until signed by President Pierce on May 30, there was no doubt of the final outcome. In Hartford, Connecticut, a center of New England abolitionism, unhappiness over the passage of the bill was expressed by the ringing of the city's church bells for an hour at sunset. The Boston *Liberator* published an impassioned editorial on May 26 which said, in part:

> The deed is done—the Slave Power is again victorious. . . . And so, against the strongest popular remonstrances—against an unprecedented demonstration of religious sentiment—against the laws of God and the rights of universal man—in subversion of plighted faith, in utter disregard of the scorn of the world, and for purposes as diabolical as can be conceived of or consummated here on earth—the deed is accomplished. A thousand times accursed be the Union which has made this possible!

While abolitionist and free-soil newspapers were complaining about the bill, the proadministration and southern newspapers were expressing pleasure over the opening of the two territories. They believed that the popular sovereignty theory was the only answer for handling the slavery question and that the federal government should not dictate to the states on the matter. Perhaps they underestimated the determination of the free-state advocates, because the passage of the bill kindled a fire that failed to go out. It was fed to a certain extent in the new territory of Kansas for seven years and became an important part of the sectionalism that led to civil war in 1861.

FREE-STATE AND PROSLAVERY SETTLERS

There was little in the way of permanent settlement when the territory was opened. The only legal residents were missionaries, people dealing with Indians as agents or traders with the approval of the federal government, and the army and its civilian employees. Several mission stations were in operation, and Forts Leavenworth, Larned, and Riley served as the outposts of federal authority in the area. Fort Scott, which had been opened in 1842, was not an active military post when white settlers began immigrating to the territory, although it would be reopened during the Civil War. Kansas Territory was a new land for businessmen and farmers and many of them were soon to be in political conflict with each other and in cultural conflict with the Indians. Included in the population were a number of free African Americans.

The first settlers in Kansas Territory came from western Missouri. Many of them were sympathetic with the institution of slavery and saw the possibilities of extending slavery into Kansas. (The first territorial census [1855] listed 192 slaves.) However, an equal number of Missourians came to Kansas simply because they were looking for opportunities in a new region and many of them were antislavery. The towns of Atchison and Leavenworth were first settled primarily by Missourians and most of the public statements on politics that came from these communities were proslavery.

Antislavery supporters in the North made several efforts to combat southern influence, and one of the best organized was the Emigrant Aid Company of Massachusetts, which soon changed its name to the New England Emigrant Aid Company. Its chief support came from Amos Lawrence, Eli Thayer, and Thomas Webb, all New England abolitionists with money and political influence. The company operated something like a modern travel agency. Groups were formed in response to the company's newspaper advertisements and transported to the West at reduced rates. Later the company raised money to purchase sawmills, to support newspapers, and to build hotels in which emigrants could stay. Local agents were sent to Kansas to meet the pioneer groups and to advise them about available land.

The settlers who came to Kansas through the company's efforts were largely responsible for the founding of Topeka and Lawrence. The first party set out for Kansas from Worcester, Massachusetts, on July 17, 1854, and they were described as "picked New Englanders" who would "fix a character of the truest kind on any community." On July 28, they reached Kansas City, Missouri, held a meeting, and agreed to go to the Wakarusa River valley where a site had already been tentatively chosen for a settlement. They camped on Mount Oread on August 1, and although it was hot and windy they decided that there they would stay, naming the settlement "Wakarusa," soon to be known as Lawrence.

Most of the pioneers were pleased with their new homes but unaccustomed hardships, homesickness, and summer heat discouraged the faint hearted. However, most stayed and within a few short months they were joined by hundreds more. Typical of the enthusiasm expressed by the new settlers is this quotation from a letter written by a member of the first party:

> Plenty of limestone is found here. . . . Fine red freestone and white marble for building is taken out of the hills. Also stove coal is taken out of mines by the Indians and sold. The banks of rivers and ravines are covered with timber. . . . Large fish are caught in the Kansas and other rivers, weighing from 10 to 100 pounds each. They are called cat fish. My advice to farmers and mechanics is to sell all they have and come to Kansas. Bring as much money with them as possible, to develop the resources of the soil.

Before very long the immigrants found that they had strong political differences with some of their Missouri neighbors. In Weston, Missouri, a

$200 reward was offered for the delivery of Eli Thayer to that town. The Liberty, Missouri, *Democratic Platform* mentioned the Weston reward and added its remarks on July 13:

> Attention is directed to the articles from the Weston papers offering
> a reward for one Eli Thayer, principal of the Massachusetts emigrant
> aid society, an association for colonizing Kansas with Abolitionists
> and Northern paupers, at the exclusion of citizens of slave holding
> states. We hope the individual may be found and meet with just
> such a course of treatment that one of his sort deserves—hanging!

Despite the troubles—both physical and political—the company continued to send settlers, who in turn attracted more free-staters. Many of them were swept up in the Kansas-Missouri border difficulties, which played a large part in the territorial history. Under the company's auspices came a good many people who later gained fame in Kansas history and who made solid contributions to the state's advancement. Among those were Cyrus K. Holliday, one of the founders of Topeka and builder of the Santa Fe Railroad, and Charles Robinson, first state governor of Kansas.

One of the most interesting organized efforts to populate Kansas Territory with free-state settlers was the Connecticut Kansas Colony. This group, organized in New Haven, Connecticut, settled the community of Wabaunsee and was also known as the "Beecher Bible and Rifle Colony." The latter name was acquired because the famous abolitionist preacher, Henry Ward Beecher, and his congregation in the East contributed Sharps carbines and Bibles to the group. C.B. Lines of New Haven, the principal organizer, served as the colony's president when the settlement was made. His colonists were described by an eastern writer as a noble group, "mostly large, athletic men, with strong hands and strong hearts." Lines wrote a series of letters back to New Haven, describing the settlement's beginning. One of those letters gave an excellent picture of the difficult life of the settlers:

> Our men have generally staked out their claims. The surveyors are
> at work finding the boundaries . . . and we hope in a very few days
> to complete the arrangement and see every man located upon his
> farm. . . .We have had dry weather until within the past week and
> the rains coming unexpectedly, found many of the company poorly
> prepared with shelters. At the close of the first rainy day a number
> were thoroughly wet and obliged to locate for the night as best they
> could. The tents we had were crowded to their utmost capacity,
> while the few cabins within our reach were also resorted to. . . . The
> nearest one is not over eight feet by ten . . . and has barely room for

a bedstead, table, stove and barrel, and yet the kind hearted owners . . . relinquished the bed to two of our sick men . . . .

Among the variety of dwellings found here, I notice one today occupied by a very respectable man, which consisted of a box in which he brought fruit trees into the territory—seven feet long, three feet wide and three deep—with a slight roof fixed over it, leaving one side entirely open. In this box is his bed, across the end of it his chest . . . and yet he pursues his daily toil, is cheerful and looks forward to better times. . . .

Despite such living conditions Lines and his friends were not discouraged, and the colony prospered. Although the community of Wabaunsee now is very small, the "Beecher Bible and Rifle Church" still stands and is a reminder of the pioneering efforts made by the Connecticut settlers.

Organized groups were also responsible in part for the settlement of Manhattan, but generally towns in Kansas Territory grew up because individuals promoted them and their locations were such that they attracted population. A fertile valley, a good landing place on the Missouri River, a well-known point on a trail, a river crossing, or a place for a water-powered mill were the kinds of features that influenced the selection of a town site.

Several Kansas towns were strongly free-state or proslavery, reflecting the beliefs of their founders. In addition to free-state towns such as Lawrence and Topeka or the proslave Atchison and Leavenworth, Doniphan and Kickapoo could be called proslave; Osawatomie and Oskaloosa, free-state. However, after four years had passed most of the residents of these towns just considered themselves Kansans.

TERRITORIAL POLITICS

The political situation in Kansas Territory from 1854 until 1859 is one of the most confused— and confusing—in American history. Ten men served as governor or acting governor during the territorial period and most of them had a great deal of difficulty keeping political peace because of the heated arguments over Kansas' future as a free or slave state.

Andrew H. Reeder, the first territorial governor, arrived in Kansas from Pennsylvania

Gov. Andrew Reeder as he fled the territory in disguise.

in 1854 and called for an election in November of that year to choose a delegate to Congress. On election day Missourians came in great numbers and, voting illegally, elected a proslavery candidate. Another election, held in March 1855 to form a legislature, was also taken over by illegal Missouri voters. The first territorial legislature was unanimously proslave. Although Governor Reeder was unhappy with the election he recognized the elected legislators.

Many of the illegal Missouri voters and some of the people they elected were referred to as "Border Ruffians" by the free-staters who were offended by their clothing and manners. A perhaps overdrawn description of the Border Ruffian was written for the New York *Tribune*, April 23, 1857, by a Kansas observer:

> I have taken occasion of late to visit some of the border towns . . .
> and inspect the inhabitants. They are a queer looking set, slightly
> resembling human beings, but more closely allied, in general
> appearance, to wild beasts. An old rickety straw hat, ragged shirt,
> buttonless corduroys with a leather belt and a coarse pair of mud-
> covered boots constitute a "full dress." They never shave or comb
> their hair, and their chief occupation is loafing around whisky
> shops, squirting tobacco juice and whittling with a dull jack knife.
> They drink whisky for a living, and sleep on dry goods boxes . . . and
> delight in robbing hen-roosts, and pilfering from Free-State men.
> They generally carry a huge bowie knife and a greasy pack of cards,
> and expatiate at length on their exploits in Kansas among the
> d——d Abolitionists. They are generally about six feet high,
> spindle-shanked and slab sided. It would be an insult to the brute
> creation to call them brutes although it must be confessed that there
> seems to be no little congeniality between them and the porkers, so
> much so, indeed, that they frequently spend the night in close
> proximity, in some convenient mud hole. . . .They are "down on"
> schools, churches, and printing offices, and revel in ignorance and
> filth. After visiting them, one cannot but feel the truth of the
> doctrine of total depravity, so far as it applies to parts of the human
> family.

The first legislature met in the town of Pawnee, which had been improperly established within the boundaries of Fort Riley military reservation and had as one of its promoters Governor Reeder. In the building now known as the First Territorial Capitol, the legislators met for four days, July 2–6, and their chief accomplishment was to adjourn to the Shawnee Methodist Mission where they completed the session. The governor's message to both houses was not well received, and a proslavery editor from Atchison wrote: "Nine-tenths of the citizens of Kansas would rather see him hanging to a tree, than filling the gubernatorial chair."

In July and August the legislature passed what became known as the "Bogus Laws," including the Missouri slave code that provided severe penalties for those who freed slaves or who spoke out against slave holding. The free-staters called the laws "bogus" because of the illegal elections and decided to organize a separate government. In the fall of 1855 the Free-State party came into being and a free-state constitution was written at Topeka, with Charles Robinson serving as governor. This added to the political confusion, for there was now a government recognized by the federal authorities and a second existing outside the laws of the United States. Each tried to completely discount the other. At about the same time proslavery people formed a "Law and Order" party. The traditional Democrat and Republican party labels were abandoned in this period by most of the people active in politics—they were either free-state or proslave.

While the people actively involved in this political maneuvering viewed the situation seriously, there was a slightly ridiculous aspect to the whole business. The congressional delegate election of 1855 is a good example. Both the Proslavery and the Free-State parties nominated candidates: John W. Whitfield, proslavery, who had been the territory's delegate in the previous congress, and Andrew H. Reeder, free-state, by then the ex-governor of the territory. Since neither party would vote in the other's election, held a week apart, both men claimed the seat and went to Washington. The House of Representatives finally decided that both should receive expenses for their trips to the capital but that neither could be accepted as a delegate. As a result Kansas had no representative in the 34th Congress.

Early in 1856, Lecompton was designated the "permanent" territorial capital and since it was only twelve miles from Lawrence, a free-state stronghold, tensions continued to increase. In April, Sheriff Samuel Jones of Douglas County, still a legal resident of Missouri and a strong proslaveryite, made several arrests of free-staters in Lawrence. That night he was shot and wounded. He consequently arrested several more people and put them in jail at Lecompton, charging them with treason. Several others for whom he was looking managed to escape, including former governor Reeder, who got out of Kansas disguised as a woodcutter.

During the spring of 1856, Kansas was visited by a congressional investigating committee, which issued a report criticizing the illegal election activities and stating that the Topeka free-state government reflected the wishes of the majority of Kansas residents. Despite this opinion the

Topeka constitution was not accepted by Congress as suitable for Kansas's admission to statehood. However, the Topeka government kept operating even though its legislature was closed down by U.S. troops on July 4, 1856.

The next effort to write an acceptable constitution came in the summer of 1857 when proslavery delegates gathered in Lecompton. The convention finished its work in November and produced a document that, had it been accepted, would have brought Kansas into the Union as a slave-holding state. The constitution was submitted to a vote of the territorial residents on December 21, 1857, and since the free-staters all stayed home and refused to vote, the constitution received overwhelming approval at the polls.

In January 1858, Kansas voted for state officers under the Lecompton constitution and also on a special constitutional referendum that had been proposed by the territorial legislature. This time the proslaveryites did not vote and the free-staters defeated the constitution. However, President Buchanan was not willing to accept the second vote. He sent the document to Congress on February 2, 1858, where it met strong opposition. A compromise was offered by Congress that provided for yet another Kansas election. Finally on August 2, 1858, the Lecompton constitution was voted down decisively and another attempt to gain statehood was finished.

The territory was famous for its outspoken newspaper editors, and politics always gave them something to write about, no matter which side they favored. One of the best exchanges at the time of the debates on the Lecompton constitution took place between Sol Miller, free-state editor of the White Cloud *Kansas Chief,* and Thomas J. Key, a Lecompton delegate and editor of the *Kansas Constitutionalist* at Doniphan. They called each other liars (among other things) and Key finally wrote this sentence about Miller:

> The editor of the *Chief* wishes us to bring him into notice. . . .We would gently hint to the cross-eyed, crank-sided, peaked and long razor-nosed, blue-mouthed, white-eyed, soft-headed, long-eared, crane-necked, blobber-lipped, squeaky-voiced, empty-headed, snaggle-toothed, filthy-mouthed, box-ankled, pigeon-toed, reel-footed, goggly-eyed, hammer-hearted, cat-hammed, hump-shoul-dered, blander-shanked, splay-footed, ignoble, Black Republican, abolition editor, to attend to his own affairs or we will pitch into him in earnest.

The White Cloud editor apparently got the last word when he replied to Key on September 10, 1857:

We did not exactly tell the truth about him. We said his name was Thomas Jefferson Key. We beg Thomas Jefferson's pardon—it should have been Thomas Jack-ass Key! (No insult intended to jack-asses generally.) . . .To think that such wretches are sent to form a Constitution for the government of decent people—the thought is humiliating! . . .

Thomas J. Key occupies a position which makes him public property—or, rather, a public nuisance—and we intend to take a long pole, with a hook and a spike in one end of it, and haul him about, and turn him over, and hold up his rotten, filthy carcass to the gaze of the public, until it makes all decent men gag, and turn from it in disgust!

There were other uncomplimentary remarks made on both sides, but the politics of the territory quieted down after the Lecompton fight ended. In 1858 there was another unsuccessful attempt to write an acceptable constitution by a convention that met first at Minneola in Franklin County and reconvened in Leavenworth. Politicians were less vocal and less bitter by 1859 when the fourth and final constitutional convention met in Wyandotte.

Two months before the delegates assembled in Wyandotte (now a part of Kansas City) to write the constitution, an important event took place that altered the general political situation. In May 1859, the Republican party in Kansas was organized at Osawatomie, and the purely local Free-State party no longer existed. Kansas Republicans still declared themselves as antislavery but they also supported what would be national planks in the Republican platform, including the construction of a transcontinental railroad and free homesteads for settlers. Horace Greeley, in the midst of a trip through the West, was present at Osawatomie and spoke to the organizers of the party. By the time the Wyandotte convention began the delegates were calling themselves Republicans and Democrats, and while they had differences of opinions they could approach these with reason and logic.

The Wyandotte constitution was written during July 1859, and two months later the people of the territory adopted it by an overwhelming vote. It was then sent to Congress where it was bitterly opposed by southern senators. Finally, as civil war approached and southerners went home to their seceding states, Congress approved the constitution. It was signed by President Buchanan on January 29, 1861.

The Kansas constitution follows closely the Ohio constitution, probably because fourteen members of the convention were originally from Ohio. It was written by young men—sixteen of them under thirty. The old leaders of both the free-state and proslavery factions were not in attendance, not even Charles Robinson, the Topeka government's chief executive. There were controversial issues, one of which centered around the establishment of the state's boundaries. A delegation from Nebraska petitioned to have the northern boundary set at the Platte River, and the Democrats were agreeable. The Republicans, however, were afraid that this would add too many Democrats to Kansas and perhaps delay statehood, so it remained at the 40th parallel. The western boundary was also in question since the territory extended to the Continental Divide in what is now Colorado. Again the Democrats wished to include the greater amount of territory, but the Republicans overrode them and set the western line where it is today.

There was a great deal of competition for the location of the state capital, but finally Topeka was chosen. Some delegates wished to exclude African Americans from Kansas but that did not pass, although suffrage was limited to white citizens and slavery was not allowed. The question of liquor sales was debated, but prohibition was defeated. Married women were given property rights but no women were given the right to vote. The question of woman suffrage came in for a great deal of discussion and the fight for the vote was led by Clarina Nichols, a nationally known newspaperwoman. Generally, the campaigning women were met by male arguments that followed the lines of these comments about Mrs. Nichols and her ideas by the Topeka *Tribune*, June 30, 1859:

> To say the least, we admire the skill which she displayed . . . but we cannot subscribe to her platform, believing . . . that justice and all the universally existing senses of right will always give to the women all the rights they can justly claim, consistent with the exercise of their duties in the position which it is evident to everyone that nature designed them to fill. Woman would never obtain that influence which she now exerts should she place herself, or be placed, in that most dangerous and exposed position—the right of elective franchise. She is never so strong as when clad in the armor of her own weakness. . . .
>
> Home—there is the true woman's sphere; administering with gentle hands to the

Clarina Nichols, champion of women's rights.

wants of the little ones . . . and if so it be, to soothe the feverish
brow of the husband.

Suffrage for both women and blacks in Kansas would have to wait.
Despite all the abolitionist activity and talk of a "free" Kansas, much of the
concern about blacks was involved only with slavery and not with their
total rights.

Although most questions at the Wyandotte convention were settled
satisfactorily there were Democrats who had political objections to the
document even though they approved the constitution as a "model instrument." When time came for the delegates to sign the document the Democrats refused and the Kansas constitution carries only the signatures of
the Republicans who were there. John A. Martin, secretary of the convention and later governor of Kansas, said:

> Each party, I think, was guilty of one blunder it afterwards seriously
> regretted; the Republicans in refusing to include the South Platte
> country within the boundaries of Kansas; the Democrats in refusing
> to sign the Constitution they had labored so diligently to perfect. . . . I
> am confident that within a brief time after the Convention ad-
> journed, there were few Democratic members who did not seriously
> regret their refusal to sign the Constitution.

In spite of this unfortunate omission, the fact remains that the Wyandotte constitutional convention produced a document that was eventually accepted by the federal government and has served as the basis for
Kansas government from 1861 to the present.

THE ACTS OF VIOLENCE

There were other events that gave the name "Bleeding Kansas" to the
territory. On November 21, 1855, Charles W. Dow, a free-state man, was
shot and killed by Franklin Coleman, proslavery, ten miles south of
Lawrence. This was the beginning of the "Wakarusa War." Dow's friend,
Jacob Branson, was arrested by proslaveryites because he attended a free-
state protest meeting, but he was rescued by free-staters. Sheriff Jones of
Douglas County called on Governor Wilson Shannon for assistance in
putting down "lawless action."

The citizens of Lawrence became alarmed and they began to fortify
the town against possible attack. Free-state militia companies arrived from
several towns while the proslavery militia set up camp two miles east of
Lawrence in support of the sheriff and governor. The siege of Lawrence

The Free State Hotel, Lawrence, in ruins after the raid by proslaveryites in May 1856.

lasted for approximately a week with each side spending most of its time drilling and waiting. On December 8 and 9, James Lane and Charles Robinson negotiated a truce with Governor Shannon, and both forces began to disband. The "Wakarusa War" was over and only one person lost his life after the killing of Dow. The significance of this almost bloodless conflict lay not in what actually happened but in what might have happened. In November and December 1855, eastern Kansas resembled a powder keg but fortunately no one lighted the fuse. But the Kansas newspapers and the Eastern press picked up the news and magnified it. Because of the competing political factions the "war" received tremendous publicity outside the territory.

Free-state residents of Lawrence continued to annoy proslaveryites. The town's newspapers were outspoken in their criticism of proslavery leaders and policies. As a result of this contempt for the territorial government, a proslavery-stacked grand jury of Douglas County, meeting May 5, 1856, stated that the two newspapers and the Free State Hotel were nuisances and concluded that "said nuisances may be removed."

On May 21, a deputy U.S. marshal, accompanied by a large posse, rode into Lawrence and arrested three men, none of whom offered any protest. Later in the day the despised Sheriff Jones visited the town with armed men and four pieces of artillery. Jones's hatred for Lawrence was intense, and he deliberately chose to interpret the nuisance declaration of the grand jury as an order to destroy. Accordingly, the two newspaper offices and the hotel were wiped out. Stores were broken into and Charles Robinson's house was burned. Jones is supposed to have surveyed the destruction and commented, "This is the happiest day of my life, I assure you."

Proslavery newspapers considered the conquest of Lawrence a great victory, and several stories about the incident were openly gleeful. The free-state papers of Lawrence were somewhat handicapped in making a reply since their printing equipment was resting in the Kansas River. Only two people were killed, one on each side, and only one of them by a gunshot, but the destruction of businesses was so great that again Lawrence and Kansas were in the national news.

A much bloodier event took place only three days after the destruction of Lawrence. On the night of May 24, five proslavery men were killed near "Dutch Henry's" crossing on Pottawatomie Creek in Franklin County. John Brown was a leader of the party that disposed of the settlers. He was accompanied by four of his sons and three other free-staters. The group, in company with a larger band, had been on its way to help defend Lawrence when word was received that the difficulties there were over. The main party decided to go on but Brown, with his followers, turned back. It was said that he announced he would rid the vicinity of its proslavery residents.

That night of murder added fuel to the fire of political controversy and it set off several other acts of guerrilla warfare. Many free-staters felt

This drawing depicts the Marais de Cygnes massacre in Linn County, May 1858, in which five free-state men were killed by Missourians.

Battle of Hickory Point in Jefferson County, 1856, from a Samuel Reader watercolor.

that it was a good answer to the Border Ruffians who had used high-handed methods in dealing with free-state voters and property. One writer said that "no other act spread such consternation among the Ruffians, or contributed so powerfully to make Kansas free. Hitherto, murder had been an exclusive Southern privilege. The Yankee could argue and make speeches; he did not care to kill anybody." At first no one knew that Brown was responsible for the killings but when the proslavery forces found out about him they marked him as one of their chief enemies.

Brown came to the territory late in 1855 and stayed only about three years. But in that time he was involved in several armed skirmishes and also managed to free some slaves in Missouri and to send them north. He was the leader of the free-state forces during the Battle of Black Jack (near Baldwin) at the end of May 1856, and he led the defense of Osawatomie when that town was raided by proslavery forces on August 29 of that same year. Although he had never been very successful in the East before coming to Kansas, his fanaticism and his acts of violence against proslavery people made him a legendary figure by the time he left the territory in 1859. By then he was already laying plans for his attack on the federal arsenal at Harper's Ferry, Virginia, and little else occupied his mind until he met his death by hanging on December 2, 1859.

Other "battles" that took place in 1856 included one at Franklin, near Lawrence, in June and one at Hickory Point, north of Oskaloosa, in September. There was a raid on Grasshopper (now Valley) Falls and there was property damaged, horses stolen, and settlers frightened, but the bloodshed remained at a minimum. One should not get the impression that it was an easy time in which to live in Kansas. If only one person had been killed that would have been cause for worry and sorrow. But the fact remains that many Kansans never heard a shot fired in anger and that much of the talk about bloodshed was only talk.

Except for the arguments over constitutional questions and a certain amount of proslavery nervousness because James Lane, a militant supporter of the Topeka government, seemed to be leading a great many free-staters into Kansas (Lane's "northern army," some called them), things were much calmer in 1857 and early 1858. One last act of violence took place on May 19, 1858. Five free-state men were killed and five others wounded about four miles northeast of Trading Post in Linn County. The incident was known as the Marais des Cygnes massacre, and it was said that nothing in the Kansas struggle did more to inflame the nation.

The murders were committed by proslavery partisans from Missouri. The massacre was widely publicized in the East, and John Greenleaf Whittier memorialized the incident in a poem published by the *Atlantic Monthly* in September 1858. Kansas papers were filled with stories that reported the killings with varying degrees of accuracy. The free-state press could not say enough in condemnation of the Missourians. Even proslavery editors were appalled, and the comments about the massacre indicated that there was a change taking place in Kansas Territory. For example, the *Kansas Weekly Herald* of Leavenworth, Kansas' first newspaper and a rabid proslavery one, carried this critical article on May 29:

> The details are horrible in the extreme, and revolting to any one who has not the heart of a savage. The report states that these men were made prisoners one by one, and their captors, when a fit opportunity and place was presented, shot them down in cold blood. Such cowardly proceedings as these are a disgrace to a civilized country, and only in keeping with the characters of fiends and monsters. No excuse can be offered in justification. We believe that the Proslavery men in that quarter have been harrassed and persecuted by their enemies, but no principle of retaliation can justify them in such acts of cowardly murder.

The territory was growing up and more and more people were realizing that the political differences need not be settled with guns and fists. The year 1858 still held excitement and controversy and even another "battle"—the Battle of the Spurs near Holton that involved John Brown, freed slaves, and a pursuing posse. However, not a shot was fired and the posse rode hurriedly away, thus giving the incident its name. In 1859 a relative calm settled on Kansas, making the Wyandotte constitution possible.

LIFE GOES ON IN THE TERRITORY

The population of the territory was increasing, and more towns were springing up. Life in Kansas was not easy for a great proportion of the settlers. Money was often in short supply, housing was frequently crude, doctors were scarce, and profits from business and farming generally uncertain.

The federal government was engaged in surveying the public lands in the territory, and most individuals who bought farm land purchased it under the Pre-emption Act of 1841 at $1.25 per acre. The act allowed settlers on the land to purchase up to 160 acres at that price before a public land auction for the region was held. As was always the case in a new area there were some arguments over land holdings, so neighborhood associations were formed to protect claims.

If a settler had a legal problem he could find a lawyer in most towns but he had to wait until a member of the three-judge territorial court came to his area if a court appearance was necessary. The same Kansan could order a several-course dinner in a number of restaurants or he could spend a night in a very good hotel if he happened to be stopping in one of the river towns such as Leavenworth and Atchison. The Planters' Hotel in Leavenworth was one of the finest in the West. He could also eat bad meals and stay in worse hotels in most other communities. The newcomer might have been fooled by advertising before he arrived in Kansas and expect a thriving city only to find a miserable collection of small buildings with very few people.

There are dozens of letters and diaries written by territorial pioneers that give realistic views of life in Kansas between 1854 and 1861.

The Planters Hotel, Leavenworth. Opened in 1856, it served many famous guests, including Abraham Lincoln. It was torn down in the 1950s.

Representative of such records that refer to life on a farm is this letter, written in 1856:

> Our cabin is 16 feet square, and is eight logs high . . . with a window on the north, and doors on the east and west sides, with chimney on the south; it is built up on the outside of logs, and on account of the saw mill not getting into operation, we have had no floor as yet. The roof is covered with split clapboards which makes it tight against rain, but not of snow; the high winds which we continually have here, blows the snow through the smallest crevice. The logs, which are laid one upon the other, are *chunked* between, and over the chunking, plaster or mud is laid, which we call *daubing;* upon the whole, I consider our cabin about as tight as the end of a wood pile. Our table and chairs are of my own make, but I would not own this were I anywhere else. Our bedstead is made in backwoodman's style; it is formed by driving sticks with crotches at the end into the ground, and laying poles length and crosswise into these crotches, and then boards are placed across to hold up the bed, which is stuffed with hay and [corn] husks. Our cooking utensils consist of an old fashioned cake pan, frying pan, and an iron kettle. . . .We cook by an open fireplace, having no stove. . . .
>
> We have the fever and ague, and are taken with a chill all over, pain in the bones . . . after which comes the shake itself, which almost tears us to pieces. A hot fever follows, with sweats, headache and weakness. . . . In the fever and ague we take quinine or Peruvian bark. . . . I killed our fatted calf about the first of January, salted one-half and the other half remains fresh; this, together with potatoes, beans, hulled corn and milk . . . we succeed to meet the demands of hunger.

The struggle to survive was overshadowed by the news of the discovery of gold in western Kansas early in 1858. The rush to the Rockies began. Kansans and easterners began to look west and the first successful attempts at mining brought thousands of emigrants to Kansas. They headed for the eastern slope of the mountains to seek their fortunes in the part of Kansas that became Colorado. By fall, 1858, all the newspapers of the Missouri valley were filled with news from the Pike's Peak and Denver regions and reports of gold seekers. This item from the Atchison *Freedom's Champion*, September 18, is typical:

> The gold fever is raging in every town in Kansas: . . . Later accounts only tend to confirm the first reports, and it is now definitely settled that gold is not only found in Kansas, but that it exists in such

This 1859 photograph is of emigrants preparing to leave St. Joseph, Missouri for the Pike's Peak goldfields.

quantities as to prove profitable to engage in searching for it. . . . A company of twenty will leave Atchison in about ten days. Companies are also forming in Kansas City, Leavenworth, Doniphan, Sumner, St. Joseph and other points.

By the summer of 1859 the new towns of Denver and Auraria were filled with miners and the businessmen who supplied their needs. Some miners made money but more did not. Prices were high, gamblers and saloon keepers prospered, and law enforcement was a problem. Kansas merchants engaged in outfitting people for the mines had more cash than ever before, and a national depression that began in 1857 was overshadowed in Kansas by the gold rush. However, by the end of 1859 discouraged miners were leaving the gold fields, having failed to make the fortunes of which they had dreamed. The next big rush would not take place until after Kansas had given up the area to the new territory of Colorado.

In that same year, during the first week in December, Abraham Lincoln came to Kansas. He spoke at Elwood, Troy, Doniphan, Atchison, and Leavenworth, and his remarks were well received. Lincoln's speeches dealt with the major purpose of the Republican party—to prevent the extension of slavery. In Atchison he commented that John Brown was guilty of treason and had paid the proper penalty for his actions at Harper's Ferry. Lincoln spoke about the theory of popular sovereignty and about the evils of states seceding from the Union. At the time he was considering his chances as a presidential candidate in 1860 and his Kansas speeches were a warm-up for the campaign. Although Kansans liked him the delegation from the territory to the 1860 Republican convention did not support his nomination.

And so the territorial period drew to a close. Kansans had endured a great deal, but they had seen tremendous changes in only seven years. They were ready for statehood in January 1861, but if they were perceptive at all they realized that civil war on a national scale was rapidly approaching. Within five short months the new state would be deeply involved in the fight to preserve the Union.

Suggestions for Reading

There is a tremendous amount of material dealing with the territorial period published in the *Kansas Historical Collections*, the *Kansas Historical Quarterly*, and *Kansas History*. More recently in *Kansas History* are these articles which shed new light on the era: Nicole Etcheson, "'Labouring for the Freedom of This Territory': Free-State Kansas Women in the 1850s" (Summer, 1998); Richard B. Sheridan, "From Slavery in Missouri to Freedom in Kansas: The Influx of Black Fugitives and Contrabands Into Kansas, 1854–1865" (Spring, 1989); and Dale E. Watts, "How Bloody Was Bleeding Kansas? Political Killings in Kansas Territory, 1854–1861" (Summer, 1995). The following books supplement those materials. Richard O. Boyer, *The Legend of John Brown* (1973); William Y. Chalfant, *Cheyennes and Horse Soldiers: The 1857 Expedition and the Battle of Solomon's Fork* (1989); Allen Crafton, *Free State Fortress* (1954); G. Raymond Gaeddert, *The Birth of Kansas* (1940); Samuel A. Johnson, *The Battle Cry of Freedom* (1954); James C. Malin, *John Brown and the Legend of Fifty-Six* (1942); Lawrence R. Murphy, *Frontier Crusader—William F. M. Arny* (1972); Stephen B. Oates, *To Purge This Land With Blood, A Biography of John Brown* (1970); James Rawley, *Race and Politics: Bleeding Kansas and the Coming of the Civil War* (1969); O. G. Villard, *John Brown* (1929); Don W. Wilson, *Governor Charles Robinson of Kansas* (1975); *Territorial Kansas: Studies Commemorating the Centennial* (1954).

6

The First Years of Statehood

When Kansans received the word that the president had signed the admission bill, January 29, 1861, they stood on street corners and cheered, they danced, they sang, and they fired cannon to signal their joy. One editor wrote: "We are citizens of the United States once more—partners in 'Hail Columbia,' 'Yankee Doodle,' the stars and stripes, the Declaration of Independence, and the Fourth of July!" Another added, "Hurrah for us, we ourselves! Hurrah for the New Star! And three times three again for the NEW STATE OF KANSAS!"

However, Kansas had its problems. There had been a long period of drought as the territorial era drew to a close, and from June 1859 until November 1860 it was said that not enough rain fell "to wet the earth at any one time, two inches in depth." By the fall of 1860 the ground was bone dry and so were wells, springs, and streams. Crops failed, many Kansans were completely without money, and thousands of settlers packed up and went back East. It was obvious that outside help would be needed. Under the leadership of Thaddeus Hyatt of New York, and William F. M. Arny and Samuel C. Pomeroy of Kansas, the Kansas Relief Committee distributed food, clothing, medicine, and seed to save untold numbers of people. One pioneer woman wrote that "little hungry children and their grief worn parents . . . would have gone down to the graves" had people in the East not provided help. Another writer, watching Kansans receive relief supplies in Atchison, said: "Great, stalwart men, gaunt, lean, hungry looking, weary, sad, tired, and dispirited; poorly clad, and in all respects filling one with the conviction of suffering patiently borne and long repressed."

There were opinions expressed that the need for relief was not as great as some thought, but in general all rural areas suffered. The relief program and the distribution of supplies came in for criticism, too, and Samuel Pomeroy was accused of increasing his own wealth by selling relief supplies and putting donated money into his pocket. However, no proof was ever given to support those charges, and the Kansas Relief Committee pulled a lot of people through the difficult times from the fall of 1860 to the spring of 1861.

A matter of primary concern to Kansans was the establishment of the new state government. Some of the Free-State party controversies of the territorial period carried over into statehood with the conservative element of the Republicans led by Charles Robinson and the radicals by James Lane. The two men had often clashed in the 1850s. The first state election saw Robinson elected governor while Lane and Samuel Pomeroy became the state's first U.S. senators. Martin Conway, also a man with an antislavery background, was the first Kansan elected to the U.S. House of Representatives. Most men who had earlier been slavery sympathizers, and who stayed in Kansas, took up the cause of the Democratic party, but its strength was slight.

There were problems in getting the new governmental machinery to run smoothly, but things went along well until early in 1862 when rumors began to circulate that Governor Robinson and other state officials had

Atchison, a center of overland traffic, as it appeared at the time of the Civil War.

engaged in illegal activities concerning the sale of state bonds. The rumors led to a full-scale investigation and impeachment charges were filed against the governor, the auditor, and the secretary of state. The bonds in question, issued by the state in 1861, had been sold to the U.S. Department of Interior. Robert Stevens, who arranged the sale, received a commission. The arrangements with Stevens were not exactly legal but the state had been unsuccessful in selling the bonds in any other way and Kansas desperately needed the money that the bonds brought.

When James Lane took a hand in the bond investigation many Kansans felt that the whole business was his idea to eliminate Robinson as political competition. One member of the legislature said that the sale was wrong but that the thing was a "humbug" by the time the session ended, and many other legislators agreed with him. Lane's supporters made a great deal out of the scandal while Robinson's followers said that he had been treated unfairly. The impeachment trials were not held until June 1862 and certainly factional politics were present. Governor Robinson was acquitted and the other state officers were found guilty on only one count. The political careers of all three were finished although Charles Robinson would try again for state office in later years. James Lane, now in control of the Republican party in Kansas, was able to have Thomas Carney of Leavenworth elected governor.

THE CIVIL WAR

As Kansas was getting started as a state, the secession movement was developing in the South and fear of what might happen to the Union was widespread. Kansans were almost unanimous in their sympathies for the Union and even those who had opposed Abraham Lincoln at election time upheld his position as he took office. The editor of the Fort Scott *Democrat,* loyal to the party for which he had named his newspaper, probably summed up Kansas and Union sympathies as well as anyone on March 9, 1861:

> The principles of our party are as dear to us now as ever. . . . But another question has arisen, more engrossing and absorbing than all others combined, which overrides party allegiance, and absolves us from fidelity to partisan interest. . . . We have but one duty—that is TO OUR COUNTRY! No party can absolve us from our imperative duty to the Constitution and Union. . . .
>
> We are not willing to give up the Union for 500 parties. . . . We will, therefore, yield a liberal and cordial support to any party, man, or set of men, whose efforts honestly tend to the preservation of our glorious Union.

Officers of the Eighth Kansas Infantry, 1863. Second from left is Capt. Edgar P. Trego, for whom Trego County is named. He was killed in action at Chickamauga. In the center is Col. John Martin, later governor of Kansas.

> And now, as the destinies of our country are committed . . . to Mr. Lincoln, we stand prepared and pledged hereby to support with patriotic zeal and earnestness, any and all measures of his administration having in view the restoration of peace to the distracted interest of our country. . . .
>
> Peace with our neighbors, and quiet within our own borders we must have; and the Union restored and reconstructed, if within the limits of human possibility.

In Washington, Senator Lane was working hard to establish good relationships with President Lincoln. On April 14, 1861, the day Fort Sumter surrendered and the Civil War began, Lane enlisted more than a hundred men in a military group known as the "Frontier Guard." The company was to serve as a special guard for Lincoln and the White House. Most of the members were Kansans looking for jobs in Washington but one of the privates was Senator Pomeroy, who was so fat that a belt could not be found to fit him.

The Frontier Guard camped out in the East Room of the White House, and remained in service for three weeks. By the end of that time Washington was filled with Union troops and the danger of a Confederate attack on the capital did not appear imminent. There is no question about Lane's motives in organizing the company—they were purely political and personal—but maybe the guard did help to calm the nerves of some Washington residents even though it was of little military value.

When the Civil War began Kansas had no troops under arms. Recruiting began at once and military companies were organized in many Kansas towns. Senator Lane thought he saw an opportunity to take over military as well as political leadership—after Governor Robinson had recruited two regiments of volunteers for federal service—and offered the president two regiments for three years' service, or the length of the war. Lincoln had the secretary of war commission Lane a brigadier general of volunteers with authority to raise troops. Although Lane soon had to give up his commission in order to retain his seat in Congress he had time to organize "Lane's brigade," which included three volunteer regiments.

On August 10, 1861, Kansas troops saw their first action at the Battle of Wilson's Creek near Springfield, Missouri, under the command of General Nathaniel Lyon, who lost his life in the engagement. The Union troops were outnumbered by the Confederates under General Sterling Price, and General Lyon did not get the reinforcements he badly needed. The Kansas regiments fought bravely but suffered heavy casualties in this first major battle of the war in the West.

In the fall of 1861 communities in eastern Kansas suffered a number of raids by the Confederates. Both Humboldt, which had just barely recovered from an attack the month before, and Gardner were raided in October. A report from Humboldt said that the Confederates "after taking whatever they could make available in the way of dry goods and groceries . . . announced their intention of burning the town. The hellish work commenced, and before they desisted 21 dwelling houses, stores and a mill were consumed—more than one-half the buildings."

This kind of guerrilla warfare was carried on throughout much of the war and it was not limited to the Confederates. At almost the same time Humboldt and Gardner were attacked, Kansas troops swept down on Osceola, Missouri, and at other times they raided widely in the western part of that state. The Seventh Kansas Cavalry was especially notorious for such "Jayhawking," and while they freed slaves they also stole horses and other property, sometimes from Missourians who were not particularly sympathetic to the Confederacy.

Confederate outlaws led by "Bloody Bill" Anderson committed several crimes, including

Gov. Charles Robinson

An artist's conception of the devastating raid on Lawrence by the Confederate guerilla force under William Quantrill.

murder, along the Santa Fe Trail during the summer of 1862, while the notorious William C. Quantrill raided Olathe in September. This kind of warfare reached it peak on August 21, 1863, when Quantrill almost wiped out Lawrence and left 150 of its citizens dead. With about 300 men, Quantrill hit Lawrence at dawn. The Confederates shot down every man they saw and fired into windows as they rode by. Near the center of town they surprised a camp of black recruits for the Union army and literally rode them into the dust. The guerrillas broke up into small groups to loot, burn, and murder. Most of the killing took place in the west part of town where a band led by George Todd operated. At first the men of the town thought that the guerrillas intended to kill only soldiers, blacks, and active "jayhawkers" and consequently many who might have escaped remained in their homes and became easy victims. Some of the men escaped by hiding under buildings, in wells, or in the fields at the edge of town. Banks, stores, and saloons were all looted, along with dozens of houses. Much of what could not be carried off was burned and the town was covered with smoke. By nine o'clock in the morning it was all over and Quantrill escaped into the Missouri hills.

The plight of one Lawrence family is vividly described in this letter written by Erastus Ladd immediately after the raid:

When they came to plundering and burning, the streets were comparatively clear. When they were near my house, or along the street, I would go into my cellar; and when they were temporarily absent, I would come up and watch the progress of affairs from the windows or porches. . . . In the course of time it came our turn. I was in the cellar. A devil came to the door with a cocked revolver in his hand, and called Eliza out. He demanded if I was in the house. She told him I was not. He demanded her money, jewelry and arms. She gave him what she had. He then broke up some chairs, and tore up some books, piled them up in the dining room and in the kitchen and set them on fire. He was a perfect demon. She begged for five minutes time to get out some things. He would not give her a moment. I heard the flames crackling and roaring over my head. I expected, however, that I should be able to escape through the outside cellar door, which I had fastened on the inside, after he should have left the house, and before I should suffer from the heat. . . . He then went to the next house. Eliza got some water and put out the fire in the dining room and partially in the kitchen. . .

When the fellow had gone I came up . . . took an observation, saw that the fellow was out of sight. . . . Took the children's wagon, put Emma in it, and Georgie in her lap, took Winnie by the hand, and Eliza, and we went boldly out into the street . . . went along the road out of town for about two miles and were not disturbed. . . .

I will not attempt to describe the desolation which I saw on return to our town. . . . I could not describe it if I would. . . . Many of our best men were murdered. All, except one, of our best blocks of buildings have been consumed, a large portion of our town destroyed, and all of it sacked and plundered. . . . Eliza and the children came in towards night of that day, and, through the kindness of friends, we have had a home, or rather several stopping places until yester-day, when we moved into a part of a house. We have three small rooms, blackened with smoke, and glass most all broken by the heat . . . for which we pay nine dollars per month. By buying, borrowing, and (not begging) donations, we have got a few things to keep house with. . . .

Wm C. Quantrill

Quantrill made one more raid into Kansas. On October 6, 1863, he attacked a temporary military post at Baxter Springs. The attack was thrown back by the small Union force there but within a short time Quantrill's men again went into action, this time against the personal escort and headquarters wagon train of General James G. Blunt. Blunt, Kansas' only major general, was on his way to Fort Smith, Arkansas, when he was surprised by Quantrill who had his Confederates dressed in Union uniforms. Blunt's force was broken up completely and suffered heavy losses. Among the people killed by Quantrill and his men were unarmed members of an army band. Again Quantrill escaped from Kansas and although many different stories were told about what finally happened to him, he presumably was killed by Union troops in Kentucky near the end of the war.

A number of Kansas volunteer regiments became a part of the Union army serving in the South during 1862. Three regiments and an artillery battery made up an all-Kansas brigade that saw action in Kentucky, Tennessee, and Mississippi. A brigade commanded by General Blunt fought at Rhea's Mills, Cane Hill, and Prairie Grove in Arkansas. Several Kansas units were in the Indian Territory, partly to control tribes sympathetic to the Confederacy, and in 1863 Kansas troops participated in the battles of Elm Creek, Cabin Creek, and Honey Springs, all in the Indian Territory. General Grant used some Kansans in the Vicksburg campaign of 1863 while the Eighth Kansas Infantry took part in the heavy fighting at Chickamauga.

The Eighth Regiment's participation at Chickamauga on September 19 and 20, 1863, was described by one of its officers:

On the morning of the 19th, after marching near eight miles, most of the way on double quick, we were suddenly turned to the right and marched near one mile into the timber when we were formed into line of battle. . . . Soon after being formed into line we were ordered forward, but had scarcely advanced fifty yards when the enemy poured a terrible fire upon us from behind a ledge of rocks where they lay concealed.

Many of the men fell at the first fire, but the others, promptly returning the fire, pressed forward vigorously, and, not only maintained their ground, but had nearly penetrated the lines of the enemy, when our

Gen. James G. Blunt

brigade commander seeing the terrible fire to which the line was exposed gave the order to fall back. Reforming the line we again advanced under a perfect shower of bullets, sometimes driving the enemy, and in turn being driven by them, until we had fought the ground over and over again. . . .

The enemy being largely reinforced we took a position farther to the west on the edge of the timber, where we resisted every effort of the enemy, and finally drove them entirely from that part of the field. . . . Before dawn next morning we were moved into position on the road to Chattanooga where we remained until nearly 12 midday when we crossed the road and took position behind a low rail fence. Scarcely had we taken our position, however, when the enemy rose up in front of us, where they had been concealed in the tall woods, and poured upon us a heavy enfilading fire. The fire was quickly returned and with good effect; whole lines of the enemy falling at every discharge. This continued for a short time and the enemy was almost effectually checked in our front, when the troops on our right and left gave way and . . . the enemy appeared in heavy force upon both flanks; when unsupported and almost surrounded, we were compelled to leave the field or fall into the hands of the enemy.

We fell back in disorder until we reached the ground formerly occupied by us in the morning. From here we were ordered to the support of the right of General Thomas but before reaching the field we were ordered forward. . . . There were many instances of personal

Samuel Reader, a soldier in the Kansas militia called into service for defense against the Price Raid, painted this scene of action at the Battle of the Blue, October 1864.

bravery and valor displayed upon the field but all did their duty
well. . . . The regiment entered the battle with four hundred and six
officers and men; our loss . . . is two hundred and twenty.

In the words of one Kansas writer at the time, the Eighth won for
itself "a name that will not die." Today a visitor to the battle fields of
Chickamauga in Georgia and Lookout Mountain at Chattanooga, Tennessee, finds references to the Eighth and its gallantry. A monument hon-
oring the regiment stands on Missionary Ridge, high above Chattanooga.

On August 25, 1863, Union General Thomas Ewing issued Order
No. Eleven, which was designed to clear the Missouri border counties of
disloyal residents and cut down on guerrilla activity along the eastern Kansas
line. The order was praised by Kansans and condemned by a great many
Missourians, including some Union sympathizers. Ewing did not intend
for homes to be destroyed but unfortunately some of the Union troops
involved did burn property and treat some of the residents badly. Although
the action served the Union's purpose it left a great deal of bitterness that
lasted through several generations.

In the fall of 1864 the Confederacy planned an all-out attack in Mis-
souri. It was a last-ditch effort, for by then the war was going badly for the
South on all fronts. An army commanded by General Sterling Price threat-
ened Kansas City and Fort Leavenworth. Governor Carney called out the
Kansas militia to help strengthen the regular federal forces in the area.
General Samuel Curtis, commanding the Department of Kansas, organized
his men into two divisions and met Price along the Blue River near Kansas
City, Missouri. Battles took place at Byram's Ford and Hickman's Mills on
October 22, and the next day the Battle of Westport was fought on ground
that now includes Loose Park in Kansas City. The Battle of Westport has
been called the last full-scale battle of the Civil War in the West. Price
was beaten and forced to retreat south along the Kansas-Missouri line.

The Confederate general rested his troops at Trading Post in Linn
County, but, on the morning of October 25, he was pushed from this position by pursuing Union troops under Generals Curtis, Blunt, and
Pleasanton. Price retreated until he reached Mine Creek, just south of
Pleasanton, where he was forced to halt because his wagons bogged down
in the mud of the creek. In order to save his wagons and supplies he turned
back with two divisions and prepared to fight, but before he could complete the move he took the full force of a cavalry charge. Panic broke out
among the Confederates and they discarded their weapons and fled across
Mine Creek—described by one observer as "fleeing like a herd of buffalo."
Over 500 Confederates were captured, and Price's army just missed being

completely wiped out. He attempted to make one more stand near the Marmaton River but by then the Union forces were almost as confused as the Confederates and no major engagement took place. Price continued his flight and the final threat of a Rebel invasion of Kansas was ended. About 25,000 men were involved in the chase of Price and the Battle of Mine Creek, more than in any other Kansas action.

The final year of the war was uneventful for most Kansas soldiers because they were not involved in the eastern campaigns that brought defeat to the South. Several regiments finished the war in Arkansas, Missouri, the Indian Territory, and Kansas. Two regiments ended up on the Plains, with the Eleventh seeing active duty against Indians in Wyoming and fighting at Platte Bridge. The battle-hardened Eighth ended the war in Tennessee and Alabama and was not discharged until several months after the war was over.

By the time the South surrendered, Kansas had contributed twenty-three regiments and four artillery batteries to the Union army, more than 20,000 men and two-thirds of all the adult males in Kansas. Kansas also suffered nearly 8,500 casualties and had the highest military death rate of any of the states in the Union. Along with the white troops recruited in Kansas the state provided three African-American units and three regiments of Native-American troops. Many of the natives who served the Union were not from Kansas but were members of tribes who fled to Kansas from areas controlled by the Confederates.

Several tribes split their allegiance when the war began. For example, there were Union and Confederate Osages and Cherokees. Some of them fought on their own rather than being regularly enlisted, and one group of Osages loyal to the Union wiped out a small Confederate force near Independence in May 1863. Other groups of noncombatant Indians spent much of the war in Kansas simply because they found life unbearable in the South to which they had moved previously. Among these were some of the Wichita tribe who had emigrated from the Kansas area long before white settlement took place.

The black troops from Kansas received high praise from all who were associated with them. General Blunt, following the Battle of Honey Springs in the Indian Territory, wrote:

> I never saw such fighting done as was done by the negro regiment. They fought like veterans, with a coolness and valor that is unsurpassed. They preserved their line perfectly throughout the whole engagement and, although in the hottest of the fight, they never once faltered. Too much praise can not be awarded them for their gallantry.

Cyrus K. Holliday, adjutant general of Kansas during the war, added: "Though suffering severe losses, and fighting at great disadvantage, owing to the merciless treatment they were sure to receive if taken prisoners . . . they faltered not, but with a steadiness and a gallantry . . . have earned an honorable reputation among the defenders of the Union."

On the homefront during the Civil War a few people involved in supplying the army profited from military activity, but mostly it was a time of sacrifice. Many farms and businesses were maintained by women and children while husbands and fathers were serving the Union. One traveler through Brown County in 1863 wrote:

> We occasionally saw a woman at work in the field. Sometimes you see a well-fenced farm unploughed and unplanted. The answers to questions on all such subjects are: "Her husband has gone to the war"—"the owner is in the service." The prairies are themselves the witnesses of the patriotism of our people. The woman who takes the plough to let her husband protect the flag . . . is deserving of higher honors than any that have ever been showered upon the head of conqueror. We have such women in Kansas. All through this northern tier [of counties] you hear of wool-pickings, wood-bees and other parties got up by the ladies for the help of families made destitute by the remorseless hand of war. The benevolence of the women at home is worthy of the patriotism of the men in the field. . . .

CONFLICT WITH PLAINS INDIANS

Following the war there were serious difficulties between Indians and whites in the West. Increasing settlement from the late 1850s on meant that Indians felt greater pressure. After Colonel John Chivington and his Colorado volunteers massacred Black Kettle's Cheyennes at Sand Creek in eastern Colorado in 1864, Indian retaliation against whites increased. Indian raiders made life miserable for settlers and travelers along the Smoky Hill and Santa Fe trails and in the valleys of the Solomon and Saline rivers. In order to make peace there was a conference in 1865 between government officials and hundreds of Indians representing five Plains tribes on the Little Arkansas River near Wichita. But the talks had no lasting influence and both sides soon charged the other with violating the treaties, which said that the tribes should restrict their hunting to areas south of the Arkansas River.

To combat the Indians more effectively the government established Forts Dodge, Harker, Hays, and Wallace, supplementing the posts already in existence—Leavenworth, Riley, Larned, and Zarah. In 1867 General W. S. Hancock was ordered into the field to bring the Plains Indians into line with the federal government's Indian policy. He left Fort Leavenworth in March with infantry and artillery. At Fort Riley he was joined by General Custer and the Seventh U.S. Cavalry. At Fort Harker, near Ellsworth, he added more troops and the entire expedition marched to Fort Larned. Hancock hoped to impress the Cheyenne and the Sioux with his show of military power but the Indians conferred with him peacefully and then simply disappeared during the night. He was completely outmaneuvered and the expedition did not impress anybody.

By July, reports from Fort Wallace indicated that the army was hard pressed to cope with the angry Plains tribes. Supplies were short at Forts Harker and Hays and it was apparent that more peace conferences would have to take place. In the meantime, Custer and the Seventh had marched through southwestern Nebraska but had little luck in dealing with the Indians. It was during this campaign that Custer decided to return to Fort Riley to see his wife because he was worried about reports of a cholera epidemic in Kansas. He left his troops without proper permission and as a result was court martialed and suspended from duty for a year.

Another treaty commission was formed by the government to bring peace to the Plains. In October 1867, at present Medicine Lodge, the commission met with the leading chiefs of the Comanche, Kiowa, Arapaho, Cheyenne, and Apache tribes, while 15,000 Native Americans waited in camp nearby. Among the leading native spokesmen were Satank and Satanta (Kiowa), Little Raven (Arapaho), and Black Kettle (Cheyenne), while the government was represented by four generals, a U.S. senator, and Indian agents. Both sides pointed out the faults of the other—there was blame on both sides—and finally another set of agreements was reached and separate treaties were signed with the tribes.

The commissioners talked about reservations and limited hunting grounds for the Indians while the Indians still voiced their complaints about the Sand Creek affair and encroachment on their lands. One of the most expressive statements came from Satanta. He was quoted by Henry M. Stanley, the newspaperman who later gained fame as the discoverer of Dr. Livingstone in Africa, in his report for the St. Louis *Missouri Democrat,* October 25, 1867:

> The Commissioners have come from afar to listen to our grievances. My heart is glad, and I shall hide nothing from you. I understand that you were coming down here to see us. I moved away from those disposed to war, and I also came from afar to see you. The Kiowas and Comanches have not been fighting. . . .
>
> The Cheyennes are those who have been fighting with you. They did it in broad daylight, so that all could see them. If I had been fighting I would have done so also. Two years ago I made peace

with General Harney, Sanborn and Colonel Leavenworth at the mouth of the Little Arkansas. That peace I have never broken. When the grass was growing this spring, a large body of soldiers came along on the Sante Fe road. I had not done anything, and therefore, was not afraid.

All the chiefs of the Kiowas, Comanches and Arapahoes are here today. They have come to listen to the good word. We have been waiting here a long time to see you and we are getting tired. All the land south of the Arkansas belongs to the Kiowas and Comanches, and I don't want to give away any of it. I love the land and the buffalo and will not part with any. I want you to understand also that Kiowas don't want to fight, and have not been fighting since we made the treaty. I hear a good deal of fine talk from these gentlemen, but they never do what they say. . . . I want the papooses brought up just exactly as I am. When I make peace, it is a long and lasting one; there is no end to it. We thank you for your presents. . . .

When I look upon you I know you are all big chiefs. While you are in the country we go to sleep happy and are not afraid. I have heard that you intend to settle us on a reservation near the mountains. I don't want to settle there. I love to roam over the wide prairie and when I do it, I feel free and happy, but when we settle down, we grow pale and die.

Hearken well to what I say. I have laid aside my lance, my bow and my shield, and yet I feel safe in your presence. I have told you the truth. I have no little lies hid about me, but I don't know how it is with the commissioners; are they as clear as I am? A long time ago this land belonged to our fathers, but when I go up to the river I see a camp of soldiers, and they are cutting my wood down or killing my buffalo. I don't like that, and when I see it my heart feels like bursting with sorrow. I have spoken.

Satanta, Kiowa chief.

Despite the eloquent speeches by both sides at the council, both knew that the Medicine Lodge meetings were simply a part of the continuing conquest of Indian lands as the settlement of the frontier moved westward. Although both sides made promises and the government handed out several thousand dollars worth of gifts, within a year warfare broke out on the Plains once more.

By the summer of 1868 the Indians were unhappy and restless. Railroad building, the

A journalist's drawing of the Medicine Lodge treaty talks in 1867.

advancing line of settlement, and the destruction of the vast buffalo herds by white hunters all combined to make the land less attractive and productive for the Indians. Determined to hold their land , they retaliated by raiding settlements and railroad construction crews.

To combat the rising rate of attacks Colonel George A. Forsyth, stationed at Fort Harker, was authorized to recruit a force of frontiersmen to be used as scouts. Volunteers were not hard to find in central and western Kansas and Forsyth soon had his group on the march. He chased some Cheyennes who had raided a wagon train near Fort Wallace and met them in combat on September 17 at what became known as the Battle of Beecher Island or the Battle of the Arickaree. Forsyth's men dug in on a sandy island in the Arickaree Fork of the Republican River just across the Kansas line in Colorado and the Cheyennes kept them pinned down there until September 25 when a rescue force finally arrived from Fort Wallace. Forsyth lost five men, including Lieutenant Fred Beecher for whom the little island was named. Sixteen others were wounded. Indian losses were unknown but the famous warrior Roman Nose was killed.

It was in this period that new all-black regiments appeared on the Plains. Known as "Buffalo Soldiers," troops from the Tenth U.S. Cavalry were assigned to Fort Larned in 1867. For years to come soldiers like them from the Ninth and Tenth cavalry served at posts in Kansas and elsewhere in the West. Led by white officers and often discriminated against, they compiled an enviable record and gained the respect of their commanders and their Indian opponents in the field. A monumental sculpture at Fort Leavenworth now stands as a memorial to their service.

Approximately two hundred civilian and military deaths occurred in 1867 and 1868 as a result of warfare with Indians, more than had been recorded for the previous twenty years. The situation became so serious that Governor Samuel J. Crawford resigned his office in November 1868 to lead the Nineteenth Kansas Volunteer Cavalry regiment against the tribes. Cooperating with regular army troops, the Nineteenth took part in the winter campaign of 1868–1869, which led to defeat for the Cheyennes at the Battle of the Washita in the Indian Territory. By the end of 1869 the conflict had quieted down, at least in Kansas, and for the next five years Kansas settlers and Plains Indians were at peace.

THE CONTINUING POLITICAL PICTURE

After the war the ranks of the Republican Party were increased by the Union veterans who moved to Kansas. In fact, Kansas became a one-party state, a situation that would not change noticeably for many years to come. Within the Republican Party there was renewed conflict as Charles Robinson battled James Lane, even after Robinson left office in January 1863. Lane held the upper hand. He influenced state conventions and the selection of candidates for office and was reelected to the Senate in 1865. In July 1866, his political power ended when he committed suicide because of failing health and financial difficulties.

Governor Crawford appointed Edmund G. Ross, a Lawrence newspaper editor, as Lane's successor. Although he was not a politician Ross was a respected journalist, a territorial pioneer, and a Civil War veteran. His choice as senator was cheered by most Kansans. However, many of those same people were to turn against him on May 16, 1868, when he voted on the side of President Andrew Johnson at his impeachment trial. Impeachment charges had been brought against the president because he disagreed with leading Republicans about the Reconstruction of the South after the Civil War. He was publicly critical of Congress and removed Secretary of War Stanton from his cabinet, which the Senate said he could not do under the provisions of the 1867 Tenure of Office act.

There was a great deal of speculation in Washington about how the Senate, sitting as the impeachment court, would deal with the charges

against the president. Among the senators who did not indicate how they would vote was Edmund G. Ross. Because of Kansas's stand on slavery during the years before the war and because of the state's role in the war and its strong Republican leanings, most people assumed that both Senators Pomeroy and Ross would vote to convict Johnson. However, Ross cast his vote for acquittal and was subjected to abuse by Republicans in Washington and at home. The story that Johnson was saved by Ross's

Edmund G. Ross

vote alone is slightly exaggerated because some Republicans voted with him and others might have done so if necessary. Ross's vote did come at the right time on the roll call to provide the needed number for acquittal.

It was an act of great personal courage. Ross ended his own political career with his vote for Johnson. He was accused of accepting bribes to vote for acquittal but his vote was given honestly and was in support of the constitutional principles in which he believed. Ross later wrote: "I almost literally looked down into my open grave. Friendships, position, fortune, everything that makes life desirable to an ambitious man were about to be swept away by the breath of my mouth, perhaps forever."

At home, editorials such as this one from the Oskaloosa *Independent,* May 23, 1868, expressed the attitude of Kansas Radical Republicans:

> On Saturday last Edmund G. Ross, United States Senator from Kansas, sold himself, and betrayed his constituents; stultified his own record, basely lied to his friends, shamefully violated his solemn pledge . . . and to the utmost of his poor ability signed the death warrant of his country's liberty. This act was done deliberately, because the traitor, like Benedict Arnold, loved money better than he did principle, friends, honor and his country, all combined. Poor, pitiful, shriveled wretch, with a soul so small that a little pelf would outweigh all things else that dignify or ennoble manhood.

Ross left the Senate in 1871 and returned to Kansas where he went back into the newspaper business and made an unsuccessful effort to run for state office. He left the Republican party because he disagreed with the administrative policies of President U. S. Grant and, in the early 1880s, moved to New Mexico Territory where he served a term as territorial governor. The bitterness against him in Kansas died eventually but he stayed in New Mexico and was successful as both a newspaperman and a lawyer until his death in 1907.

Except for the attempt to remove Johnson, Kansas politics were relatively peaceful in the late 1860s. The Republicans mended their differences under Nehemiah Green, who became governor when Crawford resigned to fight Indians, and under James M. Harvey (1869–1873) Kansas was the first state to ratify the Fifteenth Amendment to the U.S. Constitution, giving blacks the right to vote, and the state legislature made arrangements to repay Kansans for losses they suffered during the Price Raid of 1864.

Progress in the 1860s

During the 1860s Kansas recovered from drought and depression and by 1870 population, farms, crop values, and business were on the increase. Settlers had moved west and south to places such as Hays, Beloit, Wichita, and Winfield. Towns, large and small, were concerned with building public schools. In Topeka, construction began on the state capitol and by the end of 1869 the east wing was complete and state government had moved into its new offices. Baker and Highland universities and St. Benedict's College, established during the territorial era, were joined by other new colleges. Lincoln College in Topeka (now Washburn University) was founded in 1865 and Ottawa University a little later. Bluemont College at Manhattan became Kansas State Agricultural College in 1863 and Lawrence was selected as the location for the state university in that year. The State Normal School at Emporia (now Emporia State University) was opened in 1866 and several other private colleges that no longer exist were begun during the 1860s.

At Manhattan the new state college announced that "every possible effort will be made to make the facilities for acquiring a full and thorough education in this institution equal to those of any other in the country." Its aim was to promote "the highest welfare of the student, physical, mental and moral" with an administration that would be "firm but mild and parental." Tuition was $5.00 for "higher English, Algebra, Geometry, Languages, etc." and expenses for board and room were estimated to range from $2.00 to $8.00 per week. At Emporia the new building was described as a "proud monument of the interest the people of the state feel in the cause of popular education" and a "fine temple for the instruction of the teachers of common schools."

The 1860s were years of optimism for most Kansans. The editor of the Junction City *Union* probably expressed the general feeling very well when he wrote on August 8, 1863:

> Her farmers are full of hope; her business men wear smiling faces; speculators are on the alert; and all things speak of the bright prospect which is before her. Our prairies look greener, our streams larger, our trees taller, and our rich soil turns from the ploughshare richer than ever.
>
> Homesteads are taken, farms are bought, town lots are changing hands. Our cattle increase, flocks of sheep are creeping in, and grain ricks stand in every field. Yes, we are prospering; we have struggled through the order of a new country, and we are coming triumphant. . . .

No other state offers superior inducements to the settler. We have the healthiest climate in the world. . . . Our granaries are full to overflowing. . . . Millions of acres of the finest land on the continent lie open. . . .

The great Continental Railway which is destined to connect the Atlantic and the Pacific will . . . pierce these broad acres, affording an expeditious and ready outlet to the markets of the East for all our products. . . . Long trains of cars will be bearing our cattle and grain to the markets of the world.

Suggestions for Reading

Edward Bumgardner, *Edmund G. Ross* (1949); Lumir F. Buresch, *October 25 and the Battle of Mine Creek* (1977); Albert Castel, *A Frontier State at War: Kansas, 1861–1865* (1958); Albert Castel, *William Clarke Quantrill* (1962); Albert Castel, *Civil War Kansas: Reaping the Whirlwind* (1997); Dudley T. Cornish, *The Sable Arm* (1956); Samuel J. Crawford, *Kansas in the Sixties* (1911); Lawrence A. Frost, *The Court-Martial of General George Armstrong Custer* (1968); Thomas Goodrich, *Bloody Dawn: The Story of the Lawrence Massacre* (1991); Thomas Goodrich, *Black Flag: Guerrilla Warfare on the Western Border, 1861–1865* (1995); Douglas C. Jones, *The Treaty of Medicine Lodge* (1966); William H. Leckie, *The Buffalo Soldiers* (1967); Gerald W. McFarland, *A Scattered People: An American Family Moves West* (1985); Jay Monaghan, *Civil War on the Western Border* (1955); John H. Monnett, *The Battle of Beecher Island and the Indian War of 1867–1869* (1992); Leo E. Oliva, *Fort Hays, Frontier Army Post, 1865–1889* (1980); Leo E. Oliva, *Fort Wallace: Sentinel on the Smoky Hill Trail* (1997); Mark A. Plummer, *Frontier Governor: Samuel J. Crawford of Kansas* (1971); Wendell Stephenson, *The Political Career of James H. Lane* (1930); David K. Strate, *Sentinel to the Cimarron: The Frontier Experience of Fort Dodge, Kansas* (1970); Paul Wellman, *Death on the Prairie* (1934); Lonnie J. White, *Hostiles and Horse Soldiers* (1972). Also, Leo Oliva's books on Fort Scott and Fort Larned, mentioned in previous chapters, also apply here. In addition, Chapter Six of John F. Kennedy, *Profiles in Courage* (1965), is an excellent summary of Senator Ross's action concerning the Johnson impeachment and Eugene W. Berwanger, "Ross and the Impeachment: A New Look at a Critical Vote" *Kansas History* (Winter, 1978) adds to that. Hard times in early Kansas are discussed in detail in Joseph G. Gambone, "Economic Relief in Territorial Kansas," *Kansas Historical Quarterly* (Summer, 1970). Many articles in both the *Kansas Historical Collections* and the *Kansas Historical Quarterly* deal with the Civil War, and the *Report of the Adjutant General of the State of Kansas, 1861–1865* (1896) contains rosters and histories of the Kansas volunteer regiments. More recent military studies include: Gary L. Cheatham, "'Desperate Characters': The Development and Impact of the Confederate Guerrillas in Kansas," *Kansas History* (Autumn, 1991); David Dixon, "A Scout With Custer: Edmund Guerrier on the Hancock Expedition of 1867" *Kansas History* (Autumn, 1981); Mike Fisher, "The First Kansas Colored—Massacre at Poison Springs" *Kansas History* (Summer, 1979); John T. Langelier, "'Knowing No Fear': Buffalo Soldiers of the American West" *Kansas Heritage* (Autumn, 1997). Settlement during the 1860s is dealt with in James R. Shortridge, "People of the New Frontier: Kansas Population Origins, 1865" *Kansas History* (Autumn, 1991).

7

The Development of the Railroads

Kansas shared in the widespread railroad promotion that was found in most of the United States just before the Civil War and in the twenty years that followed the conflict. From the opening of the territory, people were talking about the increased business and settlement that railroad building could bring to the American West and to this area in particular. Most of the promoters had visions of their railroads becoming a part of a great transcontinental network.

News of proposed railroads began to appear in Kansas newspapers in the late 1850s. In July 1857, a meeting was held in Leavenworth to discuss the construction of a line that would connect with the Hannibal and St. Joseph Railroad, still under construction in Missouri. At almost the same time, delegates from three Kansas towns and Platte City, Missouri, gathered in Lawrence to consider a railroad survey from Lawrence to Delaware, in Leavenworth County. This was to be a first step toward the completion of a line from Chicago to the "heart of Mexico."

Another meeting took place in Emporia on July 21, with Cyrus K. Holliday the principal speaker. Holliday, later the first president of the Santa Fe, was then president of the Topeka and St. Joseph Railroad—a company with a name but no tracks. Settlers came in great numbers and they discussed railroad prospects at length. That afternoon Holliday spoke to the group and pointed out the advantages Emporia could gain if it supported his plan. The Emporia *News* reported on July 25:

The Topeka and St. Joseph road, when completed, would bring us within a few hours' ride of Chicago, and thence along the Great Lakes to New York. This road would be but sixty-six miles long, connecting at St. Joseph with the Hannibal and St. Joseph road, which would be running in one year's time. The extension of the Topeka and St. Joseph road to Emporia would open a vast region of country, rich in agricultural production and natural resources. . . . Col. Holliday concluded by saying that he was confident, from the observation he had taken of the country between this place and Topeka . . . that a railroad could be constructed between the two points very cheap, comparatively—as cheap as through any portion of Kansas which he had seen.

Railroad fever reached new heights during 1859. The Elwood and Marysville Railroad, originally chartered in 1857 as the Marysville and Roseport, began construction in 1859, building west from the Missouri River as an extension of the Hannibal and St. Joseph, which by then had reached the river. Other lines were planned and more meetings were held in an effort to make dreams become reality. Since the Elwood and Marysville was the first railroad to begin construction it received a great deal of attention and it increased the optimism of those involved in rail promotion.

The Elwood and Marysville was supposed to build to Fort Kearny, Nebraska, and then extend to Denver, Colorado, and Fort Laramie, Wyoming. The laying of track proceeded slowly but on April 23, 1860, a locomotive named the *Albany* was ferried across the Missouri to Elwood. The next day other rolling stock came across the river, and the citizens of Doniphan County celebrated. "About four o'clock the engine was coupled to the cars, the cars were crowded by a dense mass of men, and amid the ringing of bells, shrill screechings of whistles and deafening cheers, the first train of cars rolled over a Kansas railroad." The great plans never came to pass. The railroad got no farther than Wathena, only five miles, on its way to the Rockies. Nevertheless, it was the first step in Kansas railroad building.

Cyrus K. Holliday

On June 13, 1860, crowds gathered in Atchison to celebrate the futures of three railroads—the Atchison and St. Joseph; the Atchison, Fort Riley and Fort Union; and the Atchison and Pike's Peak. There were 10,000 people in town to watch a parade, hear speeches and a 100-gun salute, and to eat and drink. The day ended with a dance and the Atchison paper said that the celebration was "one of the grandest affairs of the kind upon record—a perfect carnival." Atchison thought it was in the railroad business for good and let the world know about it.

THE UNION PACIFIC

By 1861 the territorial legislature had chartered fifty-one railroad companies but the coming of the Civil War put a stop to construction. Then on July 1, 1862, President Lincoln gave his approval to the Pacific Railroad bill. It provided federal aid for the construction of a transcontinental railroad and provided for three feeder lines that were authorized to build through Kansas and eventually connect with the main line in central Nebraska. According to the act the Union Pacific was to build west from the 100th meridian in Nebraska to the west line of Nevada while the Central Pacific was to build east from western California to the Nevada line. East of the 100th meridian several roads were to build connecting links from the Missouri River, including the Leavenworth, Pawnee and Western. The L. P. & W. could build from the Missouri River up the valleys of the Kansas and Republican to Fort Kearny, Nebraska, using financial aid from the federal government.

The L. P. & W. had been chartered in 1855 but did not begin construction until September 1863, and by that time it had changed its name to the Union Pacific, Eastern Division. The work was under the supervision of Samuel Hallett who realized he was under pressure because the first hundred miles had to be finished by November 1864. A great many delays took place because materials did not always arrive by steamboat at Kansas City when they were supposed to and the weather could be a problem. Construction plans suffered another blow in July 1864, when Hallett was murdered by one of his own employees. However, his brother, John Hallett, took over the construction responsibility and finally the rails reached Lawrence on November 27. Two weeks later the first passenger train steamed into the Lawrence depot and a city-wide celebration took place.

It was another year before the tracks got to Topeka, and it was almost that much longer again before they reached Junction City. In the meantime, work was underway on the branch from Wyandotte to Leavenworth and the federal government changed its requirements so that the road could build west along the Smoky Hill River instead of northwestward along the Republican. Denver became the U. P.'s main target, with Shoemaker, Miller & Co. as the new contractors.

The change in construction plans brought happy response from Kansans who were interested in a through east-west connection, and comments similar to this one from the Manhattan *Kansas Radical*, July 14, 1866, were common:

> The route over the Smoky Hill will be the main route from the Atlantic to the Pacific. Nature so decrees. Freed from the sterility and barrenness of the northern track, from its cold and furious storms and winters, and scarcity in supply of fuel and water, it must be the main track. Being so it puts Kansas in the center of the Union...and will draw to it rapidly and steadily a dense population. For our State, indeed, it is a material triumph, the extent of which no mind can calculate!
>
> We rejoice. It does our heart good to have Young Kansas so benefited. With this grand continental road, and other great improvements certain to be made, we venture to predict, that two decades shall not pass without witnessing her the rival of the most populous and wealthiest States in the Union!

As the Union Pacific continued to make its way across Kansas, flooded streams, heavy snows, careless workmen, and angry Plains Indians combined to make progress slow at times. Military protection was limited, so the tribes found it simple to attack construction crews hoping to slow the "Iron Horse" as it moved through the buffalo hunting country. In 1868 there was a story told that some Indians tried to capture a locomotive by taking telegraph wire and stretching it across the track with two or three braves on either end. Nobody ever said what happened to the wire holders!

Railroads meant settlement, and many towns were born or were made larger and more important by the coming of the railroad. There were also towns that lasted only as long as the railroad paused in its construction at a certain place. These end-of-track towns consisted of tents and poorly constructed buildings. For a while during the winter of 1867, end of track was in Trego County at a place named Coyote. When the U. P. moved on, the town moved and became Monument in Logan County. Sheridan, also in Logan County, was the next "instant town," and for more than a year it was one of the wildest and toughest places in the American West. This description of Sheridan, written for the New York *Tribune*, December 11, 1869, makes plain what the town was like:

Sheridan is at present the most remarkable place in America, or in the world . . . where legitimate business centers, and where the most reckless of men and women gather, in order that in the absence of law and in the unprotected state in which property necessarily is placed, they may reap a harvest of plunder. It will remain to a great extent unchanged until the road advances, when they will move on. . . .

Sheridan is composed of two half streets, some 300 feet apart, the railroad track being in the center. There are large commercial houses engaged in the Sante Fe trade. . . . Some of the stores are as much as 150 feet long, and wide in proportion, and I saw one where tons of Mexican wool were stored waiting shipment. . . .

Beside these houses there are a few hotels and several buildings belonging to the railroad, and the rest are saloons and gambling establishments, more than 50 in number, all open and apparently doing good business. In almost every one are women. Fiddles and accordions are playing, glasses jingling; and there are billiard and roulette tables and other gambling devices. The men are able-bodied and strong; few are more than 35; the majority are less than 30 years old. . . . Of course they are well armed and ready at any moment for attack or defense; but I saw none who were either offensive or aggressive, although I have every reason to believe that they would commit murder on what we would call the slightest provocation, for they have been so audacious and bold that men of property have been obliged to resolve themselves into a Vigilance Committee and hang fifteen or twenty.

Back of the town is a small graveyard, where they have been buried, and only a few days before I arrived one of them was hanged to the trestlework a little out of town. For some time past the engineer has been in the habit of moving the morning train slowly over this spot, in order that the passengers might have a chance to see if any one was hanged by the neck. . . . Among the aggressive acts of these men it is related that at a hotel one asked a gentleman sitting opposite for the butter, and as he was not heard, he presented a small pocket pistol at the head of the gentleman, and, with his finger on the trigger, said: "Pass the butter."

At present these fellows are in subjection and property and life are as safe as elsewhere; but should they even threaten to be revenged, or to do any unlawful act, they will be dealt with in the most summary manner. . . .

By January 1870, train service reached Eagle Tail Station (now Sharon Springs) and shortly after that the railroad moved its equipment from Sheridan to Kit Carson, Colorado. The businesses followed and Sheridan disappeared, leaving "no streets, and no other vestiges of former habitation, except empty cans and old boots." On August 15, 1870, the railroad, by then called the Kansas Pacific, reached Denver. There was rejoicing in the Colorado capital and all along the line through Kansas. The Rocky Mountains were tied to the Missouri River by an iron road. In 1880, long after a connecting line had been built from Denver to Cheyenne, the Kansas Pacific became a part of the vast Union Pacific system.

EARLY RAIL TRAVEL

Early railroading on the Kansas (Union) Pacific was difficult. O. P. Byers, a pioneer Kansas railroader, wrote some years later:

> While it served its purpose it was in strange contrast with the modern railroad. Steel rails and the airbrake had never been heard of. The maximum speed of passenger trains was eighteen and freight trains nine miles per hour. Little effort was made to keep cars in repair, and one of the most stringent rules was that trainmen must see before leaving the terminal that enough brakes were in working order to hold the trains down the grades. . . .
>
> The "link and pin" [which had to be worked by hand on each car] was the only known coupler in passenger as well as in freight trains. Water for locomotives was a very serious problem. The well of that day was as crude as the road itself. All were shallow, under the belief that water could not be had except in certain favorable locations. . . .
>
> The first sleeping cars were operated in 1876 and were named Kit Carson, Prairie Queen, Globe, Atlas and Dexter. Each was fifty feet long and contained eight sections. They were regarded as palaces and a great luxury. In addition to these sleepers, emigrant cars made of very old coaches with wooden bunks were operated in mixed trains [freight and passenger], the passengers furnishing their own bedding. The company furnished a large emigrant house at Salina where families might remain, furnishing their own conveniences, while the men were searching for land.

Travelers commented that passenger cars, even ones that required first-class tickets, were often dirty, crowded, and poorly maintained, and those comments applied to several different railroads. However, Clarina Nichols, the woman's rights leader, was more favorably impressed with the immigrant cars than with regular coaches. In May 1872, she took a trip from Kansas City to the Pacific Coast and said:

On the Immigrant cars we had at no time more than a dozen fellow passengers. . . . They were, without exception, men and women of good address, . . . persons of education and culture. . . . All together we were sort of a family party.

A California friend suggested our coming on the Immigrant train, as being less crowded at this season of the year, . . . more safe from accidents, the seats as comfortable, the cars as cleanly and more roomy, in short, that being designed for the accommodation of immigrating families, we would be allowed privileges not to be had on 1st and 2nd class cars. . . . So we took our mattresses and blankets and personal luggage into the car with ourselves. . . . The weather was not very cold and the car always warm enough. Fare from Kansas City to San Francisco $62. Freight 6 cents per pound, and no extra charges.

RAILROAD EXPANSION

Although Atchison had celebrated its rail possibilities before the Civil War, work did not finally get started on the Atchison and Pike's Peak Railroad until 1865. Two years later it became known as the Union Pacific, Central Branch, and ran one hundred miles to Waterville in Marshall County. During that time it had received $640,000 from the federal government for construction. Waterville was the end of the line for several years but the Central Branch finally built west through Concordia and Downs, ending at Lenora in 1879. Not long after that road came under the control of the Missouri Pacific and a branch line was built from Downs to Stockton. The Central Branch never reached Pike's Peak but it did become extremely important to the northern Kansas counties through which it ran.

Several roads were built in northeastern Kansas in the 1860s and 1870s, including the St. Joseph and Denver City that became the Union Pacific's line between the Missouri River and Marysville and on into Nebraska. The Missouri River Railroad ran from Wyandotte north through Leavenworth, Atchison, and Hiawatha to join the Missouri Pacific at the Nebraska border and eventually it was a part of the Missouri Pacific system. These successful efforts increased interest in other parts of the state, particularly in southern Kansas where hopes were high for north-south connections.

Much of the railroad discussion in the western United States involved east-west lines but there were people in Kansas who had visions of railroads connecting Wyandotte, Atchison, Leavenworth, and Lawrence with the Gulf of Mexico. From this kind of thinking came three railroads: the

Missouri River, Fort Scott and Gulf; the Leavenworth, Lawrence and Fort Gibson; and the Union Pacific, Southern Branch. The Missouri River, Fort Scott and Gulf began life as the Kansas and Neosho Valley, but in 1868 its name was changed and eastern businessmen invested in its future. Management of the road was under the supervision of James F. Joy, an experienced railroad capitalist. In May 1870, the Missouri River, Fort Scott and Gulf reached Baxter Springs and became a vital part of the southeastern Kansas commercial scene. The road went through two more name changes and eventually became a part of the St. Louis and San Francisco, or "Frisco" system, which became a part of the Burlington Northern in 1980.

In Leavenworth and Lawrence promoters were asking what could keep them from building a railroad to the Gulf coast. They organized the Leavenworth, Lawrence & Fort Gibson to build to the southern border of Kansas but the Fort Gibson in the name indicated that they really wanted to go beyond Kansas, at least as far as the military post in the Indian Territory. The road got a big boost when the state gave it land along its right of way and was helped further when the voters of Douglas, Franklin, Anderson, Allen, Osage, and Lyon counties approved buying stock in it. A Lawrence editor wrote that this was not to be a local road "but a great connecting link between Galveston Bay and all the country from thence to the Atlantic and Pacific." In December 1867, the Leavenworth, Lawrence and Fort Gibson reached Ottawa from its connection with the Union (Kansas) Pacific at Lawrence but it did not get to Coffeyville and the border until 1871. By then it, too, had changed its name, to the Leavenworth, Lawrence and Galveston, and James F. Joy had become involved in its construction. It would go through one more name change before it became a part of the Santa Fe in 1880.

The Union Pacific, Southern Branch, that became the Missouri, Kansas and Texas in 1870 (the "Katy"), was incorporated in 1865 but construction did not begin until 1867. The first shovelful of dirt,

A "Katy" poster, advertising land granted to the road by the federal government.

marking the start of construction, was turned by the railroad's president on October 15, 1867, and Junction City joined the other towns in Kansas that participated in rail celebrations. The Katy's original main line from Junction City south through Council Grove and Emporia was abandoned in 1957 but for many years it was important to southern Kansas.

This road obtained land grants from both the state and federal governments and began a race for the state line. If it could get there before the Missouri River, Fort Scott and Gulf it would gain the right to build on through the Indian Territory to Texas. The Katy ran a close second, reaching Chetopa on June 4, 1870, and the state line two days later. However, the other line had mistakenly entered land held by the Quapaw Indians, where no road was supposed to be, so the federal government awarded the Katy the right to continue southward. Later in the 1870s its connections and branch lines gave it access to Kansas City, St. Louis, and the Gulf of Mexico. Parsons became an important center of activity on the Katy with large shops and offices that were not reduced in size and importance until several years after the Second World War. The Katy ceased operations at the end of 1988, and its trackage was acquired by the Missouri Pacific and ultimately by the Union Pacific.

THE ATCHISON, TOPEKA AND SANTA FE

The development of the Atchison, Topeka and Santa Fe took place largely because of Cyrus K. Holliday and his interest in rail transportation. Holliday, with Atchison and Topeka businessmen, chartered a railroad in 1859. In 1863 they obtained a government land grant for more than two million acres. The grant required that the railroad be completed across the state by March 3, 1873. Although there was a need for speed on the part of the Santa Fe there was very little cash available for construction. Finally, in the summer of 1868, a building contract was signed. The railroad also received permission to purchase land from the Potawatomi tribe, which could be resold at a profit, thereby adding to construction funds.

Work began in November 1868, as grading crews headed south from Topeka and bridge builders started to cross the Kansas River so that rolling stock could be brought over from the Union (Kansas) Pacific's track north of the river. On March 30, 1869, the Santa Fe's first locomotive, appropriately named the *Cyrus K. Holliday,* crossed the river hauling flatcars loaded with rails. By late April track had been laid beyond Pauline. An excursion was held and the guests had a good time, with one reporting for the Topeka *Daily Commonwealth*, May 1:

We left the city at three o'clock and soon were steaming over the prairies at the rate of fifteen miles an hour. We crossed the Shunganunga over a substantially built bridge, and all the streams and rivers we crossed were either bridged or culverted in the most substantial manner. . . . The ties are of oak and walnut and the rails are 56-pound iron. The grade cuts and embankments are unusually wide and the . . . grades are gradual and easy. Hills and stone quarries have been plowed through and deep and wide ravines have been filled with earth to make way for the road bed. It was apparent to all that . . . its proprietors designed it for service. . . .

We reached the end of the track in about thirty minutes where the track-layers were busily at work securing the iron to the ties at the rate of one-half to three-quarters of a mile per day. Carriages were awaiting us here to transport us to the Wakarusa five miles distant. . . .

We must not forget to mention that the excursionists were liberally supplied with refreshments by their entertainers. The excursion was a pleasant one, and judging from the sparkling eyes, the lively sallies of wit, the jokes, the repartees and the hilarity that generally prevailed, we know that all gladly welcomed the substitution of the iron horse for the Indian pony, the buckboard and the tri-weekly (make a trip one week and try to make another the next) stage.

The Rock Island's *Golden State Limited* loading at Pratt in 1923.

Three months later Thomas J. Peter, the road's superintendent, was able to announce the Santa Fe's first regularly scheduled service. Two trains ran from Topeka to Carbondale and back, one of them a passenger train and the other a "mixed" train—freight and passengers. In September 1869, the Burlingame *Osage Chronicle* could say "All Hail, All Hail . . . Cars in Burlingame at Last! . . . Hold Us, or we Bust." Again it was two trains a day each way—twenty-seven miles in approximately two hours.

It took another year for the Santa Fe to reach Emporia and another after that to build to Newton. With Newton as the temporary western end of track, work on the line between Topeka and Atchison increased but not rapidly enough to satisfy Atchisonians. Grading on the branch was done by Thanksgiving 1871, but no rails were on hand then and service did not begin between Atchison and Topeka until May 1872. The Atchison and Topeka portions of the railroad's name had been fulfilled but it was still a long way to Santa Fe.

Construction west of Newton began in late fall, 1871, and in 1872 the tempo picked up because the Santa Fe was facing its deadline for reaching the western Kansas line. Building two miles of track a day the crews marched on, connecting infant towns as they went—Hutchinson, Peace (Sterling), Ellinwood, Great Bend, Larned, and Dodge City among them. Bad weather, horse thieves, and shortages of money and supplies combined to make Santa Fe construction difficult. But on December 28, 1872, the railroad reached the Kansas-Colorado border. J. D. Criley, chief of the construction crews, sent T. J. Peter, by then the general manager, this message:

> We send you greeting over the completion of the road to the State
> line. Beyond us lie fertile valleys that invite us forward, and broad
> plains die away in the distance, dotted with mingling herds of bison
> and cattle, awaiting our further advance. The mountains signal us
> from their lofty crests, and still beyond, the Pacific shouts amen! We
> send you three cheers over past successes, and three times three for
> that which is yet to come.

By the beginning of 1873 the Santa Fe Railroad had built 470 miles of track and was involved in the operation of the Wichita and Southwestern, a connecting line from Newton to Wichita. Survey parties were already in eastern Colorado selecting a route to Pueblo. However, there was little money for additional building, and the national depression that hit in 1873 did not help matters. It was 1876 before the Santa Fe ran a train to Pueblo but work was more rapid through the rest of the 1870s. A controversy developed between the Santa Fe and the Denver and Rio Grande over control of Raton Pass as a route to Santa Fe, but the Kansas road won and reached Santa Fe in February 1880. Two years later the company was running trains to the Pacific coast.

In the meantime there were mergers and consolidations of lines in eastern Kansas. These, combined with the leasing of the Kansas City, Topeka and Western Railroad, gave the Santa Fe connections with the East through Kansas City, which became the eastern end of the Santa Fe in 1875. There the road stayed until the 1880s when a decision was made to build on to Chicago. By 1888 the Santa Fe was connecting in Chicago with the eastern roads and was truly a transcontinental line.

As the Santa Fe grew its service improved and it became one of the nation's most famous passenger carriers. In 1876 the railroad began its relationship with Fred Harvey, whose food and hotel service became equally famous. Harvey opened a lunch room in the Topeka depot in 1876 and in the same year started a hotel at Florence. Harvey service on Santa Fe diners and "Harvey Girls" serving in depot and hotel dining rooms became American institutions and a part of the Santa Fe story for most of a century.

By the beginning of the twentieth century, Santa Fe lines reached into Mexico, to the Gulf at Galveston, and to several California points. In the late 1920s it acquired the Kansas City, Mexico and Orient line that had started life in Kansas in 1901. The Santa Fe also was involved in hotels, steamships, and mining operations over a period of years. It had financial difficulties in 1893 and was reorganized in 1895 as the Atchison, Topeka and Santa Fe Railway Company. Into the 1990s it was part of a farflung business operation with a variety of interests but still very much a railroad. In 1983 the holding companies of the Santa Fe and the Southern Pacific merged, but the Interstate Commerce Commission denied a proposed merger of the railroads.

Between 1986 and 1996 the Santa Fe sold over 1,300 miles of branch line track to shortline railroads including the Topeka-Atchison route. The purchaser did not utilize the line, and it was abandoned in 1993. The Interstate Commerce Commission allowed a merger of the Santa Fe and the Burlington Northern in August of 1995, but the actual corporate change did not take place until January 1, 1997. A pioneer in Kansas transportation history no longer stood as a separate entity.

THE ROCK ISLAND AND MISSOURI PACIFIC

The 1880s saw a great increase in Kansas railroad mileage, much of it coming because of the rapid expansion of the Chicago, Rock Island and Pacific and the Missouri Pacific railroads. The Rock Island, using its subsidiary the Chicago, Kansas and Nebraska Railway, built from Elwood on the Missouri River through Horton to Topeka in 1886 and 1887.

Under the direction of Marcus A. Low the Rock Island track-laying crews sped on to Herington. From there a line was built to Wichita and Caldwell while another went to Liberal. A branch was constructed from McFarland, west of Topeka, to Belleville and a main east-west route laid out from Horton through Fairbury, Nebraska, to Colby and Goodland and on to Colorado Springs, Colorado. Within less than three years the Rock Island was operating more than 1,100 miles of line in Kansas, a fantastic record. Herington, Caldwell, and Horton were among the important Kansas points on the Rock Island and prospered because of that. However, the large shops at Horton were shut down in 1939 when the railroad cut back its operations for financial reasons.

The Rock Island declared bankruptcy in 1979, and its lines were divided and sold to various buyers. The St. Louis and Southwestern (the Cotton Belt), a part of the Southern Pacific system, purchased the main east-west line in 1982. The Oklahoma, Kansas, and Texas bought the trackage from Herington to Caldwell and the Oklahoma border in that same year. The Mid-States Port Authority, an association of Kansas counties, acquired the line in the northwestern part of the state, also in 1982. The Chicago, Rock Island, and Pacific ceased to exist as a railroad in 1983.

The Missouri Pacific was the last major railroad to build extensively in Kansas, with most of its construction coming in the dozen years before 1892. Much of the Missouri Pacific's expansion came through subsidiary companies and leased lines with financing arranged by the eastern capitalist, Jay Gould. Gould, known in American business history as one of the "Robber Barons" because of the vast amounts of money he took out of a variety of companies, was interested in making more money from central Kansas along a route that would divide the areas served by the Union (Kansas) Pacific and the Santa Fe between Kansas City and Colorado.

The subsidiary companies were organized under Kansas laws, local money was obtained if possible, and when the line was built the Missouri Pacific took over its operation. A branch was opened from Paola to Ottawa in 1880 and main line construction began from both Ottawa and Council Grove. In 1886 those two towns were connected, and west of Council Grove construction was handled in sections by the Topeka, Salina and Western; the Kansas and Colorado; and the Denver, Memphis and Atlantic. The Denver, Memphis and Atlantic, known in western Kansas as the "Darling Mary Ann," reached Horace in Greeley County in August 1887. It was open to the state line before the year was over, connecting with the Colorado portion of the road, which went to Pueblo.

In 1982 the Missouri Pacific merged with the Union Pacific but retained its identity as a wholly-owned subsidiary until the final merger on January 1, 1997.

St. Joseph and Grand Island depot at Home City, Marshall County, 1910. The St. J. and G. I. became a branch of the Union Pacific.

RAILROADS AND TOWNS

The importance of a railroad to a new community and the enthusiasm that greeted the arrival of the tracks is well illustrated by this story from the *Greeley County Gazette*, Horace, August 4, 1887:

> Last Tuesday was a day that will never be forgotten by any citizen now living in Horace as long as life lasts, or memory holds her sway. . . . At about five o'clock the Denver, Memphis & Atlantic railroad company laid their track into the town, in the presence of hundreds of our own citizens, men, women and children, together with scores of visitors from our neighboring towns, Tribune and Greeley Center, who seemed to take pleasure and rejoice with us over this event. . . .
>
> In the afternoon our citizens from all the towns and the country around began pouring into town. The streets were thronged by two o'clock. Very many people went east a mile or so to meet the engine and watch the laying of the ties and track. The rapidity of this work seems incredible. . . . As they approached Main street, the whole town with all its visitors, moved south to witness the arrival of the engine on Main street. At about the hour above named the track was thrown across the street and the train brought to a standstill amid the cheers of the multitudes in attendance. An invitation was then extended to the railroad men to visit the town and partake of refreshments, this was accepted and about three hundred marched up town and partook of the hospitality. . . .

The extreme cordiality existing between the people of Horace and those of our neighboring towns coupled with the almost unanimous support of the people of the whole country, practically settled the whole county seat question in this county. . . . Our consolidated town companies made immeasurably stronger by their union grow enthusiastic over their prospect here and promise every effort that they can command shall be put forth to make this the best town in western Kansas, with their railroad strength unlimited capital. With the aid of all the people . . . it requires no prophetic eye to see that in the immediate future Horace will be the Gem City of the best county in western Kansas.

Horace did become an important point on the Missouri Pacific but it did not achieve the status that its editor hoped for in 1887. When steam locomotives gave way to diesels, and fuel and water stops were fewer between Kansas City and Denver, it became less important and by the 1970s not much was left of the booming community of the 1880s.

More than a thousand railroads were chartered in Kansas. Probably no more than two hundred of them ever laid track, and by 1900 railroad control was held by the big companies. For some years there were several short lines in operation, including a narrow gauge originally called the Kansas Central that ran between Leavenworth and Miltonvale. It became standard gauge in 1890, and its name was changed to the Leavenworth, Kansas and Western, known to the people in the areas it served as the "Look, Kuss and Wait." By 1935 it had disappeared.

Connecting with it at Blaine in Pottawatomie County was an eight-mile long interurban line from Westmoreland called the Kansas, Southern and Gulf, which used automobiles fitted with railroad wheels to pull its trains between 1912 and 1918. There were other interurban lines and street railways that helped speed travel over short distances. There were also railroads that never built a mile of track but whose names indicated that they were planned on a grand basis. For example, a charter was issued to the Pensacola, Ness City and Puget Sound, which was to run from Florida to the Pacific Northwest by way of Ness City, but it never ran anywhere.

Railroads were eager to increase the Kansas population because more people meant more business. Consequently, they were leaders in promoting the sale of land, both that which they owned and that offered for homesteading. Millions of acres, granted by both state and federal governments to encourage railroad construction, were controlled by the railroads along with thousands more which they had obtained through the purchase of Indian reserves. Even though the railroads generally sold at reasonable prices on liberal payment terms they were criticized for some of their land practices.

Often large amounts of land were sold to speculators or promoters, which individual farmers felt was unfair. Other land was not offered for sale at all for several years and consequently did not take its place on the tax rolls of either local or state government. Complaints also came because the railroads were very influential in politics and in a variety of ways, including free passes to office holders, got legislation passed favorable to them. Since they controlled the transportation system of the West they could charge whatever rates they pleased and their charges became so high at one point that they almost wiped out farm profits. In the eyes of many westerners the railroads changed from heroes to villains between the 1860s and the 1880s and they became one of the principal targets of farm groups during the political unrest of the late nineteenth century.

Railroad financing and regulation has always been complicated and often difficult to understand. Probably it is enough to remember that the roads were built with money that came in three different forms and some roads had all three: subsidies from national or state governments, which came primarily in the form of land grants; funds raised by the sale of bonds by county or city governments; and capital from private investors. In Kansas, regulation and taxation came through the Board of Railroad Commissioners and the Board of Railroad Assessors. Those state agencies evolved and developed through the years and have been called by other titles, with most of the regulatory power finally coming under the modern Kansas Corporation Commission.

The entire nation has seen great changes in railroading in the years following the Second World War, particularly in passenger traffic. The famous trains, individually named, that once crossed Kansas in all directions no longer run. Towns that once had eight and ten passenger trains a day have not seen one for many years and only the limited service provided by Amtrak exists in the 1990s. Many branch lines have been abandoned altogether. The Rock Island's *Rockets* and *Golden State Limited* are long gone as are the Katy's *Texas Special*, the Missouri Pacific's *Eagles*, the Frisco's *Florida Special*, and the Union Pacific's *Portland Rose* and *City of St. Louis*. The Santa Fe's *California Limited*, which set record-breaking times using steam, and its many *Chiefs* have given way to the faster airplane.

Many branch lines have been abandoned altogether since 1950, and abandonments in the 1990s totaled more than 1,000 miles. In 1999 two major railroads dominated in Kansas—the Union Pacific and the Burlington–Northern-Santa Fe. The Kansas City Southern still operated eighteen miles in Kansas (to Pittsburg) connecting with its main line in Missouri. With the merger of the Union Pacific and the Southern Pacific, the Cotton Belt and the Denver and Rio Grande Western (which had only trackage rights in Kansas) became a part of the Union Pacific in 1997.

Fortunately for many communities and for Kansas agriculture several new short lines came into being beginning in the 1980s. In some cases they purchased trackage, and in others they arranged for leased lines from the major roads. The Kyle Railroad System, under lease arrangements with both the Union Pacific and the Mid-States Port Authority, operates more than 500 miles of track, which includes much of the old Central Branch and Rock Island lines in north central and northwestern Kansas. The Cimarron Valley Railroad serves the towns on the former Santa Fe branches from Dodge City southwest to the Colorado and Oklahoma borders. The Central Kansas Railway has service on approximately 1,000 miles of track, including the Missouri Pacific's old east-west main line and parts of the former Rock Island west of Wichita. Other short-line roads include the Kansas Southwestern, the Southeast Kansas Railroad system, the Northeast Kansas and Missouri, Garden City Western, Hutchinson and Northern, Nebraska, Kansas and Colorado Railnet, and the Missouri and Northern Arkansas. In August of 1998 the Union Pacific announced plans to buy back from the Northeast, Kansas and Missouri 107 miles of track from Upland in Marshall County to St. Joseph, Missouri, for use by its coal hauling trains.

There are three operating roads which could be classed as "tourist": the Midland Railway, from Baldwin to a point north of Ottawa; the Dodge City, Ford and Bucklin; and the Abilene and Smoky Valley, from Abilene to Woodbine. These offer rail fans an opportunity to relive the past.

For well over a century the railroad was the most sophisticated form of ground transportation ever developed. It still provides the backbone of American freight service and remains one of the state's major employers. The romance of the transcontinental passenger train is no longer a part of the Kansas scene.

Suggestions for Reading

George L. Anderson, *Kansas West* (1963); Keith L. Bryant, Jr., *History of the Atchison, Topeka and Santa Fe Railway* (1974); Allison Chandler, *Trolley Through the Countryside* (1963); Robert Collins, *Ghost Railroads of Kansas* (1997); James H. Ducker, *Men of the Steel Rails: Workers on the Atchison, Topeka & Santa Fe Railroad, 1869–1900* (1983); William E. Hayes, *Iron Road to Empire: The History of the Rock Island Lines* (1935); James L. Marshall, *Santa Fe: The Railroad That Built an Empire* (1945); V. V. Masterson, *The Katy Railroad and the Last Frontier* (1952); H. Craig Miner, *The Rebirth of the Missouri Pacific, 1956–1983* (1983); H. Craig Miner, *The St. Louis-San Francisco Transcontinental Railroad* (1972); I. E. Quastler, *Missouri Pacific Northwest: A History of the Kansas City Northwestern Railroad* (1994); Joseph W. Snell and Don W. Wilson, *The Birth of the Atchison, Topeka and Santa Fe Railroad* (1968); William E. Treadway, *Cyrus K. Holliday* (1980); Lawrence L. Waters, *Steel Trails to Santa Fe* (1950).

Also recommended are these *Kansas Historical Quarterly* articles: George L. Anderson, "Atchison and the Central Branch Country" (Spring, 1962); Peter Beckman, "Atchison's First Railroad" (Autumn, 1954); Robert W. Richmond and Joseph W. Snell, "When the Union and Kansas Pacific Built Through Kansas" (Summer and Autumn, 1966); A. Bower Sageser, "Building the Main Line of the Missouri Pacific Through Kansas" (Spring, 1955); and David G. Taylor, "Thomas Ewing, Jr., and the Origins of the Kansas Pacific Railway Company" (Summer, 1976). O. P. Byers, "When Railroading Outdid the Wild West Stories" *Kansas Historical Collections*, vol. 17, covers a variety of subjects concerning early railroad operations. The Santa Fe's role in agricultural promotion is thoroughly analyzed in Constance L. Menninger, "The Gospel of Better Farming According to Santa Fe" *Kansas History* (Spring, 1987).

Of great help in understanding the changes in Kansas railroad development and ownership is a publication of the Kansas Corporation Commission, compiled by Vernon Wenger, *A History of Railroad Construction, Ownership and Abandonment Within the State of Kansas*. It has been updated to 1998. The Corporation Commission also issues a railroad map of the state, with 1998 the most recent one.

The Cattle Trade:
Trail Herds, Towns, and Ranchers

At the end of the Civil War Texas cattle ranchers were faced with a major problem. They had on their ranges approximately five million head of Longhorns, which would bring high prices if they could only be sold in the markets of the North. There was a shortage of beef, and northern dealers would be happy to buy Longhorns if they could be shipped to St. Louis, Chicago, and New York. Transportation was the problem. Steamships could carry only a small number of cattle. Railroads had not then reached Texas and with the shortage of money in the South it seemed that it might be several years before there was a rail connection with St. Louis. The practical solution was to drive herds of Longhorns overland to eastern cities or to a point on the railroad where they could be loaded and sent to market.

TRAIL DRIVING

Some trail driving had been done before the Civil War but never on a large scale. During the 1850s small herds from Texas and the Indian Territory were driven into or through Kansas for sale to the U.S. Army at Forts Leavenworth and Riley while others went on into Nebraska, Iowa, Illinois, or Minnesota. There was an outbreak of Texas Fever, caused by ticks carried by the Longhorns, in 1858 and Kansas farmers were angry when their cattle were infected. The Longhorns were immune to the disease but not the Kansas animals. The Kansas territorial legislature passed a law in February 1859, that no person would be permitted to drive any infected cattle into or through Kansas, but the law was broken in 1859 and again in 1860 and more Kansas cattle died of Texas Fever. Some Longhorns were shot down by Kansas farmers and there were armed encounters between Kansans and Texans. However, during the Civil War few herds came north.

In 1866 large Texas herds were headed north. Most of them took the Shawnee Trail that ran from Texas across the Choctaw Nation and past Fort Gibson to a point near Baxter Springs, Kansas. From there it ran on northeast to Sedalia, Missouri, where the Missouri Pacific Railroad was available for shipping. When the Texans reached the Kansas line just below Baxter Springs they again met Kansas farmers who were still opposed to Longhorns with Texas Fever. Some of the drovers gave up and sold their herds cheaply while others held their cattle in the Indian Territory just

Railroads and Cattle Trails of Nineteenth-Century Kansas
This map shows the Chisolm and Western Cattle trails and their terminals on Kansas railroads, 1867–1885. Baxter springs and Coffeyville received a minor portion of the total trade from those Texas droves who used the older Shawnee Trail to the Kansas border.

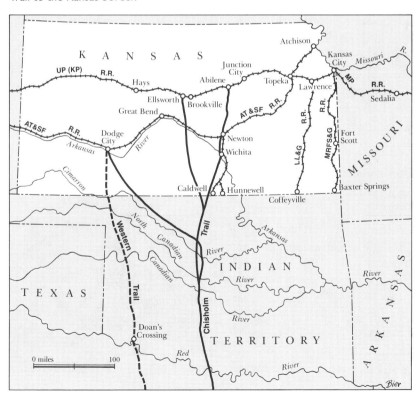

south of the town. This situation gave Baxter Springs a brief career as a cowtown, and gamblers, saloon keepers, and dance hall girls gathered to take the cowboys' money.

Of the approximately 260,000 Longhorns driven north during the summer of 1866 only a small percentage reached a profitable market. As a result, very few herds were started north in the spring of 1867. On February 26, 1867, an act was passed by the Kansas legislature that said that no one could drive Texas cattle into the state between March 1 and December 1, except through that part roughly south and west of present McPherson.

In spring, 1867, Joseph G. McCoy, a young Illinois livestock dealer, heard about Texas cattle and the possibilities of establishing a market for them. He came west and after looking at several towns decided that Abilene, on the Union Pacific Railroad, was the best place to locate a shipping business. In choosing Abilene, McCoy actually violated the new Kansas law for the quarantine line ran several miles west of the little town. However, since there were so few settlers in the vicinity at that time no one opposed his choice and Governor Samuel J. Crawford gave his approval.

McCoy bought land for his stockyards and began to build corrals. He sent a rider south to contact drovers and advertise Abilene. By the first of September he had a stockyard that would hold a thousand head of cattle, and before the month was over he had also completed a hotel, the Drovers' Cottage. The first herd to come directly up the trail from Texas was owned by Colonel O. W. Wheeler and two partners. On September 5, 1867, the first rail shipment of twenty cars left Abilene for Chicago. Joseph McCoy had opened a new era in the cattle business.

THE CHISHOLM TRAIL

The route that brought the cattle to Abilene was an extension of the Chisholm Trail. Originally used by Indians, traders, and the army, the trail had run from the Canadian River north to Jesse Chisholm's trading post on the Little Arkansas River at present Wichita. Later it was extended to other Kansas

Jesse Chisolm

Members of a roundup crew take time out for a bath.

towns, and Chisholm's name was commonly used for the entire trail from several Texas points to Caldwell, Wichita, Newton, and Abilene.

The trail entered Kansas near Caldwell and ran north past Wellington and Wichita to Abilene. After years of use it was two hundred to four hundred yards wide and lower than the surrounding country. It was as bare as a city street and marked by bleached skulls and bones of Longhorns, broken down wagons, and a few cowboy graves.

The size of the herds that came from Texas varied from under a thousand head in early years to three or four thousand during the later period. A herd of two thousand would string out for a mile or two in length and the width of the line would vary from a few Longhorns walking side by side to a group several yards wide. At times the clouds of dust raised by the herds could be seen for several miles across the prairie, and Kansans told of hearing the herds coming for hours before they actually appeared. The noise of the cattle's hooves sounded like thunder in the distance.

A trail drive was a giant undertaking. In the spring the drover gathered the cattle that he intended to market and they were then branded for the road. Herds usually started north as early as March or April and reached the shipping point by June. Most of the shipping was done in the summer and early fall. The distance from the Red River to the Kansas cattle towns was from 300 to 350 miles and the drive was made in 30 to 40 days.

The cowboys who drove the herds were generally young men, many in their early twenties. They were expert riders who had both courage and endurance or they would not have been able to stand the hardships of the drive. They were paid from twenty-five to forty dollars a month, plus their food, prepared at the chuckwagon.

When a trail herd reached the town at the end of the drive nearly all the members of the crew were free to go into town and spend the money they had earned on the trail. The cowboy usually got a haircut, a bath, and new clothes and when he had attended to those details he was ready for the nightlife offered by the cowtown. Liquor, women, and a card game were the chief interests of many of the cowhands but many others were sober, sensible men who stayed out of trouble. One Westerner, familiar with the trail crews, wrote:

> When these boys reached the terminus of their drives, this little
> settlement was a metropolis to them and they sought to enjoy
> themselves as best they could with such means as were available.
> One of the things to which they were exposed was cheap whiskey,
> which had been made for profit and not for consumption. They
> drank the same as any other class of men drank. Some took one
> drink and some took many. The ones who took too much told the
> world not only what they were but what they claimed to be. Few of
> these boys caused any trouble, but the ones who did had their
> iniquities charged up to all the rest.

The cattle themselves, the Longhorns, were unique. They had their beginnings in the cattle brought to North America by the early Spanish explorers. By the 1860s they had also acquired some blood from American stock imported into Texas. The Longhorn was long-tailed, and long-legged, and it came in a variety of colors. Its horns were tremendous. A railroad station agent at Abilene said that the horns were so long that it was sometimes hard to get the animals through the railroad car doors for shipment.

Abilene

The Abilene first seen by McCoy in 1867 was an unattractive little village. He described it as a "small, dead place consisting of about one dozen log huts," but soon it was doing thousands of dollars worth of business and was widely known. Its streets and businesses were packed with cowboys, cattle buyers, merchants, and undesirable characters. McCoy wrote: "No sooner had it become a conceded fact that Abilene as a cattle depot was a success, than tradespeople from all points came to the village, and, after putting up temporary houses, went into business. Of course, the saloon, the billiard table, the tenpin alley, the gambling table—in short, every possible device for obtaining money in both an honest and dishonest manner—were abundant."

The year 1867 was a poor one for the cattle market, even though McCoy shipped 35,000 head. Heavy rains caused coarse trail grass with little food value. Rivers were flooded, stampedes were frequent, and when the cattle reached Abilene they were thin and worn. The eastern corn crop was poor, and few farmers wished to buy feeders so the Texas stock went directly to the butchers. No profit was made on the first shipment and the second sold at $300 less than the freight charges.

In spite of his losses, McCoy made his plans for 1868. He sent men to Texas to talk to ranchers, and he advertised widely. The railroad publicized its rates and route. In the spring of 1868 a survey party went south to mark the trail from the Arkansas River to Abilene. The surveyors met the year's first herd of Longhorns and guided it to Abilene.

The season of 1868 saw 75,000 head of Longhorns driven north and the town's boom was really underway. A year later approximately 350,000 cattle came out of Texas and about half of them were shipped from Abilene. By 1870 the town had been incorporated as a third class city, had a mayor, and a board of trustees. Its night life in the "Texas section" south of the railroad tracks was so wild that the city was forced to hire a peace officer, Thomas J. "Bear River" Smith.

Smith had several years of experience as a lawman and he used his fists rather than a gun whenever possible. He did a good job for Abilene until he was shot and nearly beheaded by a half-crazy local settler. Smith was succeeded by James Butler "Wild Bill" Hickok, who was hired in April 1871. He kept the peace very well and spent a great deal of his time playing cards in the Alamo saloon. Hickok did have one unfortunate experience on the job when he shot a special policeman by mistake. With

James B. "Wild Bill" Hickok, peace officer and buffalo hunter.

the coming of winter and a lack of business Abilene dismissed Hickok in December 1871, saying it no longer needed his services.

Abilene's monopoly of the cattle business was broken in 1870 when the Missouri River, Fort Scott and Gulf Railroad built into Baxter Springs and that town became a shipping point for cattle using the Shawnee Trail. The season of 1871 was the last big one for Abilene. More settlers had come into the area and there was a great deal of opposition to the trail drivers. The Texans were forced to take their herds to other towns, principally Newton and Ellsworth, both of which became important trail points in 1871.

What kept Abilene in the middle of the cattle business in 1871 was the tremendous volume of Longhorns coming out of Texas. Even with Newton, Solomon, Brookville, Salina, and Ellsworth sharing in the trade Abilene had all it could handle because an estimated 600,000 head came north that year. Not all of those were shipped from Kansas. Many of them were trailed on north to Nebraska and to the states and territories farther to the northwest to be used as rangestock.

Newton and Ellsworth

Newton, on the Santa Fe Railroad, had only one big season, 1871, but in that short time it was probably the toughest town in the West. Its gambling houses and saloons ran wide open and gunfights were frequent. One shooting affair, called Newton's "general massacre," ended with several men either dead or wounded. The incident threatened to start a street war between Texans and townspeople but fortunately further trouble was avoided.

By 1872 many Abilene businesses had followed the cattle and the Kansas (Union) Pacific Railroad west to Ellsworth, which shipped 40,000 head that year. From 1873 to 1875 it was known as the "liveliest town on the Plains." Ellsworth had a population of about 1,000 and a genuine stone sidewalk in front of its Grand Central Hotel. It also had a race track and most of the same opportunities for wine, women, and song offered by the previous markets. The Ellsworth *Reporter*, July 25, 1872, described the town:

> This little border town . . . is not the most moral one in the world.
> During the cattle season . . . it presents a scene seldom witnessed in
> any other section. It reminds one of a town in California in the
> early days when gambling flourished and vice was at a premium.
> Here you see in the streets men from every state and from almost
> every nation—the tall, long-haired Texas herder, with his heavy

jingling spurs and pair of six-shooters; the gambler from all parts of the country, looking for unsuspecting prey; the honest emigrant in search of a homestead in the great free West; the keen stock buyers; the wealthy Texas drovers; deadbeats; pickpockets; [and] horse thieves.

The year 1873 was even bigger than 1872. Only 350,000 head came north in 1872 because of the severe winter of 1871; many drovers had planned to hold their herds in Kansas through the winter months but blizzards and cold killed thousands of cattle. But prices were high and a good corn crop farther north meant that there was a demand for feeder cattle. The money made in 1872 encouraged drovers in 1873 and 450,000 head were on the trail to Kansas that spring.

Ellsworth was not the only shipping point. In June 1871, the Leavenworth, Lawrence and Galveston Railroad was finished to the southern border of Kansas and advertised the advantages of shipping over its line from Coffeyville. In 1873 it was estimated that between 50,000 and 80,000 head were diverted in the Indian Territory and trailed to Coffeyville.

WICHITA

The principal competition for Ellsworth, beginning in 1872, was Wichita, which was reached by the Wichita and Southwestern Railroad that year. The city council hired a representative to go to Texas and tell ranchers about the city's advantages, and local businessmen sent Joseph McCoy (by then a Wichita resident) north and east to persuade buyers to come. In June the first shipment of eighteen carloads left Wichita and by the end of the 1872 season nearly 80,000 head had gone out over the new railroad that became a part of the Santa Fe system.

Wichita, founded in 1868, was growing. It had nearly 2,000 residents, sidewalks on both its main streets, a small schoolhouse, and plans for churches. It followed the same pattern as the other cowtowns. Posted outside the town was a sign that read: "Everything goes in Wichita. Leave your revolvers at police headquarters. . . . Carrying concealed weapons strictly forbidden." Wichita's tough district, known as Delano, included among its residents such characters as "Rowdy Joe" Lowe and his wife Kate, E. T. "Red" Beard, and for a while, Wyatt Earp, a member of the local police force. Gunshots and violence were a part of the Wichita scene and at times local vigilantes had to help enforce the law.

Both Ellsworth and Wichita were determined to outdo each other in 1873. The Kansas Pacific Railroad surveyed a new route for cattle from the Indian Territory leading west of Wichita directly to Ellsworth and shortening the distance from the Red River. It branched off from the Chisholm

Trail in the Indian Territory and ran north by way of Kingman and Ellinwood.

An estimated 150,000 cattle were trailed to Ellsworth in 1873 but only about 30,000 were shipped from there while Wichita loaded 65,000 head. Smaller amounts were shipped from other Kansas Pacific towns and the Santa Fe also loaded cattle at Great Bend and Hutchinson. It was a good year for the owners who had sold their herds during the summer but a bad one for those who still had cattle in late September.

By the first of October a financial panic and depression hit the West. Every business suffered, the cattle trade especially. There were large numbers of cattle awaiting the opening of the packing season and the fall market and most of their owners were in debt to banks. The banks were short of money so they could not extend loans. The owners of herds had only one choice—put the cattle on the market and hope to pay off the mortgages. Thousands of head were sold at a penny a pound to be "tanked—hide, horns, and hooves taken off, and the rest of the carcass rendered. Nearly half the cattle that came to Kansas were put on range in western Kansas or driven on into Colorado.

Joseph McCoy estimated that the panic cost the Texans fully two million dollars and he wrote:

> To a man whose sympathies ran with the cattlemen, it was like attending a funeral of friends daily, to stand upon any of the cattle marts and witness the financial slaughter of drovers and shippers. . . . Many cattle that were forwarded east did not sell for scarce more than freight and charges. A single firm lost one hundred and eighty thousand dollars in three weeks' shipments.

As the 1874 season opened the market was still suffering. Buyers were inactive, the Kansas City market was dead, and prices were so low in Chicago that cattlemen could not break even by driving herds from Texas. Some ranchers by that time were shipping to the packing plants directly from a few places in Texas because the Missouri, Kansas and Texas Railroad had been completed to Denison, Texas, by 1873.

Wichita gained the biggest share of the shipping business in 1874, with the drive less than half that of the disastrous 1873. Wichita's dominance continued in 1875 but that year marked a change in several aspects of the cattle trade. Ellsworth was nearly finished as a shipping point because there were so many settlers in central Kansas. The Santa Fe was shipping more cattle than any other company, and railroads in eastern Kansas had taken over much of the business that once went to the Kansas

Pacific. The Longhorns themselves had been upgraded with the introduction of better breeding animals. Texas cattle were not as long and lean as they had been when the long drive began.

DODGE CITY

Probably the biggest change was the opening of Dodge City as a cattle town in 1875. For the next ten years the town would truly be the "cowboy capital" of the world. Established in 1872, just before the Santa Fe Railroad arrived, Dodge City had done a booming business in buffalo bones and hides and was the civilian community for Fort Dodge. The cattle trade increased its property and its violence. Its status as a cattle market was also helped by an act of the 1876 legislature, which moved the quarantine line west and cut Wichita out of the trade.

As a result of the shift to Dodge City the trails changed. In 1876 many of the herds left the Chisholm Trail at Belton, Texas, and went northwest by way of Fort Griffin. They crossed the Red River at Doan's Ford and went through the Indian Territory to Dodge. Some cowmen took their herds farther north on the Chisholm and then cut over to Dodge City. But

The Dodge City "Peace Commission," 1883. Standing, left: W. H. Harris, Luke Short, W. B. "Bat" Masterson, W. F. Petillon. Seated: Charles E. Bassett, Wyatt Earp, M. F. McClain, Neil Brown.

most of them used the new route, commonly called the Western Trail, which ran on north to Ogallala, Nebraska.

Thousands of cattle were shipped from Dodge City between 1876 and 1885 with the peak years being 1883 and 1884. Thousands more were driven through Dodge to stock the northern ranges or for shipment from other points. Dodge City was a busy town. Its hotels, saloons, and stores were filled with customers. So was its "boot hill" cemetery, in use during the town's early years. The number of people who died from gunshot wounds in Dodge City is unknown but estimates range as high as twenty-five for the first year of the cattle trade.

No town in the West can claim such a list of gunmen and peace officers as Dodge City. Wyatt Earp, the Masterson brothers, Doc Holliday, Bill Tilghman, Luke Short, and many others played a part in its rowdy history. Some of those men lived on both sides of the law and made their livings by gambling, buffalo hunting, and questionable businesses during the times they were not employed on a cowtown police force. For example, William B. "Bat" Masterson figured in this Dodge City *Times* report, June 9, 1877:

> Bobby Gill done it again. Last Wednesday was a lively day for Dodge. Two hundred cattle men in the city; the gang in good shape for business; merchants happy, and money flooding the city, is a condition of affairs that could not continue in Dodge very long without an eruption, and that is the way it was last Wednesday. Robert Gilmore was making a talk for himself in a rather emphatic manner, to which Marshal [Larry] Deger took exception and started for the dog house with him. Bobby walked very leisurely—so much so that Larry felt it necessary to administer a few paternal kicks in the rear. This act was soon interrupted by Bat Masterson, who wound his arm affectionately around the Marshal's neck and let the prisoner escape. Deger then grappled with Bat, at the same time calling upon the bystanders to take the offender's gun and assist in the arrest. Joe Mason appeared upon the scene at this critical moment and took the gun. But Masterson would not surrender yet and came near getting hold of a pistol from among several which were strewed around over the sidewalk but half a dozen Texas men came to the marshal's aid and gave him a chance to draw his gun and beat Bat over the head until the blood flew. . . . But Masterson seemed possessed of extraordinary strength, and every inch of the way was closely contested, but the city dungeon was reached at last, and in he went. If he had got hold of his gun before going in there would have been a general killing.

Loading Texas longhorns, just off the Chisholm Trail, at Abilene.

Four months later Bat Masterson was on the Dodge City police force. Ed Masterson, Bat's brother, was always on the side of the law and died as a result of a gunfight in 1878.

The theater, mostly of the variety show type, was popular in Dodge City. One stage favorite was Dora Hand, a young actress, who was the central figure in one of the town's tragedies. One night in October 1878, she was shot accidentally by a Texan who fired through a wall of a building where he thought James H. "Dog" Kelly, first mayor of Dodge, was sleeping. Kelly was not there and the bullet intended for him killed Dora instantly. A posse led by Wyatt Earp and Bat Masterson caught the killer but he was acquitted because evidence was insufficient for conviction. Dora's funeral was the biggest one Dodge City had ever seen. While she was a part of the seamy side of Dodge she was well liked and the tough frontier town paid its respects to her.

In the spring of 1881 Dodge City had a street fight in which the principal participants were Jim and Bat Masterson on one side, with two saloon characters in opposition. A great many shots were fired but only one man was wounded by Bat, who was fined $8.00 and court costs. The Dodge City "Peace Commission" came into being in 1883 as a result of an argument that involved, among other things, the Long Branch saloon and the girls who worked there. Finally, the situation got so far out of hand that the governor's office was involved and there was a serious question about whether or not peace could be kept in Dodge City. A commission, made up of several famous gunmen, was formed to assist in law enforcement, and Dodge City returned to normal.

Business was dull in Dodge City in 1884, so to help revitalize the town's prestige, a bull fight was planned for July 4. A dozen ferocious looking Longhorn bulls were gathered and genuine bull fighters were brought in from Mexico. Spectators arrived from all over the state, the grandstand was filled, Dodge City's cowboy band played enthusiastically, and some of the bulls performed as planned. This exhibition was the first and, perhaps with one exception, the only real bull fight ever staged in the United States.

Even though the celebration boosted Dodge temporarily the town was on the downhill grade as a roaring cowtown. The Santa Fe Railroad could see that the Texas cattle business in Kansas was dying and looked for other kinds of freight. The Western Trail was practically closed to traffic in 1885. Most of the gamblers, gunmen, and "sporting women" moved on to greener pastures in the West and Dodge City changed from the most sinful city on the Plains to a solid business and farming community.

The Chisholm Trail, which seemed to have reached the end of its life in 1880, enjoyed a revival for a few years when Caldwell became a prominent cowtown. The "Border Queen," as Caldwell was known, was so near the southern boundary of the state that the restrictive laws had little effect, and in two years—1882 and 1883—nearly 100,000 cattle were shipped from Caldwell on the Santa Fe. One Caldwell editor wrote, "Dodge City has lost the cattle trade."

Caldwell claimed to have the largest and best opera house west of Kansas City but its other features were similar to all cowtowns. Business was good and there was plenty of riotous living, along with some shooting. The town had a marshal named Henry Brown who closed his career by trying to rob a bank at Medicine Lodge while on vacation from his police duties. Marshal Brown's activities were viewed dimly by Medicine Lodge residents who shot and killed him.

Caldwell served as headquarters for the Cherokee Strip Live Stock Association, an organization of cattle growers who leased land south of the Kansas line from the Cherokee Indians until 1890, when the federal government stated that the leases were illegal. For a brief period Hunnewell and Kiowa shared a little of Caldwell's glory, and part of its wildness.

THE END OF THE CATTLE DRIVES

Kansas quarantine laws in 1884 and 1885 put an end to overland driving through the state. The 1885 act prohibited the entrance of cattle from Texas and the Indian Territory between March 1 and December 1, which meant that the drives were finished. Cattle could not be driven during the short winter period remaining. A plan for a national cattle trail from Texas to the Canadian border was discussed in Congress but it did not pass and the Kansas cowtowns were finished. The "long drive" was eliminated by other factors, including the steadily marching line of homesteads and farms into western Kansas. Farmers did not like Texas herds and barbed wire eventually proved to be an effective barrier against the cattlemen. Too, by the mid-1880s, Texans had several railroad points available in their own state that made the drive unnecessary.

The death of the drives did not mean that the cattle business ended in Kansas. The state's rich pastures still served as feeding grounds for stock raised locally or brought in by rail. Even before the end of the trails cattlemen formed associations or "pools," which gave them better protection against rustlers and provided for cooperative roundups and registration of brands. Among the Kansas pools were the Smoky Hill in Lane County, the Forrester in Gove County, the Barber County Stock Growers Association, the Turkey Creek pool near Caldwell, the Western Kansas Stock Growers Association with headquarters in Dodge City, and the Comanche County pool, perhaps the largest of all the Kansas organizations.

The Comanche pool covered parts of Barber County and the Cherokee Strip in the Indian Territory plus most of Comanche County. Its offices were in Medicine Lodge and its operating headquarters at Evansville, a settlement in Comanche County that no longer exists. Like other pools it had a board of directors and officers. It owned horses, wagons, and equipment but the cattle were the private property of the individual members of the pool. The Comanche pool lowered the cost of beef production, experimented with cross breeding, and made money for its members. However, neither it nor the other pools could exist after the country was filled with settlers who fenced their 160-acre farms.

For a time Kansas had large ranches that attracted both people and money from the East and the British Isles. A good example was the ranch of several thousand acres in Hodgeman County, established by Henry S. Mudge of Boston. Outside capital was also invested in ranches in Chase County and other Flint Hills areas.

The ranching boom reached its height in the 1880s but then came crashing down. The winter of 1886–1887 was a cruel one and cattle died by the thousands. Ranchers were ruined, a period of low prices set in, and the widespread enthusiasm for ranching and speculation in cattle cooled off. Hard times continued into the 1890s but toward the end of that decade prices rose and profits increased. But the days of extremely large-scale production and profit were gone. For the most part, cattle raising went back into the hands of individual farmers and stockmen.

The state has continued to be a leader in cattle raising since the open range disappeared. The Flint Hills have always supported cattle, and in recent years Kansas feedlots have provided beef for tables all over the world.

Even the peak years of the trail driving period did not bring the numbers of cattle that have been raised in Kansas annually since the end of the Second World War.

The trails, the towns, the herds, and the men who drove them contributed greatly to the cattle industry of the entire nation and all have lived in American literature and history. The cowboy became a genuine folk hero who is still a television and movie favorite. He is joined in fiction by the gunfighter, who has always been more mythical than real but who is important in western literature. The packing industries of Kansas City, Chicago, and a dozen other cities were built by the driving of cattle to northern markets and, as a result, beef became the staple meat item in American diets—something that was not true before the Civil War.

As Everett Dick, noted historian of the West, wrote several years ago:

> The long trail was not a mere cow trail; it was a step in the course of empire. It played a part in that unfolding process which developed the great Plains and made of the Mississippi Valley the bread basket of the world. The long drive became majestic, not only because of its physical proportions, but also on account of its social and political effect.

The cowboy was a pioneer in every sense of the word. What the backwoodsman was to the timbered country of the East, what the forty-niner was to California, the cowboy was to the prairies.

Suggestions for Reading

Edward E. Dale, *The Range Cattle Industry* (1930); David A. Dary, *Cowboy Culture* (1981); Robert K. DeArment, *Bat Masterson* (1979); Everett Dick, *Vanguards of the Frontier* (1941); J. Frank Dobie, *The Longhorns* (1941); Philip Durham and Everett Jones, *The Negro Cowboys* (1965); Robert R. Dykstra, *The Cattle Towns* (1968); Joe B. Frantz and Julian E. Choate, Jr., *The American Cowboy, the Myth and the Reality* (1955); Wayne Gard, *The Chisholm Trail* (1954); C. Robert Haywood, *Victorian West: Class and Culture in Kansas Cattle Towns* (1991); C. Robert Haywood, *The Merchant Prince of Dodge City: The Life and Times of Robert M. Wright* (1998); Jim Hoy, *Cowboys and Kansas: Stories from the Tallgrass Prairie* (1995); Joseph G. McCoy, *Historic Sketches of the Cattle Trade of the West and Southwest*, ed. by Ralph P. Bieber (1940); Nyle H. Miller and Joseph W. Snell, *Why the West Was Wild* (1963); Donald R. Ornduff, *Casement of Juniata* (1975); Joseph G. Rosa, *Wild Bill Hickok: The Man and his Myth* (1996); The editors of Time-Life Books, *The Cowboys* (1973); Charles L. Wood, *The Kansas Beef Industry* (1980); John F. Wukovits, *The Black Cowboys* (1997); Frederic R. Young, *Dodge City: Up Through a Century in Story and Pictures* (1972). Also of interest are: C. Robert Haywood, "Comanche County Cowboy: A Case Study of a Kansas Rancher" *Kansas History* (Autumn, 1981); and David L. Wheeler, "Winter on the Cattle Range: Western Kansas, 1884–1886," *Kansas History* (Spring, 1992).

9

The Frontier is Settled

Conditions in eastern Kansas were not much different from those in the settlers' native states, but the open prairie farther west presented a variety of new difficulties. Wood was scarce, water had to be taken from deep wells because stream flow was uncertain, and farming operations had to be adapted to the tough buffalo grass sod. From this new area of farmland and infant settlements came innovations that were unique to the Great Plains—windmills, barbed wire, and buildings constructed of sod. The so-called "sod house frontier" finally stretched from the Canadian border to the Texas Panhandle and into eastern Colorado and Wyoming. The heart of it was western Kansas and Nebraska.

The passage of the Homestead Act by the federal government in 1862 gave a great push to western settlement. It provided 160 acres to any person who was the head of a family or was 21 years old, who was a citizen or had declared the intent to become one. One had only to pay a $10 filing fee, live on the land for five years and cultivate and improve it. At last, except for the $10, American settlers could get the free farmland they had been asking for since the Revolutionary War. The Homestead Act was supplemented and followed by the Timber Culture Act of 1873, which offered 160 acres to anyone who would plant 40 acres in trees and maintain them for 10 years. Although only a small percentage of Kansans took advantage of the second act it did make some impression on the settlement of the western part of the state.

At the time the homestead bill was being considered in the United States Congress, a speech encouraging its passage was made by Samuel C. Pomeroy, senator from Kansas. It was, of course, a time when the country was torn by Civil War and there were those members of Congress who had pointed out that it might be an unfavorable time to dispose of public lands, although money was needed to support the armies of the Union. According to Senator Pomeroy, the money was really not important but the settlement of the land was. The development of the West was vital to the progress of the nation. His speech, a part of which follows, is an excellent example of nineteenth-century congressional oratory and represents the feelings of most Westerners serving in Congress in the 1860s:

> This, then . . . is the question I propose to discuss, involved in the passage of this homestead bill, namely, that the speedy settlement of the country by actual occupants of the land, though they be "small-fisted farmers," taking a homestead without expense or benefit to the Government, will produce more revenue to the country, and vastly more increase its wealth and productiveness, than any present or prospective sale, even though $1.25 be realized for every acre. For my own part, I believe it should not be the policy of the Government to derive a revenue from the sale of the land, any more than from the sale of the air or the sunshine. These natural elements and auxiliaries of human life are God's great gifts to man, and the Government may as well bottle up the one as deed away the other. . . .
>
> I am, sir, for opening these lands for the landless of every nation under heaven. I care not whether he comes to us from the populous cities of our older states, or from the enlightened though oppressed nations of Europe. . . . To me he is an American, if he has an American heart in his bosom; if he be inspired with American impulses and American hopes, and yields himself joyfully to the moulding influence of American civilization.
>
> Now, then, I ask, how can the public lands be used so as to best increase the wealth of the country, and so be the better able to consume the imports of the country . . . as well also, as to meet the taxes imposed by the Government? And here let it be observed that the wealth of a nation does not consist in the money paid into its treasury, exacted, as it often is, from half-paid toiling millions, nor in an endless unoccupied public domain, running to waste with wild men and wild buffaloes. But wealth consists in flocks and herds, cultivated fields, in well paid labor, and well directed energy. . . .
>
> This bill, enacted into a law, shall give civilization and life throughout the silent gorges and gentle sleeping valleys, far away into the deep recesses of the continent. Where it leads the way

there shall go in triumph the American standard, the old flag of the Union. And when once thus planted, it shall never again be trailed in the dust. The proudest bird of the mountain is upon the American ensign, and not one feather shall fall from plumage here. She is American in design and an emblem of wilderness and freedom. . . . Our great western valleys were never scooped out for her burial place. Nor were the everlasting, untrodden mountains piled for her monument. Niagara shall not pour her endless waters for her requiem; nor shall our ten thousand rivers weep to the ocean in eternal tears. No, sir, no. Unnumbered voices shall come up from river, plain and mountain, echoing the songs of our triumphant deliverance, while lights from a thousand hill tops will betoken the rising of the sun of freedom, that shall grow brighter and brighter until a more perfect day….

The bill became law and a great many Americans took advantage of it although most of them had to wait until after the Civil War. Not everyone who moved to Kansas in those years following 1865 filed on a government homestead, however. Many still took land under the earlier Preemption Act while others bought land from those railroads that had been given federal land subsidies—the Santa Fe, the Katy, and the Kansas Pacific. One of the reasons the railroads had been granted the land was to assure them a source of income once they had completed their lines through Kansas. By selling the land they did not need they could regain a part of the money they had used in constructing their lines. The railroads wanted to make profits so they did not sell the land at prices that could be considered "give aways" but good farmland at a reasonable price was certainly a bargain. Railroad land prices ordinarily started at two dollars an acre and sometimes went as high as ten dollars.

THE HARDSHIPS OF PIONEERING

The land where pioneers experienced the most difficulty lay west of where U.S. Highway 81 runs today (roughly, the western two-thirds of the state). In the first half of the 1870s there was trouble again with the Plains Indians who resented the increasing settlement. The Indians saw their land usurped by snorting locomotives and people they considered alien; they saw the buffalo herds, which had provided their entire existence, threatened with extinction.

Settlers hunted the huge animals for their meat and robes, for both food and profit. Professional hunters killed the buffalo to supply eastern markets with the valuable hides, and many people shot the buffalo for sport only, utilizing neither the meat nor hide. Great hunting parties, such

Thrill-seeking tourists shooting buffalo from a Kansas (Union) Pacific train, 1871.

as the one organized to entertain the visiting Grand Duke Alexis of Russia in 1872, served only to quicken the animals' extermination and, consequently, to further anger the Indians. As the buffalo were killed, the nomadic tribes became increasingly hostile, and they sought revenge by raiding white farms and settlements.

The year 1874 was the worst year for hostilities in Kansas after 1870. Groups from the powerful Plains tribes, such as the Cheyennes, raided along the Smoky Hill and Saline rivers and, at times, made life miserable for settlers. Troops from the Kansas military posts spent weeks in the field campaigning against a native foe that usually disappeared as quickly as it had come. Some settlers were killed, along with a few soldiers, some white people were captured, and some property was destroyed and stolen by the raiders. But always the railroads kept expanding, settlement kept developing, and the buffalo continued to die. The army's concentrated campaign against the Indians that followed the defeat of George Custer's Seventh Cavalry regiment on the Little Big Horn in 1876 spelled virtual defeat for the Indians. The military, and a great many settlers, believed that the disappearance of buffalo would mean the disappearance of Indians, and that is one reason why the slaughter of the animals continued unchecked. Finally the tribes were forced to agree to the wishes of the federal government and they took their places on reservations and conformed, more or less, to the patterns outlined by their conquerors.

In Kansas the Indians native to this part of the Great Plains disappeared in the 1870s. The Osages and the Kansas no longer ranged through central Kansas but were placed on lands in present Oklahoma. The true nomads—the Cheyennes and Arapahos, Comanches and Kiowas—who used the buffalo as their complete department store and who had been described as the world's finest light cavalry, found that they could not cope with the encroachment, civilian or military, and were also forced to accept the confinement of boundaries set up by the government. Except for one last (and futile) incident, free Indians were finished in Kansas. The only representatives of the once powerful Native Americans who would remain in the state were remnants of the Potawatomi, Kickapoo, and Iowa, Sac and Fox tribes, all of whom had come to Kansas as eastern emigrants following 1830.

The one remaining contact Kansans had with "wild" Indians came in 1878 when a small band of Northern Cheyennes, fleeing from their Indian Territory reservation, attempted to make their way home along a route that lay through western Kansas. Led by chiefs Dull Knife and Little Wolf, the band of starving Indians frightened innumerable Kansans although they were more concerned with survival than warfare. Pursued by troops from Fort Dodge, the Indians made a stand at "Battle Canyon," north of Scott City, and killed Colonel William Lewis when he led his men into a situation from which there was no easy retreat. Only in Decatur County, near Oberlin, did the Cheyennes murder white settlers. The fate of the Cheyennes was sealed, however, for they did not find the freedom they sought when they reached their homeland north of the Kansas border and once again they became captives.

Most Kansas settlers in the 1870s faced three other hazards—drought, depression, and grasshoppers. Drought and depression would continue to be problems in the 1880s and the 1890s. A shortage of rainfall was understandable to most people because it was something they had experienced in other areas. However, dry periods in which crops did not grow brought great financial hardship to both farmers and merchants. Although times of depression did not necessarily come directly from periods of drought, local weather conditions could contribute to economic difficulties. A Kansas farmer who was having money troubles had little chance of recovering if he could not produce a crop.

There were recurring cycles of "boom and bust" in Kansas and over the whole American West. There was a national depression in 1873 that affected Kansas, but by 1875 good times had come again. The same kind of alternating situations continued through the 1880s, with a depression in 1887 following extremely good

William F. "Buffalo Bill" Cody, professional buffalo hunter and army scout. Courtesy of Leavenworth Public Library.

times in 1885 and 1886, and in the 1890s, with the hardest financial blow falling in 1893. Railroads and other growing businesses overexpanded from time to time while the weather hit other extremes—such as the blizzards of the mid-1880s, which killed both livestock and people. Despite the settlers' variety of troubles they were generally optimistic during periods of prosperity, and they would buy more than they could afford or borrow money for purposes of expansion, only to find that a new economic low left them in difficulties from which there was no escape.

Regulation of banks was not common in the late nineteenth century despite the fact that some people realized earlier American depressions had been brought on partly by poor banking practices. Banks often lent money without getting proper security for the loan, or they charged such high rates of interest that the borrowers, hoping for continuing good times, found that they could pay neither the principal nor the interest in hard times. In the late 1880s and the early 1890s more than 11,000 mortgage foreclosures were reported in Kansas, most of them on livestock and personal property rather than on land. Yet, it was generally the land that had to go if the other loans could not be paid, and so a great many lending companies became so heavily loaded with real estate that they, too, failed.

Still, most Kansans could understand their economic regressions, but they were not prepared for the grasshopper invasion of 1874. Grasshoppers were not unknown on the Plains during the years of settlement before 1874 and, in fact, there had been occasions when grasshoppers had been more than a mere nuisance to Kansas farmers. None of those earlier experiences was impressive enough to prepare people for 1874 and nobody was ready to battle this strange occurrence—this "plague of locusts" that descended in mid-summer on the land from the Dakotas to Texas.

The grasshoppers appeared suddenly in late July and August in such great numbers that at times they blotted out the sun. They came on the wind and under their own power and their approach was described as sounding like a rainstorm. In some places they were said to cover the earth to a depth of four to six inches and they attacked corn fields, gardens, and pasture grass. People watched in amazement and consternation as food and grain disappeared almost instantly. Cattle and horses were tormented by the hoppers, which crawled over them and into their eyes, ears, and nostrils. Clothing was eaten off people's backs and the soft wood of tool handles was devoured.

Damage caused by the insects was great all over Kansas but the eastern portions of the state did not suffer as much as the western counties. The plague was worst in areas where a majority of the settlers were recent arrivals. Almost all were poor when they came west and they had not had time to build up the financial resources necessary to combat such a disaster.

One of the best descriptions of the invasion was given by a Jefferson County resident, and the feeling of helpless horror that pressed down upon those settlers is clearly expressed by these paragraphs:

> We were at the table; the usual midday meal was being served; one of the youngsters who had gone to the well to fill the water pitcher came hurrying in, round-eyed with excitement. "They're here! The sky is full of'm. The whole yard is crawling with the nasty things." Food halfway to the mouth fell back upon the plate. Without speaking the whole family passed outside. Sharp spats in the face, insects alighted on the shoulders, in the hair, scratchy rustlings on the roofs, disgusted brushing of men's beards, the frightened whimper of a child, "Are they going to eat us up?" Turkeys gobbling the living manna as fast as their snaky heads could dart from side to side; overhead, the sun, dimmed like the beginning of an eclipse, glinted on silvery wings as far as eyes could pierce; leaves of shade trees, blades of grass and weedstems bending with the weight of clinging inch-long horrors; a faint, sickening stench of their excrement; the afternoon breeze clogged with the drift of the descending creatures.
>
> Not much was said, children huddling against their mother, whose hand touched lightly the father's arm. . . . The garden truck had disappeared, even the dry onions were gone, leaving smooth molds in the ground empty as uncorked bottles. Fruit hung on the leafless branches, the upper surface gnawed to the core. The woods looked thin as in late autumn. Someone called attention to the pitted earth here and there. . . .
>
> Water troughs and loosely covered wells were foul with drowned hoppers. Neighbors passing spoke of strange happenings. A young wife awaiting her first baby, in the absence of her husband . . . had gone insane from fright, "all alone in that sun-baked shanty on the bald prairie.". . .

The victims did not sit back and wait to be eaten, but generally their efforts to fight the insects were in vain. Kerosene was used as an insecticide and sticks and boards were used to beat the grasshoppers. The hoppers were raked into piles, like leaves, kerosene poured over them, and the piles lighted. This eliminated great numbers of hoppers, but there were simply too many.

To combat the destitution in western Kansas, after the grasshoppers finally went away, Governor Thomas Osborn called a special session of the legislature. An act was passed that authorized counties to issue bonds for local relief, but aid was not sufficient to ease the situation completely. As a result, the governor called on all Americans to help. Thousands of people responded and sent money, along with supplies, which were hauled by the railroads at no charge. A state Central Relief Committee spent several thousand dollars on seed corn and wheat, which were distributed to Kansas farmers.

Governor Osborn reported in 1875: "As our prosperity had been unparalleled so likewise was the disaster in waiting for us. . . . The brave hearts and strong arms of our people will, however, in time, overcome the severity of the disaster and in so far as it affects the state generally, to that remedy we can safely entrust it." The grasshoppers came again in 1875 but in lesser numbers, and they were not nearly so destructive.

Westerners always seemed to have the ability to make fun of difficult situations and Kansans were no exception. Tall tales about the grasshoppers were told many times. There were stories circulated that grasshoppers had eaten hooves off horses and cattle and that pigs had lost their noses. The whole experience had been so fantastic, however, that sometimes it was difficult to separate fact from fiction. For example, it is true that locomotives could not get traction on rails made slippery by the great numbers of insects but this kind of tall story was most common:

> A few weeks ago a woman dug up a panful of dirt in which to plant some flower seed. She put the pan under the stove, and went out to see a neighbor. Upon her return . . . she found 7,000 bushels of grasshoppers generated by the heat, literally eating her out of house and home. They first attacked the green shades on the windows, and then a green painted dust pan. A green Irish servant girl, asleep in one of the rooms, was the next victim, and not a vestige of her was left. The stove and stovepipe followed, and then the house was torn down so they could get at the chimney. Boards, joists, beams, plastering, clothing, nails, hinges, door knobs, plates, tinware, everything, in fact, the house contained was eaten up, and when she arrived within a mile of the place, she saw two of the largest hoppers sitting up on end, and playing mumbly-peg with the carving knife, to see which should have the cellar.

There were other stories—they went on and on—just as there were stories about blizzards and floods and bumper crops. They were a part of the settling process, and they made people forget some of the things they had endured. The same kind of folklore manifested itself in the grim years of the 1930s when much of the same area of the Plains again experienced drought and grasshoppers.

ADAPTATION AND INNOVATION
IN WESTERN KANSAS

As has already been noted, this was a time of great adjustment. All the difficulties and shortages that were met by the settler called for changing attitudes and adaptations that particularly fitted the kind of living that these people experienced on the Great Plains. It was a lonely time and a time of separation from friends and from members of one's own family.

On the treeless plains hundreds of families built dugouts and sod houses. They broke the ground by turning the sod over with a "breaking plow" which, instead of a solid steel moldboard, had three curved rods that turned the sod grass side down. For building, pieces of sod were generally about three inches thick, a foot wide, and two to three feet long. The pioneer laid the sod so that the joints and layers tied into each other. Doors and windows were provided for wherever possible and the roof was usually a combination of wood and paper (or tar paper) covered by a layer of sod, grass side up. While these buildings do not sound very attractive they were warm in winter, cool in summer and surprisingly waterproof. Often the occupants whitewashed the interiors or papered them, sometimes using newspapers for wall paper. Flooring ranged from bare dirt to boards to rag carpeting, made by the women in the family. Sometimes combinations of sod, wood, and stone were used in building, particularly if the settler decided to make his home on a hillside where the earth would provide a part of the structure.

Southwestern Kansas homesteaders pose before a familiar backdrop of sodhouse and windmill.

The following letter, written from Morton County in far southwestern Kansas in the 1880s, illustrates very well what a great many Kansas pioneers experienced:

> I am writing in my far western home, the one I love best. Let me describe it to you. It is what we call in Morton county a dugout. Ours is dug four feet down, and has a frame part about five feet high on top of the ground. It is 12 X 20 inside, with a white-washed ceiling and a canvas partition. . . .
>
> It is hard work to come west to make a home. . . . I'll tell you how we manage: there are four of us. My husband and two little boys…and myself comprise our family. This year everything was a failure in this country. Everybody left that could, but we have a few cattle and enough corn stalks to keep them alive till grass comes….Some mornings there would be fourteen wagons going east, but they are not all gone, for we are here yet. Last spring everything was fine; good prospects for plenty in the fall; but the hot winds came and the rain did not. Out of the eighty acres of spring crops we planted we got nothing but corn stalks, not an ear of corn or a kernel for the seed. We may be thankful for the stalks, as some did not even get stalks. We are 47 miles from the railroad and the only way to get a living is to freight. It takes four days to go to the railroad and back with a load. My man has gone for a load now. While he is gone I take care of thirteen head of cattle, two pigs, one colt, and milk four cows, do my house work, make lace and crazy patch. This morning I sawed a new stove-pipe hole through the roof and put up a tin to run the pipe out through. The boys are at school. I sleep with a double-barrelled shot-gun loaded in the closet and a revolver handy. My nearest neighbor is one mile northeast. . . . It is hard work, hard work, I tell you, and little pay. We have already had a bitter touch of winter. It began by raining. . . . Then the snow came and the wind with it, and for four days and nights kept snowing and blowing. . . . Through it all stock had to be looked after and run under shelter. When they get out in a storm they drift with the wind, and get lost, often killed. Times are hard but I am generous and when you come out west just stay awhile at our dug-out.
>
> You shall have pancakes and meat grease for breakfast—maybe a little coffee. Light bread for dinner, and mush and milk for supper the year round, with occasionally a young jack-rabbit fried with some milk-gravy. . . .

The people made do with what they had so far as food was concerned, often existing on even less than what the housewife described in her letter.

When crops failed they improvised, and while they may not have liked what they ate, they did survive.

They also made do concerning their medical care. Doctors were scarce and those who were in western Kansas were often far from their patients. Many pioneer women died in childbirth and many children did not live past their very first years. Measles, diphtheria, influenza, smallpox, and severe cases of dysentery were often fatal on the frontier since medicine and proper care were so difficult to come by. Settlers often used home remedies that had been handed down from parents and grandparents and some of them were effective. Although some forms of home medication sound strange today it is true that certain herbs and roots could ease physical disorders. Turpentine, kerosene, and whiskey were, at times, effective disinfectants and antiseptics, and cobwebs really did help to stop bleeding when applied to a wound. There were patent medicines available, some of which were effective in the treatment of both men and animals, but most of them did not cure all the things that their advertising claimed.

Kansans dug deep wells so that they might have a water supply on a homestead that did not boast a running stream, and they generally got the water to the surface by using a windmill. The windmill was, not very many years ago, a familiar sight on most Kansas farms, but now it is a disappearing piece of machinery. In the nineteenth and early twentieth century it harnessed what seemed to be an ever-present Kansas resource, the wind, and provided water for household use, livestock, and the irrigation of crops. Its value was tremendous to Great Plains settlement.

Along with the shortage of water came a shortage of fuel since there was little timber in the semiarid geographical area. Only small trees grew along the streams in western Kansas and consequently pioneer settlers had to find a substitute for wood as fuel. Some of them took stalks of grain or hay and made twisted bundles, which they used in their stoves. There was even a stove designed to burn hay. Others burned corn cobs. At times even this kind of fuel was insufficient and it was discovered that the dry manure of buffalo or cattle could be used to make a good clean fire. So "chips" came into common usage and a great number of stories were told about them.

As another evidence of the good humor that came from simple living this story stands out. It appeared on April 15, 1879, in the Pearlette *Call* of Meade County, written by the editor to inform old neighbors back in Ohio about the living conditions in the West:

> You know wood is scarce in Meade county, and coal expensive, hence you will doubtless wonder what we do for fuel.
>
> Those who can afford it buy coal in Dodge . . . while others, having teams, get some wood in the canyons east of us.

But most of us burn chips—buffalo chips we call them, but the majority of those we find were doubtless dropped by Texas cattle, when passing north.

These chips make a tolerable fair fire, but of course burn out very rapidly; consequently to keep up a good fire you must be continually poking the chips in and taking the ashes out. Still we feel very thankful for even this fuel.

It was comical to see how gingerly our wives handled these chips at first. They commenced by picking them up between two sticks, or with a poker. Soon they used a rag, and then a corner of their apron. Finally, growing hardened, a wash after handling them was sufficient. And now? Now it is out of the bread, into the chips and back again—and not even a dust of the hands!

The story is funny, but true, and thousands of Kansas meals were cooked over fires that got their heat from chips.

COMMUNITY AND AGRICULTURAL DEVELOPMENT

It may appear that everything in Kansas was related to some kind of hardship in the last decades of the nineteenth century. That is not true although it must have seemed so in certain areas at times. Kansans enjoyed an active social life, often centered around a church or a school in rural areas. At the same time that they were fighting Indians and grasshoppers they were organizing libraries and churches, holding literary meetings, building substantial public school buildings, and developing colleges. In

A pioneer housewife gathering buffalo chips for fuel near Lakin, 1893.

the larger communities of eastern Kansas they were attending plays and concerts and holding parties.

The farther one got from the towns along the Missouri and the Kaw rivers the less elegant the entertainment became. While a masquerade ball, accompanied by dinner, was a likely occurrence in a place like Topeka in the 1870s, dances farther west were more likely to receive this kind of notice:

> A group of splendid ones is on the floor and loving mated—the gents encircle their partners' waists with one arm. The ladies and gentlemen closely face to face. They are very erect and lean a little forward (Music.) Now all wheel and whirl, circle and curl. Feet and heels of gents go rip rap, rip rap, rip. Ladies' feet go tippity tip, tippity tip, tip. Then all go rippity, clippity, slippity, flippity, skippity, hoppity, jumpity, bumpity, thump. Ladies fly off by centrifugal momentum. Gents pull ladies hard and close. They reel, swing, slide, look tender, look silly, look dizzy. Feet fly, tresses fly, hoops fly, caresses fly, all fly. It looks tuggity, huggity, pullity, squeezity, pressity, rubbity, rip.
>
> The men look like a cross between . . . beetles and jointed X's. The maidens tuck down their chins very low, or raise them exceedingly high. Some smile, some giggle, some frown, some sneer, and all sweat freely. The ladies' faces are brought against those of the men or into their bosoms, breast against breast, nose against nose, toes against toes. Now they are again making a sound, like georgy-porgy, deery-peery, didy-pidy, coachey-poachey. "This dance is not much but the extras are glorious." If men were women, there would be no such thing as dancing. But they are only men, and so the thing goes on by women's love for it.

Obviously, not all dances in Kansas would have been described like this for the stately waltz existed at the same time as more boisterous music, but this description is a representative report on the kind of entertainment found in the rougher frontier environment. Settlers had picnics, parades, and speeches on the Fourth of July and Memorial Day and they had New Years' Eve parties and well-attended Christmas and Thanksgiving dinners. They had spelling bees and house warmings, and they socialized at weddings, funerals, and birthdays.

As the population grew new counties were created by the legislature and new towns came into being. From 61 counties in 1870 the number grew to 106 in 1888. In 1893, when Garfield County became a part of present Finney, the number was reduced to 105, which the state has today. County borders and names changed frequently, and governmental organization often came several years after boundaries were defined.

Kansas law stated that a county could be organized by proclamation of the governor when its population reached 600. The governor could also designate a temporary county seat and name temporary officials until such time as an election was held. The way was open for a variety of fraudulent schemes, especially in the counties of Barber, Comanche, Ness, and Harper. Promoters certified that 600 people were residing in these counties when it was not true. The attorney general's office conducted an investigation in Comanche county and reported that the county "has no inhabitants and never had." But a representative had been elected to the legislature and a bond issue of several thousand dollars voted. Similar things took place in the other counties mentioned, and the promoters put the bond money in their pockets, and the legal organizations that came later found themselves in debt from the moment they began to do business.

The ordinary Kansan, who spent most of his time trying to make a decent living for his family, was aware of politics on all levels, and at times he got deeply involved. The selection of a county seat was often difficult because factions within a county were generally promoting a specific community, and they realized that possession of the county courthouse could help insure the future of a town. County government would provide jobs and draw trade from those people who came to the county seat for the purpose of transacting their legal business.

In most cases locating the county seat was done peacefully. In several counties, however, spirited contests took place, some of which led to shooting and bloodshed. In Stevens County, where Hugoton and Woodsdale competed for the seat of government, six men were killed, and the militia was sent in to restore order. Among those killed was Samuel N. Wood, founder of Woodsdale and a colorful, controversial character throughout his life. He had been a free-state leader during the territorial years, an outspoken editor in Cottonwood Falls and Council Grove, a railroad promoter, and an advocate of woman suffrage. Leoti and Coronado, in Wichita County, were involved in a similar struggle, as were Sherman, Grant, Hamilton, Gray, and Pratt county towns. Records were stolen, ballot boxes tampered with, and there were outbursts of violence. In Logan and Morton counties there were debates about the county seats until the middle of the twentieth century when Oakley and Elkhart finally replaced Russell Springs and Richfield as the courthouse sites.

The western editorial style that flourished in the territorial years continued for the next several decades, and some of the most uncomplimentary paragraphs were written by editors in towns where county seat competition was strong. While they may never have fired any shots in anger they fired some mighty blasts from their newspaper columns. From Garfield

County, where Ravanna and Eminence were in competition, came these words from the Eminence *Call* editor, May 25, 1888:

> Ye scavengers of hell and subjects of perdition, whose souls are steeped in infamy and become so ulcerated that at the opening of the mouth the poisonous vitrious pours forth from the putrified barnacles within. Truth is to you a domestic enemy and virtue a foreign foe. . . . There is no meanness so damnable that you will not employ and no lie so infamous that you will not promulgate to accomplish your purpose. But the hand writing is upon the wall and you can not mistake its meaning. Behold, the end is near and . . . you will have to bow down at the knee of Eminence.
>
> Let us review your character for a moment and see how you stand before the county except that little nucleus around Ravanna of lying whelps and perjured villains. You say there was no fraud committed in the election for County Seat. Did not the judges of election swear that there was votes counted for Ravanna for county seat that was never polled? Let the testimony speak for itself ye lieing whelps. Where is the eighty-three votes you stuffed the ballot-box with? . . .
>
> Did the infernal combination of villains who constitute the board of election give Eminence credit for all the votes she received for county seat? . . . The testimony shows that we put over 90 witnesses upon the stand that confirm this truth. . . . Oh, Ye fiends incarnate! How long do you presume to impose upon the confidence of your friends and credulity of the people? Has not the past convinced the people that you are . . . "a liar and the truth is not in you." . . .
>
> You say we have been dragging the case along. It is truly said that we have been pulling you and the dragging has been like dragging a thomas cat by the tail and if you do not pull loose soon your putrid corpse will be dropped into the pit dug for us and the contest will be ended.

Garfield County and the two towns died, and one might speculate on the average life span of editors who wrote such paragraphs. Some of them were shot or horse-whipped but most survived to write more colorful editorials. This period of frontier settlement was a period of "growing pains" for a youthful state but as the years passed Kansas obviously was acquiring more sophistication in its social life, its politics, and its agriculture. The towns with the power to last began to acquire the look of permanency, and sod buildings were replaced with frame, brick, and stone ones. Public schools

Students and teachers of Buzzard's Roost school near Jennings, Decatur County.

grew and developed and high schools began to appear in communities that in their beginnings had only part-time grade schools. Theaters and opera houses in towns, both large and small, played host to touring professional actors and musicians, including some who were internationally famous.

In agriculture two kinds of farming drew increased attention. One was called "dry farming" and involved a kind of cultivation that was supposed to catch the available moisture in winter and also prevent erosion from the wind. The second, and more important, aspect was irrigation. Western Kansas had a good supply of water beneath the ground level even though its stream beds were often dry in the summer. In the 1880s a number of irrigation projects were attempted.

One of the most involved was a canal, planned by Asa T. Soule, which was supposed to run from Ingalls, in Gray County, into Edwards County, using water from the Arkansas River. Although construction was completed on much of the canal the river's flow declined because of water being diverted upstream in Colorado and consequently the project had to be abandoned. Several companies were organized to promote irrigation and the state government encouraged further projects. A great many individual farmers, using windmills and ponds, successfully irrigated limited acreages and grew bumper crops on land that had previously provided only minimal production. Most important, those irrigation experimenters showed the way for projects of far greater scope, which were developed in the years to come.

Kansas farmers also tried new crops. They added to their standard corn and wheat production a variety of sorghum grains such as milo, and they began to grow soybeans, alfalfa, and sugar beets. New strains of hard, winter wheat, combined with improvements in the American flour-milling industry, made Kansas wheat production increasingly important. All of these crops would remain principal sources of Kansas farm income.

The fields in which these crops were grown had to be enclosed and, again, innovation played a part. Some Kansans planted Osage Orange hedges, something they were familiar with in an earlier period in either an eastern part of the state or in the states east of the Missouri River. The hedges, still seen today with the familiar "hedge apples," provided a barrier that kept livestock from wandering out of pastures or into cropland. Farmers also strung barbed wire, a development of the 1870s, on wooden fence posts where they were available, or they used posts made of the limestone, which they found in many of the central and western Kansas counties. Postrock limestone, soft enough to quarry by hand and cut with an ordinary saw but particularly enduring when exposed to the air, provided unique fence posts for hundreds of Kansas farmers.

Kansas agriculture lent itself to the kind of tall-tale folklore that has already been discussed. On January 7, 1886, the *Thomas County Cat* of Colby published this article from Hamilton County under the title "Eden Restored":

> It has been discovered that western Kansas is the Eden from which Grandfather Adam and Grandmother Eve were driven for fooling with the commandments. . . . The stump of the identical tree under which Mrs. Adam was beguiled by the serpent, is just south of the river in Hamilton county. . . .
>
> The soil is just as fruitful as in ye olden time and produces prodigiously. Sunflowers can be seen that will make a dozen rails and a whole lot of hard work. Potatoes grow so big that they can only be roasted by building a fire on the windward side and when one section is done, waiting for the wind to change. Cabbage leaves are used for circus tents, and hoop poles are made out of timothy stalks. Jack rabbits grow as large as a horse, and the tail feathers of a wild goose make excellent fence posts. Wheat is larger than corn in most states, and it is dangerous to plant rye, as the roots have to be grubbed out before the ground can be plowed again. A man planted a turnip one mile from the railroad last summer and the railroad company sued him for obstructing their right of way before the middle of July.
>
> Pie plant makes excellent bridge timbers, and pumpkins are in good demand this winter for barns and houses. Pea pods are used as ferry boats on the Arkansas river, and onion seeds are much sought after for walling wells and terrace work. Rye straw, properly con-

nected, makes superior pipe for drainage, and the husk of the berry when provided with rockers, makes unique baby cradles. North of Coolidge are several lakes of strained honey and we often have showers of rose water and cologne in the early part of the year. The settlement of western Kansas is restoring Eden to its primitive glory and man to his first estate.

It is unlikely that many settlers were encouraged to settle in western Kansas because they read stories like that but certainly the exaggerated enthusiasm and the good humor of the local promoter cannot be questioned.

CRIME AND CRIMINALS

During this time two groups of criminals received national attention and reflected the image that so many people had of the "Wild West." In 1871 a family named Bender—John, his wife, son, and daughter Kate—built a small house west of Parsons. Partitioned into two rooms by a piece of canvas, it had a table, stove, and a small stock of groceries in front. In back were beds, a sledge hammer, and a trap door above a cellar. Kate, a physically attractive girl who was supposed to have healing powers, was apparently the leader of her murderous family.

The Bender house was located on a main traveled road, and travelers who stopped for a meal were seated on a bench backed up against the canvas. Between 1871 and 1873, several of them disappeared, and when area residents became suspicious of the Benders, the family fled. A search of the property revealed eleven bodies buried in the garden, and all of them had skulls crushed by hammer blows. What happened to the Benders is not known. Either they escaped completely or they were found by neighbors who killed them and did not talk about it.

In 1892 the Dalton gang was robbing trains in Oklahoma and southern Kansas, much as the James boys had operated in the West at an earlier time. The Katy Railroad was offering a reward of $40,000 for the gang. Then, on October 5, 1892, the Daltons rode into Coffeyville and robbed the town's banks of nearly $25,000. Citizens shot at them as they tried to escape, and four of the outlaws were killed along with four of the men who stopped them. The fifth robber, Emmett Dalton, was wounded, captured, and sentenced to life imprisonment. After fourteen years he was pardoned, and he later played a leading part in a movie about the raid.

KANSAS AND THE OPENING OF OKLAHOMA

Even as Kansas was being filled with settlers there were some Kansans who, like many other Americans, were looking toward the south and present

Land seekers in camp near Arkansas City, waiting for the 1893 opening of Oklahoma.

Oklahoma. Boomers tried for ten years, 1879–1889, to open parts of the Indian Territory to settlement.* Most prominent among them was David L. Payne, a Kansan who was compared with Moses as he attempted to lead people to a "promised land." In 1880 Payne and several friends formed the Oklahoma Town Company and, ignoring the federal government, made the first of several invasions into the territory. It was not until 1889 that a portion of the Indian Territory was legally opened for settlement. Payne did not see his dreams fulfilled because he died at Wellington in 1884.

The last great American land rush on September 16, 1893, filled the Cherokee Outlet (more commonly called the Cherokee Strip), a piece of Indian land 59 miles wide and 150 miles long, south of the Kansas border and west of the Arkansas River. Eager landseekers lined the outlet's borders, waiting for the starting signal. Near Arkansas City 70,000 people pressed against lines of U.S. army troops. Settlers using horses, buggies, wagons, trains, and bicycles tried for good starting positions. At high noon the army fired rifles to indicate the run was on and "strippers were stripping through the Strip." The Arkansas City *Republican Traveler* said five days later that "the great Cherokee Outlet is now the home of one hundred thousand American citizens." As people gathered to make the Oklahoma run, Arkansas City, Caldwell, Wellington, Winfield, and a half-dozen other places were crowded and their merchants busy.

Everything leveled off as the nineteenth century came to a close in Kansas. Basically the frontier was gone, even though there were still thou-

*The term "boomer" can be applied to anyone involved in the promotion of an area, particularly if fast growth is a factor. "Sooner" was also used for the first Oklahoma settlers who got there sooner than the land was legally opened or sooner than others who rushed to settle.

sands of acres available for settlement. There were still problems to be met but there had been a vast improvement in the lot of most Kansans between the close of the Civil War and the beginning of a new century. The crudeness was disappearing and a new day was coming.

Suggestions for Reading

Good commentaries on the Indian situation in the 1870s will be found in William Y. Chalfant, *Cheyennes at Dark Water Creek: The Last Fight of the Red River War* (1997); Lonnie White, *Hostiles and Horse Soldiers* (1972); and Mari Sandoz, *Cheyenne Autumn* (1953). The disposition of public lands is well covered in Roy Robbins, *Our Landed Heritage* (1942). Settlement and everyday living are graphically described in Everett Dick, *The Sod House Frontier* (1937), John Ise, *Sod and Stubble* (1936); T. A. McNeal, *When Kansas Was Young* (1922), Walter P. Webb, *The Great Plains* (1931); C. Robert Haywood and Sandra Jarvis, eds., *"A Funnie Place, No Fences:" Teenagers' views of Kansas, 1867–1900* (1992); and Charles R. King, "Childhood Death: The Health Care of Children on the Kansas Frontier," *Kansas History* (Spring 1991). Other books that have some bearing on this period are C. Robert Haywood, *Trails South: The Wagon-Road Economy in the Dodge City-Panhandle Region* (1986); John R. James, *The Benders in Kansas* (1995); Lawrence H. Larsen, *The Urban West at the End of the Frontier* (1978); James R. Mead, *Hunting and Trading on the Great Plains, 1859–1875*, edited by Schuyler Jones (1986); H. Craig Miner, *West of Wichita* (1986); Grace Muilenburg and Ada Swineford, *Land of the Post Rock* (1975); Barbara Oringderff, *True Sod* (1976); and Homer E. Socolofsky, *Landlord William Scully* (1979). More generally, an excellent work is James R. Shortridge, *Peopling the Plains: Who Settled Where in Frontier Kansas* (1995).

Kansas county seat wars are discussed in the *Kansas Historical Quarterly*: Henry F. Mason, "County Seat Controversies in Southwestern Kansas" (February, 1933) and Calvin F. Schwartzkopf, "The Rush County-Seat War" (Spring, 1970). The relationship of Kansas to the opening of Oklahoma is discussed in three *Quarterly* articles: Berlin Chapman, "The Land Run of 1893, as Seen at Kiowa" (Spring, 1965); Jean C. Lough, "Gateways to the Promised Land" (Spring, 1959); Nyle H. Miller, "The Cherokee Strip Run: From Cameron and Bluff City, Harper County, Kansas" (Summer, 1973); and in Stan Hoig, *The Oklahoma Land Rush of 1889* (1984). Descriptive of community founding in western Kansas is C. Robert Haywood, "Pearlette: A Mutual Aid Colony," *Kansas Historical Quarterly*, (Autumn, 1976).

The role of women in settlement is well told in Sandra Myres, *Westering Women and the Frontier Experience, 1800–1915* (1982); Glenda Riley, *The Female Frontier: A Comparative View of Women on the Prairie and the Plains* (1988); Marlene Springer and Haskell Springer, *Plains Woman: The Diary of Martha Farnsworth, 1882–1922* (1986); and Joanna Stratton, *Pioneer Women* (1981).

10

Immigrants on the Prairies

In the years between the Civil War and 1890 the population of Kansas increased by more than a million, a number of whom were recently from Europe. The state has never had a large foreign-born population, but its European immigrants have added to the state's economic and social life. Most numerous were the people of German (or German-Russian) background who settled widely over the state, especially in the late 1870s.

THE MENNONITES

Most prominent among the Protestant German-Russians were the Mennonites. For the entire period of their history most of the Mennonites had been farmers, just as they are today. Their religious beliefs were formed in Holland and Switzerland during the Reformation, and their theological leadership was first provided by Menno Simons. Because of their love for peace and their policies of nonresistance they became easy targets for persecution by both Protestants and Catholics. Forced out of their original homes they first settled in the delta of the Vistula River, protected by Polish and Prussian nobles. They transformed a marshland into an agriculturally productive area. For two hundred years they lived in peace.

At the end of that period they were forced to move again because of the pressures of Prussian militarism. Catherine the Great of Russia offered them free land, religious toleration, and exemption from taxes and mili-

Mennonites in temporary quarters, 1875.

tary service if they would develop and farm the plains of the Ukraine. So they moved into that part of Russia in the 1780s and prospered. They developed large-scale wheat production using hard winter wheat and eventually their product took over the European markets.

Within a century their dreams were dealt another severe blow. In 1871 a law was enacted that called for universal military service, something completely contrary to Mennonite thinking. One man, Cornelius Jansen, wrote to Mennonites who had settled in Pennsylvania, Indiana, and Ohio seeking information about conditions in the United States. The more he learned the more he was convinced that his people's future lay in the American West, and he worked hard to convince them of that. His campaign was discovered by the Russian government, which encouraged him to leave. He finally settled in Nebraska and became a prosperous farmer and rancher.

In the spring of 1873 the Mennonites sent an official committee to tour the United States. They could not have chosen a better time, for the Santa Fe Railroad was eager for settlers on its land-grant property. The Santa Fe appointed C. B. Schmidt, a German resident of Lawrence, as its commissioner of emigration, and it was through Schmidt's efforts that the greater numbers of Mennonites came to Kansas. Many were still concerned about military responsibilities in the United States, but when they found that Kansas would exempt them from militia duty and that the federal government made allowances for conscientious objectors their fears were put to rest.

One of the first groups to leave Russia for Kansas was the Krimmer congregation, led by Jacob Wiebe. In late summer 1874, they bought land from the Santa Fe and began their Marion County settlement, which they called Gnadenau—Meadow of Grace." There, very near the present town of Hillsboro, they withstood the hardships caused by the grasshopper invasion and drought and before long they prospered. They grew wheat, watermelons, and sunflowers (for seed), and they planted trees. They lived in long houses which were partitioned so that they served as storage shed and barn as well.

By the end of September 1874, nearly two thousand emigrants had arrived in Topeka. The Santa Fe housed them in a large building until they could select tracts of land and move on to them. Their clothes and their speech were strange, but their minds were sharp and their money was good. Many of the Kansans who viewed them with amazement or who ridiculed them would soon find that they were settlers to be respected and admired. They bought approximately one hundred thousand acres from the Santa Fe and much of south-central Kansas took on a new look. Among their contributions was their hard winter wheat, "Turkey Red." It became the foundation on which the state's great wheat production is based, although that original seed has been replaced by many different hybrid varieties. The Mennonites not only grew the wheat, they ground it into flour, first using small windmills and later larger mills such as those developed by Bernhard Warkentin in Halstead and Newton.

The Mennonites came in great numbers for several years and they settled principally in Marion, Harvey, Reno, McPherson, and Barton counties. Communities such as Yoder and Goessel reflect their Mennonite origins, although the language, dress, and customs have changed. After the Mennonites were well established, education became a prime concern, and they supported schools and founded colleges—Bethel, Tabor, and Hesston. At times they have suffered for their policies of nonviolence, particularly during the First World War, but they have served the nation in many other ways during wartime.

Noble L. Prentis, a well-known Kansas editor and historian, visited the Mennonite settlements when they were new and again in 1882, when they had acquired permanency. He commented in the Atchison *Champion*, May 4, 1882:

> In 1875 the Mennonites were still a strange people. They retained
> the little green flaring wagons they had brought from Russia, and
> were attempting to live here under the same rules they followed in
> Russia. The village of Gnadenau was the most pretentious of their
> villages. It was a long row of houses, mostly built of sod and

thatched with long prairie grass. A few of the wealthier citizens had built frame houses, furnished with the brick ovens of Russian origin which warm the family and cook the food for all day with two armfuls of loose straw. . . .

The site of the villages seemed selected with care. . . . It was summer in Kansas, and of course the scene was naturally beautiful, but the scattered or collected Mennonite houses, with their bare walls of sod or boards, amid patches of broken prairie, did not at all add to the charm of the scene. . . . Still there was an appearance of resolution and patience about them, taken with the fact that all, men, women and children, were at work, that argued well for the future. . . .

A great change had taken place in the country generally since my last visit. The then raw prairie was now, barring the fences, very like Illinois. At last, after driving about ten miles, Mr. Muntefering announced the first Mennonite habitation, in what seemed the edge of a young forest, and I then learned . . . that the Mennonites had abandoned the village system, and now lived "each man to himself." . . . The old sod houses had given way to frame houses, sometimes painted white, with wooden window shutters. The houses had no porches or other architectural adornments, and were uniform in appearance. . . .

We went to the house of Peter Schmidt. Had I been an artist I should have sketched Peter Schmidt, of Emmathal, as the typical prosperous Mennonite. He was a big man. . . . He was very wide, fore and aft; wore a vest that buttoned to his throat, a sort of brown blouse, and a pair of very roomy and very short breeches, while his bare feet were thrust into a sort of sandals very popular with the Mennonites. . . . Peter Schmidt showed all his arborial treasures, apples, cherries, peaches, apricots, pears, all in bearing, where seven years ago the wind in passing found only the waving prairie grass. . . . He started in the prairie with $800; he now has a farm worth $4,000. . . . A happy man was Peter Schmidt, and well satisfied with his adopted country, for when I managed to mix enough German and English together to ask him how he liked America as compared with Russia, he answered in a deep voice, and with his little smile: "Besser." With a hearty good bye to Peter Schmidt of Emmathal, we pursued our journey, passing many houses, hedges, and orchards. . . .

We made few more halts, but drove for miles with many Mennonite houses in sight, and the most promising orchards and immense fields of the greenest wheat. I have never seen elsewhere such a picture of agricultural prosperity.

GERMAN-RUSSIANS IN WESTERN KANSAS

Similar in many ways, although their church was Roman Catholic, were the German-Russians who came to Ellis and Rush counties in the 1870s and 1880s. They, too, were antimilitaristic and good farmers who lived at first in Kansas in communal groups as they had in Russia. The first large group came in 1876 and spread out on both sides of the Smoky Hill valley. Their roots were in the Volga River country and their towns reflected the names of places they had lived in Russia—Herzog, Liebenthal, Catherine, Pfeifer, Munjor, and Schoenchen. As time went by they built many churches. Native limestone buildings with tall steeples marked the countryside with the most famous church constructed by the parishioners at Herzog, now Victoria. Known as the "Cathedral of the Plains," Victoria's St. Fidelis Church was built between 1908 and 1911 with the help of every male in the congregation over the age of twelve.

It is estimated that 75 percent of the farmers in Ellis County today are of German-Russian descent and in the surrounding areas there are many people who trace their origins to the same regions of Europe. There was a Protestant German-Russian emigration into southwestern Russell and northwestern Barton counties that spilled over into Rush and Ness counties. And there were Pennsylvanians with German backgrounds who moved west, settling in Russell County particularly.

Many of these people suffered an anti-German reaction from some of their neighbors as the First World War began. Although great numbers of them left Russia because they did not like the militaristic nationalism of Czar Alexander they did not necessarily hold pacifistic views like the Mennonites. Consequently, many served in the armed forces, but they still were criticized by unthinking people for their use of the German language.

German-Russian family which settled in Liebenthal, Rush County.

A Scandinavian Heritage

Pioneers from Sweden also came to Kansas in large numbers. There were Swedes in central Kansas before the Civil War but it was not until 1868 that the first groups began to emigrate, partly because of famine in Scandinavia. Kansas profited from the activities of immigration companies in New York and Chicago that had agents in Europe who encouraged settlement in the American West. The railroads also promoted Scandinavian immigration with both the Santa Fe and Kansas Pacific issuing publications in Swedish that pointed out the advantages of living in Kansas.

Swedish land companies were formed in the United States to purchase land in Kansas for settlement. The Swedish Agricultural Company of McPherson County was organized in Chicago in 1868 and bought thirteen thousand acres from the Kansas Pacific in McPherson and Saline counties. There were other groups, including the Scandinavian Agricultural Society of Chicago, which bought land along the Republican River and colonized New Scandinavia in Republic County, the present town of Scandia. Among the individual leaders who encouraged their fellow Swedes to settle in Kansas were the Reverend Olof Olsson of Lindsborg and Dr. Carl Swensson, founder and president of Bethany College. They saw a bright future for Swedes in central Kansas and referred to *framtidslandet,* the land of the future, in their letters to Sweden.

The largest number of Swedes were Lutherans and the first church founded by that denomination was at Mariadahl in Pottawatomie County, although Swedish Lutheranism centered in the Smoky Hill valley, with Lindsborg at its heart. There were sizable numbers of other Protestant Swedish groups and most of them became, through mergers, a part of larger American denominations. It was an interest in religion, combined with education, that led to the founding of Bethany College in 1881. Dr. Carl Swensson wrote:

> I saw how God had blessed our settlements in this beautiful,
> flourishing, and liberty-loving state. But how our children and
> youth should obtain the necessary Christian education was a
> question not easily answered. Without the elevating influence
> exerted by a good school to mould the character of students and
> others, we would evidently be in danger of sinking into the worship
> of the almighty dollar and materialism. In addition, among our
> youth, how many gifts that would otherwise be hidden and deterio-
> rate, would not such a school disclose, gifts to benefit and gladden
> the community and the church of God. Finally, after consulting the
> members in the vicinity and laymen who were interested in the

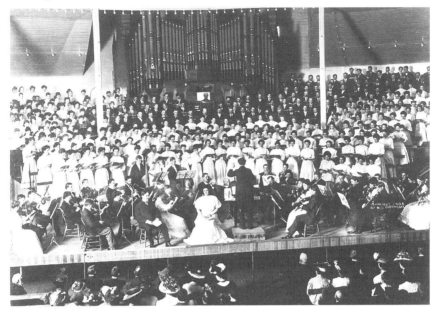

Lindsborg residents on stage at Bethany College for a performance of Handel's *Messiah* in the early 1900s.

work, all of whom with one accord seconded the project, we ventured upon the undertaking!

Bethany's and Lindsborg's greatest fame has probably come through the annual performances of Handel's *Messiah*, beginning in 1882. Many of the world's most famous singers have taken part in the Holy Week performances, which have become a Kansas tradition. For years the Swedish communities were bilingual, but English became the common language in business, religion, and education with the passage of time. Still, the Swedish traditions have not been lost, and the annual *Svensk Hyllningsfest* at Lindsborg helps emphasize the food, clothing, music, and dance that came to America with the original settlers.

Other Scandinavians from Norway and Denmark began to come to Kansas at about the same time as the Swedes. There were a few Danes here in the 1850s, but the larger numbers arrived in the 1870s and 1880s. Cloud, Marshall, and Osage counties had Danish communities, but the most distinctive one was Denmark in Lincoln County, founded in 1869. There was also a Danish Socialist colony in Ellis County, which lasted only a short time in the late 1870s. Most of these people were farmers and craftsmen who were almost completely absorbed into the overall Kansas population in the twentieth century.

Bohemian gymnasts, members of an Ellsworth County Sokol.

THE BOHEMIANS

Another fairly large group of foreign-language immigrants came to Kansas from what became Czechoslovakia. Most were from Bohemia but some came from Moravia. They first took land in Ellsworth County in 1874, and in the following two years many of them came to that area. They were encouraged by Francis Swehla, who came to Kansas from Iowa, and who wrote forty years later:

> While teaching my first public school in my log cabin on my claim
> in Nebraska, I was reading in my newspapers of our people organiz-
> ing companies in the large cities to move out and settle on land, to
> go to farming, because there was a financial panic in this country. . . .
> Some went to Wisconsin; some to South Dakota and northern
> Nebraska; some came through Kansas on the Atchison, Topeka &
> Santa Fe railroad as far as Larned . . . but there was trouble in each
> and every direction. Discord and disagreements followed. It seemed
> very hard for the exploring parties to find, to their satisfaction, the
> "Promised Land, flowing with milk and honey" and still harder to
> please all the home-seekers. It is no wonder when we consider
> where these people had been all their lives. In Bohemia . . . all the

people live in cities, towns and villages except a few foresters. . . .
Hence they had never seen isolated farm dwellings.

Customs and habits are second nature, and solitude seemed to
frighten such people. An American farmer in a well-settled country
seemed to them a poor human lost in a wilderness. . . .

So after I decided to locate a Bohemian settlement in and around
Wilson, Kan., then called "Bosland" by the Kansas Pacific Railroad
Company, I wrote up the location showing everything I could in its
favor. The main things were temperate climate; good soil; free land
from Uncle Sam, or cheap relinquishments of improvements by
previous settlers; railroad land at from $2.50 to $5.00 per acre; good
and plenty of water. . . . A paradise for poultry, cattle, horses, sheep,
hogs, etc. I kept my pen going, publishing my reports in Bohemian-
American papers until I drew the attention of the farm clubs formed
in the cities and of all the reading public. Soon letters came pouring
in wanting answers, and I had lots of writing to do. . . .

Those first Bohemian settlers did not come directly from Europe but
moved to the West from homes in larger cities—Detroit, Chicago, and
New York. They occupied areas in Ellsworth County, and some of them
went into Russell County. In 1877 the first group came directly from Europe, and for the next few years they helped settle the region around Lucas
and parts of Lincoln County.

The Bohemians at first were mostly mechanics and merchants, but
many of them turned successfully to farming. They were devoted to the
development of both minds and bodies and formed musical groups, libraries, and the Sokol, an athletic organization. In Ellsworth County much of
their social life centered around the *Ceská Siñ*, the Bohemian Hall, and,
like the Swedes, they have worked to preserve many of the traditions and
customs of their European background. Bohemian communities came into
being in widely separated parts of the state, from the northwestern counties of
Decatur and Rawlins, to Sumner County in the south, with others locating in
Republic, Washington, Trego, Rush, Marshall, and Marion counties.

SOUTHERN AND EASTERN EUROPEANS

Kansas has not had a large number of immigrants from southern or eastern
Europe, yet those who came have made an impression on and contributed
to the communities in which they settled.

In southeastern Kansas, particularly in the mining areas, families from
Italy and some from the European east did settle, and many of their descendants still reside there. The same is true in Kansas City.

South Slavic immigrants have made a lasting impression on Kansas City. Croatians, Serbians, and Slovenians came from what is now Yugoslavia, and most of them at first worked in the meat packing plants. In the Strawberry Hill area of the city the Croatian community that began in the late nineteenth century is still identifiable, and there has been a strong effort to preserve some customs, especially in food, music, and dance.

Strawberry Hill is well chronicled by the paintings of Mary Ann Grisnik, better known as Marijana. She is not an academically trained artist, yet she is not really a folk artist. She is an artist who offers pictorial narratives of life on Strawberry Hill, which are valuable to the student of folk culture. Her works have been exhibited widely, and many of them are in the permanent collections of the State Historical Society at the Kansas Museum of History, Topeka.

FRENCH PIONEERS AND THE SILKVILLE EXPERIMENT

French settlers in Kansas have received little attention from historians, but in a limited area their influence was felt for a number of years. Settlement of French-speaking people in the Cottonwood River valley began during the territorial period. Most of them came from France, though there were also Belgians and Swiss, but they were all considered part of the "French colony." These people did not come as one group but as individual families who emigrated over a period of forty years.

The first French immigrants settled in the valley in 1857 and the colony grew steadily until 1885 when there were more than sixty families. They lived mostly near Cedar Point in Chase County and in the vicinity of Florence in Marion County although there were French families in Cottonwood Falls and Marion. The first families established a town called Cottonwood City on the river but it did not grow and eventually disappeared, with the townsite land absorbed into the surrounding farms. After 1885 few new families came to Kansas. Younger people intermarried with other Kansans so that the colony lost its identity, but descendants still live in the Cottonwood valley.

Efforts were made by members of the colony to encourage additional French emigration in the 1870s and 1880s but no great numbers of settlers came. The colony included many different kinds of people: some of great talent and from noble families. The diversity of the colonists is illustrated by this quotation from the 1890s:

> One day I was with a Frenchman who had settled in Kansas a long time ago. After a long walk over the grounds he said to me, after

Earnest Valeton deBoissiere (with white beard) and some of his Silkville colonists.

proudly glancing around him, "you see, Sir, what I have done here. In the time of the Indians I began with my two arms, defending my cattle and crops against them; sometimes selling my plough-oxen to get a few measures of flour, to keep me from starving; yet I never learned anything but my trade of cabinet making in my home in Burgundy." I asked him if many of his neighbors began farming for the first time on their homesteads. "Why, down in that valley through which you came to get here," he replied, "one farmer was once a waiter, another a salesman at Pygmalions in Paris, a third a journeyman printer from New York, another is an old sailor, who deserted, and I can point out to you . . . old soldiers, merchants, and so on."

There were some early families of French descent in Topeka and others in Leavenworth, where there was a French-language newspaper published in 1858–1859. Later a French settlement developed in southeastern Kansas around Frontenac. The most unique French settlement was at Silkville in Franklin County, where Ernest Valeton deBoissiere founded a community in 1869 that successfully engaged in the manufacture of silk.

DeBoissiere, a former French army engineer, came to the United States in 1852 and settled in New Orleans. He made money but because he was outspoken about blacks' rights he had trouble getting along in the South. One story is that he came to Kansas because he was encouraged to do so by Horace Greeley and that he found Franklin County interesting because it had a river with a French name, the Marais des Cygnes—Marsh of the Swans.

He was a free thinker who envisioned a Utopian community where all would share in the responsibilities and the rewards. He found his first winter in Kansas colder than what he was used to and he wrote:

> I am living on the wild prairie. . . . I sleep in a small garret at the top of a rough frame house, as cold as the outside atmosphere. . . . It is a severe life for me, used to the mild climate and every comfort of

Southern France, but I think that the sufferings of the flesh are
nothing and preserve the predominance of the spirit.

Although the weather was different from that of France, deBoissiere
felt that it was enough alike to experiment with silk worms. He planted
mulberry trees, which flourished, and he imported silk worms from France
and Japan. He also brought over French immigrants as colonists. He built
a three-story, sixty-room building to house the settlers and then he added
a silk factory, barns, a winery, an ice house, and a school house. The worms
multiplied, ate the mulberry leaves, and spun their cocoons of silk, and the
looms turned out 250 to 300 yards of finished material a day. At the Philadelphia Centennial Exposition in 1876 the silk was awarded medals for its
high quality, ranking with silk produced in France, Italy, and Japan. Unfortunately, competition with the cheaper labor of the foreign countries
made it impossible to continue the Silkville manufacturing.

The colony then turned to the dairy industry, concentrating on the
manufacture of cheese, and again it turned out quality products. But members of the colony were beginning to find that they could make more money
elsewhere in the new country, and so they moved away. Private enterprise
became more important to them than the communal life of Silkville.

In 1892, deBoissiere disposed of Silkville, giving it to a lodge for use
as an orphans' home. Controversy arose over the title to the property, and
eventually it passed into private hands. Today it is a part of a farming and
ranching operation, and some of the original buildings are still in use.
DeBoissiere died in his native France in 1894.

The unique colony and its early success in silk production started a
new industry, and during the twenty years before 1900 more than forty
counties had silk projects. In 1887, the state legislature appropriated $13,000
to start a silk station at Peabody, and the State Board of Agriculture organized a special silk commission. It was thought that silk would become one
of the state's most profitable products, but ten years later the legislature
decided that the industry could not survive because of the high cost of
labor. The Peabody silk station was closed.

SETTLERS FROM THE BRITISH ISLES

Unlike most of the national groups that came to Kansas, the English did
not come in colonies but emigrated mostly as families or individuals. There
were, however, two exceptions, Victoria and Runnymede. Victoria was
begun in 1873 by George Grant, a Scottish silk merchant who believed
that Englishmen could profitably raise cattle and sheep in Ellis County on
land obtained from the Kansas Pacific Railroad. Grant also believed that he
could make a great deal of money for himself through both land and livestock.

Several different stories have been told about how much land Grant acquired from the Kansas Pacific but it appears that he finally bought about 31,000 acres over a period of five years, 1872–1877. The Kansas Pacific agreed to build a railroad station, loading pens, and accommodations for colonists, and Grant was to receive special privileges for travel on the railroad. There is some question about the size of Grant's herds of livestock and while the totals of both cattle and sheep are impressive—thousands of head—many of those did not belong to Grant alone but to several other investors in the Victoria project.

When George Grant died in 1878 he left generous amounts of money to many people, but he also left tremendous debts that had to be paid off. When the estate was finally settled there was little money left. Not everything Grant did was poorly planned nor did he engage in speculation only for personal profit. The Victoria colony never grew to the size that its promoters hoped for but a number of British emigrants did help populate west-central Kansas. And Grant's experiments in breeding and feeding both sheep and cattle did add to the agricultural progress of the West. He proved that sheep could successfully winter on the Kansas plains and his blooded Durham short-horns and black polled cattle (called both Angus and Galloway) helped upgrade western stock and won prizes in national competition.

Victoria was no different from many other communities started in America by foreign investors and speculators. George Grant was no different than hundreds of other individuals who saw a chance to make money while also encouraging settlement. There was for some years the flavor of the British Isles in Ellis County, and the English settlers were looked on with favor by the people who came in contact with them. Victoria, named for the English queen, still exists, but its inhabitants are mostly the descendants of the settlers of Herzog. The German-Russian Catholic community provided the people but the English name remained.

At Runnymede, in Harper County (where a post office had been established earlier), an Irishman named F. J. S. Turnly bought land in 1887, and he offered (for a $500 fee) to teach the sons of British gentlemen the secrets of successful farming. After learning what they needed to know to survive in the West they could buy farms of their own and Turnly would advise them. The editor of the Harper *Sentinel* visited Runnymede and wrote an enthusiastic story about the settlement on August 15, 1889:

> Numerous driveways, rather on the English manor style, were
> platted out, trees planted on each side have grown until the
> driveways have become pleasant thoroughfares in country life,
> indeed. Soon after the purchase of the land and the establishment
> of an American home, Mr. Turnly concluded to establish an

agricultural training school for his fellow countrymen. . . . He has made several trips across the big water in the interest of this laudable enterprise, offering inducements that has brought about forty young and enterprising Englishmen of good family to the Runnymede colony. . . . About two years ago Mr. Turnly founded the town . . . and secured a postoffice and established a grocery store; other branches of business were soon established. . . . The colony will probably establish a large creamery during the coming winter and a prospect hole will be sunk for oil, coal, gas or salt. The town stands on high ground and the two principal streets are graded in first-class shape. . . . The young men of the colony are well educated and industrious and we have no doubts concerning Runnymede becoming a town of considerable proportion as time rolls by, a surrounding rich agricultural country, being tributary to it. . . .

The establishment of Turnly's English colony and training school . . . is certainly a great benefit to this section of Kansas, as it naturally draws the attention of the best people of England to this locality. The letters the boys write home are no doubt full of glowing and entrancing descriptions of this new fertile land where there are homes for thousands of the good people of the crowded Mother country and in time hundreds of them will locate here.

Unfortunately, most of the young men from England were so well supplied with money that they found it easier to be idle than to work. They raced their horses, they had frequent parties, and they "rode to hounds" on the Kansas prairie although they would have found more jackrabbits than foxes to chase. One colonist wrote that they "had a good time while it lasted" but it lasted no longer than 1892 when most of the families in England decided that their sons were learning very little about agriculture. Although Runnymede is still shown on the map, in a slightly different location, the only reminder of the colony is a church building that has been moved to Harper.

A third English settlement that lacked the glamor of either Victoria or Runnymede but proved to be more lasting was Wakefield in Clay County. Wakefield combined organized promotion with individual emigration, beginning in 1869. The founders of the settlement incorporated the Kansas Land and Emigration Company and encouraged English families to come. The company bought land from the Kansas Pacific and then sold it to settlers. Groups came in 1870 and 1871 and they experienced the usual hardships, including the grasshopper plague of 1874. One of the residents wrote that "the dry continental climate, with its fitful and violent changes of temperature, proved very trying to the English settlers." A number of them left after 1875, and some of the land went back to the railroad because of Wakefield's financial difficulties. Today Wakefield combines both the old and new on the banks of Milford Reservoir with families in the area who trace their Kansas beginnings back to the original English settlers.

Wakefield had one unique aspect, for part of its residents were orphaned young men from London, sent to Kansas to begin a new life. The Junction City *Union* took notice of the arrival of these unusual immigrants on December 11, 1869:

> This week we have to record a new era in the history of emigration. Last Tuesday, 21 boys from 16 to 19 years of age, the first deputation from the "Home and Refuge for Destitute Children," London, arrived under the superintendence of Mr. Reuben Cox, and received a hearty English welcome . . . as they landed at the railway depot. . . . It having become known in the city that these representatives of London reform were on their way from New York, great interest was felt in the new movement. . . . It was a matter for general remark that the boys all looked so clean and healthy, notwithstanding their three weeks voyage in . . . the steerage of an emigrant ship, and a week's journey by rail. . . .
>
> The London organization from which these boys are drafted, was originally founded by W. H. Williams, and enjoys the honorable advantage of having for its president, England's noblest friend of the friendless, Lord Shaftesbury. . . .
>
> We sincerely wish such philanthropists Godspeed in all their labors for the real good of their fellow men. . . . The welcome given on this side of the Atlantic to England's sons furnishes another proof of the bond of good friendship existing between the peoples of the two countries.

Other emigrants from Great Britain who came in any number were from Wales. There were Welsh moving to Emporia in 1857, the year of the town's founding, and they continued to come through the 1860s and 1870s. They also established homes in the vicinity of Arvonia, Reading, Burlingame, and Carbondale. The Welsh published newspapers, organized Congregational and Presbyterian churches, were active in both business and agriculture, and were noted for their musical groups and performances. Also contributing to the growth of Kansas were people from Holland, Poland, Yugoslavia, and Hungary. From Italy came people who settled primarily in southeastern Kansas and in the Kansas City area.

THE MEXICAN AMERICANS

Much remains to be done in recording the history of Mexican Americans in the state, but these particular Kansans have become a significant part of the population in many counties during the twentieth century. The 1900 federal census for Kansas listed only seventy-one residents of Mexican origin, but that number grew by several thousand for each of the next three or four decades.

Most of the Spanish-speaking immigrants who first came were recruited by the major railroads to work on the construction and maintenance of their lines, and many came first as temporary residents. In the early 1900s, 98 percent of the Santa Fe's track crews in some parts of the West were of Mexican origin and in many Kansas railroad centers Mexican Americans became a permanent part of the community. They came to escape poverty and while their living conditions in Kansas were often poor they were better than in Mexico, particularly during times of political revolution in that country.

Until the Second World War Mexican Americans in Kansas were generally limited in employment to the railroads, meat packing, salt mining, and sugar beet production. Since the early 1940s, however, the descendants of the original families have moved into other occupations and have become involved in independent farming and in all business and professional walks of life. The railroad employee had not disappeared, but their jobs, by the 1970s, were better, and better paid, than the ones first

In several communities Kansans of Mexican descent have kept their traditions alive. This scene is from the annual fiesta held in Garden City.

immigrants had. Often discriminated against, particularly when they first came, Mexican Americans have found some improvement in the Kansas social climate. Conditions have changed enough so that Mexican Americans have been elected to public office in Kansas communities. Like some other Kansans with foreign backgrounds the Mexican Americans have been concerned with the preservation of their customs. In several cities annual fiestas help keep traditions alive.

Early in its history Kansas had a notable family with its roots in Mexico. Miguel Otero and his sons were involved in the operation of wholesale merchandise and overland freighting companies, doing business with Kansas towns and military posts during the 1860s. One of the sons, also named Miguel, later served as governor of New Mexico.

MINOR RELIGIOUS COLONIZATION

There were other colonies founded by religious groups. Members of the Society of Friends (Quakers) were instrumental in starting Sterling and large numbers of Dunkards (German Baptists) and River Brethren moved into central Kansas and into Franklin and Norton counties. Mormons started a colony in Stafford County, which became St. John, and Catholics of Irish origin founded Atwood, Bird City, Tully, and Pomona. There was a Jewish colonization effort made at Beersheba in Hodgeman County in the 1880s, promoted by the Hebrew Union Agricultural Society and designed to help Jewish immigrants from Europe escape both anti-Semitism and the confinement of a big-city ghetto. A combination of factors, including the settlers' unfamiliarity with life on the Plains and financial hardships, led to the abandonment of Beersheba after less than four years.

NICODEMUS AND
OTHER AFRICAN-AMERICAN SETTLEMENTS

Although the heaviest immigration of African Americans to Kansas did not come until the 1870s, there were some who came during the preceding decade to join the limited numbers present since the opening of the territory. The Lawrence *Tribune* made this note on November 19, 1868:

> A party of forty-five colored people, great and small, arrived in
> North Lawrence a day or two ago, from Cass county, Michigan, and
> also another party of about the same number, from . . . Missouri.
> They came here with the intention of buying homes, and apparently
> possess ample means for the purpose. One of the Michigan party
> informed us that they all owned good farms in that state, which they

sold at forty-five dollars per acre, and are now willing to pay the same price here if necessary. . . . They appear to be intelligent and industrious and will make excellent citizens.

Before the 1870s the bulk of the African-American population was centered in the eastern Kansas towns. Opportunities were limited, and most black adults were employed as laborers or in housekeeping duties. There were some black farmers in the eastern counties and there were black soldiers serving at Kansas forts. In the 1870s an unusual colonization movement took place involving blacks from the South, inspired and assisted by Benjamin Singleton, a former slave who returned to Tennessee to aid his people.

A planned black immigration to Kansas developed from 1873 to 1878 that brought about the establishment of colonies in Cherokee, Graham, Hodgeman, and Morris counties. Then for two years, beginning in 1879, additional African Americans came to Kansas in great numbers. Many were poor and could not even provide their own food and housing. A Freedman's Relief Association was organized by Governor John P. St. John, which was aimed at helping them in their new home. More settlements were started in Wabaunsee, Chautauqua, and Coffey counties. This was the "Negro Exodus" and the people were known as "Exodusters." The term has been applied by some to the entire black emigration movement but that is not correct. The term should be used historically only in relation to the blacks who came from the Deep South in 1879 and 1880.

The largest and perhaps the most interesting community to result from the African American migration was Nicodemus in Graham County. In 1877, W. R. Hill, the founder of Hill City, enlisted the aid of Negroes in Topeka and together they encouraged blacks to settle in Graham County. A group of freedmen in Scott County, Kentucky, were interested, for they believed that their opportunities for a self-sufficient life might be better outside the South. They named their town for a legendary slave who was supposed to have purchased his freedom in America.

Their first years in Kansas were times of poverty and bad weather. Few of the new farmers had wagons and there were only three horses in the colony. Stores from which they could buy supplies were miles away and in any case many of them had no money to buy groceries. As a result of hardship some of the first settlers left for the eastern part of the state or returned to the South. The first spring, some of the fields were broken and cultivated with hoes, and some

Benjamin Singleton

One of the settlements produced by Singleton's work was Dunlap, Morris County. Black families were coming to the area until the 1890s. This family farmed near Dunlap.

of the first harvesting was done by hand. Most of the men also found jobs in other towns to help support their families.

Signs of progress became apparent after a while. Methodist and Baptist churches were started and in 1879 a school district was organized, the first in Graham County. The dugouts and sod houses were replaced by frame and stone houses. Businesses opened, including a bank, a hotel, and two newspapers. In 1880 there were nearly five hundred black residents of Graham County, many of them living within the town limits of Nicodemus. Crops continued to be good, as was business, and Nicodemus was caught up in the booming times of the 1880s. Hopes were high that either the Missouri Pacific or the Union Pacific would build to Nicodemus, but neither did, so the little community was at a decided disadvantage. Although some of the merchants moved away, the town's decline was not rapid at first. In the twentieth century the population dwindled and even the post office, opened in 1878, was discontinued in 1953.

One of the biggest events in the western half of the state was the annual Emancipation Day celebration at Nicodemus on August 1. Politicians seeking office were always on hand to make speeches and there were carnivals, baseball games, music, and food in great quantities. Blacks and whites joined together to have a good time and to commemorate the end of slavery in both the British Empire and the United States. An annual celebration is still held there, and politicians still appear along with former residents who trace their roots to the pioneer settlement.

Even though Nicodemus was never large it produced its share of well-known Kansans. The clerk of Graham County, E. P. McCabe, became state auditor of Kansas, the first representative of his race to be elected to state office in a northern state. The Sayers family attained prominence as teachers and lawyers and Gale Sayers, famed Kansas University and Chicago Bears football player, is a product of one branch of that Nicodemus family. Lorenzo Fuller, whose family was originally from Graham County, gained prominence as a musical performer and composer, and Veryl Switzer, athlete and educator, can claim Nicodemus origins. Whatever their fields of endeavor, members of Nicodemus families have made significant contributions to the state of Kansas through the years.

Today little remains of the original community although a few families still live on the townsite, which has been designated a National Historic Site. However, the history of Nicodemus is a study in pioneer courage. A Kansas writer of the 1880s said that Nicodemus might fade from the scene "but to those who know the truth of history, the name will always recall the bravest attempt ever made by people of any color to establish homes in the high plains of Western Kansas."

A similar pioneering effort took place at Morton City, near Jetmore in Hodgeman County. Some of those black settlers were also from Kentucky and 107 of them arrived in the spring of 1878. Their town did not live as long as Nicodemus. They did, however, take up individual homesteads and they were joined by additional immigrants, some of whom came from Ohio. Eventually, many of the settlers and their families scattered to various western Kansas communities—Dodge City, Garden City, Kinsley, Larned, and Ness City. Members of succeeding generations moved farther away but some of the names from the original Morton City colony, the Bradshaws for example, may still be found on the High Plains. Also, there were a number of skilled workmen among the Hodgeman County blacks who built buildings that still stand in Jetmore.

The state's effort to provide separate higher education for African Americans led to the establishment of Western University in 1892 at Quindaro in Wyandotte County. It existed until the 1940s. The Kansas Industrial and Educational Institute, Topeka, began as a private school for blacks in 1895 but was taken over by the state in 1917 and renamed the Kansas Vocational Institute. Later it became Kansas Technical Institute (a junior college) and was closed in 1955 as a result of the *Brown* v. *Board of Education* decision.

It is obvious that the Kansas population has varied backgrounds and all of those people who had beginnings other than native, white America have made valuable contributions to the state's development and culture. A twentieth-century historian said: "Each of these immigrant groups has contributed something to the building of Kansas as it is. Their language, their customs, and their folkways have been woven into the pattern of Kansas culture, and the state is richer because they have come into it."

Suggestions for Reading

Robert G. Athearn, *In Search of Canaan, Black Migration to Kansas, 1879–1880* (1978); Jennie Chinn, *Images of Strawberry Hill* (1985); Thomas C. Cox, *Blacks in Topeka, 1865–1915* (1982); James C. Juhnke, *A People of Two Kingdoms: The Political Acculturation of the Kansas Mennonites* (1975); Emory Lindquist, *Smoky Valley People* (1953); Cynthia Mines, *Riding the Rails to Kansas: The Mexican Immigrants* (1980); Nell I. Painter, *Exodusters* (1977); Gustav E. Reimer and G. R. Gaeddert, *Exiled by the Czar: Cornelius Jansen and the Great Mennonite Migration, 1874* (1956); Ruth Sorenson, *Beyond the Prairie Wind: History, Folklore, and Traditions from Denmark, Kansas* (1996); Abe J. Unruh, *The Helpless Poles* (1973); Randall B. Woods, *A Black Odyssey: John Lewis Waller and the Promise of American Life, 1878–1900* (1981).

There are not many book-length studies of the ethnic groups and their contributions to Kansas but several articles in the publications of the State Historical Society offer good information. Included in the *Kansas Historical Collections* are: Thomas P. Christensen, "The Danish Settlements in Kansas," vol. 17; William J. Chapman, "The Wakefield Colony," vol. 10; Francis S. Laing, "German-Russian Settlements in Ellis County, Kansas," vol. 11; J. C. Ruppenthal, "The German Element in Central Kansas," vol. 13; and Francis J. Swehla, "Bohemians in Central Kansas," vol. 13.

The following will be found in the *Kansas Historical Quarterly*: Fred R. Belk, "The Final Refuge: Kansas and Nebraska Migration of Mennonites From Central Asia After 1884" (Autumn, 1974); Carolyn B. Berneking, "The Welsh Settlers of Emporia: A Cultural History" (Autumn, 1971); Phillips G. Davies, editor, "Welsh Settlements in Kansas" (Winter, 1977); Nyle H. Miller, editor, "An English Runnymede in Kansas" (Spring and Summer, 1975); Alberta Pantle, "Settlement of the Krimmer Mennonite Brethren at Gnadenau, Marion County" (February, 1945), and "History of the French-Speaking Settlement in the Cottonwood Valley"(February, 1951); William E. Powell, "European Settlement in the Cherokee-Crawford Coal Field in Southeastern Kansas" (Summer, 1975); A. James Rudin, "Beersheba, Kansas: 'God's Pure Air on Government Land'" (Autumn, 1968); Norman E. Saul, "The Migration of the Russian-Germans to Kansas" (Spring, 1974); Glen Schwendemann, "Nicodemus: Negro Haven on the Solomon" (Spring, 1968); Randall B. Woods, "After the Exodus: John Lewis Waller and the Black Elite, 1878–1900" (Summer, 1977).

Kansas History contains the following: Henry J. Avila, "Immigration and Integration: The Mexican American Community in Garden City, Kansas, 1900–1950" (Spring, 1997); Brian P. Birch, "Victoria Vanquished: The Scottish Press and the Failure of George Grant's Colony" (Autumn, 1986); Marilyn D. Brady, "Kansas Federation of Colored Women's Clubs, 1900–1930" (Spring, 1986); Nupur Chandari, "'We All Seem Like Brothers and Sisters': The African-American Community in Manhattan, Kansas, 1865–1940" (Winter, 1991–1992); Donald M. Douglas, "Forgotten Zions: The Jewish Agricultural Colonies in Kansas in the 1880s" (Summer, 1993); Gary R. Entz, "Image and Reality on the Kansas Prairie: 'Pap' Singleton's Cherokee County Colony" (Summer, 1996); Daniel C. Fitzgerald, "'We Are All in This Together'—Immigrants in the Oil and Mining Towns of Southern Kansas, 1890–1920" (Spring, 1987); James L. Forsythe, "George Grant of Victoria: Man and Myth" (Autumn, 1986); James L. Forsythe, "The English Colony at Victoria, Another View" (Autumn, 1989); Kenneth M. Hamilton, "The Origins and Early Promotion of Nicodemus: A Pre-Exodus All Black Town" (Winter, 1982); David A. Haury, "German-Russian Immigrants to Kansas and American Politics" (Winter, 1980); C. Robert Haywood, "The Hodgeman County Colony" (Winter, 1989–1990); Sara J. Keckeisen, "Cottonwood Ranch: John Fenton Pratt and the English Ranching Experience in Sheridan County, Kansas" (Spring, 1991); Linda J. Pohley, "Cultures in Harmony: Welsh Choral Music in Nineteenth Century Kansas" (Autumn, 1994); Don W. Rowlinson, "An English Settlement in Sheridan County, Kansas: The Cottonwood Ranch" (Autumn, 1989); Eleanor L. Turk, "Selling the Heartland: Agents, Agencies, Press, and Policies Promoting German Emigration to Kansas in the Nineteenth Century" (Autumn, 1989); and Eleanor L. Turk, "The Germans of Atchison, 1854–1859" (Autumn, 1979).

Prohibition to Populism, 1870–1900

Much of the political controversy in the thirty years before the beginning of a new century centered around prohibition. Arguments about the sale of liquor were not new in the 1870s. In the territorial period (1854–1861) liquor sales were attacked by temperance forces, particularly women, and at times angry citizens marched on saloons. In January 1857, a group of Lawrence women decided to take matters into their own hands and proceeded to destroy all the liquor they could:

> On Saturday . . . at half past ten in the forenoon, about forty of the ladies of Lawrence commenced a tour of inspection to the reputed groggeries. The first place visited was Mr. Rowley's saloon. . . . A general demolition of demijohns and bottles ensued, and all liquor found was destroyed. The party then proceeded to Mr. Fry's bakery; a barrel of ale was found here and was spilt on the ground. At this stage of the proceedings Mr. Fry appeared on the street, flourishing a brace of revolvers, threatening to shoot everybody that had been engaged in the destruction of his property. Several other establishments were visited in rapid succession by the ladies, and small quantities of liquor found in them were destroyed.

A number of Kansas communities were "dry" from the time of their founding, but there was no statewide law against liquor sales in the 1850s and the 1860s. The Kansas State Temperance Society first met in 1861 and the Independent Order of Good Templars, a national temperance group, was organized in Kansas shortly thereafter. A Prohibition party, formed in 1876, nominated a candidate for governor but he got only 393 votes out of 121,000. Other temperance groups came into being in the 1870s, including the Women's Christian Temperance Union, commonly referred to as the WCTU.

Several meetings were held under the sponsorship of these organizations, and, in September 1878, a huge gathering took place in Bismarck Grove, just outside Lawrence. One of the principal speakers was the Republican nominee for governor, John P. St. John of Olathe. Although his party had not taken a firm stand for prohibition, St. John was outspoken in its favor. He called for a vote of the people:

> The saloon keeper is not at fault, nor the hard drinker altogether. It lays with us temperance men and women. We have not nerve enough. We should vote it out. I have no quarrel with a man who is honest in his convictions, but I believe no man in Kansas sells liquor because he prefers to. We have a very absurd statute that a man who sells liquor without a license is the greatest of sinners while a man who sells with a license is pure. The traffic is either right or wrong. If it is right there should nothing be said about it, if it is wrong all the laws in the land cannot make it right.

By the time the meetings adjourned at Bismarck Grove thousands of Kansans were ready to back St. John for governor and to work for prohibition. In that same speech St. John called on the women of Kansas to help the cause of prohibition and also announced that he was in favor of women having the right to vote, which was a new attitude for major gubernatorial candidates in Kansas.

PROHIBITION AND PARTY POLITICS

St. John and the Republicans won easily in 1878, and the new governor took his views on liquor to the legislature. In his January 1879 message to both houses he said:

> The money spent annually for intoxicating liquors would defray the entire expenses of the state government, including the care and maintenance of all its charitable institutions, agricultural college, normal school, state university and penitentiary. . . . If it could be fully accomplished, I am clearly of the opinion that no greater

blessing could be conferred by you upon the people of this state than to absolutely and forever prohibit the manufacture, importation and sale of intoxicating liquors as a beverage.

The legislature of 1879 put the question on the 1880 general election ballot, though not without some difficulty. In the senate there were no opposing votes but when the question came up in the house there was argument. Although Governor St. John and his followers worked hard to convince the representatives that the prohibition question should go to the voters, a two-thirds majority did not develop on the first house roll call. When the next vote was taken the measure still lacked one "yes." Then the wife of George Greever, representative from Wyandotte County, approached her husband and pleaded with him to change his vote. She convinced him and the question went to the people. The amendment passed by approximately eight thousand votes and Kansas became the first state in the Union to have constitutional prohibition.

The legislature of 1881 passed the laws necessary for the regulation of prohibition, but those laws were difficult to enforce. The whiskey-selling saloon was no longer legal but beer was still available and until 1909 liquor could be sold by drugstores for medicinal purposes. Newspapers outside Kansas commented about the many things that liquor seemed to cure—cholera, cancer, tuberculosis, the common cold, rheumatism, and indigestion. There were also people selling liquor illegally since there were simply not enough officers to make prohibition effective.

The Republican party was strongly for prohibition in 1882 while the Democrats supported temperance but said that the liquor law and its enforcement were bad and that the question should be resubmitted to a vote of the people in 1884. It did not get on the ballot. John P. St. John had a final part to play in the prohibition story of the 1880s. He did not think that the Republican party took a strong enough stand on prohibition so he ran for president on the national Prohibition party ticket in 1884.

The 1884 election was notable because of the campaign tac-

Kansas supporters of prohibition gather at Bismark Grove near Lawrence, 1878.

tics used by both parties and the phrases that were coined. Grover Cleve-land, the Democrat, was accused of fathering an illegitimate child, which led to the verse, "Ma, Ma, Where's My Pa? Gone to the White House, Ha, Ha, Ha." James G. Blaine, the Republican, was referred to as "the conti-nental liar from the state of Maine." He got into trouble when his party called the Democrats the party of "Rum, Romanism, and Rebellion" in reference to prohibition, Catholicism, and the Confederacy. In the midst of this was St. John the Prohibitionist. He drew enough votes away from Blaine so that Cleveland won and became the first Democratic president in more than twenty years.

Except for two years in the 1880s, the Republicans owned the governor's office from 1870 until 1893. James M. Harvey, who served two terms ending in 1873, went into office with the party in harmony but left it during Republican factional discord. No major problems arose in state government during his terms and one of the legislative achievements of his administration was the creation of the State Board of Agriculture. Thomas A. Osborn found administrative life far more difficult between 1873 and 1877 for the state suffered through the 1873 depression, a drought period, governmental scandals, and the grasshopper plague of 1874. How-ever, Governor Osborn did not lose either personal or party prestige. The legislature in that period created the institution that became the Topeka State Hospital and also established its membership at 125 representatives and forty senators. Osborn later served the United States as minister to Chile and Brazil.

George T. Anthony lasted only one term as governor, primarily be-cause of a strike against the Santa Fe Railroad in April 1878. Anthony sent troops to Emporia, against the wishes of local officials, and, after an Emporian was shot accidentally, public opinion was against the governor. The two terms of John P. St. John were notable for reasons other than his crusade against the liquor trade. The governor's chief contribution came through the Freedman's Relief Association. He wholeheartedly supported the organization that assisted poverty-stricken black settlers in Kansas. In 1882 St. John announced his third-term candidacy for the governorship. The break with the two-term tradition and his support of woman suffrage led to his defeat and for the first time Kansas had a Democratic governor.

George W. Glick, a prominent and respected Atchison lawyer and farmer who was interested in experimental agriculture had run for gover-nor on the Democratic ticket in 1868. Glick was antiprohibition and some Republicans charged him with being in the hands of the liquor interests and with pardoning "miserable dramsellers," but there is no evidence that he made any illegal arrangements.

He was concerned with railway regulation, particularly as it pertained to agriculture. His program, adopted by the legislature, set a fair maximum freight rate for coal, wheat, corn, and cattle, along with other regulatory laws. As a cattleman Glick was interested in the appointment of a state veterinarian and a livestock sanitary commission. The legislature of 1883 rejected that idea, principally because Senator Kelley from Neosho Falls, a cattleman, objected. The senator's theory was that the pure Kansas atmosphere would protect cattle against disease.

Within a year the state was faced with an epidemic of hoof and mouth disease, and it hit the "pure atmosphere" of Woodson County. Kelley called on Glick for help and on March 11 he attended a meeting at Neosho Falls where a neighbor of Kelley's made the mistake of asking the governor what they should do. Glick is supposed to have replied, "Senator Kelley, in his superior wisdom, defeated a bill which would have helped you at this time. Ask *him* what to do." A special session of the legislature met that month and passed a bill providing for a state veterinarian and a livestock sanitary commission. Glick also worked for nonpartisan employment in state institutions and he recommended a civil service law, but he had too much opposition in the legislature. He was easily renominated by the Democrats in 1884 but the Republicans were again at peace with each other, and he lost to a fellow Atchisonian, John A. Martin.

Martin was an admired newspaperman and a Civil War hero who had played an important part in Republican politics since the Wyandotte constitutional convention, where he served as secretary. During his first term, state and local boards of health were established, the state assumed additional responsibility for orphans and for mentally retarded children, and examining boards for the licensing of dentists and pharmacists were created. In 1886 the Missouri Pacific Railroad was hit by a strike and Governor Martin helped negotiate a satisfactory settlement between management and labor.

As the 1886 election approached, some of Martin's political enemies accused him of being against prohibition even though he stated publicly that he was for it. Apparently his thinking on the subject had changed over the years, and he assured the Republican party that he supported its prohibition stand. The controversy did not have much effect on his nomination or election because he won a second term easily. Before he left office women were given the right to vote for city and school officials and although the state was in an economic depression when he stepped down Martin was given credit for a progressive administration.

The Republicans held the governor's office for two additional terms under Lyman Humphrey of Independence, who had the backing of Cyrus Leland, the powerful national committeeman from Kansas. The Democrats were divided and a new group, the Union Labor Party, was competing for votes. Humphrey had no trouble winning his two terms. However, conservative Republicans and Democrats were about to face an entirely new situation as unhappy farmers and their leaders began to engage actively in politics.

SCANDAL IN STATE GOVERNMENT

Certain periods in American political history are marked by scandal and corruption, and the 1870s was one of those periods. The administration of President Grant was notorious for its political deals and misuse of funds at the national level but similar questionable activities were going on in state governments too. Kansas was no exception, and three state officials and two United States senators were involved in scandals that led to their downfall.

In 1872 the state auditor, Alois Thoman, received funds taken from money appropriated by the federal government to compensate Kansans for losses suffered during the Price Raid of 1864. He also registered bonds for three towns in Cherokee County that did not exist and put the state money in his own pocket. Two years later, the state treasurer, Josiah Hayes, was involved in several different illegal actions involving state money, and he resigned to avoid conviction under impeachment charges. The treasurer's office had trouble again in 1876 when Samuel Lappin was charged with forgery, counterfeiting, and embezzlement over the handling of school bonds from four counties.

Lappin sneaked out of Topeka and hid in Chicago for a time before he was arrested and brought back. He escaped from the Topeka jail and made his way to South America where he lived for four years. In 1884 he was arrested in Tacoma, Washington, and returned to jail in Topeka. Finally the case was dismissed because witnesses had died and the money had been recovered.

Questions were raised about the election of Alexander Caldwell to the U.S. Senate in 1871. At that time senators were elected by the state legislature, not in a general election, and it was thought that Caldwell reached the Senate because he paid the right people. Caldwell defended himself, saying:

> My character has been unjustly, cruelly, outrageously assailed. The foulest scandals of the street have been gathered up and scattered broadcast over the country. I simply desire to say to the Senate now that I shrink from no scrutiny. Sir, I hurl back these charges with scorn and indignation, and I have nothing but contempt for the mean, mercenary, and despicable motives which prompted them. No living man can confront me and say that I have ever done aught to warrant these assaults.

Senator Caldwell's words were impressive but both the state legislature and Congress felt that he was illegally elected. He resigned in March 1873 to avoid being expelled and was replaced by temporary appointments until Preston Plumb of Emporia entered the Senate where he served from 1877 until his death in 1891.

Another senator who had problems in the 1870s was Samuel C. Pomeroy, also accused of vote buying. His election in 1867 had been questioned by some of his political enemies but no proof was given that he was improperly elected. In 1873, the other members of the Kansas delegation in Congress were not in favor of the Pomeroy faction of the Republican party and there was pressure exerted to keep him out of the Senate. However, it seemed he still had enough influence with the legislature to insure his reelection.

A political bombshell was exploded when one of the legislators, A. M. York, charged that Pomeroy had offered him $8,000 for his vote. Although Pomeroy admitted giving the legislator the money he denied that it was a bribe but was intended for business investment. Pomeroy lost his support in the legislature because of the bribery charge and was replaced in the Senate by John J. Ingalls. The investigation of the Pomeroy case involved both the legislature and Congress, as had the Caldwell case. The Kansas investigators said Pomeroy was guilty, but the three Republican members of the Senate committee stated that they were not convinced of Pomeroy's guilt. However, it made little difference because Ingalls had been elected and the Senate committee report did not come out until one day before Pomeroy was to end his term. The scandal finished Pomeroy in politics but he was immortalized by Mark Twain in a novel entitled *The Gilded Age*. Twain's Senator Dilworthy, a fictional Pomeroy, illustrates corruption in Congress during the Reconstruction period.

THE RISE OF POPULISM

The People's party—the Populists—did not suddenly burst on the American political scene. Rather, it was the end result of an extended period that saw the beginning of several reform movements, some of which took the form of political parties. There were the Liberal Republicans of the 1870s, the Independent Reform, Greenback, and Union Labor parties, all of which maintained similar stands on what was wrong with the American economy and the people who controlled it.

To refer to Twain's novel again, America was living in a "Gilded Age" during the 1870s, 1880s, and 1890s. It was a period when much of the development of American society was affected by the growth of industrial capitalism and the opportunities given to that growth. After 1872 there was no income tax, no inheritance tax, and no excess profits tax on corporations. Individuals built tremendous private fortunes and the businesses they controlled dominated both society and politics. It was a period when the theory of social Darwinism was popular. Darwin's biological and evolutionary thesis about the survival of the fittest was applied to men and business. Men were born with unequal abilities, and the ones who worked the hardest and made the most money would dominate. Any attempts by government to equalize Americans were against the laws of nature. The rich got richer and the poor got poorer but no particular sympathy was given to those who did not make money.

In this atmosphere American farmers were apt to be victimized by big business (particularly by the railroads), by the interest they had to pay on their mortgages and other loans, and by the nation's high protective tariff that made the manufactured goods bought higher in proportion to the prices received for farm products. They complained, rightfully so, that railroad rates were too high and that too much money was controlled by too few people. They did not always understand some of the other things they complained about, such as the tariff, but many of the complaints were legitimate. They talked about cooperative efforts in buying and selling, though much of the time these cooperatives did not work to their satisfaction. They joined a variety of organizations, including the Grange and the Farmers' Alliance and eventually rebelled against both the Republican and Democratic parties.

In 1890 the Farmers' Alliance became the People's party. Populism has always been related to unhappy farmers and much of its voting strength came from rural America. However, its leadership was mostly from other occupations, particularly lawyers and editors. Its most forceful spokesmen and the people it elected to office were not farmers, unless they had gone into agriculture after other careers. There were doctors, small businessmen, and several women who led the fight for political, social, and economic reform. In fact, many of the rural members of the party had little interest in reform except as it affected their own mortgages. By 1890 more than 60 percent of the taxable acres in Kansas were mortgaged, which meant that most farms of 160 acres were under heavy indebtedness.

The Republican party, all-powerful in Kansas, feared little from the new political movements until 1890 when the House of Representatives fell to the control of the Populists, and non-Republicans won five out of the seven congressional seats. Among those elected to Congress was Jeremiah Simpson of Medicine Lodge, known as "Sockless Jerry" because of a speech in which he referred to his Republican opponent as a prince who wore silk stockings while he, Simpson, had none. Simpson had a varied career before he became a rancher in Kansas and he was anything but sockless, gaining a reputation as one of the best-dressed members of Congress.

A year later there was enough Populist strength in the legislature to elect William Peffer to the United States Senate and send John J. Ingalls, the Republican, home to Kansas. Ingalls had served his state admirably in the Senate and he was a brilliant speaker but he reflected the kind of Republicanism that the Populists despised. Peffer represented the best in Populist leadership. He had farmed, taught school, practiced law, and edited newspapers in Fredonia, Coffeyville, and Topeka. He had worked for reform for several years, hoping that it would come through the two regularly organized political parties. When he no longer believed that either the Republicans or Democrats could bring the changes he thought necessary he became a Populist. He was a colorful character with an extremely long beard, which someone suggested could be used as a Christmas tree.

Another Kansan went to Washington during this period. In 1889 David J. Brewer of Leavenworth was appointed to the United States Supreme Court where he served with distinction. He was no Populist, and the court at the time was very conservative, but Brewer was progressive in many of his views toward both social and political issues.

While Kansas was the heartland of Populism, the People's party gained strength in several states and in 1892 entered the national political arena with presidential and vice-presidential candidates. In 1892, at the national convention in Omaha, the aims of Populism were stated in its platform:

> The conditions which surround us best justify our cooperation; we meet in the midst of a nation brought to the verge of moral, political, and material ruin. Corruption dominates the ballot box, the legislature, the congress, and touches even the ermine of the bench. . . . The urban workmen are denied the right of organization for self-protection. . . . The fruits of the toil of millions are boldly stolen to build up colossal fortunes for a few. . . . From the same prolific womb of government injustices we breed the two great classes of tramps and millionaires. . . .

Populist "Sockless" Jerry Simpson at a debate with Republican Chester Long at Harper, 1892.

The national power to create money is appropriated to enrich bondholders; a vast public debt, payable in legal tender currency, has been funded into gold-bearing bonds, thereby adding millions to the burdens of the people. Silver, which has been accepted as coin since the dawn of history, has been demonetized to add to the purchasing power of gold by decreasing the value of all kinds of property. . . .

We believe that the powers of government . . . should be expanded (as in the case of the postal service) as rapidly and as far as the good sense of an intelligent people and the teachings of experience shall justify, to the end that oppression, injustice, and poverty shall eventually cease in the land. . . .

We believe that the time has come when the railroad corporations will either own the people or the people must own the railroads. Transportation being a means of exchange and a public necessity, the government should own and operate the railroads in the interest of the people.

We demand a national currency, safe, sound, and flexible, issued by the general government only. . . . We demand free and unlimited coinage of silver and gold at the present legal ratio of sixteen to one. . . . *

We demand a graduated income tax. . . .

The land, including all the natural sources of wealth, is the heritage of the people, and should not be monopolized for speculative purposes.

Completely endorsing this platform, the Kansas Populists met on June 5, 1892, and nominated Lorenzo D. Lewelling of Wichita for governor, along with a full slate of candidates. The Populists gained a great advantage when the Democratic state convention decided to endorse all the Populist candidates instead of nominating their own. Obviously, the Republicans were in trouble at election time in 1892.

THE POPULISTS AT WAR
WITH THE REPUBLICANS

The entire Populist ticket was swept into office, and the party also won four congressional seats and controlled the state senate. In the House of Representatives it was a different story, although at first it appeared there

---

*The phrase "sixteen to one" referred to the theory that sixteen parts of silver should be minted into coins by the government for every one part of gold minted.

would be a Populist majority. Governor Lewelling's inaugural address offered a ringing challenge to Kansans to improve their government:

> The problem of today is how to make the State subservient to the individual rather than to become his master. Government is a voluntary union for the common good. It guarantees to the individual life, liberty, and the pursuit of happiness. If the Government fails of these things, it fails in its mission. It ceases to be of advantage to the citizen; he is absolved from his allegiance, and is no longer held by the civil compact.

The Republicans claimed sixty-four seats in the House of Representatives but the Populists charged that there had been illegal elections, a charge that quite possibly was true but one that was difficult to prove. Cooler heads in both parties advised a peaceful state government but as is generally the case in times of political excitement the participants were not guided by reasonable thinking. The floor leaders of both parties called the house to order, separate motions were made and carried, two sets of officers were elected, and two sets of messengers sent to inform the Senate and the governor that the house—or houses—were ready to do business. The situation was a farce. Both houses continued to meet in the same room, agreeing only on a division of time. The governor gave his official recognition to the Populist house, as did the majority of the Senate. The Populists unseated ten Republicans, and the Republicans retaliated by unseating four Populists. Each party published its own review of the proceedings, proving the other guilty. Finally, after the session was more than a month old, the Republican house brought matters to a head.

After a resolution was adopted stating that Ben Rich, clerk of the Populist house, had disturbed the peace of the legislature he was arrested by the sergeant-at-arms at his hotel. He was "rescued" by Populist friends, and both sides began to muster their forces. The Republicans swore in several sergeants-at-arms and the Populists appointed a number of guards to protect state property while the governor called out the militia.

The next morning members and employees of the Republican house gathered at the Copeland Hotel on Kansas Avenue and marched to the statehouse. A few guards tried to stop them but were swept aside, and the door of the house was smashed open with a sledge hammer. The militia arrived but since it was composed almost entirely of Republicans, most of the units deserted Governor Lewelling. After forty-eight hours of armed but fortunately bloodless hostilities the "war" was over. The Republican house stayed in the hall, the proceedings against the clerk were dropped, and the Populists met in another room in the capitol. Both houses proceeded with business, separately, and the question of legality of the legislature was left to the state supreme court.

During the "war" the Kansas City, Missouri, *Star* commented on February 15:

> The strained situation at Topeka suggests a new use for Kansas avenue; too wide for a street and hardly wide enough for a cornfield, it would make a fairly roomy battlefield for the close and desperate fighting in which the Republicans and Populists will doubtless indulge if they ever get at it. The contending "Houses" surging back and forth across the avenue while the blood quietly trickles down the gutters into the Kaw would be a sight to stir the blood of age and a new feature in representative government for a free and intelligent people.

The Populist house passed a railroad freight rate bill, provided for the Australian ballot,* and enacted a law long demanded by farmers, which gave debtors eighteen months in which to redeem their land after it had been sold under mortgage. The ballot and the mortgage bills became law because the Republicans passed the same measures but railroad reform died. In the supreme court the Populist lawyers argued strongly for their side but the court upheld the Republicans and only one house reconvened, with the Populists outnumbered.

Governor Lewelling was savagely criticized by the Republicans during his one term in office. J. K. Hudson of the Topeka *Daily Capital* called him both a socialist and a communist and accused him of attempting to wipe out true Americanism. However, the governor had his defenders, including the editor of the Topeka *Hurykain* who wrote on December 23, 1893:

> No man since 1860 has been set upon, abused, lied about, and villified like the governor of this state. . . .
>
> Today a meaner, more vile, wicked, and d——d lot of curs, lickspittles, and fiends, from the hypocrite in the pulpit, down to the low bum and pothouse politician . . . are traducing and trying to ruin a man no less kind, gentle, and pure in all his daily walks of life, than was the lamented martyred Lincoln. And what for. Just for the sake of the loaves and fishes of office and the money paid them by their masters. . . . Editors stab him in the back and abuse even his family. . . .

---

*An Australian ballot is what is in use today. It is printed at public expense, lists all candidates, is available at the voting place, and is marked secretly by the voter.

Political thugs, mangy curs, lousy cattle, carrion buzzards, and filthy swine from the ranks of the Republican party . . . hound him on every side. The men who spat in the face of Christ and buffeted him on his road to Calvary were saints when compared with the ragtag curs who thus hound a man for no other reason than that he is noble, honest, truthful, pure and a Populist. . . .

Gov. Lewelling will live in the memory of his countrymen when the rotten carcasses of his foes will be forgotten by all in Heaven, Earth and Hell, except the Devil alone.

Despite their success in the 1892 elections, the Populists and the Democrats decided that they would go their own ways in 1894. The Democrats nominated David Overmyer, with a platform that was against both prohibition and woman suffrage. The Populists renominated Governor Lewelling. The Republicans, realizing their mistakes of 1892, reunited their factions and nominated Edmund Morrill, a Hiawatha banker, who won easily.

During the entire time of active Populism in Kansas two women helped the cause greatly. Mary Elizabeth Lease, who is supposed to have said that farmers should raise "less corn and more hell," was a spell-binding speaker, a former Republican, and one of the few women lawyers in the

state. She was an experienced orator before she took up the Populist cause, and she impressed even her political enemies, although they found it difficult to compliment her. William Allen White, who opposed her politically, said that "she put into her oratory something which the printed copies did not reveal. They were dull enough often, but she could recite the multiplication table and set a crowd hooting or hurrahing at her will."

The other noted female Populist was Annie Diggs,wife of a Lawrence post office worker. She had been an active worker in the WCTU and wrote a Farmers' Alliance column for a Lawrence newspaper. Known as "Little Annie" to many of her co-workers she was described by a Kansas writer:

Imagine a little woman, slender, almost to fraility, barely five feet tall and weighing

Mary E. Lease.

only ninety-three pounds. Picture . . . a face on which shines the light of zealous endeavor and enthusiastic championship of a beloved cause; rather thin lips, an intellectual forehead from which the hair . . . is brushed back pompadour like; twinkling eyes which alternately squint almost shut, then open wide as she expounds her favorite doctrines of socialism; a trifle nervous, a soft voice and an occasional musical little laugh as she talks. . . .

Mrs. Diggs was not as powerful a speaker as Mrs. Lease but she was intellectually talented and convinced people of the value of Populism. Both women achieved national reputations and led other women into the political fight. Leadership for the party also came from Ben Clover of Winfield; W. F. Rightmire, G. C. Clemens, and Dr. Stephen McLallin of Topeka; John W. Breidenthal of Labette County; W. F. "Ironjaw" Brown of Kingman; and Frank Doster of Marion. There were many others, convinced of the justice of Populism, who labored long and hard on both the local and state level but they did so less colorfully.

As the 1896 election approached the Republicans were reasonably confident that they could reelect Governor Morrill while the Populists found themselves once again bedfellows of the Democrats since both parties were endorsing the cause of "free silver." The Democrats had a new national leader, William Jennings Bryan, who thrilled audiences with his speeches attacking the Republicans and gold. There were a number of Populists who did not really want to align themselves with the Democrats but it was their only hope if they wished to regain the governor's office. They finally chose John W. Leedy as their gubernatorial candidate, although the Coffey County farmer was not as strong a leader as some oth-

Dickinson County Populists on their way to a political rally in the 1890s. The populist program of political and social reform attracted many Kansans, particularly farmers.

ers, especially Frank Doster, who was nominated for chief justice of the state supreme court and later elected. Leedy was also elected.

THE FALL OF POPULISM

On August 15, less than two weeks after the Populists named their slate of candidates and reached agreement with the Democrats, William Allen White of the Emporia *Gazette* wrote an editorial that received national attention, "What's the Matter with Kansas?" White, then the staunchest of Republicans, was tired of the Populists and he wrote:

> Go East and you hear them laugh at Kansas, go West and they sneer at her, go South and they "cuss" her, go North and they have forgotten her. Go into any crowd of intelligent people gathered anywhere on the globe, and you will find the Kansas man on the defensive. . . . Kansas just naturally isn't in it. She has traded places with Arkansas and Timbuctoo.
>
> What's the matter with Kansas?
>
> We all know; yet here we are at it again. . . . We have another shabby, wild-eyed, rattle-brained fanatic who has said openly in a dozen speeches that "the rights of the user are paramount to the rights of the owner"; we are running him for Chief Justice, so that the capital will come tumbling over itself to get into the state. We have raked the old ashheap of failure in the state and found an old human hoop-skirt who has failed as a business man, who has failed as an editor, who has failed as a preacher, and we are going to run him for congressman. . . . Then we have discovered a kid without a law practice and have decided to run him for attorney general. Then for fear some hint that the state had become respectable might percolate through the civilized portion of the Nation, we have decided to send three or four harpies out lecturing, telling the people that Kansas is raising Hell and letting the corn go to weeds. . . .
>
> We don't need population, we don't need wealth, we don't need cities on the fertile prairies, you bet we don't! What we are after is the money power. Because we have become poorer and ornrier and meaner than a spavined distempered mule, we, the people of Kansas, propose to kick; we don't care to build up, we wish to tear down. . . .

White wrote later that he was angry because a group of Populists had annoyed him on the streets of Emporia and as a result he published the editorial. White also publicly apologized for many of the things he had said, and he later became an admirer of Frank Doster, whom he had first described as the "wild-eyed, rattle-brained fanatic." As a Progressive Republican in the early years of the twentieth century White would agree with much for which Populism had stood.

The Populist party, like political organizations that preceded and followed it, fell victim to its own disagreements. Populists disagreed on candidates for office and on principles. Some of them supported the course of the United States in the Spanish-American War but many of them denounced it as "imperialism" and unnecessary interference in world affairs. Some were more socialistic than others and wanted the state and federal governments to play a greater part in the operation of public utilities and services. There were violent breaks between leaders, one of the most notable being a well-publicized argument between Mrs. Lease and Governor Lewelling in which each accused the other of several kinds of wrongdoing. Even if all had been harmony among Populists the third party could not have survived because it did not have enough members.

Populism served its purpose, however. It brought to the front many of the reform ideas that others had talked about, and many of those ideas would be translated into laws before the first decade of the twentieth century was ended. Through legislation, which passed with the help of concerned members of both the Republican and Democratic parties, Populists made the life of the laboring man easier and safer. Populists also helped the farmer by regulating stockyards and providing for the inspection, grading, weighing, and handling of grain. They created the bank commissioner's office, which had regulatory powers, and they adopted the Australian ballot. Perhaps their greatest contribution was getting people to think about some of the things that needed changing, such as further regulation for big business and giving women the right to vote.

Populists were accused of treason and anarchy, and there were probably some of their opponents who really did believe they would overthrow the established government. Some of their loudest critics, such as William Allen White, would be embracing many of the same causes within a few years. On the national scene the Populist congressmen were generally described, incorrectly, as ragged farmers from the West, but they made other politicians sit up and take notice. Annie Diggs wrote:

> Had it not been for the Populist in the house and senate, ready to interject questions, ready to puncture pompous bubbles, ready to tersely and clearly state his common-sense solution of national problems—had it not been for four years of persistent, patient effort of this sort, the country would be in far darker, denser ignorance than it now is.

Some of the Populists returned to the Democratic and Republican parties in the early 1900s while others became involved in socialistic movements. Populism as a third party died, but its democratic cause did not, and American government was the better for it.

When Leedy finished his one term as governor in January 1899, a Republican moved into the office. William Stanley of Wichita began his two-term administration and Kansas politics were back to normal, with Republican President McKinley carrying the state in 1900. Things would get lively again when Progressivism began to move.

During the period of ferment in which women became recognized as active campaigners for Populism there were other women working on the local level to participate in government. Susanna Madora Salter was elected mayor of Argonia in 1887, the first Kansas woman to hold such an office. Two years later women were elected mayor in Rossville, Baldwin, and Cottonwood Falls, and in 1891 Kiowa followed suit. In Oskaloosa the entire city government was made up of women for a time during the same era. Women still could not vote in state and national elections, but they could get themselves elected at the municipal level if they worked at it.

As the century closed and a new one began the liquor question again made headlines as Carry Nation took the warpath in the spring of 1900 and made the first of her saloon smash-

Left: Susannah Madora Salter. Below: Women were elected to the mayor's office and all five council seats in Oskaloosa in 1888.

ing raids, attacking three "joints" in Kiowa. Six months later her victim was the bar of Wichita's Hotel Carey and for that she went to jail. Kansas and the whole country would hear and see more of Mrs. Nation before very long. "Demon Rum" was once again in trouble in Kansas.

KANSAS BUILDS ITS CAPITOL

Although the east wing of the statehouse in Topeka was occupied in December 1869, it was not completed until 1873. In 1879 the lawmakers provided for construction of the west wing. Governor St. John, the first of the state's chief executives to be publicly inaugurated on the capitol steps, responded to the 1879 legislative act by appointing a new board of statehouse commissioners who chose an architect. The contract called for a new wing, slightly larger than the east wing, to be built of limestone from Cottonwood Falls. Work began almost immediately, and by fall the construction was attracting attention. A reporter commented that "the south side of the State House yard is filled with stone, and the stone cutters' hammers make a merry music which may be heard some distance off."

The house of representatives met in its new hall in the west wing in January 1881, although the walls were unplastered and there was a temporary wooden floor. The east and west wings were connected by a covered

The Kansas capitol, 1888. The north and south wings were still under construction and the dome was beginning to take shape.

walkway sometimes referred to as the "cave of the winds." Construction got underway on the central portion in 1884 and as the year ended the foundation was complete. At the same time the east wing was remodeled to provide a new senate chamber. The chamber, described as "the finest representative hall in the United States," cost $300,000 and there were Kansans who complained the cost was too high:

> The interior of the chamber is finished in the style of the French Renaissance, the walls being encased in marble and Mexican onyx to the height of twelve feet on all sides, above which the walls and ceiling are finished in stucco work. . . .
>
> The gas pipes are so arranged that all of the lights are controlled from the gas stand in the sergeant-at-arms' room, and when the wires are in place all will be lighted from that point, it being the intention to wire the building so that the gas may be lighted by electricity; also to wire it so that the incandescent light can be put in.

By late summer, 1886, approximately one-half of the outside walls of the main building were up, and work began on the rotunda. By the fall of 1888 the interior walls and piers of the dome were at a level with the attic story and the fourth-floor beams were in position. In May 1889, a contract was let for roofing the main building, and the dome and the work seemed to be running smoothly. Then, a short time later, it was announced that the main arch at the north entrance was cracking because of the immense weight on it. This sounded like disaster, but the damage was repaired.

Life within the statehouse had been disrupted during the 1887 legislative session by a recently employed house doorkeeper, Boston Corbett. Corbett, a former Union soldier, had killed John Wilkes Booth, Lincoln's assassin, and since 1878 he had lived a solitary life on a homestead near Concordia. Corbett was eccentric, and he guarded his home with pistol and rifle. While performing his doorkeeper duties he was also armed but apparently nobody thought much about it until February 15, when he pulled a pistol and unofficially adjourned the house. He was disarmed by local police, declared insane, and committed to the State Insane Asylum (Topeka State Hospital). On May 26, 1888, he escaped on a stolen horse and, after a brief pause at Neodesha, disappeared.

The capitol was nearly complete in 1890 except for the final decorative touches. Plans called for a fountain in the first floor rotunda, sculptures were to go above the columns north and south, and a large statue of Ceres, the Roman goddess of agricultural fertility, was to be put on top of the dome. However, Ceres created considerable controversy, and she never occupied her pedestal. There were Kansans who said her morals were questionable and so she should not be memorialized on the statehouse. The pediment sculptures for the north and south were never made, either, but no one knows why.

Another controversy over decoration involved the painting of murals on the panels inside the dome. In 1898 the Populist executive council employed an artist, Jerome Fedeli, who provided a design that included partly nude Grecian women. The Republicans used the painting in their anti-Populist propaganda. The figures were referred to as "nude telephone girls" and were painted over in 1902 and replaced with something more modest—the panels that can be seen today representing knowledge, plenty, peace, and power. The central figures now are fully clothed women. They cost six times as much as the original paintings and are not as good artistically.

Between 1866 and 1903 Kansas spent more than $3,200,000 on the statehouse and nine workers lost their lives on the job. As one examines the controversies of thirty-seven years it seems that the building may have been finished in spite of politicians rather than because of them. Yet it was done and it became a source of pride to Kansans. As one newspaperman wrote in 1890, "A Kansan need not blush for his statehouse."

Suggestions for Reading

Robert S. Bader, *Prohibition in Kansas: A History* (1986); Michael J. Brodhead, *Persevering Populist: The Life of Frank Doster* (1969); Michael J. Brodhead, *David J. Brewer: The Life of a Supreme Court Justice, 1837–1910* (1994); O. Gene Clanton, *Kansas Populism: Ideas and Men* (1969); O. Gene Clanton, *Populism: The Humane Preference in America, 1890–1900* (1991); Michael Lewis Goldberg, *An Army of Women: Gender and Politics in Gilded Age Kansas* (1997); Paul F. Harper, *The Temple of Fame: A Personal Biography of Lyman U. Humphrey* (1995); John D. Hicks, *The Populist Revolt* (1931); Scott G. McNall, *The Road to Rebellion: Class Formation and Kansas Populism* (1988); Walter T. K. Nugent, *The Tolerant Populists* (1963); William A. Peffer, ed. by Peter H. Argersinger, *Populism, Its Rise and Fall* (1992); and Burton J. Williams, *Senator John James Ingalls: Kansas' Iridescent Republican* (1972).

These articles in the *Kansas Historical Quarterly* provide information on the period covered in this chapter: Monroe Billington, "Susanna Madora Salter—First Woman Mayor" (Autumn, 1954); A. R. Kitzhaber, "Gotterdämmerung in Topeka: The Downfall of Senator Pomeroy" (August, 1950); and Robert W. Richmond, "Kansas Builds a Capitol" (Autumn, 1972). *Kansas History* offers Dorothy Rose Blumberg, "Mary Elizabeth Lease, Populist Orator: A Profile" (Spring, 1978); Marilyn D. Brady, "Populism and Feminism in a Newspaper by and for Women of the Kansas Farmers' Alliance, 1891–1894" (Winter, 1984/85); Rodney O. Davis, "Prudence Crandall, Spiritualism, and Populist-Era Reform in Kansas" (Winter, 1980); James H. Ducker, "Workers, Townsmen, and the Governor: The Santa Fe Enginemen's Strike, 1878" (Spring, 1982); Lorraine A. Gehring, "Women Officeholders in Kansas, 1872–1912" (Summer, 1986); R. Douglas Hurt, "The Populist Judiciary: Election Reform and Contested Offices" (Summer, 1981); John M. Peterson, "The People's Party of Kansas: Campaigning in 1898" (Winter, 1990-1991); Joseph F. Tripp, "Kansas Communities and the Birth of the Labor Problem, 1877–1883" (Summer, 1981); and Harold Piehler, "Henry Vincent: Kansas Populist and Radical-Reform Journalist" (Spring, 1979).

12

Progressive Politics and Progress in a New Century

Along with other Americans Kansans were concerned about the condition of Cubans under Spanish rule and when the Spanish-American War began in 1898, they were ready to take up arms. Four Kansas volunteer regiments were recruited and, continuing the numbering system begun during the Civil War, they were named the Twentieth, Twenty-First, Twenty-Second, and Twenty-Third. None of the regiments saw combat. The Twentieth spent the war outside San Francisco, the Twenty-First and Twenty-Second were stationed in Georgia and Virginia, and the Twenty-Third, an all-black unit, served on occupation duty in Cuba after the war. Although the Kansas troops were not under Spanish gunfire, those stationed in the South battled disease, particularly malaria and typhoid fever. The Twenty-Third Regiment was unique because it was not only all black but it had black officers, something to which the regular army had never agreed.

Admiral George Dewey's victory over the Spanish fleet at Manila Bay did not affect Kansans directly but it led to the writing of a verse that was repeated throughout the United States. Eugene Ware, a noted Kansas newspaperman and lawyer who also wrote poetry, heard the news of Dewey's victory while he was eating in a Topeka restaurant and he came up with the following lines:

O Dewey was the morning upon the first of May,
And Dewey was the Admiral down in Manila Bay,
And Dewey were the Regents eyes, them orbs of Royal Blue,
And Dewey feel discouraged? I Dew not think we Dew!

The Twentieth Regiment, commanded by Colonel Frederick Funston of Iola, embarked for Manila on October 27, 1898, after Spain had surrendered. Some Filipinos, deciding that they might not like United States control any better than they had Spanish rule, changed targets and kept on fighting. The Twentieth was among the units that began a general offensive against the Filipinos and distinguished itself in several battles. In crossing the Rio Grande de la Pampanga under fire, two privates of the Twentieth, Edward White and William B. Trembly, won the Congressional Medal of Honor for heroism. Because of the units record under his command, Funston (also a Congressional Medal winner) was promoted to brigadier general of volunteers and Colonel Wilder Metcalf of Lawrence assumed command of the regiment.

The "Fighting Twentieth" came home in November 1899, but the fighting continued in the Philippines. It was obvious that the Filipino leader, Emilio Aguinaldo, was a daring commander and that he might continue to evade the American army indefinitely. General Funston laid out a plan that enabled him, five other officers, and a detachment of Filipinos fighting for the United States to enter Aguinaldo's camp in disguise and capture the insurgent leader. This brought an end to combat in the Philippines, and Funston received a regular army commission. The "sneak attack" on the Filipinos brought criticism from the Americans who saw no reason to acquire the Pacific islands and it was denounced as a part of imperialistic policy.

Frederick Funston, who was a hero to Kansans, is one of the unique people in Kansas history and is worthy of further mention. He grew up north of Iola, the son of E. H. Funston, who served in Congress, and attended the University of Kansas. Funston was a member of expeditions sponsored by the U.S. Department of Agriculture that took him to the Rockies, Death Valley, and Alaska. At one time he made a 1,500-mile canoe trip down the Yukon River alone. He served as an officer in the Cuban rebellion eighteen months before the Spanish-American War began. He was an extremely capable officer and as the commander at San Francisco during the great earthquake and fire in 1906 he was universally praised as the man who saved the city from complete disaster. He undoubtedly would have played a vital role in the First World War had he not died unexpectedly in 1917.

With soldiers back home and politics less stormy than in the 1890s, Kansans had time to look around and notice that changes were taking

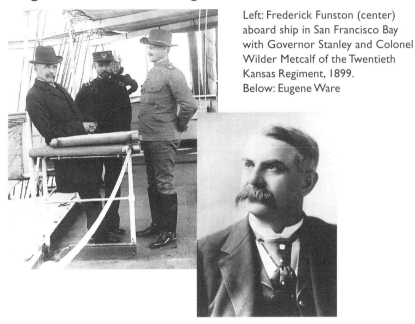

Left: Frederick Funston (center) aboard ship in San Francisco Bay with Governor Stanley and Colonel Wilder Metcalf of the Twentieth Kansas Regiment, 1899.
Below: Eugene Ware

place. As 1900 was approaching, the Topeka *Daily Capital* commented that towns with telephone systems were getting so common that they were hardly worth bragging about and the Santa Fe Railroad announced that its dining cars were being equipped with electric fans. In addition to these advances one form of recreation was gaining popularity. The inventor of basketball, Dr. James Naismith, had joined the faculty of the University of Kansas and people were taking up his new sport.

PROGRESSIVE POLITICS

William E. Stanley, in his second term as governor during the first two years of the new century, represented middle-of-the-road, conservative Republicanism, but he was a man of skill and ability who served his state well. Changes were on their way in the Republican party, however, and a new kind of leadership was emerging. William Allen White, Walter R. Stubbs, Joseph Bristow, Edward Hoch, Victor Murdock, and Henry Allen were looking for a more liberal party. They have been described as being under the spell of Theodore Roosevelt.

Roosevelt came to Kansas twice during 1900 and spoke to enthusiastic audiences. In September he made thirty-one stops and thirty-one speeches and that year Kansas could claim to be the "original T. R. state" for Kansas Republicans nominated him for vice-president. In 1904, when he ran for president, he won 66 percent of the Kansas vote cast, the biggest majority since Ulysses S. Grant.

Even though the new progressive element was unhappy with the regular Republican machine it was unable to bring much pressure on the 1902 election, and Willis J. Bailey was elected governor. Governor Bailey had no chance to run for reelection because the progressives were able to force him out in 1904 and they nominated Edward Hoch for the office.

The "new" Republicans became known as the "Boss Busters" because of their fight against the old party leadership. Most capable and outspoken among them was Walter R. Stubbs, a Lawrence building contractor and an impressive man. He was very tall and broad shouldered and was described by one reporter as having red hair that "encumbers his head as thirty bushel wheat encumbers the land on which it has grown." He added: "He looks always as if he had started for the barber shop the day before yesterday morning and had afterwards changed his mind. . . . He sheds his coat when he talks, and talks with his arms, his legs, his hair and his eyebrows, to say nothing of his booming voice."

Edward Hoch was editor of the Marion *Record* and had served in the legislature with Stubbs. At first Hoch did not want to run for governor but he was talked into it by his progressive friends. Hoch's criticism of the Republican machine was expressed in the editorials he wrote for his paper. This is a sample:

> It grows out of unwise leadership; of unfair standards of Republican-
> ism; of factional intolerance; of the multiplicity of useless offices; of
> extravagance in public expenditure; of enormous increase in
> burdens of taxation; cumulative protest against the skull and cross
> bones in politics . . . movement which would wrest our beloved
> party from the domination of leaders who care more for faction. . . .

The course of Kansas and national progressivism can be traced rather completely in the Emporia *Gazette* editorials of William Allen White. For example, White wrote on November 30, 1904:

> The most needed reform in Kansas just now is a new primary law
> which will insure honest nominations to the people of all parties.
> As the case stands now, in close counties and districts, Republicans
> vote at Democratic caucuses, generally for men whom Republicans
> believe they can defeat, and Democrats similarly vote for the
> weakest men before Republican primaries. The result is that the
> people get the weakest candidates of both parties.
>
> And the result which follows is that when the offices are filled,
> there is misgovernment, too often scrubs in office, high taxes with
> no adequate returns to the taxpayers, and in the end government is
> disregarded, laws are violated, and the people are dissatisfied.

> Honest men make honest government. . . . Unless the party
> machinery is purged, party government is bound to be unclean. . . .
> Give honest men an office as a result of an honest state-wide
> primary law, and government in this state will improve. . . .
>
> The Kansas legislature should give Kansas an honest primary law,
> a just railroad law, an equitable tax law, and an early adjournment.

Campaigning on those issues Hoch won easily in 1904 but only by a small margin in 1906. Even the "Boss Busters" had factional difficulties and Hoch was faced by a popular Democrat, William Harris, in 1906. Stubbs was speaker of the house and it was because of his forceful leadership that many important laws were passed.

Among the legislative achievements of Hoch's administration were a child labor law, the establishment of a juvenile court system, regulated hours of work for railroad employees, the creation of the state printing plant, a maximum freight rate bill, a tax commission for the assessment of railroads, and an anti-pass bill. The railroad pass question had been argued for some time. Railroads distributed free passes to politicians at all levels of government hoping that they would get preferential treatment in return, as they often did.

Also important was the primary election law, but it did not pass without a fight. Governor Hoch had recommended it to his first legislature, but it took a special session of the second one to put it into effect. Regulation of banks and protection for depositors were other things that had been needed for years. It was a point of legislative discussion under Hoch and, finally, the 1909 legislature did something about it when it passed the bank guaranty law.

In 1905 the battleship *Kansas* was commissioned by the Navy, and Governor Hoch, a believer in prohibition, first suggested that the ship be christened with Kansas crude oil rather than champagne. On August 12 the vessel was launched, and Hoch's daughter broke a bottle of Kansas spring water over the bow. In 1909 it was reported that U.S. marines did not want to serve on the *Kansas* because they thought it was bad luck that the vessel had been christened with water. To satisfy the marines and the crew, the captain bought a bottle of champagne and rechristened the ship.

The first primary election, held in 1908, saw Stubbs nominated for governor and Joseph Bristow of Salina nominated for the U.S. Senate. The reform element of the GOP defeated the machine once again and Stubbs took his "Square Deal" politics to the statehouse. Bristow also won and went to Washington to join a group of senators who would dispute regular Republicanism in the upper house while Victor Murdock of Wichita and Ed Madison of Dodge City fought dictatorial Republican leadership in the House of Representatives.

Stubbs served two terms and through the period was the leading progressive of Kansas. He applied business techniques to state government, and he helped bring some of the democratic processes up to date. The sale of stocks and bonds was regulated, a workmen's compensation law was enacted, a commission to regulate public utilities was created, and state inspection of meat packing plants was begun. Stubbs was one of the state's best governors, and William Allen White said he was right nine times out of ten in politics.

While reform politics were carried on with vigor in Kansas the same kind of feeling was taking hold of the national Republican organization, with Theodore Roosevelt leading the way. In 1910, Roosevelt spoke at Osawatomie at the dedication of a memorial to John Brown. He said very little about Brown but he talked a great deal about his "New Nationalism," which was another term for progressivism and he was applauded by the Kansas progressives.

The Republican party in Kansas split wide open over Roosevelt and Taft in 1912 and Kansans helped lead the "Bull Moose" faction of the party out of the national convention that year.* Kansas supporters of Roosevelt then became progressives with a capital "P" but the new third party could not find enough votes to elect Roosevelt. William Howard Taft was popular with the regular Republicans in Kansas, and he had been in the state in 1911, speaking on three college campuses and presiding at the laying of the Memorial Building cornerstone in Topeka. Because of the Republican split the Democrats carried Kansas, and the presidential vote went to Woodrow Wilson. Democrat George Hodges of Olathe barely defeated Arthur Capper for governor. Walter Stubbs tried for the U.S. Senate in 1912, but it was said that he spent so much time working for Theodore Roosevelt that he could not win his own race. One notable feature of the 1912 election was the adoption of a state constitutional amendment giving Kansas women the right to vote. Kansas was the eighth state to extend full voting privileges to women.

Governor Hodges, a former state legislator, generally agreed with the Progressive movement so there was no change in attitude in the governor's office. His one-term administration was concerned with additional reforms in government and since the Democrats had a legislative majority he did not have to battle the legislature. Hodges worked for better schools, stronger business regulation, court and tax reforms, and the upgrading of state hospitals and penal institutions.

---

*The term Bull Moose was applied to the progressive wing because of a statement by T. R. That he felt as "fit as a Bull Moose."

Woman suffragists stating their case in Topeka, 1916.

THE END OF THE PROGRESSIVE PARTY

After 1912 the Progressives were through as a party, although some of them would attempt to maintain a separate existence for another four years. The Republican split was partially healed during Governor Hodges' term because GOP regulars disliked seeing a Democrat in the statehouse. The Stubbs control was gone but striking changes had taken place in a dozen years. On June 26, 1913, William Allen White wrote an entertaining editorial entitled "The Chuckling Socialist," which serves as a summary of the Progressive years in Kansas:

> Kansas City, Kansas, voted to construct a municipal electric lighting plant. Yesterday, Judge Hook, of the federal circuit court, approved a plan looking to the municipal ownership of the Kansas street car system. Last week Attorney General John Dawson declared that ice, being a public utility, should be controlled by the state. Last month a bill favorably considered by a committee of Congress provided for the construction of a government railroad in Alaska, and for the government ownership and lease operation of coal mines. . . .
>
> If you were a Socialist, wouldn't you hunt a cool, shady spot between two buildings where the air poured through and sit down in a kitchen chair and chuckle and chuckle and chuckle?
>
> The really interesting part of the situation is that about half of the American Socialist platform for 1904 is now on the statute books of one third of the states, and much of it is in the platforms of at least two of the great parties.
>
> The Socialists are getting too conservative for this country. They will have to get a move on themselves or they will be without an

issue in 1916. For the Bull Moosers have stolen the Socialist thunder, and the progressive Republicans declare they are just as progressive as the Bull Moosers, and the Democrats say they are more progressive than the Progressives. Unless the Republicans and Democrats are lying about how progressive they are . . . the Socialists might as well go out of business, for all the great parties will be swiping the Socialist planks.

Which is funny. But it indicates that the people have begun thinking along economic lines, and the politicians are trying to capitalize on the popular tendencies.

White was right. It was funny, and the old line Socialists and Populists, too, must have found it so. Kansans were not unfamiliar with Socialism at that time because J. A. Wayland was publishing at Girard *The Appeal to Reason,* which he had begun in the 1890s. With a national readership, the weekly newspaper trumpeted Socialism across the nation. Also, Kate Richards O'Hare, a Kansan known to her critics as "Red Kate," was working for Socialism as a lecturer, labor union organizer, and through the columns of *The Appeal to Reason.* Those early years of the twentieth century were good ones in many ways because a good many Americans recognized some of the things that were wrong politically, socially, and economically. A theory expressed in recent years by some historians suggests that much of the reform in business practices came about because reformers had investments in those businesses. They believed that changes and government regulation would be good for business in the long run and would give them a more profitable return on their money in the future. That may well be true but the fact remains that change did come, and it was for the better. Motivation for it may not always have been a product of "Christian charity," but the overall results were beneficial to a lot of people. The Progressives lit a fire under other politicians, and they helped make life a little better for a great many people.

This does not mean that everything was right in America or Kansas. There were still many things wrong. There was still tremendous racial discrimination, and there were still vast gaps between rich and poor. Laborers in America had a long way to go toward equitable pay, reasonable hours, and safe working conditions. Still, many of those things taken for granted by Americans in the 1980s had their start in the Progressive era, and much of the push came from Kansans with reform in mind.

PROGRESS IN AGRICULTURE

At the turn of the century there were still more than two million acres available for additional settlement in Kansas, but there were also a great many farmers already on the land who were not making the kind of living that they had hoped to make. Change was necessary if the Plains were to yield the crops they were capable of producing. It was during the years before the First World War that scientific agriculture became a part of the Kansas way of life.

New varieties of seed were introduced and more sorghum grains joined wheat and corn as important crops. "Dry farming" was improved upon as farmers and scientists tried new ways to plow, plant, and conserve moisture. But the dry lands were supplemented by increasing acreages of irrigated land, watered from what then seemed to be inexhaustible supplies of underground water. New engines, run by gasoline, began to pump water, although the familiar windmill remained an important fixture on irrigated farms. From the agricultural college at Manhattan came information designed to make the life of the farmer easier and increase his crop and livestock production. Soil was tested, fertilizer experimented with, and while cattle remained important, hogs and poultry gained more attention and, as a result, their numbers increased.

Kansas agricultural products provided an impressive show at the Louisiana Purchase Exposition in St. Louis in 1904, and in 1910 the Kansas State Agricultural College won twenty-four prizes at the International Livestock Show in Chicago. Apple orchards in the northeastern Kansas counties and in Reno County were among the nation's largest. Corn carnivals were held in Kansas towns, and every county and state fair emphasized bountiful Kansas crops.

This was the period in which mechanization came to the farm and while the horse continued to be important until the 1920s, the steam-

Steam power was used for threshing early in the Twentieth century. This is a Russell County threshing outfit about 1910.

powered threshing machine and steam and gasoline tractors became increasingly common. The farmer who had plowed, sowed, and harvested with a team of horses could now do the same things much faster with a machine. By 1906, farmers in the western counties were plowing thirty-five and forty acres a day using steam tractors pulling gang plows. Wheat acreages increased because harvesting and threshing could be done more quickly.

Kansas sugar beets and broom corn became important to the world market. In Garden City in 1905, a $500,000 contract was let for the construction of a beet sugar factory, and Wichita was known as "the broom corn capital of the world." The railroads became involved with agricultural experimentation and assisted with demonstrations designed to improve farming while the state agricultural experiment stations produced new crops and provided an increasing amount of scientific assistance to the farmer.

Other changes came in farm life. Rural mail delivery began and some farms acquired telephones. The housewife found that she, too, could get information that helped her with housekeeping, food preservation, and scientific ways to improve the health of her family through Home Demonstration and Extension services which would continue for years to come. By the time Kansas farmers got caught up in the agricultural problems brought on by a world war they were living a life far different from that of the isolated homesteader of thirty years before.

INDUSTRIAL ADVANCEMENT

In southeastern Kansas there was a marked industrial growth between 1900 and the First World War. It was centered around zinc mining and smelting, coal mining, and the production of cement, glass, and brick, using natural gas as fuel. Crawford, Bourbon, and Cherokee counties, around which the industries centered, experienced both economic and population growth during the period. By 1909 Kansas was ranked fourth in salt production and mines at Hutchinson, Lyons, and Kanopolis were important producers.

However, the most important industrial advances in Kansas during those years were based on oil. Kansans knew there was petroleum in the eastern part of the state during the Civil War and for the next thirty years efforts were made to bring in wells. In 1892 the big break came when the well known as Norman No. One was drilled at Neodesha and produced abundantly. Others followed and the vast Mid-Continent oil field had been opened.

The independent drillers and producers in that area were bought out by Standard Oil in 1895, and the eastern company encouraged further production in the southeastern quarter of the state. By 1905 production had reached such proportions that prices of crude oil dropped and Standard was criticized by Kansas producers as a great monopoly. The reform-minded politicians waged war on Standard Oil, and Kansas oilmen persuaded the legislature to place controls on the company. At one point the legislature, and Governor Hoch, proposed a state oil refinery operated by prison labor, but that never came to pass.

The Kansas independent operators made life miserable for Standard Oil in Kansas at a time when many branches of big business were coming under fire from Progressives. There were independents who wanted part of the money that Standard was making and there were idealistic reformers who considered Standard an enemy because it had been greedy when it was not regulated. After the fight ended, declining production in Kansas and new wells in Oklahoma dropped the state from the petroleum spotlight. However, in 1915 a Wichita company brought in Stapleton No. One, opening the El Dorado field, which added millions of barrels of production. From that point the production and refining horizons widened and Kansas became one of the nation's leading oil states.

One of the places where a discovery of natural gas took place was Dexter, in Cowley County. In 1903 the town advertised its find but every time flames were brought near the well the gas would blow them out. For two years the name "wind gas" was used, but finally someone discovered that the gas was helium, which was why it would not burn. Beginning with the First World War the gas was used in military balloons, but Dexter did not have a helium plant until the 1920s. Since then blimps, nuclear reactors, and ballistic missiles have kept the industry alive, although the original Dexter well is no longer producing.

THE AUTOMOBILE AND THE AIRPLANE

Tied closely to the oil industry were advances in transportation. By August 1900, Terry Stafford of Topeka had completed an automobile that was simply a buggy driven by a seven-horsepower gasoline engine. Stafford joined forces with Anton and Clement Smith of Topeka, and by 1904 they were producing the Smith Veracity auto in quantity. With each passing year more powerful engines were added to the Smith cars, and there were several models available to buyers. After 1907 the Great Smith touring car was the company's most popular model, but it was a luxury automobile, selling for more than $2,600. (The Ford Model T could be purchased for $850.)

The Smith Company probably did not make more than 1,200 cars before it was forced out of business in 1912, but the Great Smith was a successful competitor in cross-country endurance races.

At least three other automobile manufacturers were located in Kansas—the Jones Motor Car Company of Wichita, the Cloughley Motor Vehicle Company of Parsons, and the Sellers Motor Car Company of Hutchinson. All three were out of business by 1920. All small manufacturers were doomed to failure because they did not have the money or the efficiency of production needed to compete with the larger manufacturers such as Ford. One Kansan did play an important part in the development of a big company. Walter Chrysler, once a resident of Wamego and Ellis, took the mechanical knowledge he acquired while working for the Union Pacific Railroad and used it to develop Chrysler automotive products.

Along with automobiles came an interest in good roads because the car needed better surfaces than did the horse and buggy. An association to promote improved roads was organized at Topeka in 1900 and some roads acquired oiled surfaces a few years later. In January 1907, a hard surfaced road sixteen feet wide was built north of Chanute, and seven years later a concrete highway was built in Allen County, supposedly the first in Kansas. There were "Good Roads Days" held in various parts of the state and local residents volunteered their services to improve the roadbeds and surfaces. One day near Beloit in 1914, five hundred citizens used two hundred teams of horses to grade and gravel nearly a mile of roadway.

Before roadmaps were in common use and highways were numbered, guidebooks were published to help the motorist. In addition to mileage the guides indicated where turns should be made. The following is taken from a 1912 guide and gives directions for driving from Topeka to Hiawatha:

Mileages		
Total	Intermed.	
0.0	0.0	TOPEKA, Kansas Ave. & 5th St. From P.O. Go north on Kansas Ave., following trolley.
1.1	1.1	Jog left on Gordon St. and immediately bear right on Central Ave.
1.5	0.4	Turn left on St. John St.
1.9	0.4	Turn right, following poles, go straight north
11.6	9.7	End of road at county line; turn left.

13.1	1.5	Turn right, following travel.
15.1	2.0	Turn left across RR, and take first right to center of
15.6	0.5	HOYT. Keep ahead through business center.
15.9	0.3	On edge of town jog left and take first right.
16.4	0.5	End of road; turn left.
16.9	0.5	Turn right, going straight north across RR, 21.8.
22.3	5.4	Turn left on Main St. To center of
22.6	0.3	MAYETTA, business center. Turn right.
23.2	0.6	Turn left with travel.
24.0	0.8	End of road; turn right.
31.4	7.4	On edge of town jog right with travel and take first left.
31.8	0.4	HOLTON, Public Square. Turn right.
32.0	0.2	Turn left, gradually curving right across RR, bearing left with road across iron bridge.
35.1	3.1	At school on left turn right, crossing RR, 36.0.
40.6	5.5	4-corners, school on right; turn left.
44.6	4.0	End of road; turn right and take first left 44.9
46.4	1.8	At Sta. on left, turn right straight through center of WHITING, cross RR, 47.3.
49.3	2.9	End of road, turn left.
51.8	2.5	4-corners; turn right.
53.8	2.0	4-corners; turn left.
55.9	2.1	Jog right 1 block, turning left over RR viaduct.
56.3	0.4	Turn left 1 block to center of
56.4	0.1	HORTON, business center. Straight north across RR, 60.8 and 68.3

| 69.9 | 13.5 | On edge of city turn left, going straight to center of |
| 70.4 | 0.5 | HIAWATHA, Court House on left. |

F. W. "Woody" Hockaday, a Wichita automobile dealer, engaged in a one-man crusade to mark Kansas auto routes before the First World War, and in 1918 he published a road map on which thirty-three marked highways in the United States were shown.

The airplane offered unlimited possibilities as far as experimentation in transportation was concerned, and Kansas provided American aviation with some of its most notable pioneers. Before success came failure for some Kansans, now long forgotten. In 1908, Henry Call organized the Aerial Navigation Company of Girard and built eight or nine planes, six of which never flew. One flew for less than a mile at an altitude of a hundred feet, but it crashed. Most of Call's planes were so heavy they sank into the ground and his expenses were so great that he went bankrupt in 1912. A Jetmore blacksmith named A. E. Hunt built what he called a "rotary aeroplane"—a helicopter of sorts. It was built of pipe and angle iron but the same principle of rotors for power is used today. All Hunt proved was that his motors could lift four hundred pounds, but his airplane weighed more than three tons, so he operated under a handicap. At Goodland two inventors came up with an airplane two-stories high, but it did not fly. One observer described the plane as having "two sets of fans, each going in opposite directions" and they should "lift the machine right off the ground." He was too optimistic—the Goodland plane stayed on the ground.

The Hunt rotary airplane at Jetmore, 1910. This mechanical marvel remained earthbound.

Other early projects were more encouraging. In 1911, three Topeka mechanics, A. K. and E. J. Longren and William Janicke, built a plane, and that year A. K. Longren made a fifteen-mile flight, reaching an altitude of a thousand feet. The Longrens manufactured planes for several years and A. K., who served as test pilot, was a popular performer as a stunt flyer at state and county fairs throughout the Midwest.

Glenn L. Martin, at one-time a resident of Liberal and Salina, acquired an airplane in 1909 and made exhibition flights. Some years later Martin founded the aircraft company that produced many military planes during the Second World War. In Kingman County, a farmer named Clyde Cessna, built a monoplane that he named *The Comet*. For several years following 1912, Cessna flew at fairs and celebrations, but in the next decade he, too, would become a prominent manufacturer of aircraft.

Cessna's exhibitions of flying in his home county drew large crowds. Kingman residents gathered to watch him on March 13, 1913, and the local *Leader-Courier* reported:

> As promised last week Mr. Cessna, the flying machine man . . .
> brought his "bird" to Kingman yesterday and took it out in the
> eastern suburbs of the city for the purpose of giving an exhibition of
> what he can do in the way of flying. The word had been sent out
> through the rural districts and quite a crowd hurriedly came. . . . But
> they were all disappointed as the wind was too strong to admit of
> the flights, although the crowd waited patiently for two or three
> hours for the wind to "lay". It was then announced that the flight would
> take place . . . this afternoon if the wind should be favorable. . . .
>
> The wind being favorable Mr. Cessna made his promised flight at
> 4:50 this afternoon, making a circle of about 3 miles over the city
> and alighting about one-fourth of a mile south of where he started
> and sooner than planned as his machine balked. About 2,500
> people witnessed the flight. He expects to give another exhibition
> shortly.

ACTIVITY ON
OTHER FRONTS

In the field of public health Kansas became known because of the activity of Dr. Samuel J. Crumbine, who became secretary of the State Board of Health in 1904. Crumbine had been a successful doctor in Dodge City, and his interest in improved public health conditions made him internationally famous. He campaigned against unscreened windows and the house fly as a disease carrier. He fought the common drinking cup and the exposed roller towel, both of which were common on railroad trains and in public places, and he attempted to replace them with disposable paper cups and towels. He attacked misleading labels on food and drugs and most of his campaigns were marked by slogans like "Swat the Fly" and "Dont Spit on the Sidewalk." He firmly believed that spitting publicly helped spread disease and was so convincing that brick manufacturing companies produced bricks for sidewalks with the slogan imprinted on them. Following the passage in 1907 of the state's Pure Food and Drug Act, Crumbine was assisted in his regulatory efforts by Professors Julius T. Willard of Kansas State Agricultural College and E. H. S. Bailey of Kansas University.

Also crusading, but for different reasons, was Carry Nation. After an initial saloon-smashing venture in Kiowa she moved on to other cities including Enterprise, Harper, Kansas City, and Topeka. In addition to personally encouraging her followers to destroy liquor by destroying places that sold it, she was involved in publishing and speaking engagements,

Left: Dr. Samuel Crumbine at the State Board of Health, 1908. Below: Carry Nation under arrest after a saloon-smashing incident in Enterprise, 1901.

some of which took her outside Kansas. Several times she was put in jail for her violent activities. Her war against alcohol gained nationwide attention, and she was the subject of both praise and criticism. She left her mark on the continuing campaign for total prohibition before her death in 1911.

Along with their increased political activity, Kansas women were making their mark in the professions of medicine, dentistry, and law. Generally speaking, women were not welcomed enthusiastically by male practitioners or educators, although the Kansas Medical College in Topeka admitted women from its opening in 1872. Dr. Deborah Longshore, a Pennsylvanian, established a medical practice in Topeka in 1879, and overcame the existing prejudice to become a respected member of the community and the Kansas Medical Society. Among the early graduates of the Kansas Medical College was Frances Storrs, a native Kansan, and she, too, was successful. Lucy Hobbs Taylor of Lawrence began the practice of dentistry in 1908, reportedly the first female graduate of a dental college.

The first two Kansas women admitted to the state's bar were Jennie Mitchell Kellogg of Emporia and Ida Tillotson of Graham County, both in 1881. After the turn of the century, the number of women in these professions continued to increase, and they gained recognition as capable practitioners.

Unique newcomers to Kansas beginning in the late nineteenth century were orphans sent west by social service organizations in the East. Thousands of children from inner-city environments were "placed out" with families in several states including Kansas. In some cases they were transported by trainloads which gave rise to the term "orphan trains." The practice continued well into the twentieth century, and some who came

A Santa Fe orphan train, about 1900.

on the trains are still living in Kansas along with many descendants of the early adoptees.

At the same time the Kansas Children's Home Society was working to find new homes for Kansas youngsters who were orphaned or lived in a state of deprivation. Founded in 1893, the society became the Kansas Children's Service League in 1926, and continues its work today. At the time the eastern orphans were coming the Kansas society expressed opposition to out-of-state efforts, believing that the problems of local children should be dealt with first. In 1901 the Kansas legislature acted to restrict the numbers and kinds of children coming from out of state and Governor Stanley said, "We cannot afford to have the state made a dumping ground for the dependent children of other states, especially New York." The Kansas organization was effective in its adoptive efforts and was a pioneer in dealing with the causes and effects of child abuse during the Progressive period.

Although progress, prosperity, and optimism were prominent in Kansas after 1900 there were two years when the weather would not cooperate. In 1903, heavy rains caused flooding in the Missouri River basin. All along the Kaw and its major tributaries cities were hard hit. The crest reached Topeka on May 29 and 30 and destruction in the capital was duplicated in Lawrence and Kansas City. Fifty-seven people died, thirty-eight of them in Topeka, and fire and a lack of safe drinking water added to the hardships of the flood itself. By the summer of 1904 most of the scars of the year before had healed, and then another flood occurred. The Kaw went over its banks, but more serious damage took place on the Marais des Cygnes, Walnut, and Neosho rivers, with Ottawa, Winfield, and Emporia among the towns most affected.

Kansas progressed educationally and culturally. Many Kansans were developing an interest in the theater and in music, from town bands to touring opera stars. Many Kansas towns built "opera houses" in the nineteenth century, but in 1907 the Brown Grand Opera House opened in Concordia, a classic example of small-town cultural landmarks. (The building was restored and reopened in 1980.) The Columbian Theater, Wamego, opened in the 1890s, and like the Brown Grand, was a cultural focal point in the years following 1900. It, too, has been restored and reopened in 1994. It features paintings brought to Wamego by its original owner from the 1893 Columbian Exposition in Chicago.

Another form of entertainment was offered by C. W. Parker. A national leader as a manufacturer of carousels and an operator of carnivals, Parker began his business in Abilene in the 1890s. In 1910 he had an argument with city government and moved everything to Leavenworth. He died in 1932, but the company lasted until 1952 under the direction of his son Paul. One of the carousels has been restored by the Dickinson County Historical Society in Abilene.

Kansas public school systems were expanding and by 1915 a high school education was available to everybody without payment of tuition. Colleges were going through a period of development and expansion of curriculum. Two more state colleges were added to the system as the western branch of the State Normal School, now Fort Hays State University, opened its doors in 1902, and the Manual Training School, now Pittsburg State University, began operation in 1903.

Progress did not stop in Kansas when a world war began in Europe but there was a marked change in Kansas attitudes as the United States moved toward international military involvement, and in the years of peace that followed 1918.

Suggestions for Reading

Barbara Brackman, Mary Droll Feighny, and Camille Nohe, eds., *Journeys on the Road Less Traveled: Kansas Women Attorneys* (1998); John G. Clark, *Towns and Minerals in Southeastern Kansas: A Study in Regional Industrialization, 1890–1930* (1970); Thomas W. Crouch, *A Leader of Volunteers: Frederick Funston and the Twentieth Kansas in the Philippines, 1898–1899* (1984); James R. Goff, Jr., *Fields White Unto Harvest: Charles F. Parham and the Missionary Origins of Pentecostalism* (1988); John Grahma, ed., *"Yours For the Revolution:" The Appeal to Reason, 1895–1922* (1990); Marvin Irvin Holt, *Linoleum, Better Babies and the Modern Farm Woman, 1890–1930* (1995); Marilyn Irvin Holt, *The Orphan Trains: Placing Out in America* (1992); Thomas D. Isern, *Bull Threshers and Bindlestiffs: Harvesting and Threshing on the North American Plains* (1990); Robert S. LaForte, *Leaders in Reform: Progressive Republicans in Kansas, 1900–1916* (1974); Sally M. Miller, *From Prairie to Prison: The Life of Social Activist, Kate Richards O'Hare* (1993); H. Craig Miner, *The Fire in the Rock: A History of the Oil and Gas Industry in Kansas, 1855–1976* (1976); George E. Mowry, *Theodore Roosevelt and the Progressive Movement* (1946); Frank Joseph Rowe and Craig Miner, *Borne on the South Wind: A Century of Kansas Aviation* (1994); A. Bower Sageser, *Joseph L. Bristow: Kansas Progressive* (1968); Francis W. Schruben, *Wea Creek to El Dorado: Oil in Kansas, 1860–1920* (1972); William Sharp and Peggy Sullivan, *The Dashing Kansan: Lewis Lindsay Dyche, The Amazing Adventures of a Nineteenth-Century Naturalist and Explorer* (1991); Elliott Shore, *Talkin' Socialism: J. A. Wayland and the Role of the Press in American Radicalism, 1890–1912* (1988); Robert L. Taylor, *Vessel of Wrath: The Life and Times of Carry Nation* (1966); Thomas D. Van Sant, *Improving Rural Lives: A History of Farm Bureau in Kansas, 1912–1992* (1993); Bernice Larson Webb, *The Basketball Man: James Naismith* (1973); William Allen White, *Autobiography* (1946).

Lewis Lindsay Dyche, for whom Kansas Unversity's natural history museum is named.

The following articles from the *Kansas Historical Quarterly* are also informative: Martha B. Caldwell, "The Woman Suffrage Campaign of 1912" (August, 1943); Thomas W. Crouch, "Frederick Funston of Kansas" (Summer, 1974); Domenico Gagliardo, "The First Workmen's Compensation Law" (November, 1950); Willard B. Gatewood, Jr., "Kansas Negroes and the Spanish-American War" (Autumn, 1971); Robert S. LaForte, "Theodore Roosevelt's Osawatomie Speech" (Summer, 1966); Patricia Michaelis, "C. B. Hoffman, Kansas Socialist" (Summer, 1975); Robert K. Ratzlaff, "LeHunt, Kansas: The Making of a Cement Ghost Town" (Summer, 1977); and Todd L. Wagoner, "Fighting Aguinaldo's Insurgents in the Philippines" (May, 1951).

In *Kansas History* are: Robert S. Bader, "Mrs. Nation" (Winter, 1984/85); Carolyn Bailey Berneking, "Pure Food and Water for Kansans: E. H. S. Bailey, the State Food Laboratory, and the State Board of Health During the Progressive Era" (Spring, 1997); Jean Folkerts, "William Allen White: Editor and Businessman During the Reform Years, 1895–1916" (Summer, 1984); John M. Hyde, "A Balm in Gilead" (Winter, 1986/87); Sally M. Miller, "Kate Richards O'Hare: Progression Toward Feminism" (Winter, 1984/85); Gail L. McDaniel, "Women, Medicine, and Science: Kansas Female Physicians, 1880–1910" (Summer, 1998); David P. Nord, "The Appeal to Reason and American Socialism, 1901–1920" (Summer, 1978); Wilda M. Smith, "A Half Century of Struggle: Gaining Woman Suffrage in Kansas" (Summer, 1981); and David L. Sterling, "The Federal Government v. The Appeal to Reason" (Spring, 1986); Paul S. Sutter, "Paved With Good Intentions: Good Roads, the Automobile, and the Rhetoric of Rural Improvement in the *Kansas Farmer*, 1890–1914" (Winter, 1995–1996).

The First World War
and a "Return to Normalcy"

Most Kansans were surprised when world war began in Europe in 1914. Like the rest of the Midwest, Kansas was isolationist; when President Woodrow Wilson issued his proclamation of neutrality on August 4, Kansans approved.

With war in Europe came an increased demand for farm products, especially wheat. Consequently, the Kansas farmer saw a great rise in his crop values. Wheat acreage rose from six million in 1913 to nine million in 1914 and the market value went up nearly $100,000,000 to $151,000,000.

When the German army crushed Belgium in 1914 Kansans quickly volunteered to help the Belgians. Farmers donated wheat, and the milling industry turned it into flour for free shipment to Belgium. Most of the Kansas counties had committees working for Belgian relief by March 1915, under the direction of Governor Arthur Capper, who was inaugurated in January of that year.

Through 1915 and 1916 most Kansans continued to support United States neutrality. The World Peace Association had active groups over the state and on February 12, 1915, a peace convention led by Governor Capper was held in Topeka. Sentiment in Kansas was mostly in favor of the Allies though there was a German minority who favored Germany.

President Wilson's plans to increase America's preparedness for defense received little support in Kansas. The Woman's Kansas Day Club, the Peace and Equity League, the United Commercial Travelers, and the Kansas State Grange were among the groups opposing military preparedness while the chancellor of the University of Kansas objected to any increase in student military training. President Wilson came to Kansas in February 1916 and spoke about national defense, but he received a cool reception. Most midwesterners felt that war in Europe would not involve the United States.

In February 1917, Germany began again unrestricted submarine attacks on shipping, and the United States cut all diplomatic relations with Germany. Kansans began to change their minds, and some even became foolishly frightened as rumors of spies and sabotage circulated. Railroad bridges were guarded by soldiers as was the Wichita water pumping station because German spies were supposedly in the Wichita area.

One of Governor Capper's chief concerns was agricultural production, and he proposed a vegetable garden in every backyard and vacant lot. He also asked that everyone conserve food and appointed a State Agricultural Council of Defense to cooperate with the U.S. Department of Agriculture.

After war was declared on April 6, 1917, canning clubs were organized and high school students were asked to help farmers at harvest time. The Defense Council announced a goal of two hundred million bushels of wheat in 1918, and farm organizations said they would do their best. By midsummer, 1917, a great deal was written about the importance of Kansas wheat. The Topeka *Daily Capital*, July 19, said:

> "Win the War with Wheat."
>
> That is the Kansas slogan. It is a battle cry that is heard in every home of the state. From Baxter Springs to St. Francis; from White Cloud to Elkhart, a determined and patriotic people have enlisted in a great industrial army to fight the battle for bread as truly and as bravely as our soldiers will fight for liberty and humanity on the battle fields of Europe.
>
> Kansas stands at the head of the class of forty-eight states in the great battle for bread. It was the first to respond to the call of the federal government to conserve and produce. . . .
>
> Will Kansas help to "Win the War with Wheat?" The answer is the wonderful page written into Kansas history during the past four months. The state council of defense movement was the initial call to the fields and gardens for greater food production and with it an appeal for saving and economy. . . . The children, too, formed a battalion in the great industrial army. In more than 12,000 schools of the state a stirring appeal from Governor Capper was read by the

High school students in Scott County aiding the war effort by working in sorghum fields.

teachers to 400,000 boys and girls. These children went home from their studies with a broader vision of life and duty, and their industry and help will add to the state's storehouse of food this year.

Tractors were rolling and plows were turning over thousands more acres of buffalo grass sod so that more wheat could be planted. Twenty-five western counties were reported to be getting ready to double their wheat acreages. In Hodgeman County it was estimated that five million bushels would be produced. Kansas farmers had the answer to the food crisis, and they also had an opportunity to "start on the road to plenty and prosperity."

Of great importance to Kansas farmers, then and for years to come, was the establishment of the Federal Land Bank of Wichita in 1917. It was the first such institution chartered in the nation. Forty years later, on March 1, 1957, the Wichita *Eagle* described its opening as "the first victory on a national scale in the farmer's long struggle for reasonable credit."

MILITARY POSTS AND SOLDIERS

Although food plans found support there was still considerable opposition to the war even after the United States entered it. There had been no draft law since the Civil War, and the new one was not very popular when it was first announced. There were a few antidraft meetings held in Kansas, though most of the protestors were women or men who were not of draft age. President Wilson was criticized by those Kansans who thought that U.S. troops should not be sent overseas, and Kansas patriotism was questioned by some easterners. But by July 1917, the state had an enlisted man in service for every 143 citizens, and Governor Capper wrote:

> Since the declaration of war, Kansas has run far ahead of her quota
> in enlistments in the Regular Army and has kept up her quota for
> the Navy. In thirty days she has recruited and mustered into service
> a third regiment of infantry; has almost completed a regiment of
> field artillery, a battalion of signal troops, a battalion of engineers
> and a motor ammunition train.

The Holton municipal band enlisted as a group in the Marine Corps and was assigned to duty as a regimental band. There were other groups of Kansans who enlisted together on the basis of their towns, their memberships in organizations, or their colleges.

Members of the Kansas National Guard had experienced active duty shortly before the United States entered the war. Difficulties on the Mexican border in 1916, including raids in the United States by Mexican revolutionaries commanded by Francisco "Pancho" Villa, had led President Wilson to call guardsmen for federal service. Approximately four thousand Kansas guardsmen were in service until early in 1917, under the overall command of General Funston, and it was not long before their numbers were increased to help form an army division.

With men going into service under the new draft law there was a great need for officers. Fort Riley was named as one of the Reserve Officers' camps to train new men. For three months in the summer of 1917, twenty-five hundred officer candidates received instruction at Fort Riley. At Fort Leavenworth a thousand student officers received engineering training, and an "aviation camp" was established to instruct officers in the new Air Corps.

In June 1917, the federal government decided to build a huge training camp on the Fort Riley reservation. Named Camp Funston in honor of the Kansas general, the installation began to take shape by the end of the summer. Thousands of wooden buildings were put up, streets were laid out, and when the work was finished, Camp Funston was capable of housing and training more than fifty thousand men.

The following description of Camp Funston under construction was published in August 1917, and gives an idea of the size of the project:

> The big city on Ogden Flats is nearing completion. The Fuller
> Construction Company, which has the contract to put up the new
> soldier's city, is making a tremendous drive to finish. . . .They have a
> vast army of carpenters and other workmen—12,000 or 15,000 we

were told Tuesday, and thousands of them are working from early in the morning until dark. . . .

The cement workers have completed their work for the infantry barracks and at the time this is being written the frames for nearly all barracks in this section of the cantonment are up. The barracks are uniform . . . and each will house 200 or 250 soldiers. They will be supplied with hot and cold water, lighted with electricity, and heated with steam.

Each company of soldiers will have a separate building in which to cook, eat and sleep, and each regiment will have a separate group of barracks. . . .

Work on the barns and stables for ten thousand horses and mules will now be pushed forward and a laundry 50 X 400 feet, equipped with machinery to do the washing for forty-five thousand men will be put up as soon as the work can be done.

Built just off the military post, between Ogden and Camp Funston, was Army City, a four-block area containing stores, restaurants, theaters, barber shops, pool halls, and other businesses to serve the soldiers. Army City was financed by private businessmen, and it gave troops in training a place to shop and relax without going as far as Junction City or Manhattan. It was considered successful by both the businessmen and the army.

Participating in the war effort were the Jayhawker Tractor Girls, organized in Salina and affiliated with the Woman's National Agricultural Legion.

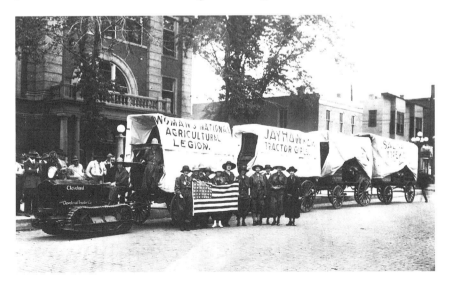

Fighting Overseas

Kansans served in many military organizations during the war but most of them were in the Eighty-Ninth, Thirty-Fifth, and Forty-Second divisions. The Eighty-Ninth was organized and trained at Camp Funston and included officers and enlisted men from the regular army along with reservists and draftees. The Eighty-Ninth arrived in Europe in June and July of 1918 and before long was in combat in the St. Mihiel offensive in France. It also participated in the Meuse-Argonne offensive and following the armistice did occupation duty in Germany until May 1919. The Eighty-Ninth suffered almost four thousand casualties in the Meuse-Argonne, then considered the largest battle in all military history.

The Thirty-Fifth Division was made up of National Guardsmen from Kansas and Missouri, but it also included draftees from both states and some men from outside the Midwest. Called into federal service on August 5, 1917, the division trained in Oklahoma at Camp Doniphan, on the Fort Sill reservation, and went overseas in the spring of 1918. For some time the Thirty-Fifth was held in reserve and saw no major action, but late in September it moved up for the beginning of the Argonne offensive. For five days the Thirty-Fifth was under fire, and by the time it was relieved by the First Division it had suffered nearly seven thousand casualties. The division saw no more major action, but it spent the winter in France and returned home in the spring of 1919. The Thirty-Fifth's homecoming in Topeka was a day for celebration, and a huge crowd welcomed the returning troops.

Troops of the Thirty-Fifth Division come home to Topeka in 1919.

The Forty-Second Division, known as the Rainbow Division because it was made up of National Guard units from twenty-six states, was assembled in New York and left for France in the fall of 1917. Its men, like the other Kansans, were participants in the Meuse-Argonne fighting and were also in the Marne and St. Mihiel offensives. Its casualties were also high and along with the Eighty-Ninth it was assigned to occupation duty in Germany.

Shortly after he returned home, one Kansas soldier described some of his experiences in Europe as follows:

> Our first winter in France will always be remembered because we did not always have adequate shelter, fuel, food, clothing or medical attention. Barracks had to be built. Fuel was almost unobtainable. Food, for the most part, consisted of canned beef, canned corn, canned beans and canned tomatoes. . . . The medical attention given by most of the army medical officers at that time consisted of a prescription of pills and the notation "duty" on the company sick book, which was neither a cure nor a comfort, but which served to make us use every precaution against sickness. . . . The government was not responsible for lack of fuel; and the lack of suitable food, clothing and medical attention was due, in the organizations or commands where such a condition prevailed, to inexperienced, inefficient and hard-boiled officers, who, as the court-martial records would show if a record of summary court cases had been kept, could almost commit murder with impunity on account of the rigid discipline and strict censorship which was necessarily maintained as a measure of defense against the enemy.
>
> On the other hand, too much cannot be said in praise of the officers and men who carried forward successfully the real work of construction, training and organization. . . . The French people watched the progress of our work and marveled. . . . We shall not forget our first trip on a French railroad in cars marked 40 *hommes,* 8 *chevaux* (meaning 40 men or 8 horses), and the time our train stopped. After waiting about fifteen minutes, we went forward to the engine and found the cab empty, due to the fact . . . that the engineer and fireman had become thirsty and had gone over to a nearby farm to get a drink of . . . red wine.

Following the forty-seven day Meuse-Argonne battle the same soldier was in the combat zone and commented:

> I stood on the crest of Montfaucon. . . . To the north could be seen the chain of rolling hills, covered here and there with patches

of wood, which had seemed impregnable with their hidden batteries and machine guns. To the west lay the silent wooded Forêt d'Argonne [Argonne Forest]. . . . To the east the heights of the Meuse [river] presented a beautiful but sad picture of waste and desolation. Then I turned to the south where towered the single bare peak of Vauquois. On the slopes of that ill-fated hill . . . I knew that Kansas boys had fought, some of them my former playmates, one a brother-in-law, and some had made the great sacrifice. . . . I stood there and breathed a prayer that they had not made the sacrifice in vain.

There were approximately 77,000 Kansans in service during the war and about 2,500 of them died. George Robb, who later served as state auditor for several terms, won the Congressional Medal of Honor as did Erwin R. Bleckly of the Thirty-Fifth Division. More than one hundred Kansans were awarded the Distinguished Service Cross. One Kansas soldier who received many honors was General James G. Harbord who served as the army's chief of supply and also commanded the Marine brigade that stopped the Germans at Belleau Wood in 1918 when it appeared Paris would fall into German hands. Two Kansans played major roles in the Air Corps. Donald Hudson became one of the first "aces" when he shot down his sixth German plane and Phil Billard, pioneer test pilot and instructor, was killed in a plane accident in France.

Allied military success in 1918 indicated that Germany was facing defeat and Americans expressed themselves on how the war should end—armistice or unconditional surrender. Governor Capper sent a telegram to President Wilson in September stating that Kansans wanted "a complete military victory that will put an end to militarism forever." A month later Capper wrote to a New York newspaper:

The sentiment practically unanimously expressed in Kansas is that the abdication of the Kaiser or the complete surrender of the German army are indispensable preliminaries to any negotiations for peace. . . . Kansas feels the allied armies should give the German people a vision of the meaning of a world in arms by marching through to Berlin and camping on German soil while the peace terms are being concluded.

Despite the strong tone of those statements, no Kansan was really unhappy when the armistice was signed on November 11, 1918. Celebrations, parades, and church services in Kansas communities marked the end of war.

ON THE HOME FRONT

The great need for wheat on a worldwide basis made agricultural planners encourage the growing of other crops for use at home, especially corn. Kansans were urged to conserve all kinds of food and they participated in the national program of "meatless Tuesdays" and "wheatless Wednesdays." Early in 1918, Monday was also named a "wheatless" day and Saturday became "porkless." Sugar and cornstarch were on the list of items to conserve, and there was a constant effort to prevent the hoarding of food supplies.

A shortage of coal, the fuel then used by most Kansans, created problems. In 1918, orders were issued by state and local governments which limited hours that certain businesses (pool halls and theaters, for example) could be open. The manpower shortage led to registration of men not regularly employed so that they could be used for jobs normally filled by the men in service. There were exceptions made under the draft law so that some men were available for farm and railroad work, and many men with farm backgrounds who were training at Camp Funston were given special leave at harvest time in 1918.

There were charges of price fixing made against businessmen and there were complaints that excessive profits were being made by companies that had government contracts for food, construction, and munitions. Former senator Joseph L. Bristow, editor of the Salina *Journal* and chairman of the State Public Utilities Commission, wrote in May 1917, that there were "hundreds of contractors, salesmen, manufacturers, and railway officials . . . out to get their share of the $7,000,000,000 authorized by Congress for financing the war." A critic of Bristow said that it was "no time to be knocking the government." Bristow replied, "This is no time to be robbing the people." Bristow was joined by Governor Capper in the effort to protect the taxpayer.

The federal government asked for four "Liberty Loans" and for one "Victory Loan," which involved the sale of savings bonds, and Kansans bought far more than their assigned quotas. Women's organizations worked for the Red Cross and European relief while church groups, civic clubs, and lodges all contributed time, money, and labor to a variety of wartime projects. They made bandages for military hospitals; they gathered clothing for children in France and Belgium; they provided gifts for servicemen; and they helped sell savings bonds.

After the United States entered the war, Kansans of German descent had a difficult time despite the fact that most of them supported the war effort. *Turnvereins*, German social and athletic organizations, bought sav-

Seneca women, members of a Red Cross group, making bandages during World War I.

ings bonds as did Mennonite churches. Many Mennonites were taken into service, but they asked for duty that did not involve carrying arms because of their religious beliefs. Other Mennonites volunteered hospital and agricultural services in place of military duty.

Protest against German influence took on ridiculous forms. There was a great outcry against the teaching of the German language in Kansas high schools and colleges, and in many cases it was dropped from the curriculum. In central Kansas an organization called the Night Riders circulated warnings against families with German backgrounds, and elsewhere houses and stores were painted yellow if German families did not appear as enthusiastic about the war as their neighbors thought they should be. In some cases this also happened to people of non-German descent.

Besides war-related problems, Kansas faced an influenza epidemic, which began in the fall of 1918 and took its toll of both soldiers and civilians. By the end of October more than 20,000 cases had been reported to the State Board of Health, hundreds of them at Camp Funston. Schools were closed, meetings were cancelled, and quarantines were enforced in many towns. The epidemic was prolonged by bitter winter weather, and new outbreaks took place into the spring of 1919. More than 5,500 Kansans died of the flu.

END OF WAR

Kansas did not take long in returning to peace. Veterans took advantage of new job opportunities while others returned to what they had been doing before 1917. Women had filled far more positions than ever before during the war because of the manpower shortage but in many cases they were wives and daughters who had substituted in business for their husbands and fathers so the labor market was not seriously disrupted.

Governor Capper again expressed Kansas sentiment when he announced that President Wilson's ideas for a League of Nations to stop war were worthwhile and that he could accept the treaty drawn up at Versailles. Before long, however, there would be leading Kansas politicians and others working against the League because they thought it was "unrealistic" and who would criticize Woodrow Wilson for his treaty negotiations. It did not take long for isolationism to return to the Midwest. Hardly anyone believed that a world war would happen again. Most Americans felt that the First World War had indeed been "a war to end all wars" and, secure in that feeling, they were completely ready to once again ignore Europe's problems.

Although partisan politics were secondary to wartime concerns, elections went on. Capper had led the Republican party back into power in Kansas in 1914 and was reelected in 1916, although President Wilson carried the state as a Democrat in that year. Kansas women had the right to vote for the president in 1916, and most political observers felt that they would vote for Charles Evans Hughes, the Republican. However, the Wilson slogan, "he kept us out of war," apparently was more convincing than Republicanism to Kansas women. Wilson undoubtedly also got a number of former Bull Moose votes from Progressives not yet completely reconciled to the GOP. The 1917 legislative session was marked by the passage of a "bone dry" law that put a final lid on the sale of alcoholic beverages. Supposedly, 150 legislators sang *How Dry I Am* when Governor Capper signed the bill on February 23, 1917.

In the 1918 election Capper moved up to the United States Senate while the Republican candidate for governor, Henry J. Allen, won easily. The Democrats managed to win one congressional seat but were badly outnumbered in the state legislature. Allen, a prominent Bull Mooser and owner of the Wichita *Beacon*, was a colorful person who had been nominated for governor while still in France working for the YMCA. He was a good friend of William Allen White, who had worked hard for his nomination. Allen was often at odds with the legislature and he lost far more legislative arguments than he won, but he made Kansas political life interesting.

Allen believed that the Kansas constitution needed to be brought up to date and he asked the 1919 legislature to call a constitutional convention. Although the legislature refused his plea, it did ratify the national prohibition and woman suffrage amendments. It also established a highway commission and provided for the registration and licensing of automobiles, which indicated that changing forms of transportation needed different laws.

THE "RETURN TO NORMALCY"

Most Kansas politicians were ready to go along with President Harding's "return to normalcy" after the war and that attitude, combined with the economic depression that came late in 1920, did not make for reforms in state government. People were more concerned about the length of dresses on public school girls, dancing on college campuses, and school teachers' smoking habits than they were about workmen's compensation or equal taxation. Intolerance was growing, and it affected education and politics and contributed to the rise of the Ku Klux Klan, an organization bitterly opposed by Governor Allen.

Kansans did take time to read their sports pages to see what Jess Barnes, Smoky Joe Wood, and Walter Johnson were doing in major league baseball. They also read about Jack Dempsey's devastating win over Jess Willard, the Pottawatomie County native, on July 4, 1919, in Toledo, Ohio. Willard had held the world's heavyweight title since 1915 when he had beaten Jack Johnson at Havana, Cuba, in one of history's most publicized prizefights. Voters also elected four women to the house of representatives for the 1921 session.

Labor disputes were increasing in the nation in 1919 and Kansas was involved because of the state's coal industry. The United Mine Workers union,which had not struck during the war, voted a strike for November 1, 1919, but President Wilson extended wartime controls and said that a strike would be illegal. The UMW called off the strike nationally but the miners in Kansas ignored the president and the union.

Miners in the southeastern Kansas counties had been well organized by Alexander Howat, a district president of the UMW and a powerful leader. By Howat's order ten thousand Kansas miners went out on strike and the coal fields were shut down. The Kansas consumer, who needed the coal, was caught between labor and management and Governor Allen tried to get the strike settled. He was unsuccessful and asked the state supreme court for an order allowing the state to take over the mines.

On November 17, Allen created a board to run the mines and asked for volunteer miners. On December 1 the mines were again open, using the inexperienced labor, which was protected by National Guard troops. State control lasted only about three weeks because the miners and mine operators reached a new wage agreement. Many of the volunteers were from Kansas colleges, both state and private. This item from the Washburn

College *Review* of December 3, 1919, refers to both the fuel shortage and the amateur miners:

> Twenty-one Washburn men left for the coal mines in answer to Governor Allen's call for volunteers, last Sunday evening, and a large number of others have signified their willingness to go when there is need.
>
> At the present writing, the coal situation at Washburn indicates that the college cannot remain in operation longer than this week, but a number of undetermined factors leaves it a matter of doubt exactly how soon the lack of fuel will force it to close down. . . .
>
> At a special faculty meeting Monday afternoon it was decided to further the cause of Governor Allen's efforts to secure fuel by granting academic credit to the men who left school to give their services in the mines. . . .

Governor Allen's concern over labor difficulties and how they affected the "public interest" led to the creation in 1920 of a unique state agency, the Court of Industrial Relations. It was not a court of law but a three-man board that could make rules, help solve problems between labor and management, and run businesses if necessary. It was to be concerned with industries involved in the production of food, fuel, and clothing and with transportation and utilities. There was considerable legislative debate over the establishment of the court but the law passed, much to the disgust of labor organizations.

Alexander Howat was especially displeased and he said:

> But come what will and whether or not my bones rot in a prison cell I am going to fight this law with the force of 12,000 miners in Kansas and regardless of the consequences give Governor Allen cause to remember that organized labor must and will have the right to cease work at its will. . . . Be the consequences what they may, there is no power on earth, injunction or otherwise, that will make me call off the strike.

Because the court was experimental it attracted nationwide attention and other states waited to see how it would work. Allen made dozens of speeches in support of the court and debated its principles in New York City's Carnegie Hall with Samuel Gompers, president of the American Federation of Labor.

Governor Allen's good friend, William Allen White, supported the Industrial Court at first but then he decided that it discriminated against labor. Because of White's participation in what the court called illegal picketing during a 1922 railroad strike he was arrested. White wrote an editorial entitled "To An Anxious Friend" in which he said that "free expression of the wisdom of the people" was all important and, in effect, that the state had no right to prohibit picketing. White was both praised and criticized for his stand. The editorial won him a Pulitzer Prize.

The Industrial Court dealt with approximately 160 cases during its existence (1920–1925), most of which had to do with the flour milling industry. It had no real effect on strikes nor did it do much for prices or production. It did do some good for labor regarding wages and hours, but organized labor never believed that the court had any lasting value. The court came to an end because of federal Supreme Court cases that overturned its rulings. It was an interesting but ineffective experiment, and it was repealed by the 1925 legislature.

In the fall of 1917 the first Kansas group of the Nonpartisan League was organized near Salina. The league began in North Dakota in 1915, mostly as a protest by small wheat farmers against the grain marketing business. It asked for state ownership of terminal elevators, flour mills, and packing plants and for state hail insurance on crops. Since this was a form of socialism, naturally the league was criticized. The controversy in Kansas came to a head in Barton County in March 1921. Opponents of the league would not let two speakers appear in Ellinwood, and near Great Bend two

Coal miners in southeastern Kansas before the First World War.

representatives of the league were tarred. The incident was described by J. O. Stevic, one of the victims:

> We underwent horrible treatment. Parsons and I had left Ellinwood and had got to Chase when the mob overtook us. They took us to Great Bend and we were turned over to another mob. We were then taken to a lonely place. Two men were stationed to each of our arms, holding them up while we were beaten by others.
>
> Then a circle of automobiles ringed about us and tar pots appeared. We were stripped to the waist and tar applied. Half blind we staggered away, hearing another mob was after us. We sought shelter in a strawstack, but at 3 o'clock in the morning we went back to Great Bend to learn the hour. We walked twenty miles on the railroad and came to a farm house. The farmer said that he doubted if we were human beings, but he took us in and two Leaguers were secured, who brought us to Salina.

The majority of Kansans were outraged by the mob action in Barton County even though many people disliked the league's aims. Governor Allen, who did not agree with the league, spoke out strongly and initiated a state investigation. However, witnesses were difficult to find and there were so many different stories told about who was involved that no one was ever prosecuted.

Because the league had not been completely sympathetic to the war effort it was attacked as an un-American organization. It was opposed by the new veterans' group, the American Legion, as well as the American Defense League. This was a period when anything not "100 percent American" was regarded with suspicion. People distrusted the league and its leaders, believing that its only accomplishment was taking money from farmers for dues for which it gave them nothing in return. Some critics compared the league to the radical, militant labor organization, the Industrial Workers of the World, and gave it a communist label. The league's leadership was not very effective in Kansas, or elsewhere, and it began to lose members in 1921. By 1922 it was pretty well finished. The farmers still had complaints, many of them legitimate, but the league had not solved any of their economic problems.

Kansas faced changing times in the 1920s, and it would seem that the state and its residents did not always understand how to cope with the changes. While there was excitement in the years just after the First World War, there was also a great deal of futility in politics and social action. Kansans had entered the Roaring Twenties with a kind of wonderment, and it would be a while before they figured out where they were going.

Suggestions for Reading

Henry J. Allen, *Party of the Third Part* (1921); Domenico Gagliardo, *The Kansas Industrial Court* (1941); James G. Harbord, *Leaves of a War Diary* (1925); Charles B. Hoyt, *Heroes of the Argonne* (1919); Clair Kenamore, *From Vauquois Hill to Exermont, A History of the Thirty-Fifth Division* (1919); Wilda M. Smith and Eleanor A. Bogart, *The Wars of Peggy Hull: The Life and Times of a War Correspondent* (1991); Homer Socolofsky, *Arthur Capper* (1962); William Allen White, *Autobiography* (1946); William Allen White, *The Martial Adventures of Henry and Me* (1918).

      The following articles in the *Kansas Historical Quarterly* are of interest for this period: Domenico Gagliardo, "The Gompers-Allen Debate on the Kansas Industrial Court" (November, 1934); James C. Juhnke, "Mob Violence and Kansas Mennonites in 1918" (Autumn, 1977); Clayton R. Koppes, "The Industrial Workers of the World and County Jail Reform in Kansas, 1915–1920" (Spring, 1975); Bruce Larson, "Kansas and the Nonpartisan League: The Response to the Affair at Great Bend" (Spring, 1968); Meyer Nathan, "The Election of 1916 in Kansas" (Spring, 1969); Herbert Pankratz, "The Suppression of Alleged Disloyalty in Kansas During World War I" (Autumn, 1976); Gregory J. Stucky, "Fighting Against War: The Mennonite *Vorwaerts* From 1914 to 1919" (Summer, 1972). In *Kansas History* is Sarah D. Shields, "The Treatment of Conscientious Objectors During World War I: Mennonites at Camp Funston" (Winter, 1981) and Judith P. Johnson, "Kansas in the 'Grippe': The Spanish Influenza Epidemic of 1918" (Spring, 1992).

14

The Changing, Troubled Twenties

The 1920s have been given numerous names, some of them not very flattering, such as, "The Aspirin Age," "The Lawless Decade," "The Era of Wonderful Nonsense," and "The Jazz Age." It was a time when Americans danced the Charleston, drank homemade liquor, wore raccoon coats, and followed the careers of gangsters and the "G-Men" who tried to arrest them.

It was also a time when conservatives feared political radicalism, and as a result racism, censorship, and religious crusades were on the upswing. The people who were concerned about what seemed to them to be a more sinful nation attacked sin with vigor and prohibition. The Ku Klux Klan became prominent on the American scene. At Kansas State Teachers College, Emporia, the dean of women ordered coeds to lengthen their skirts for dancing and "loud and moaning" music was banned at campus dances. In 1923 fifty Liberal high school students were suspended for smoking at a school picnic.

Kansans were no different from their fellow Americans during the Twenties. It was a time of great and rapid change, both good and bad, much of it normal reaction to a postwar period with quick economic ups and downs. Interest in the arts was increasing and although the time has been criticized for a lack of progressivism there were plenty of Kansans who had no intention of letting progressive and liberal thinking die.

The radio began to make a difference in home entertainment in the 1920s, and most Kansas stations of any size had musicians for live broadcasts. KGNO, Dodge City, featured the Tune Wranglers.

During the Twenties, agricultural machinery moved from the steam thresher to the more sophisticated combine, and greater numbers of tractors and trucks began to appear on farms. Travel by air began to interest more people as airplanes improved. In 1925 air passenger service began between Kansas City and Wichita with the flying time of approximately three hours. A one-way ticket cost $30.00. In Wichita, E. M. Laird, J. M. Moellendick, Lloyd Stearman, Clyde Cessna, and Walter Beech were laying solid foundations for the aircraft industry of today. Glenn Martin, the former Kansan, was predicting that within twenty years passenger planes would be flying from New York to Europe in less than a day. A decade later, summarizing progress in "The Air Capital," the Wichita *Eagle* said on November 25, 1937:

> The birth of Travel Air, Cessna and Swift, appearing in the 1925–28 period of rapid development, hinges largely about Walter Beech. He became nationally famous for flying to victory in many races. . . .
> During this period aviation captured the imagination of the American people. A bashful young soldier, Capt. Charles A. Lindbergh, flew to Paris and the nation went wild. Air races, the inauguration of air mail service, and the deeds of other fliers kept interest at a feverish pitch.
> The national enthusiasm caused an unbelievable boom in aviation here. One hundred and seventeen corporations, factories,

and clubs were directly or indirectly engaged in catering to the demands of the business. . . . There were 16 factories engaged in making planes.

Capital was easy to obtain. Eastern investors poured their money into Wichita. The old companies, organized before the boom, kept the lead. Cessna, Stearman, and Travel Air [Beech] turned out thousands of planes. . . .

An example of the enthusiasm for airplanes which had taken hold of Wichita is shown by the fact that Walter Innes, Jr., raised over $60,000 for establishing the Stearman factory in a single day— and by telephone. . . .

Kansas farms were beginning to join Kansas towns in acquiring electricity, although not in great numbers. One utility official in the state believed that all farms would have electricity in ten years, but it took a little longer than that. Concern about the environment was evident for the State Board of Health ordered cities to build sanitary sewage disposal plants for the prevention of river pollution.

THE FAMOUS AND THE INFAMOUS

In education, changes were taking place. In 1924 over one thousand school children in Logan and Thomas counties began riding school buses follow-

The 1920s saw the development of school buses. This one was used in Rice County.

ing consolidation in eleven districts. Eleven modern buildings had replaced sixty one-room, one-teacher schools. In 1925 Kansas State College celebrated the completion of fifty years of home economics teaching, and in 1926 the first municipal university in Kansas was created when Fairmount College became Wichita University. A different kind of institution, but one which would become very closely associated with education, was founded in 1925. The Menninger Sanitarium, Topeka, forerunner of the famed Menninger Clinic, was organized with the purpose of establishing, supporting, and maintaining a hospital "for the care and treatment of persons suffering from illness, disease or infirmity, and particularly those afflicted with nervous and mental diseases."

Kansans had plenty to cheer about athletically in the 1920s. John Levi, a student at Haskell Institute (a federally supported institution opened in 1884, now Haskell Indian Nations University) was named to the 1924 All-American football team. At that time Haskell was competing in "big time" football with colleges all over the United States. In the same year Walter Johnson, "The Big Train" from Coffeyville, was named the American League's most valuable player, and he led the Washington Senators to victory in baseball's World Series. In that series Virgil Barnes of Seneca was on the New York Giants' pitching staff and E. C. Quigley, a Kansas graduate of St. Mary's College, was a member of the umpiring crew. In the final game of the series, Johnson came to relieve in the ninth and hurled four scoreless innings, striking out five of the Giants he faced.

Johnson, born in Humboldt, was one of the greatest pitchers in history. He had a career total of 414 victories when he retired in 1927, and he was elected to the Hall of Fame. The Coffeyville *Morning News*, October

Walter Johnson

11, 1924, devoted much of its front page to Johnson and his win, and quoted from a telegram sent Johnson by the local Chamber of Commerce which ended, "flags are waving and everyone is yelling himself hoarse celebrating the event." Plans were announced for a homecoming celebration that was to include a baseball exhibition so that fans in the area could see "the mighty Johnson on the mound."

The first Kansas relays were held in 1923 and two years later Kansas University set what was then a world record in the quarter-mile relay. In 1925 Washburn's basketball team won the national AAU tournament and the Wichita High School basketball team won the national high school title, beating El Reno,

Officers of the Lawrence Police Department with illegal liquor confiscated during raids.

Oklahoma, 27–6. Two years earlier the Kansas City High School (now Wyandotte) team was national champion after defeating the team from Rockford, Illinois.

At a time when America's underworld was beginning to produce names that made national headlines—Capone, Dillinger, "Machine Gun" Kelly, "Pretty Boy" Floyd, and "Ma" Barker—Kansas was not to be outdone. In Finney County, north of Garden City, a family named Fleagle produced two sons who were leaders of a gang that specialized in bank robberies and murder. Jake and Ralph Fleagle were involved in a number of robberies in Kansas and on the Pacific Coast in the 1920s. In May 1928, the Fleagle gang robbed a bank in Lamar, Colorado, of $218,000 and killed three persons in the process. To take care of one of the wounded gang members, the Fleagles kidnapped Dr. W. W. Wineinger of Dighton. They then killed the doctor and fled western Kansas, but they were captured eventually. Ralph was hanged, Jake was shot by police, and the Fleagles were finished.

Kansas's other contribution to the most wanted list was Alvin "Creepy" Karpis. Karpis was a native of Canada, but he spent his childhood in Topeka, where his life of crime began. He served a term in the reformatory at Hutchinson, was involved in bootlegging liquor, spent another stretch at Hutchinson, and by the 1930s was rated "Public Enemy Number One" by the FBI. After a series of robberies, including banks in Fort Scott and Concordia, and membership in the Barker gang, he was captured by the FBI and spent more than thirty years in the federal penitentiary at Alcatraz. Bonnie Parker and Clyde Barrow, immortalized by the movie "Bonnie and Clyde," were in and out of Kansas as the Twenties ended and the Thirties began, but their criminal activities did not directly affect the Sunflower State.

THE AUTOMOBILE BRINGS CHANGE

Of great importance, as far as changing living habits in the 1920s were concerned, was the automobile. The automobile was certainly not new and many of them were on the roads in Kansas before 1920. But the car progressed in style, design, and efficiency after the First World War. Henry Ford was marketing a car for $295.00 and a lot of Kansans were buying Ford's product. The development of the automobile was good news to the Kansas oil industry. Kansas refineries were enlarged, additions were made to the Kansas pools in the Mid-Continent oil field, and several Kansas communities found that their economy was improved by a local refinery or producing field.

A car offered the individual a fast way to get somewhere without having to depend on public transportation, and most people were impressed with the new speeds. The Topeka Daily Capital, December 13, 1922, carried this report on a new record between Topeka and Kansas City:

> Major Anderson with a Packard Single Six, has set a mark which
> local speeders are likely to shoot at for a long time before it is
> equaled. And he did not do any speeding to make the record, either,
> he declared.
>
> Anderson, with his speedometer sealed at the local Western
> Union office, near Fifth and Kansas avenue, drove to the Missouri

No self service pumps were needed at this Lawrence station and garage in 1930.

end of the intercity viaduct in Kansas City, in just one hour and thirty-seven minutes.

The record was made by maintaining an average speed of about thirty-seven miles an hour almost all the way, Anderson said. No excessive speed was done, he declared. It is a great tribute to modern automobile design and modern gas engine construction, he declared. . . .

There was a noticeable increase in the loss of life, traced directly to people driving cars. Since there were no clearly defined traffic laws it was often difficult to regulate drivers and their vehicles. There were warnings issued about speeding, "U" turns, and parking, but it was hard to decide in different cities and counties just what was right or wrong. Prof. Raymond Flory of McPherson College pointed out that McPherson city officials attempted to regularize the treatment of traffic violations by saying that "all automobile accident cases would be held in court, witnesses would be summoned, and blame placed." In cases where violations of traffic laws were obvious, "the guilty parties would be fined."

The automobile generated additional interest in the improvement of roads. In McPherson County, after a square corner had been replaced by a curve, the local editor wrote, "the curve is so gradual that a motorist can go around it as fast as he cares or dares." In 1923 the hard-surfaced Victory Highway (later U.S. Highway 40) was opened in eastern Kansas from Kansas City to St. Marys, largely through the efforts of E. C. McNerney and oth-

Paving a segment of old U. S. 50 in Lyon County.

ers of Tonganoxie. In that same year a paved road was completed between Wellington and Wichita.

There were 335 miles of highways built in 1924 at a cost of more than $6,000,000, half of which came from federal funds. The "Good Roads Days" of the previous ten years were not forgotten, but the building of roads using state and federal money surpassed the efforts of local volunteers. Despite the improvements, a report issued in 1926 stated that Kansas was behind forty-six states in the building of good roads. Kansas at that point had less than 1,000 miles of hard-surfaced highways. Federal funding, matching state money, meant that more paving would come. Finally Kansas became a leader in paved road mileage. The automobile, and the roads it traveled, were vital to Kansas. Cars, trucks, and buses were increasingly a part of American life.

Many of the automobile travelers of the 1920s carried camping equipment. Consequently, they looked for places to pitch their tents at night and a number of Kansas communities began to provide campgrounds, many of them free. There was opposition to these grounds in some towns as owners of hotels and "tourist rooms" felt their business was being hurt. (The motel was not yet an American institution.) Many of the campgrounds suffered from vandalism, and within a few years their use decreased. Also, better roads and faster cars made overnight camping less necessary and so the camping habit decreased until it was revived with great popularity following the Second World War.

Kansans drove their new cars, used their tractors, bought phonographs, adopted the radio as a part of their way of life, and listened and danced to jazz music. And they went to the movies and loved them. The vacuum cleaner, the motor-powered washing machine, and the refrigerator made life easier for the Kansas housewife. And the "flapper," with her fringed and shapeless dresses, became a part of the Kansas scene. The radio had a real impact on American life and would eventually play an important role as politicians realized that this form of mass communication had unlimited possibilities. A Topeka hotel man predicted that modern hotels would have radios in every room and that many cars would be similarly equipped.

A DEMOCRATIC ADMINISTRATION

As the stormy years of the Henry Allen Republican administration came to an end in 1922, the Democrats were once again able to elect a governor, Jonathan M. Davis. Davis was a former legislator, an educated farmer, and a progressive in most of his political beliefs. But his programs, good or bad, had little chance of success because the legislature was overwhelmingly Republican. Kansas individual income was down in 1922, particularly among farm families, and a great many people felt that state expenditures needed to be greatly reduced.

The governor recommended to the legislature that the farmers' tax burdens be relieved and that the state should have an income tax, stronger bank regulation, and greater control over corporations. When the session was over Davis had vetoed dozens of bills and the legislature had turned around and passed the majority of them over his veto. By the summer of 1923 it was found that there was not enough money available to pay the bonuses awarded to First World War veterans, so a special session was called to make the necessary appropriation. Davis's term was marked by constant argument, especially when he attempted to appoint Democrats to positions in state government. Davis was renominated by the Democrats in 1924 but defeated for a second term in the general election that year. He stirred up a tremendous controversy just before he left office by forcing the State Board of Administration to remove Chancellor E. H. Lindley of the University of Kansas. The chancellor had not always agreed with the governor and the board's policies for the university. The governor made the comment that he intended to find out whether the state ran KU or if KU ran the state. After Lindley was fired thousands of students and alumni campaigned vigorously to get him reinstated. The Topeka Daily Capital expressed the general sentiment of Kansans for Lindley in this editorial, December 29:

> Gov. Davis's official explanation of his removal of the chancellor of the University just near the closing of a semester and in the middle of a college year is a damning document. By it the Governor is self-condemned. The character of the Chancellor, this disgraceful screed declares, is "unfit to occupy a place where the minds and hearts and souls of our young men and women are being developed." Then, in God's name, why did not the Governor take action, why dawdle along until his term was out, and in the middle of a college year perform this damming act of a corrupt and discredited administration, overwhelmingly rejected by the people of Kansas when they had an opportunity to pass on it in November?
>
> This slimy and disgusting assault on the Chancellor's character is merely a confirmation of the judgment of the people of the state in the late election. . . . The Governor's ugly attack in the words quoted will be resented by every friend of the University and repudiated by every member of the faculty and every student. If anything could make it baser it is the Governor's twaddle about being incapable, in his love of the University, of taking any action not in its best interest.

The governor also feuded with the Board of Health, all of whom were still serving under appointments made by Governor Allen. Finally, Dr. Samuel J. Crumbine, the Board's secretary and famed public health authority, resigned to take another job in New York. Both Lindley and Crumbine were popular with the public and although Crumbine left, Lindley was restored to his position after Davis left office. As a result of the controversy, the Board of Regents was created in 1925 to supervise state educational institutions. On the day before he left office Davis was charged with accepting bribes for issuing pardons from the state penitentiary, but he was acquitted in May 1925.

WILLIAM ALLEN WHITE'S FIGHT AGAINST THE KU KLUX KLAN

As the 1924 election approached Kansans were concerned with the growth of the Ku Klux Klan. The Klan of the 1920s was not the same organization that had been formed in the South following the Civil War as a protest against Radical Republican reconstruction. During the First World War a new Klan was organized by an extremely conservative Georgia minister named William Simmons. This organization developed rapidly and spread throughout much of the United States.

The Klan was against almost everything except what it defined as "Americanism." It was anti-Jewish, anti-Catholic, and anti-black, and it preached its undemocratic ideas wherever it could find listeners. Governor Allen had said that it was the "greatest curse that comes to a civilized people," and he had done his best to run it out of the state. But the Klan continued to grow and by May 1923, it was estimated that there were 60,000 Klansmen in Kansas with similar numbers existing in the other midwestern states. Organizers were sent into Kansas from Oklahoma but much of the operation was directed from Kansas City, Missouri.

William Allen White, in front of the Emporia *Gazette* office with the car he used in his anti-Klan gubernatorial campaign of 1924.

The Klan was involved in the railroad strikes in Kansas during 1922 as it acquired members among laboring men who opposed black strike breakers hired by the railroads. Part of labor's sympathy for the Klan came because of its opposition to Henry J. Allen. Since labor did not like Allen, because of the Industrial Court, and Allen did not like the Klan, some union members supported the Klan. Organized labor as a whole was not solidly behind the KKK. Allen brought suit against the Klan in 1922 and the crusade was carried on into 1923 by Attorney General Charles Griffith. However, the prosecutors and the courts had trouble keeping witnesses who were willing to testify against the Klan because of threats and pressures. The Klan operated in Kansas City, Topeka, Wellington, Salina, Dodge City, Galena, and Emporia, and in several other Kansas communities.

On July 21, 1923, 1,200 Klan members paraded in Topeka, robed and hooded, and on that day the first issue of a Klan newspaper was printed in the state capital. *The American Guardsman* outlined just what the Klan stood for, and it said that its "one great purpose" was to "teach AMERICANISM in its fullest sense." It said that every American should be allowed to worship God as he saw fit but implied that only Protestants could be really good Americans. Its creed follows:

The Tenets of the Christian Religion
White Supremacy
Closer Relationship Between American Capital
    and American Labor
Protection of Our Pure Womanhood
Preventing the Causes of Mob Violence and Lynchings
The Limitation of Foreign Immigration
Close Relationship of Pure Americanism
The Upholding of the Constitution of the United States
The Sovereignty of Our State Right
The Separation of Church and State
Freedom of Speech and Press
The Much Needed Local Reform

These statements came from an organization that inhibited free speech, lynched people, burned crosses on lawns, and became so concerned about the imagined power of Roman Catholicism that it distributed this bit of doggerel:

I would rather be a Ku Klux Klan with a robe of snowy white,
Than to be a Roman Katholic with a robe all black as night,
A KKK is American, America is his home,
While a Katholic owes allegiance to a Dago pope in Rome.

The Klan was concerned about what young people were doing while in parked cars outside of Topeka and wanted to cut down on such "evil activities." While the Klan had a large membership in Kansas it also had many critics who enjoyed making fun of it. One KU student wrote a song that sold nationally. It was entitled *Daddy Stole Our Last Clean Sheet and Joined the Ku Klux Klan.* Even with people laughing at the Klan it was still powerful enough to be a threat to the political and social structure of Kansas.

When the nominees for governor were announced—Davis, the Democrat, and Ben Paulen, the Republican—William Allen White filed as an independent because he thought that neither of the regular candidates would fight the Klan strongly. Although there was no evidence that either Davis or Paulen had any direct connection with the Klan, White felt that the Klan would exert its influence on the two parties. He wrote to friends that he did not really want to run for governor because the last thing he wanted was to get elected but he thought that somebody had to point out to Kansans how bad the Klan was. Three years before his candidacy, on August 2, 1921, White had written an editorial that expressed how he felt:

> It is an organization of cowards. Not a man in it has the courage of his convictions. It is an organization of traitors to American institutions. Not a man in it has faith enough in American courts, American laws, and American executive officers to trust them to maintain law and order, and it is an organization of lazy butter fingers in politics, or it would get out at the primary and the election and clean up the incompetent officials whom its members think are neglecting to enforce the law.
>
> The Ku Klux Klan in this community is a menace to peace and decent neighborly living, and if we find out who is the Imperial Wizard in Emporia we shall guy the life out of him. He is a joke, you may be sure. But a poor joke at that.

Since White was so well known his campaign attracted national attention. He was careful to avoid endorsements from his Republican friends who were also candidates for office because he knew he would divide the party to a degree. He wrote to Henry Allen: "I wanted to go out into this thing all by my little lonely against the Klan, and if I was defeated, not put the stigma of defeat on anyone else whose political future might be affected by defeat." White did divide the Republican vote but he was strongly supported by Allen, no longer a candidate, and by Victor Murdock of Wichita, who had not been a "regular" Republican since the Bull Moose days. Another notable opponent of the Klan was Frank Doster, the former Populist state supreme court judge.

Paulen won and White ran third, but he had about 150,000 votes and he did it mostly on his own since his organization was practically non-existent. He commented that Charles Curtis, U.S. Senator from Kansas and part Kansa Indian, had been criticized because he was not "pure white," and he also said: "The way the Catholics and Jews and colored people were persecuted by the Klan in Kansas was a dirty shame and I couldn't rest under it." His candidacy brought the Klan problem into the open. In January 1925, the state supreme court ruled that the Klan could not do business in Kansas without a charter. Since the secretary of state's office would not issue a charter the Klan was through in the state.

Although Ben Paulen of Fredonia had a reputation as a conservative Republican banker, his two administrations were not as conservative as many Kansans thought they would be. He fought for and obtained a modern highway commission and a tax on motor fuel to help maintain highways. The legislature also legalized the sale of cigarettes once again and in so doing gained a sizeable amount of tax revenue. If Kansans did not make the progress in education, social welfare, or tax reform that it might have, the blame was not on its governors.

Paulen's Republican successor was Clyde Reed, Parsons newspaperman. Reed had been Henry Allen's secretary and had served on the Industrial Court and the Public Utilities Commission. He was described as a "rugged individualist" and a champion of the ordinary Kansas taxpayer. One thing Reed wanted was tax equalization and he also asked for an income tax, which he thought necessary. The 1929 legislature put an income tax amendment on the 1930 ballot, but it was defeated. It was obvious during Reed's term of office that Kansas had gained virtually no new industries during the 1920s, and he attempted unsuccessfully to get an Industrial Development Commission established.

KANSAS INFLUENCE IN WASHINGTON AND THE END OF A DECADE

Two Kansans played parts in national politics during this period. In 1925 President Coolidge appointed William Jardine to his cabinet as Secretary of Agriculture. Jardine had been president of Kansas State College since 1919 and for several years before that he had been a professor and dean of agriculture at the college. His appointment met with general approval in Kansas, and the Manhattan *Chronicle* said, on February 15, 1925:

> President Jardine has been an outspoken advocate of the farmers'
> interests. In public speeches he has declared that only ten per cent
> of the troubles of the farmer can be remedied by legislation, that the

other 90 per cent must be solved by the farmers themselves and their immediate associates, the business men of each agricultural community.

When Herbert Hoover was elected president in 1928 his vice-president was Charles Curtis, the only person of Indian descent ever to hold the office. In August, after the Republican convention had given Curtis the nomination, there was a celebration in Topeka, birthplace of the nominee. The Topeka State Journal reported on August 18:

> Far overshadowing any previous event in Kansas or the middle west, thousands of Republicans are in Topeka today to participate in formal notification of Sen. Charles Curtis of Kansas as the party's nominee for vice-president. Every state in the nation, every county and community in the state is represented in the monster demonstration. . . .
>
> Never has there been such a setting for the notification of a party's vice presidential candidate. Never has such nation-wide interest been manifest in events surrounding ceremonies for a man who held second place on a national ticket. In earnest compliment to the senior Kansas senator and his record of a third of a century of public service, the Curtis notification has been made an occasion of almost presidential magnitude.
>
> Today Topeka is living again that final day of the Republican national convention in Kansas City—that day when "Her Charley Curtis" was unanimously selected as Herbert Hoover's running mate. . . .
>
> First time Kansas ever had a place on the ticket of a major national political party. Kansas is making the most of it. Topeka . . . began whooping it up a week ago. Began scrubbing up and strutting her stuff. Just like preparing for the Fourth in the old days. Or a boy with his first date. Nothing but thrills and expectancy. . . .

Curtis ran with Hoover again in 1932 and went down to defeat with the Republicans. He died in 1936, having spent most of his adult life in public service as a Republican with roots deep in his native state.

Another Kansan figured prominently in the national news during the 1920s. Harry Sinclair, who grew up in Independence and built a vast fortune in the oil industry from beginnings in southeastern Kansas in the early 1900s, was involved in the Teapot Dome oil deal during the scandal-ridden Harding administration. In return for money, Albert Fall, Harding's secretary of the interior, gave the Sinclair Oil Company the right to exploit the Teapot Dome reserves in Wyoming. Fall went to jail for accepting a bribe but Sinclair was acquitted of criminal charges. In a civil suit Sinclair was forced to give up his leases in Wyoming. Sinclair has been severely criticized for his part in Teapot Dome, and rightly so, but he should also be given credit for a thorough understanding of the oil business and for his ability to develop one of the country's leading industrial firms.

During the recession of the early 1920s, Kansas farm prices dropped below the national average. They improved beginning in 1925 and collapsed again as the nation entered the depression years following 1929. Kansas farmers were inclined toward independent action and most of them believed in the kind of self-reliance that Dr. Jardine advocated. However, their problems led them to join organizations such as the Kansas Farm Bureau as they hoped to better their situation through unified action. When the economic crash came in 1929 the Kansas farm mortgages had reached a total of 440 million dollars. In Washington the Kansas farmer had a strong friend in Senator Arthur Capper. In the 1920s Capper became a leader of the group fighting to help farmers, and he continued in that role through the 1920s.

In 1925, when things were looking up for Kansas agriculture, enthusiastic reports on the state's farm possibilities were circulated. The Kaw valley was compared to the valley of the Nile, and its promoters claimed that it exceeded the ancient land in production and fertility. Such enthusiasm had factual support, but the world's economy simply did not hold up beyond 1929 and the state's prosperity, based heavily on agriculture, went down once again in the 1930s.

The following statement helps to illustrate the changing times of the 1920s. In 1925 a small town Kansas editor wrote: "A few years ago when a man got tired of farming he came to town and bought a livery stable. Now he comes in and buys a filling station. . . .When a man's neighbors can't understand how he makes a living, they start the story that he bootlegs whiskey. . . ."

At about the same time a raid in northwestern Kansas had resulted in thirty-five arrests and confiscation of six automobiles, sixteen stills, seven thousand gallons of mash, and two hundred and fifty gallons of whiskey. Apparently, despite all that Kansas and federal laws had done in relation to liquor sales, there was no way to stop people with a thirst from trying to quench it! However, the national superintendent of the Anti-Saloon League, F. S. McBride, said in 1929 that prohibition was "the biggest Santa Claus the United States of America has ever known." He credited the national prohibitory law with abolishing slums, lowering the death rate, and raising the standard of living for "the mass of American people." There were some Kansans who agreed with him.

As the 1920s closed the Kansas housewife found prices reasonable in her favorite grocery store—a dime for a box of cereal, a quarter for two pounds of cookies, thirty-two cents for a pound of sausage, and twenty-nine-cent coffee. If she were in Wichita and did not want to cook, her family could patronize the local White Castle. "Clean and fast and cheap," the distinctive chain of hamburger stands, which became a national institution, began in Wichita in 1921. Families gathered around the radio to listen to Amos 'n' Andy, Guy Lombardo's orchestra, Uncle Dave's Children's Club, or the Kansas Farmer Old Time Orchestra. And even with the economic blows of 1929 Walt Mason, a favorite columnist of Kansans, could write at year's end:

> Farewell, old year. . . . I think you've been a good old year. Of course a poor man here and there complains that he is in despair; he says his children daily cry and cry in vain for pumpkin pie; he hunts for work throughout the town and all employers turn him down. But nearly everyone I know is earning good and ample dough; few are so poor they cannot drive their cars with pistons four or five. . . .'Tis true hot weather hurt the corn, and farmers wished they were not born; some cornfields shriveled in a night, but other crops came through all right, the cows gave milk, the hens laid eggs, enough to fill the farmers' kegs, the apple trees were loaded down with fruit they marketed in town. . . . Goodby, old year, you had your flaws, like every year that ever was, but when I view you, con and pro, I rather hate to see you go.

Suggestions for Reading

There have been few books written about Kansas during the 1920s. William Allen White's *Autobiography* (1946) and Walter Johnson's *William Allen White's America* (1947) contain some information on the era as do the various biographies of White. Homer Socolofsky, *Arthur Capper* (1962); Marvin Ewy, *Charles Curtis of Kansas* (1961); Lawrence J. Friedman, *Menninger: The Family and the Clinic* (1990); Patrick G. O'Brien and Kenneth J. Peak, *Kansas Bootleggers* (1991); Frank Joseph Rowe and Craig Miner, *Borne on the South Wind: A Century of Kansas Aviation* (1994); and William E. Unrau, *Mixed Bloods and Tribal Dissolution: Charles Curtis and the Quest for Indian Identity* (1989) are helpful. Raymond L. Flory, ed., *McPherson at Fifty: A Kansas Community in the 1920's* (1970), gives good information about a representative middle-sized Kansas town. Martha Vogt and Christina Vogt, *Searching for Home* (1979) deals with children who came to Kansas during this era via the "Orphan Trains," while Marilyn Irvin Holt, ed., *Model Ts, Pep Chapels, and a Wolf at the Door: Kansas Teenagers, 1900–1940* (1994) relates to young people with an emphasis on the 1920s.

The following *Kansas Historical Quarterly* articles shed some light on the period: Michael J. Brodhead, "A Populist Survival: Judge Frank Doster in the 1920's" (Winter, 1968); Francis D. Farrell, "Dr. Lindley's Christmas Present" (Spring, 1956); John R. Finger, "The Post-Gubernatorial Career of Jonathan M. Davis" (Summer, 1967); Charles W. Sloan,

Jr., "Kansas Battles the Invisible Empire: The Legal Ouster of the KKK From Kansas, 1922–1927" (Autumn, 1974); Jack W. Traylor, "William Allen White's 1924 Gubernatorial Campaign" (Summer, 1976); Sondra Van Meter, "The E. M. Laird Airplane Company: Cornerstone of the Wichita Aircraft Industry" (Autumn, 1970); and Clinton Warne, "The Municipal Campgrounds of Kansas" (Summer, 1963).

Mary S. Rowland has done three articles on this period for *Kansas History:* "Kansas and the Highways, 1917–1930" (Spring, 1982); "Kansas Farming and Banking in the 1920s" (Autumn, 1985); and "Social Services in Kansas, 1916–1930" (Autumn, 1984). Others are Richard C. Cortner, "The Wobblies and *Fiske* v. *Kansas:* Victory Amid Disintegration" (Spring, 1981); Grace Dobler, "Oil Field Camp Wives and Mothers" (Spring, 1987); and Patrick G. O'Brien, "'I Want Everyone to Know the Shame of the State': Henry J. Allen Confronts the Ku Klux Klan, 1921–1923" (Summer, 1996).

The early development of Haskell Institute is told in Don W. Wilson, *Governor Charles Robinson of Kansas* (1975) and two articles in *Kansas History* provide additional information: Donald J. Berthrong, "From Buffalo Days to Classrooms: The Southern Cheyennes and Arapahos and Kansas" (Summer, 1989); and Keith A. Sculle, "'The New Carlisle of the West': Haskell Institute and Big-Time Sports, 1920–1932" (Autumn, 1994).

15

The "Dirty Thirties":
Kansas and the Great Depression

The worst of the hard times did not hit Kansas immediately after the 1929 stock market crash. Grain crops were good for the next two years although prices dropped to unheard-of lows, with wheat going down to an average of thirty-three cents a bushel in 1931. The full impact of the depression was felt in the western part of the state with the coming of the drought. By 1933 subsoil moisture in Kansas was exhausted, crops did not grow, and feed for livestock was scarce. In some areas farmers were forced to use Russian thistles (tumbleweeds) for feed, and finally many of them had to give up livestock production altogether.

As the late Clifford R. Hope, Sr., who served Kansas for many years in Congress, wrote:

> None of the calamity periods can compare from the standpoint of financial loss, long lasting distress, suffering and discouragement with the decade of the 1930's.
>
> The great depression which began in the fall of 1929 affected Kansas just as it did every other part of the country, but on top of it there was superimposed almost a decade of drought and duststorms. In other words, Kansas and the neighboring Great Plains states got a double dose of misery and calamity.

The dust really began to blow in 1933 and for four years western Kansas was part of the Great Plains "dust bowl." Some days it seemed that much of the state was being blown away as Oklahoma dust settled on Kansas. Housewives used rugs and towels to seal door and window openings but nothing kept the dirt from sifting in. It covered furniture in homes, desks in schools and offices, and the merchandise in stores. In some cases it drifted around buildings and farm machinery like snow, and it aggravated respiratory illnesses and hampered all kinds of activities, including travel.

The worst year for the "black blizzards" was 1935. On March 15 of that year, a date remembered as "black Friday," a tremendous dust storm hit western Kansas but an even worse one rolled in on April 10. The Garden City *Daily Telegram* reported:

> The "Black Friday night" duster . . . was equalled if not surpassed by the intensity of the top soil blizzard which swept this region today. After a brief cessation from yesterday's blow during the early morning hours, a new storm swept in . . . and grew steadily worse until it was dark as night before noon. Bright electric signs could hardly be seen across the street.
>
> Traffic was halted, schools closed, numerous meetings and social functions postponed and virtually all business in Garden City and neighboring towns was suspended. Other than grocery and drug stores most business houses were closed and clerks had returned to their homes. Only first and second hour classes were held this morning in the public schools, including the junior college.

A "black blizzard" rolling across Morton County in 1935.

At Hutchinson the dirt was mixed with a rain shower and it rained mud balls. At Goodland and Norton there was snow blowing with the crust, which made conditions even worse. The dust drifted so badly on railroad tracks that a train was derailed between Scott City and Garden City. Near Deerfield crews had to walk ahead of trains to see if the track could be used. A funeral and a murder trial had to be postponed because of the severity of that April storm. At other times people lost their way in the clouds of dust, and some deaths were recorded.

Dust has always blown on the Plains during times of drought but the worst of the dust storms could have been prevented in Kansas in the 1930 if everyone had cooperated in soil conservation programs. In western Kansas thousands of acres were farmed by "suitcase farmers" who were on the land only at planting and harvesting times, and thousands more acres were farmed by tenants who did not have the money or machinery to invest in conservation. Some landowners worked at conservation while their neighbors did not, and it would have taken a combined effort to keep the soil on the fields. Finally, state and regional programs, with the assistance of the federal government, began to attack the problem of soil conservation and the dust storms died down.

As they had done during earlier periods of hard times, Kansans joked about dust storms. There was a story told that the crust was so thick that a prairie dog was seen digging a burrow ten feet in the air, and another said that a man was hit by a raindrop and his friends had to throw a bucket of sand in his face to revive him. The birds were said to fly backward to keep the dust out of their eyes.

The wind brought more than dust in the 1930s. Tornadoes struck several communities, with Liberal being the hardest hit in 1933. Four people were killed, and damage surpassed a million dollars. In western Kansas, where dust and drought were the worst, Garden City, Logan, and Pratt were among the towns visited by tornadoes. Other Kansas communities suffered similar fates while Kingman was a target in both 1937 and 1938.

THE DEPRESSION

Merchants felt the depression first in some areas, and cash became a requirement for trade in many stores while others set limits on charge accounts. There were Kansas banks that remained open but still did not have much money available for lending. To some people who did borrow it seemed as though it would take a lifetime to repay only a few hundred dollars. The person with a salary, even though it was cut, was better off than most farmers or blue-collar workers on an hourly wage. In Kansas, as in other states, there were hundreds of men "on the bum"—hitching rides on freight trains and seeking to earn a meal or a half-dollar by doing some small job for a businessman or a housewife. They were called tramps, bums, and hoboes, and they were always in evidence in the larger towns along railroad main lines.

Grocery prices dropped like everything else, but if one had hardly any money all prices still seemed high. Many families subsisted on very basic foods and bought only bread, milk, beans, potatoes, and a minimum of meat, but many supplemented those foods with what they grew at home. Home-canned foods were important to many households, and great numbers of families in towns raised a few chickens for their eggs and meat. The farmer who could provide feed for livestock often did his own butchering and processing and kept meat on his table. Game birds and fish also assisted family food budgets.

Periods of extreme heat and drought often made raising a garden difficult, but towns with deep wells were better off than rural areas, and gardenhose irrigation was practiced by urban Kansans. They also used water to alleviate the summer heat in their houses by building window air conditioners that were simply boxes filled with excelsior through which water ran from a hose while an electric fan on the inside, in front of the window, drew in and pushed the slightly cooler air through the room. Several days would pass in succession with the temperature over 100 degrees, and once in a while somebody would fry an egg on the sidewalk to lend a touch of humor to an uncontrollable situation. On summer nights many families moved outside to sleep, hoping for a cooling breeze.

In some counties the annual fairs were canceled because local farmers did not have enough livestock or produce to make a display worthwhile. In others the fairs went on and even though exhibits were limited, the carnivals, horse races, and baseball games made people forget for a time how tight things were. Kansans looked for things to do that did not cost much money, and they supported town-team sports, high school athletic events, and summer outdoor band concerts. One western Kansas housewife reminisced about social life in mid-1930:

> Strange as it may seem we had fun. I can remember the days when the wind and dirt would blow all day until along about sunset when the wind would go down and the air could clear. One of the neighbors would drive into the yard . . . and say "come over for supper." We would hurriedly fix a dish of something to take and the whole family would go; after supper we would play cards and really have a good time. We also had party dances in our homes; there would be two or three men available who played a violin and a guitar; we would move enough furniture out of the front room so we

would have enough room to dance. . . .Most of us managed to buy a radio, which was something new, and we spent many a night listening to the programs and music.

The drug store, the pool hall, the meeting rooms of lodges and fraternal groups, and the local American Legion or Veterans of Foreign Wars buildings were social centers, along with the churches and schools. There were still people who could afford to pay their dues to a variety of organizations that offered inexpensive entertainment, particularly in smaller communities. Young people benefited from those organizations and from their 4-H Clubs and the extracurricular groups active in high schools. Many a teenage romance flourished on nickel Cokes, free dances, and bowling at ten cents a line.

Some areas of the state suffered from an overabundance of rabbits that were destroying the already limited pastures. Consequently, jackrabbit drives were organized, and what started out to be an economic venture turned into a social event. Pens were built and residents gathered to drive the rabbits through the fields into the pens where the animals were killed. In Greeley County in January 1935, more than 1,600 rabbits were exterminated. Stores, offices, and schools were closed at times for rabbit drives and one participant said, "It's lots of fun, and does much to relieve a situation which was rapidly becoming acute." While it seems a cruel sport it did save pasture land while the rabbits provided a source of food at a time when it was needed, and, as one observer put it, the drives "gave the people something to look forward to and participate in. The emotional outlet may have been worth it all."

Kansas lost population during the 1930s but part of the loss can be traced to a declining birth rate. Some people left because of the drought, the dust, and the depression, but most of them stuck with their farms, hoping for rain and better times. Some rural Kansans who did not have a major investment in the land or whose family roots were not deep in the state sought to better their conditions on the west coast during the last half of the decade. However, there was not the mass migration from Kansas as the one from Oklahoma described so vividly in John Steinbeck's *Grapes of Wrath*.

JOHN R. BRINKLEY VERSUS REPUBLICANS AND DEMOCRATS

The depression hampered business and agriculture but it did not take anything away from the spice of Kansas politics in the 1930s. The Republicans fought among themselves in 1930 with Frank "Chief" Haucke of Council Grove winning the nomination for governor. The Democrats nominated Harry Woodring, a banker from Neodesha. Neither man was well known politically but both were young, veterans of the First World War, and active in the American Legion.

The 1930 general election probably would not have held any particular excitement for ordinary Kansas voters if an unusual third candidate had not appeared. His name was Dr. John R. Brinkley; he ran as an independent write-in candidate, and his background was unique. Brinkley had come to Kansas in 1918 and opened a medical practice in Milford where he offered to restore male sexual vitality by transplanting goat glands. Supposedly his first operation was successful for his patient finally became a father after years of frustration. Other patients, believing in Brinkley's magic, helped spread his fame. The Brinkley empire grew. He built and paid for a hospital and a drug store in Milford, he opened his own bank, and he traveled by Cadillac car or in his own airplane. In 1922 he opened the first radio station in Kansas—KFKB, "Kansas First, Kansas Best"—and his broadcasts, the "Medical Question Box of the Air, " were heard in thousands of homes within a few years. He answered letters from listeners on the air, gave lectures on all aspects of health, and arranged for his special patent medicines to be sold in several Kansas drug stores.

But the doctor's success was challenged by the American Medical Association, which took a dim view of his practices, particularly since he had never completed work for a degree at a recognized medical school. His diplomas were from schools that issued impressive looking pieces of paper but offered little in the way of regular training. The Kansas City (Missouri) *Star* and its radio station, WDAF, began a series of investigations into Brinkley's background and publicly denounced him. The Kansas Board of Medical Examination and Registration revoked Brinkley's license to practice and, fearing that his broadcasting rights might also be taken away, the "doctor" became a politician.

The ballots were already prepared for the election when Brinkley decided to run so anyone wishing to vote for him would have to write his name on the ballot. Brinkley had registered as a candidate under "J. R. Brinkley" and anyone not putting his name down

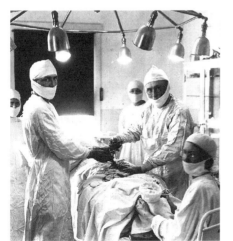

The infamous Dr. John R. Brinkley in his operating room. He is second from the right.

in that way would have the ballots thrown out. Because of William Allen White's independent candidacy in 1924 great care had been taken to protect "regular" candidates from independent, nonpartisan challengers. Brinkley used KFKB to good advantage, beaming his political speeches into voters' living rooms. His platform advocated better highways, free textbooks, a lake in every county (which he said would increase rainfall), tax equalization, cheap automobile license plates, and community health clinics. His slogan was "Clean out, Clean up, and Keep Kansas Clean." The Federal Radio Commission was trying to revoke his broadcasting license at the time, but he managed to forestall that action until after the election.

The Brinkley campaign was colorful. Although he depended heavily on radio broadcasts he did appear before large crowds, accompanied by his wife and his son, "Johnny Boy" He was also assisted by Roy Faulkner, "The Lonesome Cowboy," who entertained by singing and playing the guitar. Brinkley mixed religion with politics and made people believe that the Lord was on his side. When the final count was in, Woodring was the victor by a very narrow margin over Haucke, with Brinkley finishing a fairly close third. There is still speculation over the 1930 vote count because there were some irregularities, and perhaps Brinkley really won. The write-in votes created a counting problem, and there was some dispute on Republican and Democratic votes, but the feeling was that if the Republicans asked for a recount more Brinkley votes might have been ruled valid giving him a chance to win. Brinkley, as a write-in candidate, had no right of recount. Woodring's election was finally declared, several days later.

Brinkley's success in gathering votes led people to believe that he would run again in 1932, and they were right. Brinkley's critics pointed out that he would have difficulty in carrying out some of his plans and that much of his support came from the "lunatic fringe" of American voters. However, Brinkley was only one of several politicians in America during the 1930s who advocated unrealistic governmental changes and appealed to voters struggling to survive the depression. There are similarities between Brinkleyism and Populism, as Francis W. Schruben points out, because Populism "appealed to the underdog, the victim of social and economic injustice, just as Brinkley appealed to him at a later day."

Harry Woodring's one term as governor was not marked by any great accomplishments. He was the only Democrat elected to a statehouse office, and his efforts to cut back state expenditures were blocked by Republican legislators and department heads. The governor reduced his own salary, and in the highway department, the one place where the Democrats held control, he managed to reduce salaries. Woodring finally ordered a reduction in these salaries not fixed by law. There was talk about scandal in the highway department, which might have dated from previous administrations, but no investigation took place until after Woodring left office. At that point it was discovered that contractors bidding on state highway jobs had contributed to the support of the Democratic campaign fund. The 1931 state legislature, urged on by Alfred M. Landon, did come up with one major accomplishment when it passed a law giving the state control over the regulation and conservation of oil reserves.

Landon's work on the behalf of independent midwestern oil producers kept his name in front of Kansans, and he was nominated for governor by the Republicans in 1932. A former Bull Mooser, he had worked for and supported Clyde Reed's efforts on behalf of progressive Republicanism. Woodring had no trouble getting the Democratic nomination again and Brinkley, who had never stopped campaigning, had his name printed on the ballot in 1932 as the Independent candidate. Brinkley had sold KFKB to the Farmers and Bankers Life Insurance Company of Wichita but he was not out of the broadcasting business. Since he was in difficulties with the U.S. government he established a new station, XER, in Villa Acuna, Mexico, just across the border from Del Rio, Texas. The station's transmitter was so powerful that Brinkley could be heard in Kansas.

Brinkley Clubs supported his candidacy, along with more than two hundred Cowboy and Cowgirl Ranch Clubs, which rallied youthful Kansans to his cause. At his rallies Roy Faulkner sang and Mrs. Brinkley and "Johnny Boy" were on the platform. In addition to his sixteen-cylinder Cadillac, Brinkley had a large truck that he called "Ammunition Train No. One." The truck's sides let down to form a speaking platform and he was generally preceded by a Milford minister who testified to Brinkley's generosity, piety, and honesty. When Brinkley himself began to speak the lights were lowered except for one spotlight that made him the central figure. Brinkley bothered his opponents, and William Allen White wrote: "Are we going to bow our heads after the election; bow in shame that the intelligent, patriotic people of this state did not have the sense or the courage to avert this disgrace? Shall Kansas be greeted by a gibing ba-a-a, the cry of the billy goat, when they walk the streets of other states?"

Despite Brinkley and Woodring's energetic campaigns the Republicans won and Alf Landon moved into the governor's office. Woodring and Guy Helvering, both of whom had worked hard for the election of Franklin D. Roosevelt as president, went to Washington—Woodring as Assistant Secretary of War and Helvering as Commissioner of Internal Revenue. The Kansans who chose a Republican governor in 1932 also elected their only congresswoman, Kathryn O'Laughlin McCarthy of Hays, a Democrat. She served one term, losing to Frank Carlson in 1934.

THE NEW DEAL

On September 15, 1932, Franklin D. Roosevelt spoke in Topeka in sympathy with American farmers and the rock-bottom prices they were receiving for their products. The depression-ridden Kansans were to vote
overwhelmingly for FDR. Landon and the state legislature were no less
sympathetic to the plight of the farmer. They managed to pass a law taxing
oleomargarine not made from domestic animal or vegetable oil and a law
that barred foreclosures of mortgages and liens against real estate for six
months after March 1933.

The first Roosevelt administration opened with the "bank holiday,"
which meant that banks would be closed temporarily and withdrawals from
accounts would be limited. Governor Landon, however, beat the president
to the punch and a great majority of existing banks in Kansas had their business under control by the time the federal proclamation was issued.

A banking crisis came about in the state because funds were with-
drawn from relatively sound Kansas banks by banks outside the state.
Landon and the state bank commissioner agreed that a law was needed to
limit deposit withdrawals to 5 percent, and the governor discussed the
plan with the directors of the state banking association. The directors were
unenthusiastic until they heard that large banks in Kansas City, Missouri,
were faced with long lines of depositors wanting their money. Landon went
to the legislature, and in two hours a banking law was passed limiting withdrawals and giving state government control over the activities of all financial institutions for two years. Kansas went along with the national
holiday, and on March 13, when it ended, most of the Kansas banks operating ten days before reopened on a sound basis. Most banks stayed healthy
and depositors did not see their money go down the drain.

There were bankers who saw the newly initiated Federal Deposit Insurance Corporation (1933) as a threat to individualism but with the passage of time they realized that the FDIC and its accompanying federal
audits was beneficial to both banks and depositors. In the 1990s there was
not a bank in Kansas that was not covered by FDIC and what was then a
New Deal innovation is something that is now taken for granted.

The "alphabet agencies" of the New Deal drew scornful comment
from many Kansans, but in reality they were the salvation of the state's
residents. Governor Landon showed little hesitancy in going along with
the Roosevelt program. In fact, much of the New Deal program had been
endorsed, at least in part, by Landon. He was well aware of the need for
financial assistance in a variety of forms, such as the encouragement of
agricultural programs offering relief to the farmer and the dust bowl concerns of water and soil conservation.

The Agricultural Adjustment Act (AAA), the National Recovery Act (NRA), the Reconstruction Finance Corporation (RFC), the Public Works Administration (PWA), the Home Owners Loan Corporation (HOLC), the Works Progress Administration (WPA), the National Youth Administration (NYA), and the Civilian Conservation Corps (CCC) all had an impact on Kansas life. Farmers complained about the federal government telling them what to do concerning crops and livestock and eventually the AAA was declared unconstitutional (1936), but the allotment checks, totaling millions of dollars, received by most of those same farmers, saved their economic lives. At CCC camps in several counties unemployed young men found work that was to benefit hundreds of others. They built lakes and planted farm shelterbelts, which meant that water stayed where it fell, and soil was held where it ought to be. The NYA gave jobs to college and high school students. In spite of jokes about people leaning on shovels at federal work projects the state acquired new school buildings, courthouses, and a variety of other public structures and road improvements. In addition, a great many Kansans had a chance to draw a paycheck during times when they could not find another job, thus preserving their dignity. More people worked than loafed on those projects, some of which even gave jobs to unemployed artists, musicians, and writers, to the betterment of American cultural life. On a state basis, most of these programs were administered by the bipartisan Kansas Emergency Relief Committee (KERC).

Of lasting importance was rural electrification. The first Rural Electrification Administration project in Kansas was in Brown and Atchison counties with power generated by the Horton electric plant, beginning in April 1938. Rural electrification became known as "the best hired hand" the farmer could have, and that initial cooperative effort was followed by thirty-eight others in the state.

THE LANDON ADMINISTRATION

The 1932 general election had seen the passage of a state income tax amendment on a graduated basis, but the Kansas taxpayer had a break with lower property taxes, for this was a time when a great many westerners were "land poor." Landon pushed for a budget and cash basis law (for which the Woodring administration had laid a foundation), so that state government could be put on a "pay as you go" footing. No indebtedness could be taken on by state government unless there was money on hand in the state treasury to pay it, and each state agency was required to present a realistic budget. The governor was also concerned about the financing of local governments on a sound basis.

One of the greatest achievements of the Landon administration was the creation of the Legislative Council, an organization that provided a research agency to give legislators the answers they needed. It was the first of its kind to be established in the United States and its fact-finding powers assured that the drafting of bills was placed on a professional basis never before achieved. While Governor Landon cannot be given credit for the origination of the Legislative Council idea, he encouraged its implementation. It was the brainchild of several people associated with state government, and it was made effective by people such as Dr. Fred Guild. Now replaced by another kind of legislative liaison (the Legislative Coordinating Council), the council's foundations still remain, and legislative research is still an important part of Kansas government.

The first Landon term was marred by the Finney bond scandal although attempts made to link the governor with governmental fraud were unsuccessful and had no basis in fact. The Finneys of Emporia, Warren and Ronald, father and son, were successful financiers and close associates of important political figures in both major parties. It was discovered that the Finneys had forged municipal and school bonds and had obtained cash for their own use from the state treasury. Involved also was the state treasurer, T. B. Boyd. Landon placed troops in the statehouse and called a special session of the legislature in 1933 to deal with the scandal.

The two Finneys stood trial, along with Boyd. All three were convicted and sentenced to prison but the elder Finney committed

Above: Alfred M. Landon on the presidential campaign trail as the GOP nominee in 1936. He carried only Maine and Vermont, a victim of the Roosevelt landslide. Left: Charles Curtis campaigning for vice-president. He served in both houses of Congress, as Herbert Hoover's vice-president, and was his unsuccessful running mate in 1932.

suicide. Roland Boynton, attorney general, and Will French, state auditor, were impeached on November 21, 1933, but the senate did not convict them, and they completed their terms in office. At the time the investigation began there were nearly a half million dollars worth of forged bonds in the state treasury, and the Finneys were described as "financial dictators" of the state of Kansas.

People were still talking about the Finney bond scandal at election time in 1934, but Landon was a solid choice to repeat as governor. He had an opponent in the primary, Doctor Brinkley, who had decided to become a Republican. Landon disposed of the goat gland specialist with little difficulty. By then Brinkley was in trouble with the Mexican government, which shut down station XER. Brinkley had made twelve million dollars on rejuvenation operations alone but by 1938 his financial world collapsed, and he took bankruptcy in 1941, just a year before his death.

The Democratic candidate in 1934 was Omar Ketchum, the capable and personable mayor of Topeka. The national Democratic organization did not back Ketchum very strongly, but it was highly unlikely that he could have defeated Landon under any circumstances. The governor was reelected by large margin.

One question asked when Landon entered the governor's office for the second time concerned how far Kansas was willing to go with FDR and the New Deal. In Congress, both Senators Capper and McGill had endorsed most of what Roosevelt had offered the country. In the House the Kansas delegation was constantly concerned with agricultural problems, with Clifford Hope providing leadership. However, the Republican House members were not sold on the entire New Deal program. Whatever complaints Kansas Republicans (and some Democrats) may have voiced about the New Deal they could not afford to stray far from its aims, or from its financial assistance. Kansas congressmen voted unanimously for the Social Security Act in 1935, and in 1936 two amendments to the state constitution passed, one of which approved federal measures for unemployment insurance and Social Security.

In the statehouse Landon continued to work for more equitable taxation, water and soil conservation, and the protection of the Kansas oil market. He answered the call of Governor Marland of Oklahoma by sending a representative to Dallas, Texas, where an oil and gas compact was drawn up. With the help of Congress, the states agreed to participate in controlling oil imports and domestic production. Kansas ratified the compact and has periodically renewed its membership since. Conservation of natural resources was a part of the compact's aim but the real purpose was to insure stable prices for small midwestern producers.

On the whole, labor made progress during the 1930s, but Governor Landon did have to face one serious situation. The coal mines were quiet, particularly after the United Mine Workers replaced Alexander Howat with a less fiery leader, but in the lead and zinc areas of southeastern Kansas trouble broke out in 1935 and 1936. Acting on a request from Cherokee County officials who said pickets threatened violence, Landon sent the National Guard to preserve order. He was not happy about having to use the Guard, but he pointed out that he did not want law enforcement to break down, and there had been complaints about both strikers and local lawmen causing trouble.

Throughout Landon's second term there was talk that Landon might be a possibility for the Republican presidential nomination in 1936. Landon was nominated but no one could have defeated Franklin D. Roosevelt in 1936 with the nation still in the depths of the depression. The Roosevelt image was too solid for any Republican to combat. An interesting sidelight in 1936 was that Communist party candidate, Earl Browder, was a native Kansan.

Landon was completely realistic about his candidacy, and while he did not publicly concede that Roosevelt would win, he knew how impossible his chances were. He was handicapped by some of his supporters who made speeches that expressed a far more conservative viewpoint than his own. Kansas was excited about Landon's nomination, and thousands of people gathered on the statehouse grounds in the evening of July 23, 1936, for the official notification ceremonies. It was a blistering hot night, and the governor commented that he hoped his speech would bring rain. One reporter replied that if it did Landon would carry every state in the Midwest. It did not rain, and despite their enthusiasm over Landon's nomination, Kansans did not cast enough Republican votes for him to carry his own state. Only Maine and Vermont went Republican in 1936, and the second term of FDR's New Deal was launched. Governor Landon never again sought public office, but his interest in progressive government and politics continued. Donald R. McCoy summed up the governor's record very well when he wrote:

> No man is nominated for President without a record, and no man, once he has run this race, can retire from public life. Landon, to be sure, had done the extraordinary during the early New Deal days: he was the only Republican governor to have won reelection in 1934, and he had balanced his state's budget. These feats, and a shrewd publicity campaign, led to his nomination. But most Republicans and Democrats did not know that Landon had twice bolted his party—the only politician in American history to do this and nevertheless receive a major-party presidential nomination. He had been an active opponent of the Ku Klux Klan, a rebel who had

fought the major oil companies and the utility interests, a forceful advocate of conservation, and a fairly successful reform governor. . . .

After his nomination . . . Landon compiled another record. He tried to reconstruct his party, into a moderate rather than a conservative force. He hammered away at Republicans to recognize labor unions, to regulate the excesses of capitalism, to support essential welfare services, to champion free speech, and to seek world peace while maintaining adequate national defenses. . . .His failure to make a favorable impression on the public mind was partly because of his moderation, and partly because he was occasionally immoderate. . . .

It is for his record of a half century in politics—not for the defeat of 1936—that Alf Landon is important. In making that record, he contributed to the changes in this nation, state, and party, he reflected the ways of a politician, and he was a fascinating amalgam of moderation and independence.

In 1936 a Democrat, Walter Huxman, was elected governor, but he was faced with a Republican legislature. When Huxman took office there was a need for a new source of revenue to finance the programs for the needy, aged, blind, and dependent children, in cooperation with the federal social welfare program. Over Huxman's protests the legislature enacted a 2 percent sales tax but instead of all the money going to social welfare, much of it was used for other purposes, particularly property tax relief. It was a badly managed system and the governor was blamed for much that went wrong. At first the sales tax was paid with small, metal tokens, each worth one-tenth of a cent. Those Kansans who disliked the governor and the tax named the tokens "Huxies" He called a special session in 1938 to try to meet additional relief needs, but only two out of twenty-six days were spent on the problem, and the gap between governor and legislature grew even wider.

Although Huxman was praised by some as one of the best governors in Kansas history he was sharply criticized by anti-New Dealers who said he was a puppet of the Roosevelt administration. He was also accused of being a "wet" because he signed a bill legalizing the sale of 3.2 beer—a bill that the legislature had initiated and passed. The Republicans rallied around a new standard bearer in 1938, Payne Ratner of Parsons, and when Jonathan Davis, running as an independent, pulled away some Democratic votes, Huxman was beaten. He went on to have a long and distinguished career as a federal judge, and he was widely known and respected for his work in the courts.

In 1938 a new face appeared in Kansas politics as an independent candidate for the U.S. Senate. Gerald Winrod, a radio preacher who headed an organization known as Defenders of the Christian Faith and who had made a great deal of money from his religious activities, began to campaign on a platform that was anti-Jewish, anti-Communist, anti-Catholic, and that sounded very much like Fascism. He had made a trip to Germany and was impressed by Hitler's plans for that country. Fortunately Kansas voters had the good sense not to elect Winrod and sent Clyde Reed to the Senate instead. Although he did not run for office again, Winrod continued to preach his far-right ideas until his death in 1957.

A number of reforms in state government came about during Ratner's two terms—reforms that other governors and legislatures had only talked about. For example, several different offices that had been collecting fees and taxes were combined into a new department of revenue and taxation and a merit system for government employment, the basis for the present state civil service, was established. Even before Ratner's first term expired events in Europe were to affect the lives of Kansans and the state's economy.

HEROES AND HEROINES

Although politics was important in Kansas during the 1930s, particularly because of the national roles played by Kansas candidates and the fact that depression relief measures were tied to political philosophies, many other people and events caught the attention of Kansans.

The decade opened with a visit to Topeka by the noted African American, George Washington Carver. Called the "foremost agricultural scientist of the age," Carver had become an almost legendary figure in his own lifetime. He was credited with discoveries of how to make a variety of products from two southern crops, sweet potatoes and peanuts. Carver had lived in Kansas in his youth, attempting to get an education whenever he had the opportunity. In 1886 he took a homestead near Beeler in Ness County but two years later mortgaged his farm to go to college. At the age of thirty-two he joined the faculty of Alabama's Tuskegee Institute where he stayed until his death in 1943.

Amelia Earhart, shown here after her first solo flight, became the first woman to fly the Atlantic alone.

It was a time of heroes and heroines in the fields of aviation and athletics. In May 1932, Amelia Earhart Putnam became the first woman to fly the Atlantic alone, a feat which brought her international honors. She was born in Atchison and had become interested in flying as a girl. Her hometown paper, the Atchison *Globe*, said on May 21: "Amelia Earhart Putnam Proves Woman Can Do Anything Man Does. Let's Turn the Government Over to the Women." Following the historic solo flight she wrote books and articles, was a member of the Purdue University faculty, and became the first woman to fly from California to Hawaii. In July 1937, she took off on her last adventure, a round-the-world flight that ended when her plane disappeared somewhere over the Pacific.

Another Kansas woman who, with her husband, gained fame was Osa Johnson. For more than twenty-five years Osa and Martin Johnson brought enjoyment to adventure-loving Americans. From Independence and Chanute they traveled over the world photographing native villages and wild animals in Africa and the Pacific islands. They took thousands of pictures, made movies, wrote books, and lectured throughout the United States. Martin died in the crash of a commercial airliner in January 1937, but Osa continued working and writing for several years before her death in 1953.

Among the notable performers in Kansas athletics in the 1930s were two mile runners, Glenn Cunningham and Archie San Romani. The Elkhart Tri-State News of August 31, 1933, ran a banner headline announcing that the town was celebrating Cunningham Day, "when he arrives for a few days visit with home folk between his recent triumphal European tour and his return to Kansas University for the coming year's school work." Cunningham had run in eleven meets in Europe and had not lost a race. In the 1936 Olympics Cunningham and San Romani from Kansas State Teachers College were teammates, but they raced against each other several times in this country. Cunningham set a world record in the mile of 4:06.7, but San Romani beat him in both the 1937 and 1938 KU relays.

Jim Bausch of Kansas University was the 1932 Olympic decathlon champion and Glen Campbell and Dale Burnett of Emporia were star performers for the New York Giants in the National Football League. In major league baseball Kansas was well represented. Don Gutteridge of the Cardinals and Ray Mueller of the Pirates made headlines along with Eldon Auker, a former Kansas State star, who pitched for the Tigers, Red Sox, and the St. Louis Browns.

Kansas scored a baseball first on April 28, 1930, when the Independence Producers of the Class C Western Association met the Muskogee

(Okla.) Indians under the lights in Independence. This was the first night game played in professional baseball. Unfortunately Muskogee won 13-3.

Six-man football came to small Kansas high schools in the Thirties. It continued to be played through the 1950s until eight-man games began. However, in the 1990s a half-dozen schools still competed in the six-man category.

In the "sport of kings," Kansas had a star. Laurin, owned by Herbert Woolf of Johnson County, won the Kentucky Derby in 1938, the only Kansas horse to do so in the race's history.

THE PARADOX OF DEPRESSION

Other things brightened the depression years. The vast Hugoton natural gas fields underwent major development after 1935, helping the western Kansas economy. On January 31, 1935, the Union Pacific streamliner, *City of Salina*, began operating on a daily roundtrip schedule between Kansas City and Salina, "a new marvel of the rails which has attracted the attention of millions of Americans." It was completely air-conditioned and made the 187 miles in three-and-a-half hours. A year later the Santa Fe put its *Super Chief* into operation between Chicago and the Pacific Coast. Running at speeds up to 102 miles an hour, the *Super Chief* took less than 40 hours to make its transcontinental journey.

Studs Terkel, the social historian and commentator who has dug deeply into the reactions of people who remember the depression, points out that if there really is a "generation gap" in American society it may exist mostly between the depression generation and the present one. He is probably correct, for the 1930s still remain deeply imprinted on the minds of people who were alive then. There was never in history a period quite like that—a period that saw so many Americans plunged so deeply into poverty and that, interestingly enough, gave a few other Americans a great opportunity to increase their wealth and their land holdings.

In Kansas, farmers who had any money added acreage while some of their neighbors were forced to cook tumbleweeds like spinach or make artificial coffee from roasted barley. Kansans wanted New Deal assistance yet few of them ever completely subscribed to the Roosevelt programs. Ironically, they strove to maintain individualism while collecting aid from government agencies. They worked with their fellow Kansans to a great extent, yet they were at times indifferent to the overall problems of social welfare. Some of them worked for less than twenty-five cents an hour, and they took fifteen cents from a day's wages to see a movie, hoping that they would collect free groceries or cash on "bank night" or from some other kind of lottery. Most Kansans survived the hard times and when the rains finally came, the crops began to grow again and the economy rose, helped along by the requirements of a nation beginning to think once again about national defense. A resident of a western Kansas community particularly hard hit by the depression expressed his feelings about the times: "All were equal with no money. In sickness or problem times all helped—a people-to-people relationship, what the government says we need to do now to solve some of our social problems. We had it then. . . . All were accepted, even if you could not pay your bills or if you were a sly businessman, you all belonged."

Suggestions for Reading

Robert S. Bader, *The Great Kansas Bond Scandal* (1982); Gerald Carson, *The Roguish World of Doctor Brinkley* (1960); Grant Heilman, ed., *Farm Town: A Memoir of the 1930s* (1974); Clifford R. Hope, Jr., *Quiet Courage: Kansas Congressman Clifford R. Hope* (1997); R. Douglas Hurt, *The Dust Bowl: An Agricultural and Social History* (1981); Pascal James Imperato and Eleanor M. Imperato, *They Married Adventure: The Wandering Lives of Martin and Osa Johnson* (1992); Osa Johnson, *I Married Adventure* (1940); Donald R. McCoy, *Landon of Kansas* (1966); Keith D. McFarland, *Harry H. Woodring* (1975); George P. Putnam, *Soaring Wings. A Biography of Amelia Earhart* (1939); Pamela Riney-Kerhberg, *Rooted in Dust: Surviving Drought and Depression in Southwestern Kansas* (1994); Francis W. Schruben, *Kansas in Turmoil 1930–1936* (1969); Homer E. Socolofsky, *Arthur Capper* (1962); George G. Suggs, Jr., *Union Busting in the Tri-State: The Oklahoma, Kansas and Missouri Metal Workers Strike of 1935* (1986); Lawrence Svobida, *Farming the Dust Bowl* (1986); and Bill Wright, *Rearwin: A Story of Men, Planes, and Aircraft Manufacturing During the Great Depression* (1997).

A wealth of information is contained in the Federal Writers' Project, *Kansas: A Guide to the Sunflower State* (1939). It provides a close look at Kansas in the late 1930s. Republished as *The WPA Guide to 1930s Kansas* (1984), it has a new introduction by James R. Shortridge which puts into proper context the original work.

The following articles from the *Kansas Historical Quarterly* are of value for the history of the 1930s: James Beddow, "Depression and New Deal: Letters from the Plains" (Summer, 1977); James C. Carey and Verlin R. Easterling, "Light on the Brinkley Issue in Kansas: Letters of William Allen White to Dan D. Casement" (February, 1953); James C. Duram, "Constitutional Conservatism: The Kansas Press and the New Deal Era as a Case Study" (Winter, 1977); Clifford R. Hope, Sr., "Kansas in the 1930's" (Spring, 1970); Donald R. McCoy, "Alfred M. Landon and the Oil Troubles of 1930–32" (Summer, 1965); George H. Mayer, "Alf M. Landon, As Leader of the Republican Opposition, 1937–1940" (Autumn, 1966); and Michael W. Schuyler, "Federal Drought Relief Activities in Kansas, 1934" (Winter, 1976).

In *Kansas History* are: Larry G. Bowman, "'I Think It Is Pretty Ritzy, Myself': Kansas Minor League Teams and Night Baseball" (Winter, 1995–1996); Thomas S. Busch, "Sunflower Stars: Big Leaguers from Kansas" (Summer, 1998); Peter Fearon, "From Self-Help to Federal Aid: Unemployment and Relief in Kansas, 1929–1932" (Summer, 1990); Peter Fearon, "Riot in Wichita, 1934" (Winter, 1992–1993); Shane N. Galentine, "The Forgotten Candidate: Omar B. Ketchum and the Senate Race of 1936" (Summer, 1990); Clifford R. Hope, Jr., "Strident Victories in Kansas Between the Wars" (Spring, 1979); Donald R. McCoy, "Fifty Years On: The Politics of Kansas in 1932" (Spring, 1983); Donald R. McCoy, "Senator George S. McGill and the Election of 1938" (Spring, 1981); and Francis W. Schruben, "The Wizard of Milford: Dr. J. R. Brinkley and Brinkleyism" (Winter, 1992–1993).

16

Changing Times:

The Second World War and Its Aftermath

Most Americans, Kansans included, were caught up in their own problems in 1939 and early 1940, and they found it hard to be as concerned about the coming of the Second World War in Europe as were President Roosevelt and his advisers. They were rudely awakened in April 1940, when Hitler invaded Denmark and Norway. Within two months the Nazis had overrun Holland and Belgium and had occupied France. Only England remained to combat Germany. Public opinion was split. A few people wished to declare war on Germany immediately. Others believed that a heavily armed America could stand alone, isolating itself from Europe's troubles, and that entry into this new war would not settle anything, anymore than had the First World War.

A third opinion was held by those who formed the Committee to Defend America by Aiding the Allies in May 1940, with William Allen White as chairman. The committee proposed aiding the Allies while stopping short of active military involvement in Europe. White firmly believed that the British fleet was America's first line of defense and if Great Britain fell Hitler would control the seas, and the United States would be in great danger.

Shortly after that, Harry Woodring, by then Roosevelt's Secretary of War, was dropped from the cabinet because he did not agree with the president on foreign policy. Alf Landon, in many ways less isolationist than most of his Republican colleagues, still came out strongly with an antiwar stand, and he was widely supported by the press. Several leading Kansas Republicans, including Landon and Arthur Capper, spoke out against Roosevelt's plans for Lend-Lease to aid the Allies—not because they were against the Allies, but because they believed the president was attempting to assume dictatorial powers in foreign affairs. On the other hand, there were influential Kansans who went along with the White committee and were strong supporters of the Lend-Lease plans, which would allow the United States to "lend, lease, or otherwise transfer military equipment to nations resisting aggressors." Generally, Kansans were sympathetic to Great Britain and its stand against Nazi Germany.

The year 1940 began on a hopeful note at home. Heavy snows had put moisture back into the soil and agricultural production rose above the levels of the early 1930s before the year was over. It was a presidential election year and although Alf Landon was no longer a candidate, he was recognized as a power in the national Republican organization. Republicans interested in obtaining the nomination had to pay attention to Kansas, but Landon made no statements about whom he might support.

The Republicans decided to support Senator Arthur Capper as a favorite son candidate on the first convention ballot, which they did, but on the fifth ballot the delegation went for Wendell Willkie, who got the nomination. In September, Willkie began a 30,000-mile campaign tour starting from Coffeyville, where he had once taught school. Kansas returned to the Republican column, voting for Willkie by a wide margin, but Roosevelt stayed in the White House for his third term. Ratner was reelected governor, defeating the Democrat William Burke, in one of the state's closest elections ever.

Political activity was at a minimum in Kansas during the war years but in 1942 Republicans went to the polls in enough strength to produce the party's greatest victory in the state since 1928. They put Andrew Schoeppel in the governor's office and sent Capper back to the U.S. Senate. With the approach of the 1944 general election the Republican party in Kansas was a model of harmony, and Schoeppel was easily elected. The state went for Thomas E. Dewey in the presidential race and saw him fall to FDR, who would begin his fourth term.

In his January message to both houses the governor presented a sweeping plan for development, which included recommendations for a long-range highway construction program, improvements in state agencies dealing with social welfare, and the establishment of a state veterans' administration to cope with postwar problems. At the session's end the governor, with difficulty, had won his fight for highway improvement and state services generally were increased while additional taxes were enacted to help pay for the new programs.

AS THE WAR BEGINS

Although most Kansans did not wish to get involved directly in Europe's troubles, both political and business leaders saw the value of defense contracts in bolstering the state's economy in 1940. The Reconstruction Finance Corporation announced that it was lending money to the Stearman Division of the Boeing Aircraft Company for the expansion of production, and the Beech Aircraft Corporation received a thirteen-million-dollar contract to produce training planes for the army. Before the year was over several defense construction contracts were awarded in Kansas, and the expansion of Forts Leavenworth and Riley, needed to meet the demands for training facilities brought on by a new draft law, meant that additional millions of dollars would be spent for construction. Federal defense activities pumped fifty million dollars into the Kansas economy during 1940.

Defense industries boomed in 1941, and state officials worked to bring even more industry to Kansas. More than 25,000 aircraft workers were employed in Kansas plants, most of them in Wichita, where the next year Boeing began to turn out parts for B-17 bombers, for a time the backbone of the Army Air Force's long-range operations. Schools were established to train more aircraft production workers, and thousands of people moved to Kansas from other states seeking jobs in the industry. In August 1941, the War Department authorized the construction of a huge munitions plant near Baxter Springs, and it was joined by ammunition factories at Sunflower and Parsons. Smaller defense plants, most of them making airplane parts, sprang up at Hutchinson, Wellington, and a dozen other towns.

An Olathe campany, Kansas State Guard, 1941. The State Guard was formed after the National Guard was called to federal service.

On December 23, 1940, the Thirty-Fifth Division was called to active duty and its roster included 4,800 members of the Kansas National Guard. The division was federalized for "at least a year" under the national preparedness program, but before the year was over the Japanese had bombed Pearl Harbor and the Kansans stayed in service until war's end, although many of them ended up in units other than the Thirty-Fifth. Commanding officers were pleased with the smoothness of mobilization in Kansas and the first day's service for Topeka guard units was described by the *Daily Capital* on December 24:

> Locally, M-Day went off with neatness and dispatch worthy of the exacting officers who command Topeka's five units of the Kansas Guard. . . .
>
> "Every one of our men got right down to work. They are conducting themselves like soldiers, not a bunch of kids," said one officer describing the conduct of his men. . . .
>
> First thing on tap for all five companies was a period of calisthentics to loosen up a few unworked muscles. This activity will take up a good deal of the Guardsmen's time between now and January 2, when local units will join the rest of the state's soldiers at Camp Robinson, Little Rock, Ark.
>
> Breakfasts of bacon and eggs, potatoes, coffee and milk were then served. The rest of the morning was taken up by instructions on how to care for and "display" equipment, military courtesy and other similar subjects. Frequent rest periods were held so that the men could "get used to it gradually."
>
> Noon mess, served at exactly 12 o'clock noon, looked as good as any 35-cent meal a person could buy anywhere in the city. Cooks said the soldiers, their appetites whetted by exercise and drill in the cool outdoors, left nothing for the scraps. . . .

On that fateful Sunday, December 7, 1941, radios were playing in thousands of Kansas homes when the bombing of Pearl Harbor was announced. Kansans, like other Americans, did not understand immediately the disastrous event nor did many of them even know about Pearl Harbor's importance as a military installation. But they soon found out. As Franklin D. Roosevelt spoke to Congress and the nation about the "date which shall live in infamy," students in Kansas classrooms and their parents at home and work listened to radios with a kind of stunned fascination. High school and college classmates soon left to serve in a war, which by then was truly worldwide.

Kansas congressmen, previously reflecting the state's attitude toward military involvement, were solidly behind the president as were the state's newspapers. The Topeka *Daily Capital*, Senator Capper's newspaper, editorialized on December 9:

> Japan's perfidious surprise attack upon the United States forces the American people into a war of defense which must be waged relentlessly until victory is ours. The outrageous opening of hostilities shocked a nation that had hoped to keep out of war. . . .
>
> From now until Japan is defeated and rendered impotent to again disturb the peace of the world, all Kansans, from those in highest official positions to the lowliest layman, will do everything possible to avenge the effrontery of the Japanese militarists. . . .
>
> It means heartaches and grief to many families in Kansas, as elsewhere in the nation. The casualty lists already are bringing sad news to homes with sons in the service of their country. . . .
>
> Home defense measures become doubly important now that the Americans are engaged in war. Governor Ratner has directed the Kansas Defense Council to take precautionary measures. . . . Kansas is in no immediate danger, but her highways, railways, industries and cities form an integral part of the national defense. Whatever steps are necessary to insure continuous operation in all-out preparedness will be taken, cheerfully and loyally by Kansas citizens.

As 1941 ended the federal government announced plans to build several army air bases in the state, and Kansas became a major training ground for air corps personnel. GIs from all over the nation became a part of communities such as Garden City, Winfield, Pratt, Independence, and Liberal as they trained for combat crews. Typical of the army air fields in the state was the one at Pratt, dedicated on May 2, 1943, with 13,000 people on hand for the ceremonies. Established first as a satellite of the base at Salina, the Pratt installation became the home of heavy bomber groups until its closing at war's end. It, like all other air fields, had a great impact on the community because it not only brought troops but civilian workers for whom a "trailer city" was created. Dedication day was described by the Pratt *Daily Tribune*.

> The huge crowd overflowed out on the field and parked cars extended in closely-packed rows far down the long concrete runways. Thousands stood on the apron before a big hangar and heard Republicans Andrew F. Schoeppel of Kansas formally dedicate the field.
>
> Far out on the apron were parked airplanes of various types, from a B-17 Flying Fortress to the Small courier planes the CAP

[Civil Air Patrol] uses in carrying messages between air fields in this region.

During the course of the afternoon thousands of visitors, many of them parents of men in other army and navy camps and stations all over the world, saw barracks, mess halls, and other facilities such as those of which their own sons, brothers and husbands are familiar. . . .

The planes, especially the Flying Fortress, were surrounded by big crowds throughout the afternoon and runways were lined with spectators when the big planes moved off late in the afternoon. . . .

Top: B-29 Superfortress being serviced at Smoky Hill Army Air Field, Salina. Aircraft such as this, built by Boeing in Wichita, were the first land-based planes to bomb Japan, June 15, 1944.
Bottom: A soldier comes home. Dwight D. Eisenhower waves to a Topeka crowd from the special train taking him to Abilene, June 1945.

For thousands, it was the first time to be allowed the privilege of inspecting a military installation in time of war and they made the most of their opportunity. Soldier guides were kept busy answering questions.

KANSANS AT HOME AND IN SERVICE

Service stars, commemorating family members in uniform, hung as small banners in Kansas windows, and Kansas colleges acquired training programs designed to educate officers for all branches of the service. The USO, offering "a home away from home" for servicemen, opened its doors in Kansas communities that had neighboring military installations, and Kansas housewives could be found dispensing coffee and doughnuts to GIs on troop trains at mainline depots throughout the state.

Ground troops trained at Salina's Camp Phillips and at Forts Leavenworth and Riley, while white-hatted sailors served with the navy's air arm at the land-locked towns of Hutchinson and Olathe. Kansas schoolchildren bought war savings stamps, and adults purchased war bonds in numbers far beyond the quotas hoped for by the federal government. As in 1917 and 1918 most conscientious objectors served as noncombatants to help the national effort.

At Kansas City and Leavenworth steel fabricating plants produced landing craft; in Kansas City's Fairfax Industrial District, B-25s came off the production line; and in Wichita the Cessna Aircraft Company became deeply involved in the war effort. The crews were readied for overseas duty at the Salina air base. The combinations of manufacturing, construction, and thousands of serviceman made a vast difference in the state, in housing, finance, transportation services, and education.

Wichita became a nerve center of aircraft industry and the years of war production proved that labor recruited from rural areas could do a superior job. In 1940 there were approximately 1,200 aircraft workers in Wichita and by the end of the war some 52,000 Kansans were building planes, from little Culver trainers to B-29s. During the five years there had been no strikes and absenteeism was far below the national average. The plants had turned out 24,000 planes, and all had received efficiency awards from the army and navy.

Women became an important factor in the industrial labor force. When the song *Rosie the Riveter*, with its references to female war workers, became popular nationally, there were plenty of Kansans who could relate to it. The aircraft manufacturers employed great numbers of women, as did the munitions plants. An Associated Press story of late May 1943 reported on women at the Kansas Ordnance Plant in Parsons: "Girls and women work everywhere in the widespread clusters of buildings. Some pour melted t.n.t. Others black powder into shell cases. There are even women carpenters, who nail packing crates together. Girls everywhere run long, miniature, electrically-powered trains of small flat-bed trucks to haul explosives to and fro."

Kansans grew "Victory Gardens" that included, under a plan announced in 1943, a garden on every farm, home garden for every family in town where land was available, and community gardens for school lunches. They grew accustomed to food, clothing, tire, and gasoline rationing and to reading in their local newspapers tips on economical food preparation, helpful hints on gardening and home canning, and statements like "It's patriotic . . . and it's plain common sense . . . to keep your driving at a minimum until victory comes." They also read "Our Men in Service" columns and obituaries of men killed in action. They participated in paper and scrap metal drives. And they subscribed to slogans like "Keep 'em Flying," while they went to movies that had wartime plots and listened to popular music with wartime themes.

Kansas agriculture entered a period reminiscent of the First World War, and the old slogan "Wheat will win the war" came back into use. With the weather cooperating, the farmer was able to bring crop production to new highs in 1941 and 1942. There were some ups and downs, brought about mainly by weather extremes in 1943, but farm prosperity rose steadily during the war and good wheat crops were supplemented by bumper crops of other grains and by increased livestock marketing. On January 1, 1945, the State Board of Agriculture reported:

> People of this state may long remember the accomplishments of Kansas agriculture in 1943 and 1944. Geared for production of vital food in time of war, the industry established an imposing list of remarkable new records.
>
> These records are noteworthy for two reasons. They register the tremendous contribution of Kansas agriculture toward the inevitable victorious conclusion of World War II, and they prove that we can never judge the full potential

Kansans grew Victory Gardens similar to the one seen here.

strength of Kansas agriculture. Under the strain of . . . wartime handicaps, the industry reached almost unbelievable proportions. This suggests possibilities of even greater accomplishments, should urgent demand appear under more favorable circumstances.

Kansas began to produce great quantities of soybeans, described as a "miracle crop." In 1941 there were only 47,000 acres of soybeans in Kansas but when a great need for vegetable oils rose in 1942, Kansas farmers were asked to plant 125,000 acres. They planted 300,000 acres, harvested 15 times more soybeans than they had in 1939, and added a valuable cash crop to the continuing agricultural economy of the state.

The agricultural industries—milling, meat packing, milk and egg dehydrating, soybean processing, and (by the end of the war) alfalfa dehydrating—all worked at peak capacity with much of their production going to support the armed forces. Once again there were labor shortages in agriculture but younger students, women, and men exempt from military service helped make up the difference in the work force. Some labor even came from German prisoners of war who were in custody at a camp near Concordia. Kansas was labeled the "granary of democracy." In 1945 and 1946 the transition from war to peace began, but records established in

German prisoners of war, held in Kansas, were sent out to work as agricultural labor. This group, with army guards, was at the agricultural experiment station near Hays.

1945 were bettered in 1946 in both crop and livestock income. The wheat crops of both years were considered "miracles," according to the State Board of Agriculture. Even after the end of the war tremendous amounts of grain were shipped to Europe, and Kansas agriculture did not decline in world-wide importance.

During the war some Kansas families had greatly increased incomes as higher prices for farm crops together with expanded production, brought more money into farm homes. The added number of working wives brought family income up, particularly for those involved in wartime industries. But in some families pay went down because a great many servicemen made far less than they had in civilian life. Necessities cost more than ever before and consumer goods, despite price controls, still were higher than in the 1930s. The gigantic costs of global war required increased taxation from which there were few exemptions. By midsummer of 1944, Kansans were paying $1.25 to buy what they had spent $1.00 for in 1939. Demands on both time and money were made in Kansas by the Red Cross, USO, and other volunteer organizations, but everyone on the homefront survived. When officials of the federal government made a statement during the war about sacrifices and suffering at home a Kansas editor remarked that there really was no suffering at home; it was all taking place on the battlefields of Europe and the Pacific. Putting up with shortages and rationing restrictions was a lot easier than dodging bullets.

During the war years over 215,000 Kansas men and women were in uniform and more than 3,500 of them were killed in action. Because of a War Department policy designed to keep losses for any one American community at a minimum, service personnel from a single geographical area were not kept together but were scattered throughout the armed forces although the heart of the Thirty-Fifth Division remained Kansans and Missourians, just as in the First World War. After Pearl Harbor the division was transferred from Camp Robinson, Arkansas, to defense of the southern California sector of the Western Defense Command. In May 1944, after a year of training in the South, the Thirty-Fifth moved east for shipment to the European theater of operations, and on July 5 it went ashore on Omaha Beach. It saw combat all through France and Belgium, including the bitter fighting at Bastogne during the "Battle of the Bulge," fought in Germany, and reached the Elbe River as the war ended. Many Kansans were part of the naval war and Kansas names appeared on both naval and merchant marine vessels. The USS *Wichita*, a heavy cruiser, had a remarkable war record, and there was also a light cruiser, the *Topeka*, three frigates, and four Victory ships that bore the names of Kansas cities. More than fifty vessels were named for persons associated with Kansas and for Kansas towns, counties, and rivers.

A new vessel in the Navy's fleet was named for a Kansan in 1997. The guided-missile destroyer, *USS Ross*, memorializes the late Donald K. Ross of Lincoln, a retired naval officer who won the Medal of Honor at Pearl Harbor on December 7, 1941.

During the war Kansans watched with pride as Dwight D. Eisenhower of Abilene became the war's foremost soldier. They read his name in headlines connected with the invasion of Africa and D-Day (June 6, 1944), and they celebrated when Allied troops under Eisenhower brought the war in Europe to an end on May 8, 1945. In June 1945, "Ike" came home to Kansas, and the European theater's supreme commander received a welcome unmatched in Kansas history. His hometown reception was reported by the Abilene *Reflector-Chronicle*, June 22:

> General Dwight D. Eisenhower, back home at last among the people he grew up with, today expressed great emotion as he accepted their acclaim, then very seriously called for solid support by the American people of President Truman for his efforts to solve the war problems and unite the nation. . . .
>
> For the second day in succession in his native midwest, Eisenhower struck at isolationism, by saying:
>
> "We are not isolationists. Intelligent people cannot be isolationists, we are part of the world, and the world is part of us. Through national organization we cooperate with each other and it is through that cooperation and cooperations with nations of the world that we hope to preserve peace and make sure there are no more wars."
>
> General Ike paid heartfelt tribute to his aged mother and late father. His mother . . . unable to participate in the home-coming celebration listened in on the radio as he said:
>
> "I have wandered far, but never have I forgotten Abilene. Here are some of my oldest and dearest friends. . . ."
>
> Paying tribute to the parade that preceded his brief speech in the park where he played as a boy, Eisenhower said:
>
> "Every boy dreams of the day when he comes back home after making good. I too so dreamed but my dream of 45 or more years ago has been exceeded beyond the wildest stretch of the imagination.
>
> "The proudest thing I can say today is that I'm from Abilene."

By the time Eisenhower spoke in Abilene the United States had acquired a new commander-in-chief. Kansans had voted decisively for Franklin D. Roosevelt only once, in 1936, but most mourned his death on

April 12, 1945, and wondered how Harry Truman, the former senator from neighboring Missouri, would perform as president. Although no trace of dishonesty was ever associated with Truman there were many Kansans who remembered that his name had been linked with that of Tom Pendergast, the "boss" of corrupt machine politics in Kansas City, Missouri.

THE WAR IS OVER

Kansans generally believed that the president was following the correct course of action when he ordered the atomic bombing of Japan, and they celebrated when he announced "Japan accepts surrender" on August 14, 1945. The Salina *Journal* reported on typical Kansas reactions:

> Three words, mighty in their import, set off an impromptu celebration in Salina within a few seconds after they were uttered by President Truman at 6 this evening. Church bells burst into motion and sound. Train whistles added their voices to the din, blasting from the railroad yards in north Salina. Automobiles, quickly forming into a double parade on the main streets and extending along Santa Fe and Iron into residential areas, added to the bedlam with a continuous roar of horns.
>
> People who never saw each other before grinned happily as they passed in the parade. They waved ecstatically. Gone were thoughts of tire conservation. Gone was gasoline rationing. And gone, too, were thousands of Saline county boys, never again to join in one of the home town demonstrations. It was not an unmixed joy. Even as they gathered and laughed together there was a catch in many a throat, a hint of tears behind many a broad smile.
>
> There had been no celebration planned in Salina. It was not necessary. The news, so long awaited, . . . was spark enough to touch off all the exuberance needed. There was only the church service, city-wide in scope, which began in Memorial Hall at 8, where people of all denominations, color and creed were asked to gather and give thanks that the mighty conflict has ended. . . .

On the following day the *Journal* added, editorially:

> It will be up to us, as well as to every other nation, to rebuild our own economy, and to give such assistance to other countries as is within our power to grant without bankrupting our people or permitting our own government to be destroyed. Obviously it is the most stupendous job that the world has been called upon to undertake in all its history.

This sentiment was echoed by Republicans Schoeppel, Kansans in Congress, and Alf Landon, who said: "We have a reconstruction and rehabilitation job ahead that will tax the tremendous capabilities of our country to the limit. We must meet it." Kansans with relatives in service breathed sighs of relief, commanders of Kansas military posts gave their troops a holiday, and the thoughts of everyone turned from war and scarcity to "progress, domestic culture and pursuit of happiness," according to one state government leader.

POSTWAR POLITICS
AND A NEW FIGHT OVER PROHIBITION

The biggest single political issue in the state after the war concerned the sale of liquor. Liquor and all its side issues—repeal of prohibition, taxation, alcoholism, and law enforcement—came to the front of the political stage in the years 1946–1950. Generally speaking, it was difficult to separate liquor from politics.

Described as a Republican "sacred cow" by *Time* on September 9, 1946, prohibition had ruled in Kansas for over sixty years. The war helped boost the "wet" cause. Liquor was coming into Kansas illegally, and many Kansans coming out of service wanted to make it legal. The purchase of liquor was no problem if one knew where to find it, but prices were extremely high. Democratic leader Harry Woodring blasted prohibition in a February speech, and the Democrats began to form a wet ticket for the 1946 election. The leaders of the Kansas United Dry Forces met in Topeka to lay plans to combat the rising tide of repeal sentiment. They protested what they called pressure from "out-of-state liquor interests" and said that the people of Kansas would meet the issue "if and when their own initiative dictates."

By midsummer Woodring was saying that Kansas was "dripping wet," and he called for repeal to end a "hypocritical situation." The former Republican's outspoken stand won him the Democratic gubernatorial nomination in the August primary election. The Republicans' reluctance to talk about repeal could be traced to their respect for Senator Capper, a veteran dry leader, who did not want repeal used as a campaign issue. While Capper defended the dry position no one could ignore the fact that large quantities of liquor were being sold in Kansas. The U.S. Treasury Department reported that 570 Kansans held federal retail liquor licenses, many of which belonged to private clubs and organizations.

One political observer termed the 1946 gubernatorial campaign "one of the weirdest" in Kansas history. Woodring kept his name in the spotlight more than did Frank Carlson, the Republican candidate, but in so doing he angered a lot of people, especially church groups who were strong for prohibition. Carlson conducted a quieter campaign, stressing the point that Kansas needed to return to constructive local programs now that the war was over. Carlson did say that he would try to get the legislature to submit the repeal question to the people. When the results of the November election were in, Carlson, who had served two terms in the legislature and six in the Congress, had kept his record of never losing an election. The Republicans made a clean sweep of state offices and the congressional seats.

On January 15, 1947, Governor Carlson laid before the legislature one of the most comprehensive outlines for action ever proposed. He defined broad policies of social, economic, agricultural, and industrial adjustments. Some of the reforms he wanted had already been started by the Schoeppel administration. The governor's message carried a plea for state responsibility to veterans. He also recommended a three-day waiting period for marriage validation; stronger law enforcement policies including better highway policing; an increase in legislative pay; liberal small loan legislation; and flexible state salary schedules geared to the cost of living. He urged expansion of the rural school programs, construction at the state colleges to keep up with increasing enrollments, planning for a state office building, and development of the highway system.

The legislature wasted no time in starting work on the prohibition resubmission proposition and soon had it ready for the 1948 ballot. A fight took place over the question of consolidation and reorganization of rural school districts, and a workable solution for district unification was still some years away. State aid to education was increased as were taxes to help pay for it. The governor suffered defeat when his plan to regulate interest rates on small loans was killed. Gains were made in welfare legislation by the administration but not without a fight. Lowering the voting age to eighteen was debated and defeated. Carlson praised the 1947 legislature, saying that it had been "expensive but conservative" but he vetoed a drivers' license bill that diluted the strict requirements he advocated.

The legislature's decision to submit the prohibition question to a new vote was not the only thing that brought attention to liquor. Edward Arn, the new attorney general, began a drive to uncover bootlegging and illegal liquor sales. At Lawrence, a Kansas University student had his car confiscated because it contained wine for a wedding party. Violators in hotels and clubs were sought out, property was seized, buildings were padlocked, and people were jailed. In Russell County an investigation was carried out by Arn's office, and several raids were made on clubs.

Three days before Christmas, 1947, an incident took place that gave even more publicity to the prohibition issue. A Kansan drove to Missouri, bought some whiskey for his own use, and on his way home had his car searched by the Highway Patrol. The patrolmen explained that they had mistaken his car for that of an out-of-state bootlegger, but since they had found his whiskey they would have to arrest him. His car and liquor were confiscated by the court, and he was fined. In Wichita a group of businessmen started a fund to buy a new car for the victim and formed an "It Could Happen to Me" club, hoping that the publicity would help defeat prohibition at election time.

An organization known as the Kansas Legal Control Council was formed to "present a factual campaign for repeal" and it was out to disprove the theory that Kansans could be depended on to stagger to the polls and vote dry. The slogan "Vote Yes for Decency" was devised, and a pamphlet entitled *Beware of Dry Rot* was widely distributed. The United Dry Forces answered the council with a booklet called *They Are All Wet*, which announced, among other things, that anyone who took a drink should be put in a cage. The WCTU issued *The Black Book of Repeal*, which said that drunkenness and insanity followed legalized liquor.

The drys created more publicity with the Temperance Tornado. Led and financed largely by Willard Mayberry, Morton County rancher and publisher, the Temperance Tornado recruited teenagers and enlisted the help of famed runner Glenn Cunningham. A caravan formed and traveled 1,500 miles in twelve days, camping in parks, church yards, and on college campuses. The Temperance Tornado, sincere but not a great success, came up with such things as this bit of verse:

> Jack and Jill went up the hill
> To get a jug of likker,
> Jack went blind and lost his mind
> And Jill got sicker and sicker.

Newsweek said that the Tornado "caused more chuckles than catastrophe," and outside Lyons it was greeted with a sign reading, "The bootleggers of Lyons welcome you and assure you of their cooperation."

Most politicians avoided the Tornado, but as election day drew near, repeal looked like a possible winner. Counties that had been traditionally dry had lost population while wet counties had gained. When it was over repeal had carried by over 60,000 votes and even Barber County, once the home of Carry Nation, went wet.

On January 17, 1949, the legislature took up the matter of Governor Carlson's liquor control bill. It provided for the licensing of manufacturers, distributors, and sellers with regulation and taxation, the responsibility of a department of Alcoholic Beverage Control. Those areas that had voted dry in November 1948 could remain dry if they chose to do so, and many of them did. The Kansas liquor law was strict, and a columnist for the Kansas City (Missouri) *Star* wrote: "One consoling thought is that those who can't quite qualify to operate a liquor store under Kansas' high-minded and stringent law may be able to make the ministry." The first truck load of legal liquor arrived in Kansas on July 8, and ten days later licenses for retail stores were in the mail.

GIANT STEPS AHEAD

Among the accomplishments of the 1949 legislature, one of the busiest in history, was the creation of a twenty-year highway program, which led to a vastly improved state system of roads and a law reorganizing the administration of social welfare and mental hospitals, one of the best ever passed by a Kansas legislature. A better system of handling mental patients was developed, and social workers at the county level were given more authority in investigation of mental cases and in recommendations for treatment. Commitment laws were improved so that people sent to state hospitals were no longer considered hopeless, and mental patients were placed in the same category as any other sick persons who needed treatment. The Topeka State Hospital was raised to a teaching level and became an accredited psychiatric training center. It was obvious that Kansas institutions were fifty years behind the times and both houses and the Republicans approved the new legislation in record time.

Mental health was a major concern outside state government. In December 1946, an expansion plan for the Menninger Clinic was approved, making the already famous institution an even stronger instrument for the treatment of mental illness. Winter Hospital in Topeka, operated by the Army during the war, became a psychiatric hospital under the U.S. Veterans Administration. Its close working arrangements with the Menninger organization and the Topeka State Hospital, plus the teaching facilities of the combined institutions, made Topeka the psychiatric center of the world. Both Doctors Menninger—Karl and Will—were instrumental in these developments and Dr. Will was particularly influential in pushing the psychiatric services of the Veterans Administration.

Also in connection with medicine, the legislature listened to Dr. Franklin Murphy, then the dean of the University of Kansas medical school and later chancellor of the university, advance his ideas on rural health. Dr. Murphy pointed out that the state needed more doctors in the country and that state financial help for a program to train them would mean additional federal aid. Increased facilities were needed at the medical school if the state was to produce enough doctors to care for its population. A bill passed, the medical college was enlarged, and Dr. Murphy made an effort to get young doctors into small communities.

Kansas was faced with a serious shortage of doctors and many newly graduated MDs were reluctant to set up practice in rural areas, especially if hospital facilities were not available. Murphy's Rural Health Plan had almost immediate success as towns and counties worked to make clinic and hospital space available. Mankato was the first town to put a plan into successful operation and welcomed a doctor to its clinic in the fall of 1949. The medical school also sent its senior students into rural areas to practice for a time with established physicians, and that plan has continued in one form or another, although rural Kansas still suffers from a shortage of physicians.

Not all the political news in the late 1940s concerned the "demon rum" and legislative action. Arthur Capper retired from the U.S. Senate in 1949 and was replaced by former governor Andrew Schoeppel. Kansas Republicans once again supported Thomas Dewey for president in 1948 and believed that he would win. Even though Kansas Democrats claimed the first Harry Truman for President club they were doubtful about Truman's chances against Dewey. Both parties in Kansas were surprised, along with the rest of the nation, when the president's energetic campaigning paid off in November, and he was returned to the White House. The Democrats had an able gubernatorial candidate in Randolph Carpenter of Marion, former congressman and U.S. attorney, but Governor Carlson had no difficulty being reelected in 1948. In Congress all Kansas members were Republicans with effective leadership still in the hands of Clifford Hope, mentioned as possible Secretary of Agriculture if Dewey won. Hope, one of the state's most astute political observers, had warned Republicans that they were too confident about Dewey's prospects, but they were not inclined to listen to him.

Carlson moved on to the Senate in 1951 where he served three terms, and Edward Arn moved in that same year from the attorney general's office to the governor's chair for two terms that were marred by disagreements between Republican factions. One major change came about in state government in 1953 with a reorganization plan creating the Department of Administration, which was given centralized control over budget, purchasing, personnel, and accounting procedures.

The Democratic party in Kansas was a happy organization after the Truman victory in 1948 and the Jefferson-Jackson Day dinner, held in June 1949, was a congenial gathering. The belle of the ball was the new Treasurer of the United States, Georgia Neese Clark of Richland. She had been a national committeewoman for nearly fifteen years when President Truman announced her appointment as the first woman treasurer. She was confirmed by the Senate on June 9, 1949, and held the office until 1953. Later active in Topeka philanthropic work, she died in 1995, preceded in death by her husband, Andrew Gray.

EISENHOWER'S NEW ROLE

General Eisenhower had been mentioned as a possible presidential candidate for several years. Both parties had wanted to put him on their tickets in 1948, but he refused. In 1951 a number of prominent Kansas Republicans, including C. M. Harger of Abilene, Harry Darby of Kansas City, and Senator Carlson began to lay plans for Eisenhower at the 1952 convention. When the GOP gathered in Chicago, Eisenhower, who had resigned his command of the North Atlantic Treaty Organization, won the nomination from Senator Robert Taft of Ohio and went on to win over Adlai Stevenson in a landslide. The Abilene *Reflector-Chronicle* of November 6 announced "IKE WINS" and said:

> The home town of the next president of the United States rolled up an overwhelming 9-to-1 vote for him and then celebrated the sweeping nationwide victory of General Dwight D. Eisenhower with the wildest celebration in Abilene's colorful history. . . .
>
> Throughout the evening as the votes were being tabulated the size of the crowd grew larger downtown. About midnight, when the bulletins began to indicate an Ike landslide the throng swelled to more than 3,000 persons bubbling over with pent-up enthusiasm and waiting for the signal to explode.
>
> Then it came. Seconds after Governor Stevenson took the microphone in Chicago to concede defeat the Abilene demonstration was set off officially by a series of long blasts on the fire whistles and the old belle Springs creamery whistle—out of commission for 15 years but wired up for this great occasion.
>
> It was at the creamery where Ike spent some of his most memorable out-of-school hours as a boy. His father was a steam engineer there and Ike used to help him blow that same whistle—in fact Ike and some of his pals more than once were called on the carpet for blowing it too loud and too long on New Year's eve.
>
> Within minutes, the downtown area from Spruce to Cedar resembled Times Square on celebration night. . . . Members of the Abilene band who could light their way through the mob set the tune of the demonstration. Right in the middle of everything— adding to the color of the show with a display of huge arc lights was a CBS television crew from New York filming the proceedings for the world to see. . . .

Ike, everybody's favorite son, who left Abilene in 1911 for West Point, had reached a new high point in a distinguished career. For the first time there was a Kansan in the White House.

VARIED ASPECTS OF THE POSTWAR SCENE

A good many Kansans were widening their horizons in the late 1940s. The Kansas author, Kenneth Davis, writing in the *New York Times Magazine*, June 26, 1949, said:

> Another trend with pleasant significance is seen in the fact that Kansas, once notorious as a "hotbed of isolationism," now expresses on the popular level a burgeoning internationalism. The Kansas response to UNESCO, for example, has been so remarkable that the State Department issued the other day a special popular bulletin on it. . . . All over the state these days one hears sharp condemnation of isolationism.

One of the reasons for the success of UNESCO (United Nations Educational, Scientific, and Cultural Organization) in Kansas was its national chairman, Milton Eisenhower, brother of the general and then president of Kansas State College. UNESCO councils, devoted to international cooperation in education, communications, humanities, libraries, and the arts, spread throughout the state, and Kansans, particularly students, worked hard to increase cultural understanding around the world.

Kansas colleges, both state and private, began to bulge at the seams as ex-GIs flocked back to school with financial aid provided by the federal government. With wartime restrictions lifted on travel and with leisure time more available than it had been during the war, Kansans looked at the country around them, read more, added to their public and private libraries, and became greater boosters for museums and concerts.

While the revitalized agricultural economy was still vitally important to the state, the Industrial Development Commission and local groups worked hard to bring new industries to Kansas and to encourage the expansion of existing ones. Plants that had produced goods for war converted to the production of goods that could be used on farms and in city homes, and the aircraft industry began to turn out great numbers of planes for civilian use. A Kansas woman, Olive Ann Beech, became prominent in the industry as she assumed a role of leadership after her husband Walter's death in 1950. Manufacturing surpassed agriculture as a source of income in Kansas for the first time in 1953, a situation that would not be reversed in the years to come.

It was an enjoyable time for Kansas athletic fans. In 1946 Kansas University tied Oklahoma for the Big Six conference title in football, and in 1947 tied for the crown again and were invited to meet Georgia Tech in the Orange Bowl. On New Year's Day, 1948, the Jayhawks lost 20–14 but it was the first time a team from Kansas had ever participated in one of the postseason classics. On the Manhattan campus a new field house began to rise, and the 1949 legislature appropriated funds to begin a similar structure at Lawrence. In that period both Kansas University and Kansas State began to produce basketball teams of consistent national stature, and both had players named to All-American teams.

In the 1940s it appeared an age-old argument between Kansas and Colorado was finally settled. For years the two states had been quarreling over the water in the Arkansas River, with Kansas charging that too much water was taken out of the river before it reached the western Kansas border. In 1945, with the establishment of an interstate commission, and the settlement of a 1948 lawsuit, Kansas and Colorado hoped they had settled their differences and agreed on an equitable amount of stream flow for both sides of the boundary. However, in the 1980s Kansas again claimed that Colorado siphoned off more than its fair share of water before it reached the state line. Kansas was to get 40 percent of the stream flow—and it does, from the John Martin reservoir in eastern Colorado but not from the flow farther upstream, say residents in the western part of the state. Kansas again filed suit in December 1985. Ultimately, a court-appointed Special Master was to consider the issues of compliance and damages with Kansas claiming Colorado was in debt by 186,000,000,000 gallons. The case may again go back to trial on the basis of economics.

Rivers and plans to control them were much in the news in the late 1940s and early 1950s. Flooding had spurred plans to construct reservoirs in Kansas and by 1950 two major flood control projects had been completed, at Kanopolis on the Smoky Hill and on the Fall River in Greenwood County. During that same period arguments raged over the fate of the Blue River valley from Manhattan north because of a projected dam on the Blue to be named Tuttle Creek. Angry farmers and ranchers in the area protested against "Big Dam Foolishness" and the taking of valuable bottom lands, arguing that small dams on small streams would solve the problems. However, some became convinced that additional dams and reservoirs were needed as the Kansas River and its tributaries went on a rampage in July 1951. It was the greatest Missouri basin flood in history, and from central Kansas to eastern Missouri communities were under water. Thousands of Kansans were homeless, several died, and more than two billion dollars worth of damage was done. Railroads could not operate because of submerged tracks, and in Topeka two major bridges were swept away. Kansas City was particularly hard hit be cause of its low-lying industrial districts along the Kaw and the Missouri rivers. Despite the 1951 flood, the arguments about reservoir building continued for a time. But Tuttle Creek dam was built, a vast lake was created on the Blue River, and the town of Randolph moved to a new location in 1957 as its original site went under water.

Kansans viewed the United Nations with far less distrust than they had the League of Nations after the First World War but they also looked with dismay at the world's uneasy peace, the "cold war." In the period 1950–1953, when the cold war became hot in Korea, Kansans were again called upon to contribute to a national effort. A new group of soldiers came into Fort Riley for training, and the Air Force reactivated Kansas air bases and tailored them for jet planes. Some Kansans who had thought they were through with military service found themselves recalled to duty, while at Fort Leavenworth the Command and Staff College was involved in the education of officers from all over the free world.

Kansas was altered, as was much of the world between 1939 and midcentury, and mostly for the better although participation in world conflict was a painful catalyst for change. There were differences in land use, economy, and cultural interests, and there was a noticeable shift in population. A number of native residents left the state while many other people adopted Kansas as a new home. More and more farm people moved to town, and the number of individual farming operations decreased. The urban counties of Johnson, Sedgwick, and Shawnee increased greatly in population but some western Kansas communities experienced tremendous growth, too. Kansas presented a different face to the rest of the nation as it approached its hundredth birthday.

A Navy jet fighter airborne at the Olathe Naval Air Station in the 1950s. The base was home to the "Bitter Birds," the 884th Fighter Squadron of the U. S. Naval Reserve which included Kansans. The squadon served as a carrier-based unit during the Korean War.

Suggestions for Reading

Some of the aspects of politics in the 1940s are covered in the biographies of Capper, Woodring, Landon, and Hope and in Bader's study of prohibition, all which have been mentioned previously. There are innumerable books on Eisenhower, but these are particularly recommended: Stephen E. Ambrose, *The Supreme Commander* (1969); Robert F. Burke, *Dwight D. Eisenhower: Hero and Politician* (1986); Kenneth S. Davis, *Soldier of Democracy* (1945); Dwight D. Eisenhower, *At Ease: Stories I Tell to Friends* (1967); and Daniel D. Holt and James W. Leyerzapf, eds., *Eisenhower, the Prewar Diaries and Selected Papers, 1905–1941* (1998). Wartime aircraft manufacturing is dealt with in George Bauer, *Fairfax Ghosts: The "Bomber Builders" and Others Who Made a Difference* (1995), while problems in the Missouri basin are discussed in Kenneth S. Davis, *River on the Rampage* (1953). Thomas D. Isern, *Custom Combining on the Great Plains* (1981) contains information on agriculture for the period, as does H. Craig Miner, *Harvesting the High Plains: John Kriss and the Business of Wheat Farming, 1920–1950* (1998).

The following articles from the *Kansas Historical Quarterly* are of interest: "General Eisenhower of Kansas" (August, 1945); "U.S. Army and Air Force Wings Over Kansas" (Summer and Autumn, 1959); James L. Forsythe, "Postmortem on the Election of 1948: An Evaluation of Cong. Clifford R. Hope's Views" (Autumn, 1972); R. Douglas Hurt, "Naval Air Stations During World War II" (Autumn, 1977); Henry B. Jameson, "Making a President" (Spring, 1966); and William M. Tuttle, Jr, "William Allen White and Verne Marshall: Two Midwestern Editors Debate Aid to the Allies versus Isolationism" (Summer, 1966).

The entire Autumn, 1990, issue of *Kansas History* is devoted to various aspects of Eisenhower's career, while the Spring, 1994, issue deals with the World War II home front. In addition, the journal contains these articles: Charles William Sloan, Jr., ed., "The Newsletters: E. Gail Carpenter Describes Life on the Home Front," (Spring, 1988, through Winter, 1988–1989); Philip A. Grant, Jr., "The Kansas Congressional Delegation and the Selective Service Act of 1940" (Autumn, 1979); Michael J. Grant, "'Food Will Win the War and Write the Peace': The Federal Government and Kansas Farmers During World War II" (Winter, 1997–1998); Milton S. Katz and Susan B. Tucker, "A Pioneer in Civil Rights: Esther Brown and the South Park Desegregation Case of 1948" (Winter, 1995–1996); Christopher C. Lovett, "'Dear, I'll Be Back in a Year': The Mobilization of the Thirty-Fifth Division in 1940" (Summer, 1994); Patrick G. O'Brien, Thomas D. Isern, and R. Daniel Lumley, "Stalag Sunflower: Prisoners of War in Kansas" (Autumn, 1984); John W. Partin, "The Dilemma of 'A Good, Very Good Man': Capper and Noninterventionism, 1936–1941" (Summer, 1979); and Caron Smith, "The Women's Land Army During World War II" (Summer, 1991).

17

Kansas and the Arts

In the 1930s William Allen White wrote, "Kansas may scarcely be said to have a literature" yet White himself, through his Emporia *Gazette* editorials, became one of the most widely quoted writers of the twentieth century. White embodied all that was good about small-town, western editorial writing and reporting, but he could also comment effectively about national and international affairs. Following White's death in 1944, Rolla Clymer of the El Dorado *Times* wrote on February 3:

> He wrote many books—and they fill a well-thumbed shelf—and volumes have been written about him. Some of the most intelligent critics of his day have attempted to dissect him. . . . But they have all failed in their endeavor, and will fail, because his magic makeup ever was one to defy analysis. Men called him a sage, and while he was wise with an incisive understanding that plumbed the depths, he was more an amiable, roly-poly Peter Pan in all his ways. . . .
>
> He was the outstanding editor of his day. There is none to compare with him in the annals of Kansas—and few in the nation. He gave the country press a lustre which it had not hitherto attained; there was not an editorial chair in the country which he could not have graced. To the last day of his active life—and he was always a prodigious and zestful worker—he could out-write every

other craftsman within his orbit. . . . He constantly had the exact word at his finger tips for the precise shade of meaning he wished to convey. There was music and a classical sweep in his language that carried the majesty of the Scriptures. In fact, he often admitted to the influence of the King James version of the Bible upon his style. And then, there was always his bubbling humor—expressed in pungent phrase and with impish twist that aroused a delight all its own.

EDITORS AND JOURNALISTS

Creative fathers do not necessarily produce creative sons, but White did. William L. White, who died in 1973, won critical acclaim for his works of nonfiction and also spent many years as the editor of the *Gazette*. "Young Bill" White's *Journey for Margaret* (1941), *They Were Expendable* (1942), *Back Down the Ridge* (1953), and *The Captives of Korea* (1957) skillfully present in book form subjects taken from his experiences as a correspondent in both the Second World War and Korea. The action and suspense connected with the war's PT boats and their crews took on the aspect of a novel in *They Were Expendable*.

Another distinguished Kansas editor, a contemporary of the senior White, was Edgar Watson Howe of Atchison. Howe died in 1937, and in the sixty years he lived in Kansas he produced one famous novel, innumerable other books, and thousands of quotable comments, many of which appeared in paragraph form rather than as full-length editorials. In 1877 Howe founded the Atchison *Globe*, and in 1910 he turned it over to his son Gene, but he published *E. W. Howe's Monthly* for another twenty-two years. The *Saturday Review of Literature* once called Howe "Franklin's spiritual legatee" and his *The Story of a Country Town*, published in 1883, led American literature into what would be called American "realism." *The Story of a Country Town* is a rather grim novel about ordinary people, and it drew in part on Howe's own experiences, but it was not intended to be a reflection of life in Atchison.

Howe wrote four books as a result of his travels, and among his other volumes was an autobiography entitled *Plain People*, first serialized in the Saturday Evening Post in 1928. Howe's biographer, Calder Pickett, described *Plain People* as "a moving, prejudiced, funny, and infuriatingly un-thorough book." For years

Edgar Watson Howe

Howe contributed articles to the *Saturday Evening Post* and the *Country Gentleman*. He corresponded with and was quoted by most of the leading writers in America until his death. Howe's personal life, including his marriage, was not always happy, and he seems to have been generally pessimistic about the human race, but he was respected locally and internationally.

Howe, like White, produced a second generation to whom writing was important. Gene Howe, after editing the *Globe* for a time, moved on to Amarillo, Texas, where he became one of the leading journalists of the Southwest. A daughter, Mateel Howe Farnham, wrote a prize-winning novel entitled *Rebellion* in 1927, and before her death in 1957 produced another half-dozen novels that were called "romantic and undistinguished."

Another notable Kansas journalist who wrote extensively for national publication was Charles M. Harger, editor first of the Abilene *Reflector* and later of the combined *Reflector-Chronicle*. His work appeared in *The Outlook, Harpers,* and the *Saturday Evening Post*, and for a time he was associate editor of a financial magazine published in New York. He found time to lecture at the University of Kansas school of journalism and served his state in various ways. He was a kindly man who could still take the hide off an opponent editorially. A life-long friend of Dwight Eisenhower, he worked diligently to establish the Eisenhower Center in Abilene. Harger started many a journalist on his way to bigger and better things from the Abilene newspaper office, and the story was told that he encouraged a young teacher at Fort Hays Kansas State College to leave the classroom for journalism. The teacher was a Kansas native named Ben Hibbs who went on to hold executive editorial positions with the *Country Gentleman, Saturday Evening Post*, and *Reader's Digest*.

Although his greatest fame came from what he wrote in New York City, Damon Runyon spent his early years in Kansas towns where his father worked as a newspaper editor—Manhattan, Wellington, and Clay Center. Reporter, war correspondent, and columnist, Runyon is best remembered today for his stories that were the basis for the Broadway hit *Guys and Dolls*.

Among the other Kansas editors in what Rolla Clymer called "a golden era of Kansas journalism" were Victor Murdock of the Wichita *Eagle*, Charles F. Scott of the Iola *Register,* Henry J. Allen of the Wichita *Beacon*, Clyde M. Reed of the Parsons *Sun*, Tom McNeal of the Medicine Lodge *Cresset* and the Topeka *Mail and Breeze*, George W. Marble of the Fort Scott *Tribune-Monitor*, W. Y. Morgan of the Hutchinson *News*, Paul A. Jones of the Lyons *News*, John Redmond of the Burlington *Republican*, Harold T. Chase of the Topeka *Daily Capital*, Gomer Davies of the Concordia *Kansan*, Will T. Beck of the Holton *Recorder*, A. Q. Miller of the Belleville *Telescope*, and two generations of Anthonys at the Leavenworth *Times*. Several of them were sons of newspaper fathers and some of them saw their families carry on those newspapers into the 1980s. They reported, they interpreted, and many of them made Kansas history. It was the vision of nineteenth-century editors in Kansas—people such as Daniel W. Wilder, Sol Miller, and the senior Dan Anthony—that led to the establishment of the Kansas State Historical Society in 1875 and its collection of local newspapers that is known to researchers around the world.

More recently a number of Kansans have made their mark in broadcast journalism. The late John Cameron Swayze; James Lehrer and Elizabeth Farnsworth of the award-winning Public Broadcasting System's *Newshour*; and Bill Kurtis, who after thirty years with CBS, became a producer and narrator of documentaries for PBS and the Arts & Entertainment Network.

NOVELS, NONFICTION, AND POETRY

A noted novelist who cut his writing teeth on the staffs of midwestern newspapers was the late Paul I. Wellman. While a reporter on the Wichita *Eagle* Wellman wrote his first three books, and he continued working for himself while writing editorials for the Kansas City *Star*. His first novel, *Broncho Apache*, came out in 1936 and by 1966, nearly thirty books later, it was estimated that Wellman's work had sold more than seven million copies. Several of his novels were made into motion pictures, including *Broncho Apache*, *The Comancheros*, and *The Iron Mistress*. Wellman's knowledge of history was excellent, and his fictionalized history was basically correct. Three of his books, *The Chain*, *Walls of Jericho*, and *The Female* led

best-seller lists, and the first two have southwestern Kansas as their setting. He also wrote straight history like *Glory, God and Gold*, about the Spanish Southwest, and *The House Divided*, which dealt with America as it moved toward

For decades Chautauqua provided Kansans with summer cultural activities including music, drama, and speeches by famous Americans. This family was spending the 1897 Chautauqua season at Forest Park in Ottawa.

civil war. Although he was born into a missionary family in West Africa and spent his later years in California, his storytelling abilities were developed in Kansas, and he never lost touch with the Midwest.

Manley Wade Wellman, Paul's brother, was also educated in Wichita and worked for the Wichita *Eagle*. Among his books are *They Took Their Stand*, a popular historical study of the first months of the Confederacy, and *Candle of the Wicked*, a novel which has at its setting eastern Kansas just after the Civil War and incorporates the violent Bender family into its plot.

A unique literary figure in Kansas was Emmanuel Haldeman-Julius of Girard who gained his greatest fame as publisher of the Little Blue Books. That series of publications, which sold originally for a nickel a volume, reproduced the classics and also printed original manuscripts including some by Haldeman-Julius. Will Durant credited Haldeman-Julius with urging him to write his famed *Story of Philosophy*, but, more important, the Little Blue Books made literature available to many who were unable to afford more expensive publications.

One widely read Kansas writer of fiction during the first three decades of the twentieth century was a Topeka housewife, Margaret Hill McCarter. Mrs. McCarter came to Topeka as a high school English teacher in 1888 and remained until her death in 1938. *The Price of the Prairie* was her first novel, published in 1910, and the books she wrote over the next several years followed the same pattern of a pioneer Kansas setting with rugged, moralistic characters. She came to know Kansas very well, and her descriptions of both landscape and events are authentic.

Charles M. Sheldon, for many years pastor of the central Congregational Church in Topeka, wrote a moralistic novel, *In His Steps, or, What Would Jesus Do? The Advance*, a Congregational magazine in Chicago, bought the story and published it serially in 1896–1897 and it came out in book form in 1897. Though nobody knows how many copies of the book have been sold, estimates range from six to thirty million. Sheldon wrote other stories and pamphlets, but except for *In His Steps*, he gained the greatest attention when he edited the Topeka *Daily Capital* for a week in March 1900, as a "Christian daily." Good news was emphasized and many regular advertisements were banned—from ladies' corsets to patent medicines—and Sheldon claimed the paper could be read in any family circle because the news was "clean." Journalistically Sheldon's edition of the Capital came in for considerable criticism and editors such as Ed Howe openly made fun of it, but it went down as a unique experiment in American newspaper publishing.

A widely praised but mostly forgotten novel, *A Man of Learning* by Nelson Antrim Crawford, was published in 1928 and contained satire on midwestern life. Crawford had a varied literary and editorial career, most of it in Kansas. He taught journalism at Kansas State College and for more than twenty years was the editor of *Household for Capper Publications*, Topeka. He also edited and published *Author and Journalist*, a magazine for writers, and from the time he began teaching in 1910 until his death in 1963, Crawford wrote poetry, fiction, and nonfiction.

Three native Kansans whose novels attracted attention, beginning in the 1940s, were Kenneth Davis, Frederic Wakeman, and Joseph Stanley Pennell. Davis was born in Salina and educated at Kansas State College, and two of his books, *The Years of the Pilgrimage* (1948) and *Morning in Kansas* (1952), have Kansas settings. Frederic Wakeman, a Scranton native, has produced several novels, of which *Shore Leave* (1944) and *The Hucksters* (1946) were viewed most favorably. *Fabulous Train* (1955), set in Kansas during the depression, did not receive the recognition given his earlier works. Pennell, son of a prominent Junction City photographer, drew upon the history of his own family for *The History of Rome Hanks* and *Kindred Matters* (1944) and *The History of Nora Beckham* (1948). The two volumes were received well enough to rate Pennell a comparison with Thomas Wolfe, and Sinclair Lewis called him "the most promising American novelist to appear in a decade." However Pennell did not follow up with any works of comparable quality. Russell Laman, formerly of the Kansas State University English department, has written a novel set in Kansas, *Manifest Destiny*, and James Gunn of the University of Kansas faculty has produced several science fiction novels and short stories. One of them, *The Immortals*, served as a basis for the television programming by the American Broadcasting Company in 1969. Lee Killough, Manhattan, Elizabeth Ann Scarborough, Kansas City, and Ann Tonsor Zeddies, Lawrence, also have achieved success as science fiction novelists in recent years. Killough also has written a series of mysteries set in a futuristic Topeka.

Fictional events in a very real modern Kansas are told hilariously and skillfully in Robert Day's *The Last Cattle Drive* (1977). Day, originally from Johnson County and a former faculty member at Fort Hays State University, also has written some shorter works that use Kansas settings. The late Earl Thompson used his familiarity with Kansas, and Wichita particularly, to set the scene for several novels that reflect the very gritty and sometimes seamy side of life.

Jim Lehrer, in addition to his television reporting, has written several novels. Most of them are humorous and involve the same protagonist, an Oklahoma lieutenant governor named One-Eyed Mack. However, there are Kansas references in the books, and they reflect Lehrer's own interests. He also has written an autobiography, *A Bus of My Own* (1992), which contains delightful stories about his youthful years in Kansas. Another journalist, James R. Dickenson, who grew up in Rawlins County, has written *Home on the Range: A Century on the High Plains* (1995). It is autobiographical, but it also sets forth some of the history of western Kansas and the role of his family in the region's development.

There are two other recent memoirs of interest. Jessie Foveaux, at age ninety-eight, a resident of Manhattan for over seventy years, has had published *Any Given Day: A Memoir of 20th Century America* (1997), which chronicles her childhood, marriage, and life as the mother of eight children. Her story attracted the attention of the national press and network television, and for the first time in her life she did not need to concern herself about money. The second book is Bruce Bair's *Good Land* (1997), which deals with his life as a farm boy in Sherman County and changes in Kansas agriculture following World War II. He worked as a journalist for several years outside the state before returning to Kansas to pursue his writing career.

The settlement of western Kansas has been described graphically in Julia Siebel's *The Narrow Covering* (1956), Mela Meisner Lindsay's *The White Lamb* (1976), and Charlotte Hinger's *Come Spring* (1986). Jeanne Williams, an Elkhart native, has used western Kansas as the setting for several of her novels, which encompass a variety of time periods including the 1920s and the Dust Bowl.

Robert E. Segerhammer, who died in 1998, was a Lutheran minister with his roots in the Lindsborg vicinity. He planned a fictional trilogy dealing with a Swedish-American family and its neighbors and published two volumes, *Dugouts and Daisies* (1991) and *Swedish Mecca of the Plains* (1993). The manuscript for the third volume, "Still Pioneers," was completed prior to his death with eventual publication expected.

For many years one of the most popular mystery writers in America was Rex Stout, who grew up in Topeka. More recently, success in that genre has come to several Kansans—Sara Paretsky, originally from Lawrence; Gaylord Dold, Charles Goodrum, and S. K. Epperson of Wichita; Kevin Robinson and Randy Russell of Kansas City; Nancy Pickard, Susan Hoskins, and Virginia DeCoursey of Johnson County; and Edward Hays of Leavenworth. Paretsky's work features a female private eye, V. I. Warshawski, and Pickard and Epperson also have used women as central characters. Epperson, writing as Dylan Harson, has produced a novel, *Kansas Blue* (1995), which has a Kansas frontier setting.

Rebecca Brandywyne of Wichita and Janice Young Brooks and Julie Garwood of Johnson County have done well as "romance" novelists. Brooks's *Seventrees* (1981) uses the Shawnee Methodist Mission as its backdrop. Brooks also has written novels with non-Kansas settings, including *Guest of the Emperor* (1990), which was made into a television movie, *Si-*

lent Cries, in 1993. Using the name Jill Churchill, she joins the circle of mystery writers. One somewhat unlikely contributor to the romance genre was the late Lester V. "Sam" Roper, Jr., who served in the state legislature from Girard. He produced six other works of fiction, but under the name of Samantha Lester he published romance novels very successfully.

Harold Coyle, Leavenworth, wrote six books on modern warfare before turning to historical fiction with an emphasis on the military. In 1997 he published *Savage Wilderness,* an account of the French and Indian War. Lawrence novelist James Preston Girard's *The Late Man* (1993) is set in Wichita, and Kansas Citian Edgar Wolfe's *Widow Man* (1953) is about interracial relations in his hometown in the 1950s. Wolfe also wrote novellas and short stories. Scott Heim, from Hutchinson, received acclaim for his *Mysterious Skin* (1995) and Carol Ascher, who spent her childhood in Topeka, has a novel, *The Flood,* set in the capital during the 1950s. Steve Heller, Manhattan, has published both short stories and longer works. Janice Graham, Wichita, had written screenplays, but her first novel, *Firebird,* came out in 1998. It is set in Cottonwood Falls and the ranch country of the Flint Hills. John Ise, long a leading economist on the Kansas University faculty, also wrote *Sod and Stubble,* which deals with family life in nineteenth-century Kansas and has become a classic description of the "sod house frontier." Ise's manuscript was shortened for its original publication in 1936, but in 1996 a new unabridged edition was issued.

Richard Rhodes, a Kansas City native, won a Pulitzer Prize and a National Book Award for *The Making of the Atomic Bomb* (1988). He has written other nonfiction and several novels along with *A Hole in the World: An American Boyhood* (1990), a personal memoir. Maxine Clair, also a Kansas Citian, published *Rattlebone* (1994), an acclaimed collection of short stories based on her experience growing up in an African-American community. She is also a poet.

Richard Lee Marks, for the past several years a Topekan, has done two books best described as historical fiction: *Three Men of the Beagle* (1991), which deals with Darwin's voyage; and *Cortés* (1993), a story of the Spanish conquest of Mexico. Kansans writing suspense fiction include Al Clovis, John McCormack, and Phillip Finch. Finch, a Howard resident, had his *Sugarland* named one of the ten notable thrillers of 1991.

Don Coldsmith of Emporia has been very successful using the American Indian and the West in his popular fiction. He has published more than thirty books, most them included in his Spanish Bit Saga series. In 1990 he won the Western Writers' Golden Spur Award for the best original paperback of that year, *The Changing Wind.* Other writers of westerns include Max McCoy, Pittsburg; Cotton Smith, Mission Hills; Judy Lilly,

Salina; George Brandsberg, Manhattan; and Terry Johnston, who grew up in Arkansas City.

Beginning with Helen Dannefer Francis of Hays, there have been many Kansans writing for children and young people. Included among these are Lois Ruby, Harvey Watson, Lisa Ernst, Richie Tankersley Cussek, Harvey Watson, Ronald Bliss, Barbara Steiner, Nolan Carlson, Irene Bennett Brown, and Bill Martin, Jr. In some cases they have been the illustrators of their work. A new addition to this group in 1998 was a Topeka high school student, Anna Riphahn. She published two books which she wrote and illustrated and was selected by the Public Broadcasting System to be featured on a program on young entrepreneurs. Her life and her promising career were cut short by a fatal traffic accident before year's end.

Two physicians, Arthur Hertzler of Halstead and Samuel Crumbine of Dodge City and Topeka, made significant contributions with their autobiographies. Hertzler's *Horse and Buggy Doctor* (1938) and Crumbine's *Frontier Doctor* (1948) vividly and entertainingly report progress on the Kansas medical frontier.

Two generations of the doctors Menninger—Karl, William, Walter, and Roy—have published many times, including both scientific studies and works easily understood by nonprofessionals. Harriet Lerner, a Topeka clinical psychologist, has written several volumes which analyze and advise in understandable terms. Her first book, *The Dance of Anger* (1989) sold more than two million copies and has been followed by other successful efforts.

Clementine Paddleford became one of the nation's leading writers about food and cooking, and Roderick Turnbull—for many years farm editor of the Kansas City *Star*—produced innumerable nostalgic essays about life in a small Kansas town, many of which were included in his *Maple Hill Stories*.

William S. Burroughs, who gained notoriety as a "beatnik" writer in the 1950s and 1960s, spent the last seventeen years of his life in Lawrence. There he was recognized as an intelligent writer who produced a variety of publications reflecting his wide interests and his complex personality. He became a unique member of the community, and when he died in 1997, the people who knew him best thought of him as a real contributor to Kansas literature.

Nineteenth-century Kansas poetry was similar to much American poetry at that time—sweetly conventional and evenly rhyming, using trite words and phrases. Florence Snow, whose career spanned ninety years, was devoted to poetry and worked for its recognition, but her own poetic efforts were undistinguished. William H. Carruth gained national attention in 1895 for a poem entitled *Each in His Own Tongue*. Carruth collected poetry for publication but he was generally critical of the Kansas efforts before 1900. More realistic was Helen Rhoda Hoopes, whose Kansas imagery is clear and is expressed in unpretentious language.

Eugene F. Ware, "Ironquill," wrote many poems, some of which were serious and philosophical, but probably his greatest fame still came from *Dewey Was the Morning,* quoted in chapter twelve. Esther Clark Hill and Amy Lathrop received some recognition outside the state, and Kansas may make some claim on the famous black poet Langston Hughes who spent a part of his childhood in Topeka and credits the Topeka Public Library as the place where "books began to happen" to him.

Another African-American poet who discovered a new world in his public library was Frank Marshall Davis, a native of Arkansas City. Educated at Friends and Kansas State, he was a part of the new Negro Renaissance of the 1920s and 1930s and was first published in the *Kansas Magazine.* As both poet and journalist he was a political activist who worked to end segregation in the United States.

Perhaps the most notable woman poet in earlier years was May Williams Ward of Wellington, who received the Poetry Society of America Award in 1937 for a series of poems called *Dust Bowl,* and who published several other collections, including *Wheatlands.* William Allen White once said, "Her verse is beautiful, poignant, and understanding. She excels because she is of the prairie. She makes music of it." Mrs. Ward died in 1975.

Will Gibson, for several years a Topekan, is best known as a playwright (*Two for the Seesaw*), but he has written poetry using Kansas themes. The late Kenneth Porter, originally from Sterling, recalled his Kansas background in *The High Plains* (1938) and *No Rain from These Clouds* (1946). Active at present is Bruce Cutler, a native of Illinois who was educated in Kansas and taught at both Kansas State and Wichita State Universities. Cutler's first collection of poems was *The Year of the Green Wave* (1960), and in 1963 he wrote *A West Wind Rises,* based on the Marais des Cygnes massacre of 1858. Cutler has been described as "an assured, lyrical, reflective craftsman whose basic romanticism is attached to lands and people he has known." William Stafford, from Hutchinson, continued to write poetry that received national recognition until his death in 1994. He won a National Book Award for *Traveling Through the Dark* (1963). A reviewer in the 1970s noted that "Kansas remains his home as both a physical and a metaphysical state."

Over the past two decades the state has seen the rise of several poets whose works often use Kansas or Great Plains imagery and have brought them wide recognition and in some cases national awards. Some of them are native Kansans, while others have spent considerable time in the state because of their association with academic institutions here. Included in this group are Mark Cox, Harley Elliott, Albert Goldbarth, Steven Hind,

Jonathan Holden, Ronald Johnson, William Kloefkorn, Denise Low, Stephen Meats, W. R. Moses, Raymond Nelson, Luci Tapahonso, James Tate, Patricia Traxler, and Kevin Young.

Albert Goldbarth of Wichita won the National Book Critics Circle Award in 1992 for his collection *Heaven and Earth,* and Jonathan Holden of Manhattan received the Devins Award for *Design for a House* (1972). Another prize winner is Kevin Young of Topeka whose *Most Way Home* (1995) explores African-American life. Lucy Tapahonso, a Navajo now living in Lawrence, included both poetry and stories in her *Sáanii Dahataał: The Women Are Singing* (1993). Steven Hind of Hutchinson who grew up in the Flint Hills often reflects that region in his work, while Denise Low, a native of Emporia, has several volumes in print, and her work is especially sensitive to the natural life of the prairies and plains. William Kloefkorn now lives in Nebraska, but he is a Kansas native and his *This Death by Drowning* (1997) has its basis in his childhood.

Although many Kansas poets have published with university presses and major eastern houses, they are fortunate to have available publishing opportunities within the state. The Cottonwood Press of Lawrence, the

Gordon Parks (on chair) directing the film version of *The Learning Tree.* Courtesy of Topeka *Capital Journal.*

Woodley Press of Topeka, and the *Midwest Quarterly* of Pittsburg all have provided outlets for poetic works.

One native Kansan with a wealth of talent is Gordon Parks, who spent the early years of his life in Fort Scott. Parks is creative in photography, music, literature, and drama. He became famous as a photographer for *Life* but more people learned about him when his novel *The Learning Tree* was published in 1963. Hailed as the "fiction find of the year," *The Learning Tree* was made into a motion picture in 1968 with Parks directing, producing, and composing the musical score. Filmed in the Fort Scott vicinity, *The Learning Tree* draws on some of Parks's early experiences as it "probes the frustrations of a Negro boy in Kansas."

Parks was the first black to become a national magazine's leading photographer. His poetry has received national circulation, and in 1952 he began another career, musical composition. He wrote *Symphonic Set for Piano and Orchestra*, which was first played in Venice, Italy, before an enthusiastic audience. His autobiographical *A Choice of Weapons* (1966), is a moving account of a life that, in spite of discrimination, has been a success because of a solid family background and individual ability.

A close observer and able commentator on the Kansas literary scene was Gene DeGruson of Pittsburg State University, who died in 1997. A published poet and the longtime editor of the *Little Balkans Review*, DeGruson was also a teacher, actor, director, historian, and collector with a wide acquaintance among writers, and a walking encyclopedia of the literary world.

Similar in his interests and knowledge is Thomas Fox Averill, teacher and Writer in Residence at Washburn University. He has published two collections of short stories and has edited other works. He also has gained wide recognition as William Jennings Bryan Oleander, homespun social commentator and political analyst from Here, Kansas, because of his regular appearances on KANU, Kansas University's National Public Radio outlet. His *Oleander's Guide to Kansas*, illustrated by Pat Marrin, was published in 1996.

Kansas has been blessed with good historians over the years, most of whom appear in the suggested readings and elsewhere throughout this volume.

MUSIC AND MUSICIANS

Kansans have been singing and playing instruments since the opening of the territory. Folk singing and dancing; choral groups such as Topeka's old Modoc Club, organized in the 1870s; small town "silver cornet bands"; and the performances of *Messiah* at Lindsborg, *Elijah* at Emporia and

Winfield, and the *Seven Last Words of Christ* at Newton have provided musical opportunities for both performers and listeners in Kansas communities for decades.

Pioneer music included western ballads and cowboy and play-party songs, most of which were products of the whole American frontier. However, there are two exceptions. The official state song, *Home on the Range*, was written by two early Smith county settlers, Dr. Brewster Higley and Dan Kelley, and the words were first published in 1873 by the *Smith County Pioneer*, Smith Center, under the title *Western Home*. *The Lane County Bachelor*, often credited to Texas and other western states, apparently had its beginning in Lane County, Kansas, and humorously recounts the difficulties encountered by a homesteader living in a sod house:

> Frank Baker's my name and a bachelor I am,
> I'm keeping old batch on an elegant plan.
> You'll find me out west in the county of Lane,
> I'm starving to death on a government claim.
> My house it is built of the natural soil,
> The walls are erected according to Hoyle.
> The roof has no pitch but is level and plain,
> And I always get wet when it happens to rain.
>
> Hurrah for Lane County, the land of the free,
> The home of the grasshopper, bed bug and flea.
> I'll sing loud its praises and tell of its fame,
> While starving to death on a government claim.

Edith Bideau, a lyric soprano, was among the notable performers of the past who had Kansas beginnings. She was born in Wilson County and educated at Baker University and the University of Kansas. She was soloist with the Minneapolis Symphony and appeared with the Metropolitan Opera Company. Hazel Eden Mudge was born at Eskridge and graduated from Topeka High School. Also a soprano, she sang with the Chicago Grand Opera Company and with companies in Boston and the British Isles. Harold Challis went "from raising chickens in Atchison, his birthplace in 1876," to singing title roles in the Bayreuth Wagnerian Festival in 1914. Although he planned to stay in Germany, the outbreak of the First World War brought him back to America, where he continued to perform. Marion Talley, whose family lived in Ellis and Kansas City, retired from an operatic career in 1930 and returned to Kansas, having gained fame as one of the youngest soprano soloists at the Metropolitan Opera. Kathleen

Kersting of Wichita made her operatic debut in Milan, Italy, in 1927 when she was only eighteen. Three years later she was back in the United States to sing the role of Marzellina in Beethoven's *Fidelio* with the Chicago Civic Opera Company. She sang several years with the Chicago company, taught, and toured Europe a number of times before her death in 1965.

One of the brightest stars in opera today is Samuel Ramey of Colby, educated at Kansas State and Wichita State universities. Acclaimed internationally, he has become the most recorded American bass in history. He has performed in *Faust* innumerable times, but his talent is so versatile that his value to opera and the concert stage is virtually unlimited.

Other operatic singers include Rebecca Copley of Lindsborg, daughter of Elmer Copley who retired in 1988 as director of the *Messiah* festival after twenty-nine years. She is a soprano who has performed in Paris, at the Metropolitan Opera, and as a soloist with the Bethany Oratorio Society. James King, a Dodge City native, and a popular Wagnerian Heldentenor, sang at La Scala, the Met, and in Germany for nearly thirty years. Patricia Wise from Wichita is a lyric soprano who has sung on both sides of the Atlantic and has starred in BBC productions. Vincent Baskin from Kansas City had a promising career cut short in 1988 when he died at age thirty-five. He had starred in Opera Ebony in New York City and also had sung in Europe.

Richetta Manager, a Washburn University graduate, and Carolyn Smith-Meyer, Topeka, have been successful in European opera and also have performed in the United States. Beverly Hoch of Marion, a popular coloratura, has sung operatically in America and Europe and on the concert stage. The late Louise Sherman of Garden City had a long association with the Metropolitan Opera where she served as assistant conductor, accompanist, and voice coach. She was one of the founders of Opera Colorado in 1982. Michael Lichtenauer, from Johnson County, currently tours with "Chanticleer," the men's choral group which performs internationally.

Larry Newland of Winfield has been the assistant conductor of the New York Philharmonic and has served as guest conductor for several other orchestras across the United States. Merle Evans of Columbus was also a noted conductor, in a different field of music. Known as "the Toscanini of the Big Top," Evans led the Ringling Brothers and Barnum and Bailey Circus band for years. He died in 1988.

Robert Russell Bennett, a Kansas City native, was for years one of the country's premier arrangers and orchestrators, and he also composed orchestral music.

Samuel Ramey. Courtesy Thomas County Historical Society.

In popular music, Marilyn Maye of "If My Friends Could See Me Now" and "Step to the Rear" recording fame and a well-known club performer has roots in Wichita and Topeka; so does the progressive rock group "Kansas," which rose to continuing prominence in both the performing and recording fields in the 1970s.

Recently Freedy Johnson of Kinsley, songwriter and performer on rhythm guitar; Karrin Allyson, born in Great Bend, vocalist; and Melissa Etheridge, Leavenworth, songwriter, rock singer, and recording artist, have gained recognition in the popular field.

Kansans have contributed greatly to the jazz world. Charlie "Bird" Parker, a Kansas Citian, has been called "the most influential musician in jazz," and his alto saxophone work and compositions are enduring. Unfortunately, he died in 1958 at an early age, a victim of substance abuse. Bobby Watson, Lawrence, also an alto sax player, is a prominent composer and record producer. Coleman Hawkins, "the father of the tenor saxophone," came to Topeka in his youth to study music, and his association with the city is celebrated annually with a jazz festival. Kevin Mahogany, while not a native Kansan, is a Baker University alumnus and maintains Kansas ties. Buck Clayton, born in Parsons, played trumpet with Count Basie and Duke Ellington and had his own band in the 1950s.

Kansas audiences have embraced jazz enthusiastically. The Topeka Jazz Workshop has been in existence for many years and performs with regularity. Jazz festivals are held in several communities and on an annual basis, and Kansas high schools and colleges include jazz and stage bands in their regular music education programs.

A transplanted Texan who has been in Kansas for many years is James Rivers, a concert pianist and a Washburn University faculty member. He and pianist Julie Rivers performed widely in the Midwest in concert for several years, and they have been in demand as teachers of master's classes throughout the region. Julie Rivers composes for the piano and her recent album, *One Starry Night*, features her own compositions.

The late Kevin Oldham of Overland Park was a talented pianist and composer whose career was cut short by his tragic death. Charles Axton from Topeka, a pianist and arranger, was a successful director and conductor of musical theater in Germany beginning in the 1970s. He has returned to the United States.

The state has been fortunate in having good music departments at both its public and private colleges, which in turn have brought capable musicians and scholars who stayed for most of their careers. An example is Carl Preyer who was born in Germany but came to Kansas in 1887, teaching first at Baker and then for many years at the University of Kansas. He enjoyed a wide reputation as a composer for violin and piano, and his

Concertstueck for piano was arranged for orchestra and performed by the Chicago Symphony. Charles S. Skilton, a New Englander by birth, began a long career of teaching at the university in 1903. He wrote cantatas, oratorios, and opera, as well as orchestral music, much of it based on American folk themes and legends. His Indian opera *Bluefeather,* based on Pueblo tribal music, was produced for radio in 1930, and he wrote other compositions using Indian melodies.

Perhaps the foremost authority in the field of Indian music history and interpretation was Thurlow Lieurance. Lieurance was born in Iowa but he grew up in southeastern Kansas and was bandmaster of the Twenty-Second Kansas Regiment during the Spanish-American War. For twenty years he was a member of the music faculty at Wichita University. He traveled throughout the West recording Indian music and compiling an extensive collection of reference material, which is still useful to scholars. Lieurance produced several compositions, the most popular being *By the Waters of Minnetonka.* Arthur Finley Nevin, for a time on the University of Kansas faculty, also worked with Indian themes.

Gail Kubik of Coffeyville has received recognition for his compositions. He won an Academy Award in 1951 for the score of the animated cartoon feature *Gerald McBoing Boing* and the following year a Pulitzer Prize for his *Symphony Concertante.* A Kansan with a different role in music as it applies to eduction was the late Joseph Maddy, originally of Wellington. After study in Wichita and a chair in the Minneapolis Symphony,

Thurlow Lieurance, Wichita composer and teacher, shown here recording traditional Indian music in the Southwest.

Maddy organized the National High School Orchestra in 1926 and founded the National Music Camp and Arts Academy at Interlochen, Michigan. Maddy was credited with changing the course of both music instruction and appreciation in the nation's public schools, and the camp at Interlochen served as the model for similar operations across the country. James Dick of Hutchinson, noted concert pianist, established the Festival Hill performing arts center at Round Top, Texas, which draws musicians from across the country. Glad Robinson Youse of Baxter Springs was recognized as one of the leading women composers in the country and was especially known for her choral music.

Kirke L. Mechem, a former Topekan, has seen his orchestral works receive acclaim in the Midwest and on the Pacific Coast. The premier of his *First Symphony* by the San Francisco Symphony in 1965 brought an "unprecedented outburst of curtain calls," according to the music critic of the San Francisco *Examiner*. The symphony was performed in Topeka in March 1973, by the Topeka Civic Symphony.

The female dean of black music in America, Dr. Eva Jessye, returned to her native southeastern Kansas in 1979 at age eighty-four, to serve as an artist-in-residence and consultant at Pittsburg State University. She was the music director of the original *Porgy and Bess* and the pioneering film *Hallelujah*, and formed the noted Eva Jessye Choir. She died in 1992.

A bright chapter in Kansas musical history has been written by the symphony orchestras that have developed within the state since the Second World War. Topeka and Wichita, particularly, have developed orchestras of quality. On January 23, 1956, *Time* magazine devoted considerable space to the Wichita group, reporting that in 1945 "with wild hopes but grave doubts, seven musicians gathered . . . and laid plans to start a symphony orchestra." The infant orchestra rehearsed in a room where the players had to provide their own janitor service but as *Time* put it, "Wichita's musical life is rich and happy" eleven years later. That situation has not changed. Under able direction the Wichita Symphony developed a notable concert season, and it has continued to add to the cultural stature of the state.

The same is true of the Topeka Symphony. There had been several orchestras in the capital from the turn of the century, but in 1946, under the direction of the late Everett Fetter of Washburn University, the Topeka Civic Symphony was born. As in most community sym-

Eva Jessye

Typical of Kansas community bands in the late-nineteeth and early-twentieth centuries is this one from Norcatur.

phonies, the members are basically amateur performers although they do now receive a minimal stipend. Groups with similar interests have been formed in Salina, Kansas City, Hutchinson, Beloit, and Lawrence.

In 1960 in Topeka, accompanied by the symphony, a symphony chorus presented its first concert under the direction of the late Floyd Hedberg. The chorus continues to perform regularly. Choral groups have also been formed in smaller Kansas cities such as Garden City, and they present standard classics, modern compositions, and musical comedy, and most important, they strengthen musical life in a society that increasingly needs to sing. Kansans are being brought full circle to what their pioneer ancestors were doing when they brought town bands and *Messiah* to the Great Plains. Several Kansas communities still enthusiastically support bands, most of which perform primarily in the summer.

THE DRAMATIC ARTS

Kansas can claim a playwright of lasting distinction, William Inge, who died in 1973. Inge was born in Independence, graduated from the University of Kansas, worked for a Wichita radio station, and taught in both high school and college before his play *Come Back, Little Sheba* brought him fame in 1949. *Picnic* won him a Pulitzer Prize in 1953, and *Bus Stop* received rave reviews in 1955. All drew upon Inge's Kansas background, and all were made into motion pictures. Much of the movie version of *Picnic* was filmed in Kansas, and the Halstead *Independent* carried this announcement on May 13, 1955:

> Riverside park will be the scene of more than fifty percent of the footage of the movie "Picnic," advance men for Columbia Pictures corporation who were here making preliminary arrangements disclosed this week. Already some $5,000 worth of permanent improvements have been installed in the park. . . .
>
> Even the food that will be served the extras in the picnic scene must be real, home cooked picnic food. Charley Granucci, property master. . . explained Wednesday that delicatessen type vittles won't do. Before he left, he contacted Mrs. Marvin Stein, community leader for the Gem 4-H Club, and asked that the women of the club prepare food for the movie of exactly the same type they would fix for a picnic for their own group.
>
> Granucci needs enough picnic food to feed some 250 extras in one sequence. . . . Columbia will pay for the ingredients, and enough more to make a tidy profit for the club treasury. And on top of that, the families involved will be on the inside track when it comes to getting jobs as extras, Granucci promised.

In addition, Inge wrote *The Dark at the Top of the Stairs* for theater and the Academy Award winning screenplay for *Splendor in the Grass* in 1961. The kind of sensitive realism, which applied to both settings and characters by Inge in his plays, did not quite come across in his first novel, *Good Luck, Miss Wyckoff*, published in 1970. Again small town Kansas provides the background, but a plot involving a kind of sordid sexual tragedy is not really typical of William Inge's writing. *My Son Is a Splendid Driver*, published in 1971 and described by Inge as "a novel in the form of a memoir," is better reading.

Also prominent on Broadway for many years was Brock Pemberton,  one of the most successful producers that the American stage has ever had. Playwrights such as Maxwell Anderson and Zona Gale were first introduced to New York theatergoers by Pemberton, and he also was a founder of the USO camp shows in the Second World War. He grew up in Emporia, graduated from the University of Kansas, and learned to write on the Emporia *Gazette*. He was assistant dramatic critic for the New York *Times*, won a Pulitzer Prize for his production of *Miss Lulu Bett* in the

William Inge

A traveling dramatic troupe on stage in Kansas, 1924.

early 1920s, and was primarily responsible for the record-breaking success of *Harvey*.

When Pemberton died, William L. White wrote in the Kansas City *Star*, March 13, 1950:

> Emporia should be properly proud of the fact . . . that Brock in all of the almost forty years he has spent on Broadway remained unshakably a Kansan and an Emporian. . . .
>
> My father (William Allen White), although he pointed out that his sole contribution to this was one letter of introduction, was tremendously proud of Brock Pemberton, as was all of Emporia . . . and we basked in the fact that Brock was our exhibit on glamorous Broadway, our boy who had made good, among the bright lights of the biggest town on earth. . . .
>
> Of course our pride had its price. It was understood that any Emporian who managed to thumb his way to New York, was privileged, no matter how slightly he knew Brock to get him on the phone, and then demand aisle seats to whatever show Brock then had on Broadway. . . .

One of the first famous actors from Kansas was Fred Stone, who was born in Colorado in 1873 and lived in several Kansas communities but began acting during his boyhood in North Topeka in a tightrope act. Stone was in circus and medicine shows before he became a "song and dance" man in vaudeville. Then he moved into musical comedy winning international acclaim for his role as the Scarecrow in *The Wizard of Oz*. In April 1932, the Wichita Eagle said, "Fred Stone is one of the most widely known men in public life in this country. . . He is one of the most highly respected actors of the American stage." He played serious drama in the 1930s and retired to California where he died in 1959.

Fred's cousin, the late Milburn Stone, worked in both Broadway theater and motion pictures successfully for many years before he became one of television's most familiar faces as "Doc" on the long-running Columbia Broadcasting System's *Gunsmoke*. Milburn Stone grew up in Burrton and his characterization of "Doc" was patterned after his own country-doctor grandfather.

Sidney Toler, son of a prominent Wichita family, went on the stage shortly after finishing high school and he became familiar to millions of moviegoers as "Charlie Chan" after 1938. The Tolers were of Scottish descent but Sidney had no trouble portraying the famous fictional Chinese detective, and he once commented that "no one could imagine me doing anything but Charlie Chan." Charles "Buddy" Rogers of Olathe had dozens of leading parts in motion pictures and during the 1920s he was known as "America's Boy Friend." Reb Russell, a Montgomery County rancher, starred in several "B" westerns in the mid-1930s and performed as a trick rider and crack shot in circuses after he left Hollywood.

Hale Hamilton became a Kansan in 1899 when his parents moved to Topeka from Iowa. Hamilton scored his greatest stage success in the comedy *Get-Rich-Quick Wallingford*, and he performed frequently in Europe,

playing a command performance in England for King George V in 1918. That same year he entered motion pictures for the old Keystone Comedy Corporation and remained active in Hollywood through the 1930s. Also in comedy was Fay Tincher, described as "one of the prettiest of the younger crowd in Topeka society" in 1902. She played music halls and comic opera in Chicago and New York, and by 1917 she was not only a famous movie star but headed her own film company. Referred to as "a feminine Charlie Chaplin" Fay Tincher had a universal appeal. Louise Brooks, of Cherryvale and Wichita, starred in silent films in both Hollywood and Europe. She later had smaller roles in movies and radio soap operas.

Fred Stone

One famous film star whose Kansas connection was very brief but whose career has led to an annual celebration of his work is Joseph "Buster" Keaton. He was born in Piqua in 1895 while his parents were traveling with a tent show. For several years Iola has hosted a two-day program featuring Keaton movies, film scholars, and other silent stars' performances.

On Broadway, Norma Terris, Columbus, starred as Magnolia in the original cast of *Showboat*, a role she reprised many times. She was featured in roles at the St. Louis Municipal Opera in the 1930s and 1940s and was cast in a few motion pictures. She died in 1989. Mary Murfitt of Lindsborg has written, produced, and starred in the off-Broadway musical *Cowgirls*. The play is set in Thomas County and has enjoyed great success. Robert Sink, of Topeka and Overland Park, played Lieutenant Cable in the first touring company of *South Pacific*, and Dort Clark of Wellington was well received by New York audiences for his parts in many of the hits following World War II. Mary-Pat Green from Johnson County has had major roles on stage in *Nunsense*, *Sweeney Todd*, and *Godspell*.

Karla Burns, a singer, dancer, and actress, is from Wichita, and in 1983 was nominated for a Tony Award as a result of her appearance as Queenie in the Broadway revival of *Showboat*. Burns also created a one-woman show about Hattie McDaniel. McDaniel, who was born in Wichita, won an Oscar for her portrayal of Mammy in *Gone With the Wind*, the first African American to be so honored.

Clark Tippet, Parsons, starred with the American Ballet Theater until his untimely death in 1992. Stephanie Heston of Topeka is receiving acclaim as a ballerina and has returned to Kansas to perform. A different kind of dancer was Virginia Lee Hicks of Kansas City, better known as Jennie Lee, who starred in burlesque for thirty years.

Vivian Vance of Cherryvale and Independence was a hit as a comedienne on Broadway but is best known for her role as Lucille Ball's best friend on television's *I Love Lucy*. Vera Ralston Miles of Wichita has had a very successful career in both motion pictures and television; Patrice Wymore of Salina had featured roles in movies during the 1940s and 1950s; and Shirley Knight of Lyons has made more than 200 television dramatic appearances and movies and was nominated for an Academy Award as a supporting actress in *The Dark at the Top of the Stairs*. Also in Hollywood is Dennis Hopper, a native Dodge Citian, who won critical recognition for his direction of *Easy Rider* in which he also played a major role. Edward Asner of Kansas City, who has had many screen roles, became widely recognized as television's "Lou Grant," and served as president of the Screen Actors Guild. He is a multiple winner of both Emmy and Golden Globe awards.

Other screen actresses from Kansas who have been successful include Marj Dusay, Cynthia Sikes, Kirstie Alley, Dee Wallace, Shanna Reed, and

Marilyn Schreffler. Dusay, from Russell, has had roles in over fifty TV series and served on the Kansas Film Commission. Alley, of Wichita, first gained attention as Rebecca on *Cheers* and continues to get major roles in both movies and television. Sikes, also from Wichita, has been a cast member of TV's *St. Elsewhere* and *L.A. Law* and has had movie roles, while Schreffler, of Wichita and Topeka, worked in comedy groups, television, and was the cartoon voice of Popeye's Olive Oyl. Dee Wallace, a Kansas Citian, has played in many movies and television shows, but she is probably best remembered as the mother in the movie, *E.T.* In addition, she is a teacher of drama.

Hugh Beaumont of Lawrence worked on screen and was familiar to TV viewers as Ward Cleaver, the father on *Leave it to Beaver.* Everett McGill of Kansas City, Dennis Hayden of Girard, James Reynolds of Topeka, Paul Rudd of Overland Park, Darren Burrows of Winfield, and Jeff Yagher of Lawrence have all succeeded as actors in recent years. Reynolds stars on *Days of our Lives* and returns to Kansas to perform on stage, while Burrows was a regular on *Northern Exposure.* Gordon Jump, who stayed in Kansas for several years following army service at Fort Riley, has worked in radio, television, and movies. He is best known as the station manager on *WKRP in Cincinnati* and as the lonely Maytag serviceman in that company's commercials in the 1990s. Don Johnson, who spent his youth in Wichita, has played several roles over the years, but television viewers remember him particularly for his part on *Miami Vice*.

Michael Shane of Roeland Park has acted in television in England and on the American stage and played Friar Tuck in the move *Robin Hood, Prince of Thieves*. He also does improvisational comedy. Eric Edwards and Greg Brinkley, both of Topeka, are actors and stand-up comics. Bill Farmer of Pratt has provided the voices of innumerable animated characters including Goofy in the movie featuring the Disney dog. He, too, does stand-up comedy. Max Showalter of Caldwell for many years played character roles in both movies and television, and he is also a composer and painter.

Several Kansans are involved in screen writing, producing, and directing, including Steve Mills, Doug Curtis, Mitch Brian, Eric Darnell, and Mike Robe. Robe, originally from Arkansas City, has written and directed several television miniseries and has been instrumental in bringing movie production companies to work in Kansas. He maintains close ties to the Kansas Film Commission and to the Theater and Film Department of Kansas University, his alma mater.

Kevin Wilmott, who grew up in Junction City, had his movie, *Ninth Street*, premiered in 1998 in Kansas City, Missouri. He had written other screenplays, but *Ninth Street*, filmed in Kansas City, is based on his knowledge of his home town's African-American community.

Gregory Hill of Overland Park is nationally known as a theatrical set designer for his work on both network television and Broadway.

One Kansas, in a different branch of show business for many years, was Emmett Kelly. Kelly, who died in 1979, was born and spent his early years in Sedan and entertained millions as America's favorite circus clown.

Reminiscent of the road shows and summer stock efforts of the past are theatrical companies at work in Kansas today. Summer playhouses and civic theater groups are giving people an opportunity to perform and are enriching the opportunities for playgoers in the state.

The Topeka Civic Theater is the state's oldest, celebrating its sixty-third season in 1998–1999, but there are similar community efforts ongoing elsewhere in Topeka and around Kansas. Abilene has a professional theater group, and children's theater has been featured in several cities. All have been well received, and the quality of the production is good. The state's colleges and universities do well in this field, and at times stage original productions. For the past several years Summer Chautauqua has been recreated in many towns, aided by the Kansas Humanities Council and featuring Kansans representing national figures.

A notable product of local theater is Ric Averill of Topeka and Lawrence. Averill writes, directs, and produces a variety of dramatic presentations, many of which have strong Kansas themes. He is also an actor, and his Seem-to-be-Players perform across the country. His wife Jeanne, an actress, at times performs with the company.

ARTISTS AND THEIR WORK

Early travelers and explorers sketched and painted the Great Plains, but Henry Worrall of Topeka who began work as an illustrator in the 1860s was the first Kansas artist. Worrall was nationally known for his contributions to the popular magazines of the day. Worrall's best known drawings have been described as "journalism in pictures," but Worrall also worked in oils—both portraits and Kansas landscapes. Frederic Remington can hardly be considered a Kansan just because he lived on a Butler County sheep ranch in the mid-1880s but those years increased his love for the West where he developed some of the techniques that would later make him famous as the nation's leading portrayer of cowboys, Indians, and cavalrymen. Samuel J. Reader of Topeka, who came to Kansas as a territorial pioneer, drew and painted hundreds of subjects. His work is definitely classed as "primitive," yet much of what went on during the territorial period and the Civil War in the West is illustrated only by his unsophisticated art.

Referring to George M. Stone, the Kansas City *Star* said in 1933, "It is fortunate for Kansas that she had all through the years of her youth a

John Steuart Curry at work on the state capitol murals, late 1930s.

painter who loved her and perhaps idealized her. . . . Stone understood the Kansas of his time." A Topekan most of his life, Stone studied in Paris, traveled widely in Europe, and in company with Albert T. Reid started a school that became Washburn University's art department. Stone was the state's foremost portrait painter of governors, judges, businessmen, and their wives. He also earned the title "The Millet of the Prairies," because he represented western farmers in a similar fashion to Millet's French peasants. Stone painted murals, two of which are in the governor's office—*The Pioneers* and *The Spirit of Kansas*.

John Noble of Wichita studied in Europe and won distinction, but his most famous paintings are of the sea. One of his early works suffered an interesting fate. Noble painted *Cleopatra at the Bath,* which hung in the bar of the Carey Hotel in Wichita, and Cleopatra was done in by Carry Nation when she broke up the bar in one of her famous attacks. Kenneth Adams, formerly of Topeka, is known for work in the graphic arts as well as for painting, and Bradbury Thompson, who died in 1995, was one of the nation's leading designers and art consultants.

John Steuart Curry, who began life in Jefferson County, was a leader in the movement for realistic regionalism, along with Grant Wood and Thomas Hart Benton. Critics recognized him as a faithful chronicler of rural life because of paintings such as *Baptism in Kansas* (1928). Curry was commissioned to paint the murals in the east and west corridors of the capitol's second floor. "The theme I have chosen is historical in more than one sense," said Curry. "In great measure it is the historical struggle of man with nature. . . . It is my family's tradition and the tradition of a great majority of Kansas people. . . . " In his *Tragic Prelude* Curry depicted the early struggle for freedom in Kansas while in the west corridor he painted a pastoral scene, incorporating a farmstead and Kansas's natural resources. Of the latter mural the artist said, "I show the beauty of real things under the hand of a beneficent Nature . . . so that we, as farmers, patrons, and artists can shout happily together, 'Ad Astra per Aspera' [To the Stars through Difficulties]."

Curry was criticized because a few viewers of the murals thought his animals were not properly proportioned, and his pig's tail curled the wrong way. Others believed that his depiction of John Brown was too extreme. Curry never quite finished the paintings, but by the time he died in 1946 most of the controversy had subsided. In a completely different style, but one worthy of respect, Kansas artist David Overmyer painted eight murals in the first floor rotunda of the capitol that represent periods in nineteenth-century Kansas history. The rotunda space left unfilled by Curry now is covered with murals painted by another Kansan, the late Lumen Winter. Also a sculptor, he is responsible for the Great White Buffalo that stands near the entry to the Kansas Museum of History, Topeka.

Sven Birger Sandzen, who came to the United States from Sweden in 1894 to teach art and languages at Bethany College, was an artist about whom no controversy ever raged. He stayed in Lindsborg till his death in 1954, painting, sketching, teaching, and helping organize artistic groups and exhibitions. Sandzen, who understood and graphically portrayed his adopted region, was once described as "the one painter in the United States who bypassed the art movements of the past forty years and now reveals himself as a bridge between the impressionists and the so-called abstract expressionists." *Southwest Art*, one of the nation's most prestigious art publications, commented in August 1983, that Sandzen "produced some of the most lyrically beautiful landscapes of Western America ever painted."

Birger Sandzen of Lindsborg surrounded by art, including some of his own paintings.

Many of his landscapes may be seen at the Sandzen museum on the campus of Bethany College. Sandzen also attracted to Lindsborg, Anton Pearson, a noted wood carver whose representations of Swedish pioneer settlers helped preserve an ethnic heritage.

Henry Salem Hubbell, who was born in Paola and grew up in Lawrence, studied in Paris and Chicago and created portraits in the impressionistic manner. He taught in Pittsburgh, Pennsylvania, for many years and died in 1949. He gained fame nationally but was not well known in his native state. Paul Mannen who worked in oils and watercolor did landscapes of the Southwest and Kansas and had his paintings shown widely. He was a Kansas University graduate who lived in Topeka in the 1940s and established the art department at New Mexico State University. He died in 1976.

Albert T. Reid, George M. Stone's art school partner, was best known for his political cartooning, particularly in the 1890s and the first two decades of the twentieth century. But Reid also painted, did poster art and nonpolitical cartoons, illustrated magazines, ran two newspapers, and found time to write music. His career took him from his native Cloud County to New York, by way of Topeka, Leavenworth, Kansas City, and Chicago, and in all those places he caught the spirit of the times with his pen. Reid's skill was tremendous, and the detail in his drawings is fantastic. His cartoons recorded history wittily and graphically.

Successful cartoonists working currently include Jerry Bittle, a Wichita native, who has done editorial cartooning and is the creator of the comic strip "Geech," Mort Walker of El Dorado who produces the strip "Beetle Bailey," and Charlie Podrebarac of Kansas City whose work includes cartoons for the Kansas City *Star*. Paul Coker, Jr., Lawrence, has worked on animated television specials and has done cartoons for *Mad* magazine.

John Falter, noted illustrator and painter, whose work was familiar in magazines such as the *Saturday Evening Post* and *Country Gentleman*, was from Atchison, and his painting reflected his northeastern Kansas background. Another illustrator, Rudolph Wendelin, is best known as the creator of the U.S. Forest Service's Smokey the Bear. Byron Wolfe, who painted historical scenes dealing with the West, which are much admired, was from Johnson County. John Bashor, painter and teacher, is a product of Topeka schools and Washburn and taught at Bethany College and Montana State University. Kansas artists using western themes included Laurence Coffelt of Emporia, Charles B. Rogers of Ellsworth, and, currently, Gary Hawk of Iola.

The paintings of Topekans Mary Huntoon and Pauline Shirer have become familiar to a number of Kansans, and so have the sketches and illustrations of Margaret Whittemore. Roland "Kickapoo" Logan, who acquired his nickname because he was born in that Leavenworth County community, has a national reputation, and while he is best known for seascapes, he used the midwestern landscape in his work. The state was fortunate to acquire as a resident a native Oklahoman and well-known artist. The late Blackbear Bosin, a Comanche and Kiowa, moved to Wichita in 1940 and became internationally known for his portrayals of the Indians and their customs.

Laurie Houseman-Whitehawk, Winnebago and Sioux, grew up in Johnson County and was educated at Emporia State, Kansas State, and Haskell Indian Nations University. She lives near Lawrence and works in gouache as a painter, colorfully illustrating Native American culture, especially that of the Winnebagos.

In the field of sculpture three Kansans, Robert Merrell Gage, Bernard Frazier, and Bruce Moore, have made distinguished contributions. Gage is famous for sculptures of Abraham Lincoln, including the Lincoln statue on the state house grounds. There, also, is the former Topekan's Pioneer Woman. Frazier, a Smith County native, a graduate of the University of Kansas and a member of its faculty until his death in 1976, has among his most familiar works the sculptures on the Docking state office building in Topeka. Bruce Moore of Wichita, some of whose sculpture can been seen there, began to receive national attention in the late 1920s and early 1930s, and in later years he became a designer and artist for Steuben Glass.

At the present there are innumerable Kansas artists working in different media, several of them gaining national recognition. It would be impossible to compile a complete list, but many of them deserve special mention.

Painters who have taken great advantage of the Kansas landscape, some in both oil and water color, include Robert Sudlow of Lawrence, Mary Frances Ballard, Bea Opelka, Jack O'Hara, James Hamil, Helen Wendlandt, and Donna Carrington, all of Johnson County; Charles Sanderson of Wichita; David Melby of Leavenworth; Steve Heckman of Liberal; Kathleen Kuchar of Hays; and Joan Foth of Topeka (and Santa Fe). The late Marilyn Richter of Topeka falls into this same category. Other painters are Richard McInteer, Galen Senogles, Thomas Russell, James Fallier, John Sandlin, Colette Bangert, Charles Marshall, Sue Jean Covacevich (who is also an artist with stained glass), Jerry Thomas, Terry Maxwell, John Gurche, and Wayne Willis, a wildlife artist. Bernard Martin, a native of Hiawatha who died in 1998, was for many years one of the nation's leading painters of wildlife. Keith Jacobshagen, who grew up in Wichita and was influenced by Sudlow at Kansas University, paints Plains landscapes and is on the art faculty at the University of Nebraska, Lincoln.

Dr. John Cody, originally from Brooklyn but a long-time resident of Hays, is internationally known as an artist whose subjects are moths and butterflies.

Elizabeth "Grandma" Layton of Wellsville began drawing in the late 1970s for purposes of therapy. She was in her sixties at the time. A self-effacing person, she was little affected by the fact that her work was shown widely in the United States. She worked primarily in pencil and crayon, and one critic described her as "the Van Gogh of contour drawing." She died in 1993.

Another unique Kansas artist is Stan Herd, who grew up near Protection. He is a capable painter and muralist, but he is best known for his "field paintings," which he does with tractor, implements, and seeds. He has used twenty acres for a still life and a quarter-section for a portrait. "He paints fields with the broad strokes of a plow," according to one observer, and his art cannot be truly appreciated except from the air. His love for the land and the beauty of the agricultural environment led him to practice this unusual kind of art.

Ed Dwight, a Kansas City native once destined to be the first black astronaut, left the Air Force and turned to art for which he has gained national acclaim. Presently working in Denver but with close ties to his native state, he uses the West as a theme along with American Jazz. Other sculptors are Pete Felten, who is using Kansas limestone, and Jim Hagan, John Whitfield, James Bass, Gus Shafer, and Charlie Norton, all of whom work with metal, and to whom Kansas and the West are important thematically.

A different kind of sculptor is Bruce White of Kinsley, who grew up in Coldwater. He carves carousel horses, and his work is in demand internationally by collectors and commercial firms.

The Prairie Print Makers, organized during the Great Depression, included many Kansans, some of whom are still living. There are other forms of art in demand from Kansans, such as Margaret Lowe Burke's woodcuts and the textiles of Mary Sue Foster, Jean Bass, and Janet Kummerlein. College art departments in the state had and do have both faculty and students producing beautiful and marketable art. Some persons with college and university connections have been mentioned previously here but others are Richard Bergen, the late Albert Bloch, Robert Kiskadden, the late Jim Hunt, Jack Wright, Sheldon Carey, and Oscar Larmer. There is a Kansas Watercolor Society that encourages both amateurs and professionals, there is a Kansas association of Indian artists, and museums such as the Mulvane Art Center at Washburn, the Spencer Museum at the University of Kansas, and the Wichita Art Museum continue to be interested in exhibitions of art by Kansans.

In recent years there has been an increasing interest in folk art which includes a great variety of products, many of which are extremely attractive and sought after. One of the primary interests centers on quilting and the Kansas Quilt Project, 1986–1990, documented more than 13,000 quilts in Kansas. Some represented several generations of Kansas families, and the project led to numerous museum exhibitions and publications.

Art fairs are being held in towns from Parsons to Oberlin annually. The late Peggy Greene, for decades a popular Kansas newspaper columnist, wrote: "Art is flowering all over, in big towns and small, and moving outdoors to brighten the summer." That is still the case today. Most encouraging is that artists seem to find Kansas a good atmosphere in which to work, despite its distance from the major markets, and perhaps more talent will stay within or be attracted to the state in the future.

Suggestions for Reading

Thomas Fox Averill, ed., *What Kansas Means to Me: Twentieth Century Writers on the Sunflower State* (1990); Barbara Brackman, Jennie A. Chinn, et al., *Kansas Quilts and Quilters* (1993); Jennie A. Chinn, ed., *"Don't Ask Me My History, Just Listen to My Music": An Exploration of Kansas Folklife* (1992); Joseph S. Czestochowski, *John Steuart Curry and Grant Wood: A Portrait of Rural America* (1981); Frank Marshall Davis, *Livin' the Blues: Memoirs of a Black Journalist and Poet*, ed. by John Edgar Tidwell (1993); Sally Foreman Griffith, *Home Town News: William Allen White and the Emporia Gazette* (1989); James R. Hamil and Sharon Hamil, *Return to Kansas* (1984); Jim Hoy, comp. and ed., with photos by Vada Snider, *Prairie Poetry: Cowboy Verse of Kansas* (1995); E. Jay Jernigan, *William Lindsay White, 1900–1973: In the Shadow of His Father* (1997); Walter Johnson, *William Allen White's America* (1947); M. Sue Kendall, *Rethinking Regionalism: John Steuart Curry and the Kansas Mural Controversy* (1985); Don Lambert, *The Life and Art of Elizabeth "Grandma" Layton* (1995); Emory Lindquist, *Birger Sandzen: An Illustrated Biography* (1993); Arthur F. McClure, *Memories of Splendor: The Midwestern World of William Inge* (1989); Timothy Miller, *Following In His Steps: A Biography of Charles M. Sheldon* (1987); Barbara Thompson O'Neill and George C. Foreman, *The Prairie Print Makers* (1981); Gordon Parks, *Voices in the Mirror* (1990); Calder Pickett, *Ed Howe: Country Town Philosopher* (1968); Edna Reinbach, *Music and Musicians in Kansas* (1930); Everett Rich, *William Allen White, the Man From Emporia* (1941); Samuel J. Sackett, *E. W. Howe* (1972); Laurence E. Schmeckerbier, *John Steuart Curry's Pageant of America* (1943); Robert Taft, *Artists and Illustrators of the Old West: 1850–1900* (1953); and Howard Wilcox, *Bruce Moore: Notes Toward a Review of His Life and Art* (1975). Three publications of the Shawnee County Historical Society, edited by John W. Ripley, are informative. They are *Stage, Screen and Radio: Shawnee County, 1871–1941* (1966), *Albert T. Reid's Sketchbook* (1971), and *A Century of Music* (1977).

The *Kansas Historical Collections*, vol. 17, contains two articles of interest: James P. Callahan, "Kansas in the American Novel and Short Story," and Edna Reinbach, "Kansas Art and Artists." The following articles may be found in the *Kansas Historical Quarterly*: Frederick W. Brinkerhoff, "The Ottawa Chautauqua Assembly" (Winter, 1961); Myra E. Hull, "Kansas Play-Party Songs" (August, 1938); James C. Malin, "Eugene F. Ware, Master Poet. . . ." (Winter, 1966); Kirke Mechem, "Home on the Range" (November, 1949); John W. Ripley, "Another Look at the Rev. Mr. Charles M. Sheldon's Christian Daily Newspaper" (Spring, 1965); and John W. Ripley, "The Strange Story of Charles M. Sheldon's *In His Steps*" (Autumn, 1968). In *Kansas History* are: Thomas Fox Averill, "Oz and Kansas Culture" (Spring, 1989); Thomas Fox Averill, "Of Drought and Dust: Expressions in Kansas Literature" (Winter 1997–1998); Ronald L. Davis, ed., "Within the Shadows of Pickfair: An Interview With Charles 'Buddy' Rogers" (Summer, 1990); Ronald L. Davis, ed., "Doc Adams of 'Gunsmoke': An Interview With Actor Milburn Stone" (Winter 1987/88); Harlan F. Jennings, Jr., "Grand Opera in Kansas in the 19th Century" (Summer, 1980); Linda L. Pohly, "Early Musical Development in Wichita" (Winter, 1982); Peggy and Harold Samuels, "Frederic Remington, the Holiday Sheepman" (Spring, 1979); Mark Scott, "Langston Hughes of Kansas" (Spring, 1980); Mark Scott, "The Little Blue Books in the War on Bigotry and Bunk" (Autumn, 1978); Richard B. Sheridan, "John Ise, 1885–1969: Economist, Conservationist, Prophet of the Energy Crisis" (Summer, 1982); and John Edgar Tidwell, "Ad Astra Per Aspera: Frank Marshall Davis" (Winter, 1995–1996). The entire Spring 1990 issue of *Kansas History* is devoted to quilts and quilting.

Sue Haldeman-Julius, "An Intimate Look at Haldeman-Julius," *The Little Balkans Review* (Winter, 1981–1982) is enlightening along with John Diffily, "Birger Sandzen, 1871–1954," *Southwest Art* (August, 1983); and Robert A. McInnes, "Chautauqua, 'The Most American Thing in America,'" *Kansas Heritage* (Autumn, 1997).

18

Change, Controversy, and Commemoration

The population of Kansas grew steadily after 1860, when it was only 107,206. In ten years it tripled and by the mid-1880s reached its first million. It took another sixty years for the second million to be recorded, but by 1970 there were two-and-a-quarter million Kansans. Kansas, like other Great Plains states, saw many of its people leave between 1960 and 1970 but the population still increased 3 percent. Little change occurred in the 1970s and early 1980s, but by 1996 Kansas had acquired another 150,000 residents, and the count stood at 2,572,150. A great many young people leave the state after finishing their education and the proportion of aged persons in Kansas is increasing, although that trend has been reversed in some rural areas. Metropolitan counties are acquiring more young people, but in some rural areas there is a noticeable loss of young men and women.

During the 1960s and early 1970s many Kansas counties lost population but after 1975 the state's "out-migration" declined significantly. In the 1990s sixty counties lost population, with the heaviest decrease coming in western Kansas, although Finney, Ford, and Seward counties had substantial increases. Counties surrounding major population centers—Butler, Leavenworth, and Douglas counties, for example—experienced major growth. It was hoped that the development of new industries would attract and hold younger people, but in some areas new industry has only improved the level of living for those who stayed. Kansas is becoming increasingly urbanized and industrialized and less identifiable as a rural society.

Economic experts, local businessmen, and many politicians believe that economic development with a tax structure favorable to industry holds the proper answers for the future of Kansas. However, the state must also provide adequate funding for the arts, for libraries, for public health and welfare, and for superior educational opportunities at all levels if the quality of life is to appeal to future Kansans.

A state in transition must pay attention in every way to its people and the communities in which they live.

Environmental Control

Some Kansans have always been concerned about the environment, particularly where water is concerned, and progress has been made in cutting down pollution from industrial waste, and some streams considered dead a few years ago are now alive with fish. There are still fish kills from foreign substances in creeks and rivers but rigid regulation of runoff from livestock feedlots has helped. There is room for improvement in the constant battle to keep water clean, and there is confusion at times because state and federal standards for pollution control do not always coincide. Conservation of water is an ever-present problem and the continued lowering of the Ogallala Aquifer is a very real concern to Kansas and other Plains states.

In addition to the ongoing controversy with Colorado, mentioned previously, Kansas and Nebraska became involved in arguments over Nebraska's consumption of Republican River water. Both states filed suit in 1998 and were awaiting a hearing before the U.S. Supreme Court at this writing. This case, also, could drag on for years to come.

In recent years concern over the storage of nuclear wastes has produced lengthy arguments about the safety of residents if the federal government should utilize abandoned salt mines in central Kansas as underground nuclear dumps. A regional coalition of states was formed to deal with hazardous waste, with Nebraska designated the state to undertake that dubious task. However, Nebraska has had second thoughts, and the selection of a dump site has yet to be accomplished.

Debates, too, have taken place between ranchers and ecologists over the killing of coyotes. Is the animal a pest or worthy of preservation? That question may never be resolved. Some animals that were virtually extinct in Kansas have flourished in recent years—deer, for example. Buffalo, once "the monarchs of the Plains," do not exist in their original state, but there are several herds in Kansas, maintained by both state agencies and individuals. They are even being raised for commercial packing purposes. Among the few Americans who originally wished to preserve the buffalo were two Kansans, H. H. Stanton of Topeka and C. J. "Buffalo" Jones of

Garden City. Jones established his own herd in the 1880s and furnished animals to zoos and parks. When the federal government decided to preserve buffalo in Yellowstone National Park, early in the twentieth century, Jones was given the job of building the herd.

Environmental control is the responsibility of several state agencies including the Department of Agriculture, Kansas Water Office, Geological Survey, Department of Health and Environment, Department of Wildlife and Parks, and Corporation Commission. While the fight for an unpolluted Kansas is not ended, there has been enough progress, including a new air quality control act in 1993, to make the claim that "Kansas is clean air country."

Discussions about the establishment of a prairie national park began in the early 1960s. There were those who wished to set aside a portion of the Flint Hills for a tall-grass park, but they met opposition from ranchers who pointed out that the land has never been tilled and, except for cattle grazing on it, remains much as it was a century ago. The issue appeared dead for many years, but in 1998 the Tallgrass National Preserve was dedicated. Occupying nearly 11,000 acres in the Flint Hills, the preserve is administered by the National Park Service, although the Park Service itself (through its Trust) owns only 180 acres, which include the buildings of an historic Chase County ranch. Final plans for management of the entire ecosystem are under discussion. Together with the Konza Prairie, created farther north in the Flint Hills in the 1970s through the efforts of the Nature Conservancy and Kansas State University, Kansas is now home to huge natural laboratories offering opportunities for study to both historians and scientists.

State parks have grown in both numbers and size, particularly around major reservoirs, and the cause of historic preservation has been furthered by both national and state government. Fort Larned in Pawnee County became a national historic site in 1964, and Fort Scott in Bourbon County was designated a national historic monument the following year. Both have been restored by the National Park Service. They were joined recently by the Monroe Elementary School in Topeka, which is the *Brown* v. *Board of Education* National Historic Site. The site will be developed by the National Park Service in the near future. The sixteen historic sites administered by the State Historical Society continue to attract interest, and five of them have undergone considerable development in recent years: Constitution Hall, Lecompton; the Native American Heritage Museum, Highland; Hollenberg Pony Express Station, Hanover; Mine Creek Battlefield, near Pleasanton; and Cottonwood Ranch, near Morland. Historical organizations at both city and county levels are also involved in the preservation of historic sites and buildings. In 1990 a Heritage Trust Fund was established to aid in the promotion and preservation of properties included on the National and State registers of historic places, and it has been most beneficial.

For several years funding for state parks was inadequate, and facilities deteriorated. The 1998 legislature addressed the problem and provided for upgrading along with planning for development of multipurpose resorts at one or more of the state parks. A new wetland habitat at Milford Reservoir also was provided for, a welcome addition to the other preserves in Kansas such as the large Cheyenne Bottoms area near Great Bend, which is on the Central Flyway for migratory birds.

One of the strongest voices for environmental preservation throughout the United States came from a former Kansan. Walter Hickel, who grew up on a Kansas farm and went on to become governor of Alaska, was viewed with suspicion by environmentalists when he was named Secretary of the Interior in 1969 because of his previously expressed interest in the rapid development of Alaska's mineral reserves. He soon quieted their fears. Dismissed by President Nixon because of his outspoken opinions, Hickel summed up much of what was wrong and what needed to be done in *Who Owns America*, published in 1971.

POLITICS AND CHANGING KANSAS LAWS

The political scene has not been tranquil throughout the past four decades. In 1953 the Republican national chairman, Wesley Roberts of Kansas, resigned over questions about his lobbying activities and his part in the sale of a building at the Norton State Hospital. The building was sold to the state under unusual circumstances and the GOP felt that the deal damaged its image.

A year later a battle developed between the Republicans and Fred Hall of Dodge City, then lieutenant governor. Hall had revolted against the Republican party organization, but even so, he won the gubernatorial primary in 1954 and defeated George Docking of Lawrence in the general election. The 1955 legislative session was stormy because of anti-Hall sentiment and arguments over a right-to-work bill, which would prohibit the closed union shop in Kansas. The legislature passed the bill and Hall vetoed it, but in 1958 it became law as a constitutional amendment.

In 1956 Hall was defeated in the primary by Warren Shaw, who lost to Docking, the first Democratic governor since 1936. At the last minute Hall resigned and was appointed to the state supreme court by his successor, Lt. Gov. John McCuish. It was an astute move on Hall's part, but it was considered unethical by many. Hall left the court in less than two years and took no further part in politics.

Docking was reelected in 1958, the first Democrat to serve two terms, and he and the legislature were often at odds. In 1960 Docking lost to John Anderson, Jr., former attorney general from Johnson County. Kansas went for Richard Nixon in 1960 even though John F. Kennedy appealed to a great many members of both parties. In 1964 Kansas preferred Lyndon Johnson to Barry Goldwater for the presidency but came back to Republicanism, voting for Nixon in both 1968 and 1972 and Gerald Ford in 1976.

Anderson served two terms and was succeeded in 1965 by former Congressman William H. Avery of Wakefield, also a Republican. Avery had the courage to push through a tax increase for the improvement of Kansas schools, but that very fact was instrumental in his defeat when he ran for a second term. He was succeeded by the state's seventh Democratic governor, Robert Docking of Arkansas City, who followed in his father's steps when he won a second term. He became the only Kansas governor to be elected to a third term in 1970 and won an unheard-of fourth term in 1972. The GOP returned to the governor's office with the 1974 election of Robert Bennett for a four-year term but in 1978 John Carlin of Smolan, a Democrat, foiled Bennett's bid for reelection. Carlin had served as Speaker of the House in 1977 and 1978, the first sessions in which Democrats had controlled the house since 1913.

Carlin was reelected in 1982 and was one of the most effective governors of the twentieth century. In his eight years in office the legislature never overrode a veto. He had said he would sign a death penalty bill if one were presented, but he was unable to do so when the time came and vetoed it. The issue arose again during his tenure, and each time he vetoed it and each time the veto stood. Kansas had done away with the death penalty in 1972. He increased the emphasis on water conservation and economic development and worked for a variety of things that he thought necessary for a modern Kansas, including a severance tax on mineral production. The latter became law in 1983 after decades of debate.

In 1986 the Republicans returned to the governor's office when Mike Hayden of Atwood, a former Speaker of the House, defeated Tom Docking of Wichita, son and grandson of governors. Hayden's major campaign plank was reinstatement of the death penalty, but he had no success with its passage in the 1987 legislative session and it was not an issue in 1988. For a long period in the twentieth century Kansas did not have a death penalty provision, and in the years it did have one very few people were executed.

Another part of the Hayden campaign involved a promise to return to the voters the tax "windfall" created by the changes in the federal tax laws. However, because of revenue shortfall in 1987, the governor and the legislature agreed that those funds needed to be retained. In 1988, after a further windfall occurred, much of the legislative session was spent on the subject of alternative plans. Compromises were offered, and agreement was reached between the governor and the legislature. Kansans received some tax benefits.

Hayden stood for reelection in 1990, but was upset by Joan Finney, the popular Democratic State Treasurer, who became the state's first woman chief executive. A self-described "populist," she was often unorthodox and frequently at odds with the legislature which overrode thirty-three of her vetoes. She championed the causes of the state's Native Americans and appointed women to several administrative posts. Although still popular with Kansas voters, she chose not to run again in 1994.

In 1994 James Slattery, long-time Congressman from the second district, was the Democratic nominee, while the Republicans' candidate was Bill Graves, then serving as Secretary of State. Graves was the winner, and both houses of an increasingly conservative legislature were Republican led.

The abortion question was a heated one in legislative considerations beginning in the late 1980s. Restrictions on legalized abortion were imposed in 1992, but abortion opponents, who demonstrated frequently for their cause, worked to make the law more restrictive each session. In 1998 legislation banning partial-birth abortions was passed and signed into law.

In 1962 Senator Schoeppel died in office and was replaced by James Pearson. Six years later Senator Carlson retired and was succeeded by Robert Dole of Russell. In 1971–1973, Dole was the Republican party's national chairman and its vice-presidential candidate in 1976. He was the Senate majority leader under President Reagan until January of 1987 and was one of the leading Republican presidential hopefuls in 1988 during the first months of the campaign. In June 1996 Dole resigned his Senate seat to accept the Republican presidential nomination, but was defeated by President Clinton. He carried his home state by a solid margin. Nancy Landon Kassebaum was elected to the Senate in 1978 after a hotly contested race with former Congressman Bill

Governor-elect Joan Finney accepts congratulations on the day following her victory in 1990. Courtesy Topeka *Capital-Journal*.

Roy, the first woman to be elected to the Senate in her own right. She succeeded the retiring Senator Pearson.

Governor Graves appointed Sheila Frahm of Colby to fill Dole's un-expired term until the 1996 general election. She was a candidate to finish the term but lost the Republican primary to Sam Brownback of Topeka, a first-term Congressman. Brownback went on to defeat the Democratic candidate, Jill Docking of Wichita. In 1998 Brownback was returned to the Senate, defeating Paul Feliciano of Wichita. Nancy Kassebaum chose not to run again in 1996, and Republican Pat Roberts of Dodge City, a leader of the House, easily defeated Sally Thompson, the State Treasurer.

Republicans swept the Congressional elections in 1996, and the Kansas delegation was solidly Republican. One of the so-called "social conservatives," Todd Tiehart of Wichita, had upset veteran Democratic House member Dan Glickman in 1994. Glickman went on to become Secretary of Agriculture in the Clinton cabinet.

Reapportionment at both the state and national level has occupied legislative time. In 1961 Kansas lost a congressional seat and was reduced to five. Following the 1990 census redistricting again occurred, and Kansas was reduced to only four House seats, effective with the 1992 election. In that same year discussions about the reapportionment of the state senate began but nothing was done until the federal courts outlined the "one man, one vote" principle. The state senate was reapportioned in 1963, but the house was not, and the courts said the senate plan was unsatisfactory. A year later both houses were reapportioned with some additional representation given to the more populous areas of the state but in the mid-1960s a majority of the house of representatives was still elected by only 19 percent of the voting public. As the 1970s began there were still inequalities in the house of representatives, but early in 1974 the federal government ruled that Kansas's apportionment was satisfactory. However, the question arose again in 1979 and the legislature remapped both houses. In the 1988 legislative session the question was again under discussion, and in 1992 both legislative houses were reapportioned because of further changes in population.

Shifts in population after the war meant that hundreds of rural elementary districts were no longer able to maintain the familiar "country schools." In 1957 the legislature appropriated funds to conduct a statewide comprehensive study of education, published in 1960. Three years later a uniform school district system was established. The 1965 legislature laid the foundation for a statewide system of junior colleges, four years after legislation had provided for state aid to junior colleges and municipal universities. On July 1, 1964, the state acquired another college when Wichita University became a part of the system, and since then there have been

innumerable legislative discussions concerning the state's acquisition of
Washburn University.

Vocational education, which began in 1917, expanded greatly with a
heavy emphasis on agriculture. In 1963 a plan for area vocational-techni-
cal schools was enacted, and several were founded to serve students both
in and out of high school. Also established was a State Technical Institute
at Salina. Discussions continue on school financing, particularly as it de-
pends on property taxes, and additional unification procedures will be necessary in the future. Some educational leaders feel that Kansas schools
have gone through revolutionary changes in the past several years, mostly
for the better. Special eduction programs in the public schools have been
vastly improved since the 1970s, but legislative debates about their funding continue.

Education in Kansas was very much in the news in 1954 when on
May 17, the U.S. Supreme Court, in its decision on the case of *Brown* v.
Board of Education of Topeka, stated that separate but equal school facilities were inherently unequal and that school segregation violated the
constitution's guarantee of equal protection under the Fourteenth Amendment. Topeka had a strange kind of segregation, for it existed only in the
grade schools—junior and senior high schools had been integrated for several decades. As full integration of the races became a primary issue in the
1950s the Topeka situation provided the basis for a test case before the
Supreme Court while cases from four other states were before the court at
the same time. However, before the court heard the case, complete integration in the Topeka schools was already underway.

In spite of segregation in the Topeka elementary schools there was
little adverse reaction to the court's decision, and the president of the Topeka school board hailed the decision. However, thirty years later there
were questions being raised about racial imbalance in schools in Kansas,
and a few school districts were at odds with federal agencies and constitu-
ents over student distribution. Generally, resolution of such problems was
reached in the 1990s.

Consumer protection has been a concern of the legislature and the
attorney general's office, which established a consumer protection division, and the state keeps a close watch on prices, interest rates, and advertising claims. Concern about the rights of racial minorities brought the
establishment of the Commission on Civil Rights (now the Human Rights
Commission) that has enforcement powers in cases involving employment,
housing, and public accommodations where discrimination is evident on
either a racial or sexual basis.

There have been disagreements over methods of highway financing
and proposed routes for new roads in Kansas. Some lawmakers believe that

state bonds can supplement tax money for construction while discussions have taken place concerning the possibilities of additional turnpikes in eastern and south-central Kansas. Progress had been made with the completion of the Kansas Turnpike in 1956, financed by private capital under the state's supervision; the opening of Interstate 70 across Kansas from east to west; and completion of Interstates 35 and 135, north and south. With the completion of I-70, Kansas became the first state in the union to finish an entire interstate route. In addition, several shorter interstate connecting and bypass routes have been finished in the metropolitan areas. Kansas roadside parks and rest areas on both state and federal highways are the country's finest and have been used by some four million travelers each year.

Governor Hayden called a special session of the legislature in August 1987 for the purpose of putting together a new comprehensive highway plan. However, the legislature, including members of the governor's own party, believed the plan was too expensive and in part unrealistic. Consequently, after much acrimonious debate, the session adjourned, having accomplished nothing. The massive program was not resurrected for regular session consideration until 1989 when $4 billion was authorized.

The "liquor-by-the-drink" question continued to attract attention, and in 1970 it was again on the ballot but was defeated. Although Kansans could buy intoxicants in a liquor store, 3.2 beer in a tavern and restaurant, or a mixed drink in a private club, the "open saloon," abolished in 1880, still did not exist in the state. Finally, in 1986, the constitution was amended, and bars returned to Kansas, with certain restrictions. The vote was based on local option so in some counties the private club laws still apply, and only 3.2 beer may be sold in restaurants and taverns. Liquor store advertising regulations were relaxed slightly, and discount pricing for package goods became legal.

Legalized gambling has been a hot issue since 1969 and received much attention because of Vern Miller, who was elected attorney general on a "law-and-order" platform in 1970, the first Democrat to win that office since 1893. He was reelected in 1972. Miller became a controversial figure although members of both parties supported him. He conducted a vigorous war against drugs, gambling, illegal sale of alcohol, and crime in general. Gamblers were warned to stay away from county and regional fairs where they had often gathered, and slot machines were confiscated from places where they had enjoyed immunity for years. A law permitting the operation of bingo games by nonprofit organizations was passed when it became obvious that the attorney general intended to prosecute gambling at all levels. Miller's somewhat dramatic actions were questioned at times, and he made national headlines when he ordered Amtrak trains and commercial airlines to stop serving liquor as they traveled through and over Kansas.

Also on the ballot in 1986 were constitutional provisions for a state lottery and parimutuel betting at race tracks, and both passed. The lottery began operating in 1987 and betting began on a limited basis in 1988. Both were designed to increase revenues and to further economic development, among other things.

Race track operators had high hopes, and at first enjoyed success with both dog and horse racing. However, the proliferation of casino gambling in Missouri drew away patrons, and the tracks suffered severe financial problems.

New on the Kansas gambling scene since the mid-1990s are casinos belonging to the Iowa, Potawatomi, Kickapoo, and Sac and Fox tribes. They are highly successful thus far and are drawing customers from all over Kansas and from out of state.

The 1970 legislature, urged on by Governor Docking, put a lid on property taxes and most levies were not to exceed those of 1969 unless voters of local governmental units authorized both an increased budget and a tax levy limit. Voters could also supplement property tax revenues by authorizing local income and sales taxes, which has been done in some communities.

The period 1948–1958 was a dramatic one in the development of mental health institutions, but in recent years funding has been inadequate to maintain proper quality of care. The state was criticized severely in the 1980s by the federal government for deficiencies in patient care and was threatened with removal of Medicaid support to certain institutions. Those problems were resolved to the satisfaction of the federal authorities. In 1995 a Hospital Closure Commission was formed, and its findings resulted in the closing of the Topeka and Winfield state hospitals. Some patients were transferred to other state institutions while others were sent to private care facilities. The Winfield property has been converted to use as a state soldiers' home.

County and regional mental health clinics have grown and improved, and more communities have expressed concern for child abuse, drug and alcohol dependency, and domestic violence. Kansas, in 1980, was the first state in the Union to establish a fund for child abuse prevention programs, and the 1993 legislature passed a Habitual Sex Offender Registration act.

In Topeka another generation of doctors named Menninger continue to work, increasing the effectiveness of the Menninger Foundation and its clinic and hospital, promoting research, and cooperating with state and federal hospitals.

The Kansas prison system came under fire from the federal courts because of the extreme overcrowding. The 1988 legislature, through greatly increased appropriations for prisons, took the first step toward remedying the situation. Since then correctional facility expansion has taken place with new institutions in El Dorado and Norton, and more work-release plans have been implemented.

Other recent legislation in the field of criminal justice includes determinate sentencing guidelines, tougher sentences for murder and repeat felony offenders, expansion of victims' rights, and changes in the juvenile justice code. Kansans generally support stricter laws to deal with juvenile offenders, but the legislature has been criticized for its reluctance to spend more on juvenile detention facilities.

In 1994 Kansas reinstated the death penalty. Lethal injection is to be used for crimes of premeditated murder. By 1998 no executions had taken place although there had been three capital convictions.

In the 1990s Kansas law had made voter registration simpler and advance voting possible, relaxed the restriction on intrastate branch banking and authorized full interstate banking, provided for "charter schools" and outcome-oriented educational programs, expanded drug-free school zone limits, brought several changes in the workers' compensation area, reduced motor vehicle taxes and established additional sales and fuel tax exemptions, reduced oil and gas severance taxes, established advisory commissions on Hispanic and African-American affairs, set new highway speed limits, expanded tax increment financing to encourage business and rural housing development, established recreational trails using abandoned railway roadbeds ("rails to trails"), prohibited same-sex marriages, and required smoke alarms for Kansas residences.

A major agency reorganization took place in 1995. The Kansas State Board of Agriculture, in place since the early years of statehood, was replaced by the Department of Agriculture. The department's secretary, a cabinet position, is a gubernatorial appointee, subject to Senate confirmation. A nine-member Board of Agriculture, appointed by the governor, serves in an advisory role only. Two years later the State Grain Inspection Department was abolished, and its duties with regard to public warehouses were transferred to the Department of Agriculture.

The 1998 legislature and the governor agreed on an increase of $114 million for public education and $247 million in tax cuts. Funding for higher education was also increased. With concerns rising over health care generally and care for children in particular, Kansas took a giant step forward by providing health insurance for children in lower-income situations. This will benefit more than 60,000 Kansas children.

Welfare reform has occupied a great deal of legislative and executive thinking, especially since 1996 when the federal government revamped its program. Kansas has been reasonably successful in its quest to put some 2,000 families in a position to retain some benefits while participating in vocational rehabilitation or job-training programs. Similar efforts already have placed numbers of persons back into the workplace. Some placements have been in jobs where minimum wage is paid, and those people still find it difficult to make ends meet without some outside assistance. Private social service agencies have stepped up their programs to help fill the gap.

A longtime responsibility of the state's welfare department, foster care for children and adoptive services has been privatized with mixed results. Adoptive placement appears to be having some success, but there is much criticism of foster-care arrangements. Only time will tell whether or not privatization will work to the advantage of all concerned.

The increasing conservatism in both state and national politics in 1995 and 1996 diminished Democratic strength in the legislature and caused dissension in the state's Republican ranks. Conservatives gained control of the party structure and the leadership of the House while moderates retained leadership of the Senate. As the 1998 primary election approached, Governor Graves was challenged by ultraconservative David Miller of Eudora who had been Republican state chairman and an outspoken critic of the administration. The primary campaign was heated, and the governor spent a record amount of money to support his incumbency. Despite the conservatives' efforts, Graves defeated Miller with an overwhelming 73 percent of the vote. At the same time moderate Republicans regained control of the party at the precinct level.

In November Graves went on to beat Democrat Tom Sawyer of Wichita, the minority leader of the House. The Republicans retained three of four seats in the U.S. House. Vince Snowbarger, the incumbent conservative Republican in the Third District, was beaten by Dennis Moore, and the Democrats took that seat for the first time in nearly forty years. No dramatic change came from the state legislative House races, and the only major state office won by a Democrat was that of Insurance Commissioner, where Kathleen Sebelius, the incumbent, was reelected by a wide margin.

Kansas ratified the amendments to the U.S. Constitution giving eighteen-year-olds the vote and equal rights to women. Additionally, the state lowered the legal age of adulthood to eighteen, except for the purchase and consumption of intoxicating liquors. Since the general election of 1974 the governor and lieutenant governor are elected to four-year terms, running on a party's ticket as a team, as do candidates for president and vice-president of the United States.

The cowboy no longer rides the range in Kansas in great numbers but the cattle industry is still big business. These Herefords on a Flint Hills ranch are readied for market at the feed trough as well as on the Bluestem pastures.

DEVELOPMENTS IN AGRICULTURE AND INDUSTRY

A new term came into use in the post–World War II era—"agribusiness." Agriculture has become highly commercialized in Kansas and the term is applied to all phases of agriculture and related industries. The companies that manufacture and distribute farm supplies and the firms that process and market farm products are as much a part of agriculture as the farmer himself. Farmers spend tremendous amounts of money on machinery, seed, feed, fertilizer, and insecticides. The people who make and sell such things, plus those who store grain or work in packing plants, are part of the agribusiness.

The number of farms in Kansas has declined but farming has not. Mechanization, rural electrification, and advanced scientific methods have led to larger farms and fewer workers. It is predicted that in the year 2000 there will be only half as many farms as there were in 1986. In the 1860s a farmer supplied food for five people and by the 1990s he supplied 100 from a farm five times the size of his great-grandfather's.

The majority of Kansas farmers saw hard times in the 1980s, but the state remained in the top ten states consistently in cash receipts from farming. Still, net income continues to remain low proportionately, and many farms support more than one family. Cost of operation is so high—implements, seed, chemicals, for example, coupled with loan payments—that making a profit is often difficult. In many cases farmers acquired land when interest rates were high and market prices were up. The market went down, but the interest rates continued. This led to the demise of many farmers, some of whom were third and fourth generation on the same homestead.

By the late 1980s fewer farmers were in severe debt, but 10 percent of them still had over 40 percent of their assets in debt. Record farm earnings in 1987, recovering land values, fewer land problems, and livestock profits contributed to a brighter picture. Serious questions still remain about surpluses and government programs, however.

Irrigation has brought dramatic changes since the end of the Second World War, and the "Great American Desert" has grown greener. Approximately three million acres in western Kansas are producing crop yields not even imagined by pioneer farmers. Wells are supplemented by reservoirs built by federal agencies, by thousands of farm ponds, and by small reservoirs developed by local watershed districts.

Until the late 1950s corn was not grown in quantity in western Kansas, but now irrigated cornfields there can produce 200 bushels to the acre. Hybrid sorghums, like milo, yield regularly 150 bushels per irrigated acre, and irrigated wheat land can provide both abundant harvest and spring and fall pastures. Production of vegetables, alfalfa, soybeans, and sugar beets increased but acreage devoted to the latter crop declined sharply in the late 1970s because of low profit margin and has virtually disappeared in Kansas. The livestock feeding industry has grown tremendously, and millions of animals fed for slaughter are fattened with feed from irrigated fields. By the mid-1980s Kansas was the nation's second largest beef producer with feedlots on the High Plains at times holding more than 30,000 head of cattle. There has been increased interest in more scientific dryland farming because of concern about the lowered water table in the western third of the state.

Farmers have profited from the increased experimentation carried on by Kansas State University and the state experiment stations. Grain scientists at Kansas State currently are developing a new white winter wheat which will supplement and perhaps eventually supplant the red wheat grown in Kansas since the 1870s. The white variety is easier to mill and may allow extra plantings, according to researchers. County agents, other extension service experts, and the experimental work of seed and milling companies have been extremely helpful. Stockmen study how others in their business breed and feed animals, and through the Future Farmers of America and 4-H Clubs young people approach agriculture scientifically.

Farmers have involved themselves in cooperative movements that benefit their lives and their families. The Grange still exists, as it did in the nineteenth century, but in addition there are the Farm Bureau, Farmers Union, National Farmers Organization, and the Kansas Livestock Association. The old "Co-op" has assumed a new role through its Farmland

Industries making fertilizers, refining oil, and packing meat. The State Department of Agriculture also provides farmers with regulatory assistance and often provides a helpful official voice in difficult times.

Kansas wheat growers have been concerned with worldwide marketing, and in 1948 the Kansas Association of Wheat Growers was organized. The Kansas Wheat Commission, the National Association of Wheat Growers, and the regional Great Plains Wheat, Inc., all helped make wheat farming more profitable.

In the 1970s there were four times the number of cattle on grain feed than ten years before, and meat packing became a 770-million-dollar industry. The burgeoning packing industry has made a particular difference in southwestern Kansas since then. Garden City has had the major role in this change, but Dodge City and Liberal have had similar experiences to a lesser degree. The Iowa Beef Company's plant between Garden City and Holcomb is one of the largest such installations in the world, and the combined Garden City processing can feed a million people for a month.

These developments have brought waves of immigrants and refugees from Latin America and Southeast Asia, and Garden City's population has increased by a third since 1980. Thus far there has been a successful assimilation of these new Kansans even though it has been necessary to make numerous school and community adjustments. Western Kansas is coping very well with dramatic change.

There have been years when wheat storage facilities were inadequate, and almost every year there is a shortage of railroad cars at harvest time, and in the 1990s more grain was hauled by trucks than by the railroads.

Wheat harvest in Hamilton County, 1988. Modern combines greatly reduce the time necessary to bring in the crop. Courtesy of the Garden City *Telegram*.

Prices for both grain and livestock have reached very low levels from time to time, and feed prices have sometimes made livestock and poultry production unprofitable. The demands and the shortages and the part-time control programs of the federal government played tricks on Kansas agricultural producers in the 1970s and took them to both extremes of the profit and loss scale. Federal subsidies and fixed minimum prices at times have helped pull the farmer through, and amazingly profitable situations have occurred, as in 1973–1974 when the price of wheat per bushel rose to the highest figure in history. No Kansas farmer had even dreamed about four-dollar and five-dollar wheat since those unbelievable years of the First World War. A rapid drop in grain prices, the disappearance of operating capital due to inflation, and what many Kansas farmers felt was an unsympathetic federal government led them to join the protesting American Agricultural Movement. Some participated in the "tractorcade" to Washington, D.C., during the winter of 1978–1979.

Corporate hog farming was a point of contention in the 1990s and caused bitter fights in some cities and counties in 1998. Legislation that passed in 1994 permitted corporate production in certain types of dairy and swine facilities. In 1996 changes were made in the corporate farming laws, allowing "family farm companies," a definition that has had various interpretations. While current law imposes reasonably severe restrictions on how hog producers may operate, there are still concerns regarding both water and air pollution.

A once important crop has reappeared on the state's agricultural scene. In the 1880s Kansas was one of the nation's top ten wine producers from 7,000 acres of vineyards. Kansas's prohibitory laws forced the wineries out of business, but in 1983 the state again legalized commercial wineries, and there are now seven of them operating. Their output is still limited, but indications are that production will increase. In 1998 the Kansas State Fair held its first wine judging, which gave the industry additional exposure.

The late 1990s brought more problems to Kansas farmers. The 1998 wheat harvest produced a record yield, but prices were extremely low. The same held true for other grains and for soybeans. Foreign markets were restricted, partly because of the unsettled international situation. There was, again, a severe shortage of grain storage, and a great deal of grain was on the ground. The storage problem was complicated by a tragic elevator explosion in Haysville in June, 1998. Six workers were killed and much of a huge storage facility was wiped out. A sagging cattle market was bad news for the state's beef raisers and feeders.

U.S. flour exports diminished in 1998 which hurt the Kansas milling industry. Much of the problem was caused by increased flour exports by the European Union, especially to Africa. However, Kansas is still first in

U.S. flour-milling capacity, but that capacity needs to be utilized fully to bolster the state's economy.

Despite problems Kansas continues to show off its agriculture-related products at the State Fair and at various sites around the state. In 1998 the Three I show marked its forty-fourth year. Organized by the 200-member Western Kansas Manufacturers Association, the show alternates between Garden City and Great Bend and displays products related to irrigation, implements, and industry.

Kansas agriculture is a great industry, but the farmer is still at the mercy of the weather and the market and may be classed as the world's greatest gambler.

Kansas has ranked among the top ten mineral-producing states for several decades. Not only oil and gas but salt, gypsum, and limestone are vital to prosperity. Despite a national recession early in the 1970s, the state's economy and job market expanded, and personal income rose. Wichita's aircraft industry was at a low point in 1971, but it recovered the following year. Since then it has gone through numerous ups and downs, but its future seems reasonably secure. In 1998 aviation provided 16 percent of the state's manufacturing employment. In Wichita Boeing, Learjet, Cessna, and Ratheon (formerly Beech) employed more than 40,000 workers. Unemployment in the state is minimal and personal income is above the national average.

Along with agriculture and aircraft production the third major problem area in recent years is the petroleum industry. In the 1980s the number of workers in oil and gas drilling declined substantially, and the production of crude oil fell by several million barrels. At that time most felt that the biggest problem was OPEC, which flooded the market with cheaper oil, but many oilmen blamed the Kansas tax structure. Since then the severance tax has been reduced, and oil from the Near East is less of a problem. However, things are not very good in the state's "oil patch." In 1996 the price of crude was twenty-two dollars a barrel but by 1998 it

The Goodyear plant at Topeka is one of the nation's major producers of tires.

had dropped to just over eight dollars. Because of the low price Kansas producers have shut down many of their wells, and 60 percent fewer workers are involved in the oil and gas industry than in the mid-1980s. Natural gas continues to supply users from the Great Lakes to the Rockies.

Banking has been affected by the economic climate, especially where agriculture and oil are concerned. There were thirteen bank failures in 1985, and more followed—mostly small rural banks that were overextended in farm and ranch loans. Many of them were purchased and reopened quickly, due to federal deposit insurance, and the change in Kansas law that allowed multibank holding companies and branch banking. More bank purchases and mergers took place, and by 1998 there were fewer than 400 chartered banks in Kansas. However, there were more banking facilities than ever before because of the proliferation of branches.

By 1988 recovery was underway. To further economic growth the state created a new state Department of Commerce with broader responsibilities than the predecessor economic development agency. The Kansas Technology Enterprise Corporation was created to form a cooperative effort among universities, private industry, and the state and assist with research and promote the transfer of technology from schools to businesses. The Department of Commerce is also charged with seeking new markets for Kansas products and business and community development overall.

In the spring of 1973 Kansas products were pushed further into international trade when businessmen carried out missions to Europe and Japan, and in 1979 Governor John Carlin led a delegation to the People's Republic of China. That trip led to the establishment of a sister state relationship with Henan Province, and representatives from there have, in turn, come to Kansas. Carlin in succeeding years led trade missions back to the People's Republic, Taiwan, Japan, Europe, and all proved valuable in the long run. Governors Hayden, Finney, and Graves also embraced the idea of marketing Kansas products farther afield and have worked to further the effort.

Kansas manufacturers produce an amazing array of products from tires to cement, pipe organs to batteries, church furniture to greeting cards, automobiles to industrial chemicals, bricks to dresses, gasoline to railroad cars, plastic drinking cups to farm machinery, and elevator equipment to cellophane, and some of these are marketable abroad. Kansas business is concerned about export markets over and above agriculture, and in recent years has seen a growth in overseas trade.

Energy is always a consideration when economic development plans are made. In the early 1970s, when the country was concerned about an energy crisis, the three major power suppliers in Kansas announced plans for the construction of giant generating plants in eastern Kansas that would utilize both coal and nuclear fuel with completion scheduled for the 1980s. The building of the Wolf Creek nuclear plant near Burlington brought some protest because of the uncertainties surrounding nuclear power and the possibility of accidental disaster. The first unit of Kansas Power and Light's coal-fired plant in Pottawatomie County went on line in 1978, and the Wolf Creek plant, operated jointly by Kansas Gas & Electric, Kansas City (Mo.) Power & Light, and the Kansas Electric Power Cooperative, Inc. began production in 1985.

A Celebrating State

Kansans took great pride in their exhibits at the nation's centennial observance at Philadelphia in 1876 and at other "world's fairs." They marked the fiftieth birthday of the opening of Kansas Territory in 1904 with parades, music, and speeches, and the 400th anniversary of Coronado's entrance into what is now Kansas gave rise to a statewide celebration in 1941. In 1954 a Territorial Centennial Commission was formed, and traveling exhibits took the Kansas story into dozens of communities. Along with historical publications and commemorative pageants there were

Great floods in the summer of 1951 caused severe damage in Kansas. This view of the overflowing Kansas and Missouri rivers was taken from the Kansas City, Kansas side. Flooding also were the Kansas River's tributaries and the state's losses were an estimated $2.5 billion.

beards, old fashioned costumes, and practical jokes. In 1961, after 100 years of statehood, a celebration was devoted to notable achievements in Kansas life, and well-known Kansans who had left the state came home to assist in the birthday party. It spurred efforts in local history and led to the creation of some new local historical societies.

The Chisholm Trail centennial in 1967 saw Kansas cooperate with Oklahoma and Texas to tell the story of the great cattle drives, and the Civil War centennial was observed from 1961 through 1965. In the 1970s, Kansans with a concern for the national story participated in the American Revolution bicentennial observances and the commemoration of all American history, and in 1986 a variety of events commemorated the state's 125th birthday. With 2004 only a few years away some Kansans already are talking about the possibilities of a territorial sesquicentennial observance.

THE DARKER SIDE OF LIFE

There have been darker aspects to the recent Kansas past, including great natural disasters. In May 1955, the small town of Udall was hit by a tornado that caused dozens of deaths, and virtually wiped out the town. Three years later, El Dorado was struck and seventeen were killed, while two million dollars worth of damage was done. The tornado that hit Topeka in June 1966 was reportedly the worst in American history, as far as financial loss was concerned. One hundred million dollars worth of property was destroyed, though fewer than twenty people died. In September 1973, tornadoes swept through four north-central counties and devastation was particularly bad in Clay Center, Greenleaf, and Linn, with some loss of life. Similar storms have struck Garden City, Wichita, Manhattan, Emporia, Andover, and several other towns since 1950. The severity of these storms increased Kansas's reputation as a "cyclone state."

Kansas received some notoriety in November 1959, when Herbert Clutter and three members of his family were murdered at Holcomb by Perry Smith and Richard Hickock. The murders were national news, but became even better known when Truman Capote told the story in *In Cold Blood,* published in 1965. Smith and Hickock were joined on the state penitentiary's death row by George York and James Latham, who had murdered seven persons, including a Kansan, in the course of a cross-country trip. All four men were hanged in 1965.

Between 1950 and 1953 when United States forces were involved in Korea, Kansans again served. Camp Funston once more became an induction and army training center while the air force reactivated some Kansas facilities and enlarged them to fit the jet age. Forts Riley and Leavenworth expanded their service schools and Leavenworth's Command and General

Staff College trained Allied nations' officers as it had for some years. (It continues to do so.) During the Korean conflict James Jabara of Wichita, a World War II air combat veteran, became the first jet ace, destroying fifteen MIGs in the air.

Although Kansas was not subject to widespread violent protest during the years of the war in Vietnam, there were some demonstrations, most of which were peaceful. For example, college students gathered in an orderly manner on the statehouse grounds in May 1970, voicing their objection to United States action in Cambodia. Elsewhere that spring there were some bomb scares and street disturbances. Not directly related to anti-Vietnam feelings, those events seemed to be more a product of general unrest—student unhappiness with college administrations, complaints about racial discrimination, and severe law enforcement policies aimed at the use of marijuana. On April 20 a fire was set in the University of Kansas student union, and on another night the ROTC building at the university was damaged. In July two youths were killed in Lawrence during demonstrations against local and national policies.

Kansas National Guardsmen were affected by Vietnam when the Sixty-Ninth Infantry Brigade and the Nine Hundred Ninety-Fifth Maintenance Company were called to active duty in April 1968 and served until the end of 1969. Although the entire units were not sent overseas, hundreds of men from them did supplement regular army troops in the combat zones. Additional hundreds of Kansans, volunteers and draftees, served in Southeast Asia.

The 1990 crisis in the Near East and the United States' implementation of Operations Desert Shield and Desert Storm in Saudi Arabia called many Kansans to active duty. National Guard and Reserve personnel were deployed to U.S. bases and overseas, along with the army's First Division and other regular troops from Fort Riley. The Kansas Air National Guard's One Hundred Ninetieth Air Refueling Group played a major role in the brief conflict.

Kansas: A Land of Contrasts

Kansas in its more recent past has provided the nation with scientists—Elmer McCollum, nutritionist; Edwin Menninger, horticulturalist; Clyde Tombaugh, discoverer of the planet Pluto; and Earl Sutherland, winner of the Nobel Prize for physiology and medicine in 1971. Kansas's most famous citizen, Dwight D. Eisenhower, came home to Abilene for the last time in April 1969, while thousands gathered there in silence to pay tribute and thousands more stood at railroad stations during the night as the special train carrying his body passed by. Other notable Kansas soldiers

include Gen. Lewis Walt of Wabaunsee County, former assistant comman-
dant of the U.S. Marine Corps; Gen. Bernard W. Rogers of Fairview, formerly the Army's chief of staff and commander of NATO forces; and Frank
E. Petersen of Topeka, a distinguished pilot and the first black to serve as a
general officer in the Marine Corps. Gen. Donn Starry of Kansas City was
credited with the "intellectual rejuvenation of the U.S. Army," during its
rebuilding and modernization after Vietnam. Elizabeth Hoisington of Newton was the first woman promoted to brigadier general, while serving as
head of the WAC in 1970. The nation's space program has been well served
by Kansans—Capt. Ron Evans, Topeka; Col. Joe Engle, Chapman; and
Dr. Steve Hawley, Salina. Evans was one of the Apollo group, Engle commanded *Columbia II*, and Hawley was on the maiden voyage of *Discovery*.
The late Charles E. Whittaker of Doniphan County served on the U.S.
Supreme Court, 1957–1962. He is the only Kansas native ever to sit on
the court. George W. Haley, a Kansas City attorney and the first African-
American elected to the State Senate (1964), was named U.S. Ambassa-
dor to The Gambia, West Africa, in 1998.

A younger generation of Kansans has contributed three Miss Ameri-
cas—Deborah Bryant, Overland Park, in 1965; Debra Barnes, Moran, in
1967; Tera Dean Holland, a recent arrival to Johnson County, in 1996;
and a youthful Mrs. America, Marlene D. Cochran, Shawnee. Kelli Mc-
Carty, Liberal, was crowned Miss USA in 1991. This generation has also
seen its members win medals at Olympic games in marksmanship, track,
field, and basketball. Several of the basketball players were coached by
Forrest C. "Phog" Allen of Kansas University. Glenn Cunningham and
Archie San Romani saw their mile-run times broken by Wes Santee, Archie
San Romani, Jr., and Jim Ryun, while sprinter Thane Baker set new Olympic records, along with field-event participants Al Oerter and Bill Nieder.

The 1980s were especially exciting for Kansas basketball enthusiasts
with Fort Hays State winning the NAIA national championships in 1984
and 1985, the first Kansas team to do so since St. Benedict's (now
Benedictine) brought home the titles in 1954 and 1967. Southwestern
had won one of the early NAIA tournaments in 1939. In 1987 Washburn
was the NAIA champion. In 1988 Kansas State made it into the NCAA's
final eight and KU finished as the NCAA champion. The following year
Wichita State, perennially strong in baseball, won the College World Series.

In succeeding years KU has remained a national basketball power
while Kansas State built a nationally ranked football program, something
it had not done for decades. Pittsburg State has had continued success in
football for many years while several other Kansas smaller colleges have
done well in national competition. Fort Hays State went undefeated in
the 1995–1996 basketball season and won the NCAA Division II national

championship. Women's basketball each year continues to draw fans at all levels and Washburn and Emporia State have been recent national tournament participants in Division II.

Kansans have spent hours at their television sets watching Kansas products perform in professional basketball, baseball, and golf. Barry Sanders of Wichita has been one of the most exciting ball carriers in professional football in the 1990s, and Jim Colbert is a leading money winner on the senior golf tour.

Unique among the professionals is Lynne Woodard of Wichita and the KU class of 1981. An all-American and an Olympian, she became the first woman to play with the Harlem Globetrotters and also has played professionally in Europe and in the WNBA. Another woman notable for her success in basketball is Billie Jean Moore, a Washburn graduate. As a coach she produced national championship teams at California State-Fullerton and UCLA and led the U.S. Women's team to a silver medal at the 1976 summer Olympics.

Kansas's most recent winning Olympian is Catherine Fox of Roeland Park who came home with two gold medals in swimming from the 1996 Olympics. With a bright future in track is Maurice Greene of Kansas City whose time in the 100 meters at the 1998 Goodwill Games labeled him as "the world's fastest man."

The rodeo, an entirely different kind of sport, has been popular in Kansas for more than a century. One of the best known nationally is Strong City's, now in its sixty-first year. The Roberts family of Kansas is famous for its rodeo accomplishments. Emmett, the father, was Rodeo Man of the Year in 1979; Gerald was twice named All-Around World Champion Cowboy in the 1940s; Ken was a world champion bull rider; and their sister Marge is in the National Cowgirl Hall of Fame.

Along with their interests in individual achievements Kansans have recognized a broadening cultural horizon. They have established a Kansas Arts Commission, a Kansas Humanities Council, and a regional public library system, and they have contributed to the Eisenhower Library in Abilene, which began to build in 1959. While their chief concerns are local, they are aware of what is going on in the world economically, politically, and socially, although they may not always understand the reasons behind the changing national and international scenes. They are inclined to know more about other parts of the country than other Americans know about Kansas.

Kansas has been described as a state of mind, as has the whole American West. Kansas has a kinship with the other Great Plains states yet it is different from its neighbors. William Allen White once said that Kansans were mostly part of a "middle class civilization" and that theory probably holds true today. Kansas, like every other bit of civilization, is people—good, bad, and indifferent. As Emory Lindquist said, Kansas is more than "those who would be included in the Hall of Fame." Kansas is conservative in many ways yet has participated in some of the truly innovative movements in America in the past century, some of which Kansas started. Consequently Kansas history is filled with contrasts, and the state's conservatism has always been broken periodically by progressive thought or action.

John J. Ingalls, who came to Kansas from Massachusetts in the 1850s and stayed to serve his adopted state in many ways, expressed himself about Kansas and Kansans with great feeling and perception. He wrote: "As the 'gray and melancholy main' to the sailor, the desert to the Bedouin, the Alps to the mountaineer, so is Kansas to all her children. . . . No genuine Kansan can emigrate. He may wander. He may roam. . . . He may go elsewhere, but no other State can claim him as a citizen. Once naturalized, the allegiance can never be forsworn."

And, at another time, Ingalls summed up the state's diversity and changing patterns as well as anyone:

> Kansas has been the testing-ground for every experiment in morals, politics, and social life. Nothing has been venerable or revered merely because it exists or has endured. . . . Every incoherent and fantastic dream of social improvement and reform, every economic delusion . . . every political fallacy nurtured by misfortune, poverty, and failure, rejected elsewhere, has here found tolerance and advocacy. . . . There has been neither peace, tranquility, nor repose. The farmer can never foretell his harvest, nor the merchant his gains, nor the politician his supremacy. Something startling has always happened, or has been constantly anticipated.

Suggestions for Reading

The magazine *Kansas!* and its predecessor *To the Stars*, published by the Kansas Department of Economic Development, contain much information on industrial development and general news of the state, beginning in 1945. Also informative for this most recent period are Marvin Harder and Carolyn Rampey, *The Kansas Legislature: Procedures, Personalities and Problems* (1972); Kansas State Board of Agriculture, *Kansas Agriculture: Centennial Report* (1961); H. Craig Miner, *Discovery! Cycles of Change in the Kansas Oil and Gas Industry, 1860–1987* (1987); and Peg Vines, ed., *Kansas! Its Power and Its Glory* (1966). Of value also are Emory Lindquist, "Kansas: A Centennial Portrait," and Floyd R. Souders, "The Small Town and Its Future," *Kansas Historical Quarterly* (Spring, 1961) and (Spring, 1969), respectively, Kenneth Davis, *Kansas: A Bicentennial History* (1976) and Nyle H. Miller, *Kansas—The 34th Star* (1976) both contain information on the state in the 1970s.

The entire Spring 1996 issue of *Kansas History* is devoted to the various aspects of the importance of water to Kansas in both the nineteenth and twentieth centuries while the following books address the subject: John Opie, *Ogallala: Water for a Dry Land* (1993); James Sherow, *Watering the Valley: Development Along the High Plains Arkansas River* (1991); and John L. Zimmerman, *Cheyenne Bottoms: Wetland in Jeopardy* (1990).

Comments on changing times in Kansas may be found in Joel Paddock, "Democratic Politics in a Republican State: The Gubernatorial Campaigns of Robert Docking, 1966–1972" *Kansas History* (Summer, 1994); H. George Frederickson, ed., *Public Policy and the Two States of Kansas* (1994); H. Craig Miner, *Wolf Creek Station: Kansas Gas and Electric Company in the Nuclear Era* (1993); Paul E. Wilson, *A Time to Lose: Representing Kansas in Brown v. Board of Education* (1995); and *Newcomers in the Work Place: Immigrants and the Restructuring of the U.S. Economy* (1994). The latter volume contains information on the Asians and Hispanics in Finney County.

Appendix

GOVERNORS OF KANSAS TERRITORY
(1854–1861)

Reeder, Andrew H., Shawnee Manual Labor School. Commissioned June 29, 1854, took the oath July 7; arrived in Kansas, October 7, 1854; served to April 17, 1855; June 23 to August 16, 1855.

Woodson, Daniel, Shawnee Manual Labor School. Acting governor April 17 to June 23, 1855; August 16 to September 7, 1855; June 24 to July 7, 1856; August 18 to September 9, 1856; March 12 to April 16, 1857.

Shannon, Wilson, Shawnee Manual Labor School and Lecompton. Commissioned August 10, 1855; took oath September 7, 1855; served to June 24, 1856; July 7 to August 18, 1856, sworn in the second time June 13, 1856.

Geary, John White, Lecompton. September 9, 1856 to March 12, 1857; resigned March 4, 1857, to take effect March 20.

Stanton, Frederick P., Lecompton. Acting governor April to May 27, 1857; November 16 to December 21, 1857.

Walker, Robert John, Lecompton. Took the oath May 9, 1857; served May 27 to November 16, 1857.

Denver, James W., Lecompton. Acting governor December 21, 1857 to May 12, 1858; appointed governor; served May 12 to July 3, 1858; July 30 to October 10, 1858.

Walsh, Hugh Sleight, Lecompton. Acting governor July 3–30, 1858; October 10 to December 18, 1858; August 1 to September 15, 1859; April 15 to June 16, 1860.

Medary, Samuel, Lecompton. Took the oath December 1, 1858; commission dated December 22; served December 18, 1858 to August 1, 1859; September 15, 1859 to April 15, 1860; June 16 to September 11, 1860; November 26 to December 17, 1860.

Beebe, George M., Lecompton. Acting governor September 11 to November 26, 1860; December 17, 1860 to February 9, 1861.

STATE GOVERNORS OF KANSAS

Robinson, Charles, Lawrence (Republican), February 9, 1861 to January 12, 1863.

Carney, Thomas, Leavenworth (Republican), January 12, 1863 to January 9, 1865.

Crawford, Samuel Johnson, Garnett (Republican), January 9, 1865 to November 4, 1868 (resigned to take command of the 19th Regiment).

Green, Nehemiah, Manhattan (Republican), November 4, 1868 to January 11, 1869.

Harvey, James Madison, Fort Riley (Republican), January 11, 1869 to January 13, 1873.

Osborn, Thomas Andrew, Leavenworth (Republican), January 13, 1873 to January 8, 1877.

Anthony, George Tobey, Leavenworth (Republican), January 8, 1877 to January 13, 1879.

St. John, John Pierce, Olathe (Republican), January 13, 1879 to January 8, 1883.

Glick, George Washington, Atchison (Democrat), January 8, 1883 to January 12, 1885.

Martin, John Alexander, Atchison (Republican), January 12, 1885 to January 14, 1889.

Humphrey, Lyman Underwood, Independence (Republican), January 14, 1889 to January 9, 1893.

Lewelling, Lorenzo Dow, Wichita (Populist), January 9, 1893 to January 14, 1895.

Morrill, Edmund Needham, Hiawatha (Republican), January 14, 1895 to January 11, 1897.

Leedy, John Whitnah, Le Roy (Populist), January 11, 1897 to January 9, 1899.

Stanley, William Eugene, Wichita (Republican), January 9, 1899 to January 12, 1903.

Bailey, Willis Joshua, Baileyville (Republican), January 12, 1903 to January 9, 1905.

Hoch, Edward Wallis, Marion (Republican), January 9, 1905 to January 11, 1909.

Stubbs, Walter Roscoe, Lawrence (Republican), January 11, 1909 to January 13, 1913.

Hodges, George Hartshorn, Olathe (Democrat), January 13, 1913 to January 11, 1915.

Capper, Arthur, Topeka (Republican), January 11, 1915 to January 13, 1919.

Allen, Henry Justin, Wichita (Republican), January 13, 1919 to January 8, 1923.

Davis, Jonathan McMillan, Bronson (Democrat), January 8, 1923 to January 12, 1925.

Paulen, Ben Sanford, Fredonia (Republican), January 12, 1925 to January 14, 1929.

Reed, Clyde Martin, Parsons (Republican), January 14, 1929 to January 12, 1931.

Woodring, Harry Hines, Neodesha (Democrat), January 12, 1931 to January 9, 1933.

Landon, Alfred M., Independence (Republican), January 9, 1933 to January 11, 1937.

Huxman, Walter August, Hutchinson (Democrat), January 11, 1937 to January 9, 1939.

Ratner, Payne, Parsons (Republican), January 9, 1939 to January 11, 1943.

Schoeppel, Andrew Frank, Ness City (Republican), January 11, 1943 to January 13, 1947.

Carlson, Frank, Concordia, (Republican), January 13, 1947 to November 28, 1950, resigned. Elected United States Senator.

Hagaman, Frank Lester, Fairway (Republican), November 28, 1950 to January 8, 1951, succeeding Frank Carlson.

Arn, Edward Ferdinand, Wichita (Republican), January 8, 1951 to January 10, 1955.

Hall, Fred, Dodge City (Republican), January 10, 1955 to January 3, 1957, resigned. Appointed Justice Supreme Court.

McCuish, John, Newton (Republican), January 3, 1957 to January 14, 1957, succeeding Fred Hall.

Docking, George, Lawrence (Democrat), January 14, 1957 to January 9, 1961.

Anderson, John, Jr., Olathe (Republican), January 9, 1961 to January 11, 1965.

Avery, Wm. H., Wakefield (Republican), January 11, 1965 to January 9, 1967.

Docking, Robert B., Arkansas City (Democrat), January 9, 1967 to January 13, 1975.

Bennett, Robert F., Overland Park (Republican), January 13, 1975 to January 8, 1979.

Carlin, John, Smolan (Democrat), January 8, 1979 to January 12, 1987.

Hayden, Mike, Atwood (Republican), January 12, 1987 to January 14, 1991.

Finney, Joan M., Topeka (Democrat), January 14, 1991 to January 9, 1995.

Graves, William, Salina (Republican), January 9, 1995–.

UNITED STATES SENATORS FROM KANSAS

Lane, James Henry, Lawrence (Republican), April 4, 1861 to July 11, 1866.

Pomeroy, Samuel Clark, Atchison (Republican), April 4, 1861 to March 3, 1873.

Ross, Edmund Gibson, Lawrence (Republican), July 19, 1866 to March 3, 1871.

Caldwell, Alexander, Leavenworth (Republican), March 4, 1871 to March 24, 1873.

Ingalls, John James, Atchison (Republican), March 4, 1873 to March 3, 1891.

Crozier, Robert, Leavenworth (Republican), November 22, 1873 to February 2, 1874.

Harvey, James Madison, Vinton (Republican), February 2, 1874 to March 3, 1877.

Plumb, Preston Bierce, Emporia (Republican), March 4, 1877 to December 22, 1891.

Peffer, William Alfred, Topeka (Populist), March 4, 1891 to March 3, 1897.

Perkins, Bishop Walden, Oswego (Republican), January 1, 1892 to March 3, 1893.

Martin, John, Topeka (Democrat), March 4, 1893 to March 3, 1895.

Baker, Lucien, Leavenworth (Republican), March 4, 1895 to March 3, 1901.

Harris, William Alexander, Linwood (Democrat), March 4, 1897 to March 3, 1903.

Burton, Joseph Ralph, Abilene (Republican), March 4, 1901 to June 4, 1906.

Long, Chester Isaiah, Medicine Lodge (Republican), March 4, 1903 to March 3, 1909.

Benson, Alfred Washburn, Emporia (Republican), June 11, 1906 to January 29, 1907.

Curtis, Charles, Topeka (Republican), January 29, 1907 to March 3, 1913.

Bristow, Joseph Little, Salina (Republican), March 4, 1909 to March 3, 1915.

Thompson, William Howard, Garden City (Democrat), March 4, 1913 to March 3, 1919.

Curtis, Charles, Topeka (Republican), March 4, 1915 to March 3, 1929.

Capper, Arthur, Topeka (Republican), March 4, 1919 to January 3, 1949.

Allen, Henry, Wichita (Republican), April 1, 1929 to November 30, 1930.

McGill, George, Wichita (Democrat), December 1, 1930 to January 3, 1939.

Reed, Clyde, Parsons (Republican), January 3, 1939 to November 8, 1949.

Schoeppel, Andrew F., Ness City (Republican), January 3, 1949 to January 21, 1962.

Darby, Harry, Kansas City (Republican), December 2, 1949 to November 28, 1950.

Carlson, Frank, Concordia (Republican), November 29, 1950 to January 3, 1969.

Pearson, James B., Prairie Village (Republican), January 31, 1962 to December 23, 1978.

Dole, Robert, Russell (Republican), January 3, 1969 to June 11, 1996.

Frahm, Sheila, Colby, (Republican), June 11, 1996 to November 27, 1996.

Kassebaum, Nancy Landon, Wichita (Republican), December 23, 1978 to January 7, 1997.

Brownback, Sam, Topeka (Republican), November 27, 1996–.

Roberts, Pat, Dodge City (Republican), January 7, 1997–.

Index